I0896934

Emotion, Violence, Vengeance and Law in the Middle Ages

Medieval Law and Its Practice

Edited by

John Hudson (*St Andrews*)

Editorial Board

Paul Brand (*All Souls College, Oxford*)
Emanuele Conte (*Università Roma Tre/EHESS, Paris*)
Dirk Heirbaut (*University of Ghent*)
Richard Helmholz (*University of Chicago*)
Caroline Humfress (*St Andrews*)
Magnus Ryan (*Peterhouse, Cambridge*)
Robin Chapman Stacey (*University of Washington*)

VOLUME 24

The titles published in this series are listed at *brill.com/mlip*

Bill Miller

Emotion, Violence, Vengeance and Law in the Middle Ages

Essays in Honour of William Ian Miller

Edited by

Kate Gilbert
Stephen D. White

BRILL

LEIDEN | BOSTON

Front cover illustration: The attack on Gunnar of Hlíðarendi. Detail from the Njáls saga Tapestry designed by Kristín Ragna Gunnarsdóttir. With kind permission of Christina M. Bengtsson and Gunnhildur E. Kristjánsdóttir, project managers and owners, Hvolsvöllur, Iceland. Photo © Jóna Sigþórsdóttir.

Back cover illustration: The death of Gunnar of Hlíðarendi. Detail from the Njáls saga Tapestry designed by Kristín Ragna Gunnarsdóttir. With kind permission of Christina M. Bengtsson and Gunnhildur E. Kristjánsdóttir, project managers and owners, Hvolsvöllur, Iceland. Photo © Jóna Sigþórsdóttir.

Photo credit for the picture of Bill and his dog: Kathy Koehler

Photo credit for the frontispiece: Arlie Nuetzel

The Library of Congress Cataloging-in-Publication Data is available online at http://catalog.loc.gov
LC record available at http://lccn.loc.gov/2018010092

Typeface for the Latin, Greek, and Cyrillic scripts: "Brill". See and download: brill.com/brill-typeface.

ISSN 1873-8176
ISBN 978-90-04-34272-9 (hardback)
ISBN 978-90-04-36637-4 (e-book)

Copyright 2018 by Koninklijke Brill NV, Leiden, The Netherlands.
Koninklijke Brill NV incorporates the imprints Brill, Brill Hes & De Graaf, Brill Nijhoff, Brill Rodopi, Brill Sense and Hotei Publishing.
All rights reserved. No part of this publication may be reproduced, translated, stored in a retrieval system, or transmitted in any form or by any means, electronic, mechanical, photocopying, recording or otherwise, without prior written permission from the publisher.
Authorization to photocopy items for internal or personal use is granted by Koninklijke Brill NV provided that the appropriate fees are paid directly to The Copyright Clearance Center, 222 Rosewood Drive, Suite 910, Danvers, MA 01923, USA. Fees are subject to change.

This book is printed on acid-free paper and produced in a sustainable manner.

Contents

Acknowledgments

The editors would like to thank the following people, without whose help this volume would not have been possible: John Hudson, who helped guide the project in its early stages; Helle Vogt, who gave it much-needed momentum at a critical time; Marcella Mulder and Saskia van der Knaap at Brill Publishers, for their guidance and patience; and Belle Tuten, for the index. We also thank The Staatsarchiv Zürich, for permission to reproduce an image from Staatsarchiv Zürich B VI 190; Kristín Ragna Gunnarsdóttir, designer of the Njáls saga Tapestry, and Christina M. Bengtsson and Gunnhildur E. Kristjánsdóttir, managers and owners of the tapestry project in Hvolsvöllur, Iceland, for the two cover images; and Jóna Sigflórsdóttir, Arlie Nuetzel, Kathy Koehler, and Jamie Page for their photographic images. Special thanks to Kathy Koehler; Eva, Bess, Louie, and Hank Miller; and all the contributors, who somehow managed to keep the Festschrift a secret from Bill Miller across three continents and for nearly two years.

List of Illustrations

Figures

Table

Notes on Contributors

Stuart Airlie

is Senior Lecturer in History in the School of Humanities, University of Glasgow. He has published widely on the early Middle Ages and in particular the Carolingian period.

Ted Andersson

taught at Harvard, Stanford, and Indiana University for more than forty years and it is now emeritus at the latter two institutions. He focused on the study of early Germanic literatures with a growing interest in Old Icelandic texts, especially the sagas. In 2017 a book appeared on the sagas about Norwegian kings, and he is currently at work on the sagas about early Icelandic bishops ca. 1200. In 1981–82 he served as President of the Society for the Advancement of Scandinavian Study and in 1998–99 as President of the Medieval Academy of America.

Nora Bartlett

was for many years Honorary Lecturer in English at the University of St Andrews. The inaugural Nora Bartlett Lecture of the Scottish Branch of the Jane Austen Society of the United Kingdom took place in 2017.

Robert Bartlett

is Bishop Wardlaw Professor of Mediaeval History Emeritus at the University of St Andrews in Scotland and a Fellow of the British Academy. His books include *The Making of Europe: Conquest, Colonization and Cultural Change 950–1350*, which won the Wolfson Literary Prize for History; *England under the Norman and Angevin Kings 1075–1225*; and *Why Can the Dead Do Such Great Things?: Saints and Worshippers from the Martyrs to the Reformation*. He has presented three television series for the BBC, "Inside the Medieval Mind" (2008), "The Normans" (2010), and "The Plantagenets" (2014).

Carol J. Clover

is Professor of the Class of 1936 Emerita at the University of California, Berkeley, where she taught film in the Rhetoric Department and Old Norse-Icelandic language and literature in the Department of Scandinavian. Her publications in the latter field have chiefly to do with the sagas—their narrative form and its origins, their gender system and its effects, and, more recently, their legal cast.

She has been Kerstin Hesselgren Visiting Distinguished Professor of Sweden and a Rockefeller Foundation Bellagio Resident Fellow, has received honorary doctorates from Lund University and the University of Iceland, and is a Fellow of the American Academy of Arts and Sciences.

Jordan Corrente Beck
is a graduate of the University of Michigan Law School and currently practices law in the New York and Tokyo offices of Debevoise & Plimpton. She also edits English language translations and commentary for Stanford Law School's China Guiding Cases Project.

Lauren DesRosiers
is a graduate of the University of Michigan law school and currently practices law.

William Eves
is currently a Post-Doctoral Research Fellow at the University of St Andrews Institute of Legal and Constitutional Research. He was previously an Arts and Humanities Research Council Cultural Engagement Fellow in the University of St Andrews School of History (2016) and a Scouloudi Junior Research Fellow at the Institute of Historical Research, School of Advanced Study, University of London (2015–16). His research focusses on law in medieval England and Normandy c. 1100–1300.

John Hudson
is Bishop Wardlaw Professor of Legal History at the University of St Andrews, where he is currently Director of the Institute of Legal and Constitutional Research. He is also William W. Cook Global Law Professor at the University of Michigan Law School. He was elected a Fellow of the British Academy in 2016.

Elizabeth Papp Kamali
is an Assistant Professor of Law at Harvard Law School. Her research focuses on the medieval English common law and the history of criminal law, with a particular interest in the early criminal trial jury. Her current projects include studies of the role of criminal intent in thirteenth- and fourteenth-century English felony cases, medieval understandings of anger's operation in felony adjudication, conflict between urban customary law and the English common law in the early fourteenth century, and the influence of Roman law on the development of the common law.

Kimberley-Joy Knight
is a postdoctoral research fellow at the Australian Research Council Centre of Excellence for the History of Emotions. She is also an Honorary Research Fellow at the Institute for Constitutional and Legal Research at the University of St Andrews. Her research and publications focus on medieval emotions and gestures, hagiography, and Old Norse.

Simon MacLean
studied at the Universities of Glasgow and London, and is now Professor in the School of History at the University of St Andrews. His research focuses on the history of the Carolingian Empire and its successor kingdoms in the ninth and tenth centuries. His most recent book is *Ottonian Queenship*, published in 2017 by Oxford University Press.

M. W. McHaffie
received his PhD from the University of St Andrews in 2014, before taking up a Leverhulme Early Career Fellowship at King's College London (2014–2017), where he is now a visiting research fellow. He writes on the subjects of law, lordship, and ritual in eleventh- and twelfth-century France.

Eva Miller
completed her doctorate at the University of Oxford in 2017, in the field of Assyriology. Her doctoral thesis examined the representation of enemy punishments in the Teumman-Dunanu sequences of Neo-Assyrian king Ashurbanipal's reign. She is currently the Teaching Fellow for the History and Culture of the Ancient Near East at the University of Birmingham, and the Henri Frankfort Fellow at the Warburg Institute, University of London, where she is pursuing research into the reception of Assyria in modernist art and architecture. William Ian Miller is her father.

Hans Jacob Orning
has been professor in medieval history at University of Oslo since 2012, after serving as professor of history at University College of Volda 2005–12. His PhD (2004) was published in 2008 as *Unpredictability and Presence: Norwegian Kingship in the High Middle Ages*. He has published numerous articles on Nordic medieval history, and edited several books. In 2017 he published *The Reality of the Fantastic: The Magical, Political and Social Universe of Late Medieval Saga Manuscripts*, combining New Philology and historical approaches to late medieval Icelandic manuscripts.

Jamie Page
is Leverhulme Early Career Fellow at Durham University. A social and cultural historian of the German-speaking lands in the late Middle Ages, his broad interests include law, gender, sexuality, and popular fiction, which inform specific research projects on prostitution, masculinity, and the early emergence of the concept of 'good police' (*gute Policey*) within the cities of the southern German-speaking Empire.

Susanne Pohl-Zucker
PhD (1997), University of Michigan, is an independent historian living near Mainz (Germany). She has worked as an assistant professor of Early Modern European History at Cornell University and taught seminars as a lecturer at the University of Tübingen and the University of Frankfurt. Her published work includes articles on late medieval and early modern criminal justice in Württemberg and Zurich and *Making Manslaughter: Process, Punishment and Restitution in Württemberg and Zurich, 1376–1700* (2017).

Amanda Strick
is a graduate of the University of Michigan law school and currently practices law.

Helle Vogt
is Professor in legal history at the Faculty of Law, University of Copenhagen. Her research interests are Nordic legal history 1150–1850 and the interaction between local law and learned Christian legal ideology. Her main publications are about these areas, including *The Function of Kinship in Medieval Nordic Legislation* (2010) and *The Danish Medieval Laws: The Laws of Scania, Zealand and Jutland* (2016).

Mark D. West
is the Nippon Life Professor of Law at the University of Michigan Law School. He joined the faculty in 1998 and has served as Dean since 2013. He is the author of several books on Japanese law.

Stephen D. White
is Asa G. Candler Professor of Medieval History Emeritus, Emory University, and an Honorary Professor of Mediaeval History at the University of St Andrews. His books include *Feuding and Peace-Making in Eleventh-Century France* (2005) and *Re-Thinking Kinship and Feudalism* (2005). He has been a Visiting Member in the School of Historical Studies at the Institute for Advanced Study, Princeton; a National Humanities Fellow at the National Humanities Center; and a Visiting Scholar at the Harvard Law School.

List of Abbreviations

In citing works in the notes, short titles have generally been used. Works frequently cited have been identified by the following abbreviations:

ADIL	Archives départementales de Indre-et-Loire
ADML	Archives départementales de Maine-et-Loire
CAD	*Chicago Assyrian Dictionary*
DD	*Diplomatarium Danicum*
H	*Hirdskråen* [*The Law of the Retinue*]
Hs	*Hákonar saga Hákonarsonar* [*The saga of Haakon Haakonsson*]
HstA	Hauptstaatsarchiv Stuttgart
ÍF	Íslenzk fornrit
JEGP	*Journal of English and Germanic Philology*
KS	*Konungs skuggsiá* [*The King's Mirror*]
LHP	*Leges Henrici Primi*
MGH SS	Monumenta Germaniae Historica Scriptores
MGH SRG	Monumenta Germaniae Historica Scriptores Rerum Germanicarum
RA	*Archives d'Anjou*
RINAP	Royal Inscriptions of the Neo-Assyrian Period
RS	Rolls Series
SAA	*Cartulaire de l'abbaye de Saint-Aubin d'Angers*
SSE	*Premier et second livres des cartulaires de l'abbaye Saint-Serge et Saint-Bach d'Angers (XIe et XIIe siècles)*, 2 vols.
StaZH	Staatsarchiv Zürich
StRT	Stadtarchiv Reutlingen
Svs	*Sverris saga*

Introduction: In Search of Miller

Stephen D. White

The articles in this volume are published in honor of William Ian Miller, aka Bill Miller or simply "Miller," which is how some of us habitually refer to him in retaliation for his habit of calling people by their last names. Because the many tall stories that Miller tells on himself have grown taller with each repetition, this Introduction's preliminary remarks on his early career—which precede its review of his scholarship and notes on the articles that honor him—mix fiction and fact more freely than do the comments of Jordan Corrente Beck on Miller at Michigan Law School and Kimberley-Joy Knight on Miller at St Andrews. At the risk of interpolating false rumors, hagiography, malicious gossip, panegyric, and scurrilous innuendo into Miller's authentic—or, at least, authorized—confessions, here is one possible story about how early phases of his professional life unfolded.

As a high school student in Green Bay, Wisconsin, Miller abandoned his fantasy of playing wide receiver for the Packers when he was denied a football scholarship to college. Instead of compensating for this early failure by going into real estate or working in a local paper mill, he began the process of picking up the credentials he needed to climb the greasy pole of academic success. His irresistible rise began when he left home for the University of Wisconsin in Madison, escaped expulsion for hurling a television set out the window of a tenth-floor dormitory room, and got a BA in History in 1969. To avoid being drafted into the Vietnam war, Miller secured another 2S deferment by entering graduate school at Yale. There, he began building his reputation for being "wild" by riding motorcycles at terrifying speeds, consuming vast amounts of alcohol, and taking multiple vows of virginity that he may or may not have broken. Miller also learned much more Old English and Middle English than anyone his age could be expected to know. Though legally barred (he later claimed) from the country where he needed to research his PhD thesis, he nevertheless got a doctorate by completing a cutting-edge dissertation entitled "The Poetry of MS. Sloane 2503: A Critical Edition" (1975).

Once Miller was fully armed with a PhD, he landed a highly coveted tenure-track assistant professorship of English at Wesleyan University in 1975. However, his chances of survival there were nil. Though he was, of course, a brilliant if unorthodox teacher of Chaucer, Langland, *Beowulf*, and Icelandic sagas, he seemed certain to perish, not publish. Suffering from incurable writer's block (to name but one of the maladies he expatiated upon, to both old friends

© KONINKLIJKE BRILL NV, LEIDEN, 2018 | DOI 10.1163/9789004366374_002

and new acquaintances), Miller knew that even if he could get down on paper his many brilliant conjectural emendations in poems from Sloane MS 2503 and publish them all in *Notes & Queries*, they wouldn't satisfy a tenure committee. Besides, his "colleagueship"—on which his tenure chances would depend as well—was questionable. Even if his reputation for drinking beer, playing pinball, staying off committees, and picking fights with colleagues didn't doom him, he might well have been violating the terms of his employment when he started to moonlight as a law student at Yale.

Before Miller could be denied tenure for any number of reasons, he left Wesleyan and completed a Yale law degree (1980). He briefly practiced law back in Madison before returning to teaching, this time in law school, where, he had heard, the salaries were much higher, the publication requirements somewhat lower, and the likelihood of anyone noticing his irascibility and contentiousness virtually non-existent. But what about the old problems of writing and publication? As one can see from the bibliography at the end of this volume, neither problem was still a problem. Why not? For one thing, as soon as Miller had undergone his conversion from literature to law, he was miraculously healed of writer's block and lost some of his perfectionist inhibitions about publication. Better yet, he had found in Icelandic sagas a subject that he not only loved, but even loved to write about. Best of all, he entered legal academia just as law schools were becoming havens for unemployed PhD's with law degrees who could teach and publish on law and something else. So why not law and Icelandic sagas or rather, law *in* Icelandic sagas, especially since "law" could be construed to include blood vengeance and feud, two subjects on which Miller was already an expert?

After three years at the University of Houston Law Center, Miller got the call in 1985 to Michigan Law School, where in 1998 he became Michigan's Thomas G. Long Professor. In the meantime he was also doing short-term teaching at Yale Law School, Chicago Law School, the University of Bergen, the University of Tel Aviv, and the University of St Andrews, where he became an Honorary Professor of History in 2011. In 2016 he celebrated (or rather, mourned) his seventieth birthday and entered semi-retirement. He is now spending the remainder of his late adolescence in Ann Arbor, while making regular visits to Scotland and Slovenia.

•••

As one might have expected from this rapid review of Miller's checkered, shapeshifting, and multidisciplinary career, his published work defies easy categorization by discipline or anything else; and one shudders to think how he would have explained his "methodology" and "theoretical orientation" if he had ever needed to write a grant proposal to secure outside funding. Bemusement at Miller's multiple identities as a scholar and his lapses into intellectual intersectionality only deepens when one studies his two different websites on the University of Michigan server. In his faculty bio for Michigan Law School, he almost passes himself off as a fairly conventional legal academic with a PhD by listing his "Curriculum Interest Areas" as Interdisciplinary Perspectives on Law; Legal History; and Law and the Humanities.[1] But his personal home page comes closer to the truth by identifying his "areas of interest" as Icelandic Sagas; Medieval History; Social and Political Theory; Emotions; Vices and Virtues.[2] In his writings Miller delves into all of these subjects, while occasionally casting himself in the supporting roles of film critic, biblical scholar, translator and editor of sagas, philologist, public intellectual, hostile observer of academic life, and participant in/observer of the most embarrassing moments in his own life. He is also well known as our leading ethnographer of what he calls "honor-based" societies ranging from the Hebrew Bible's Israel to Saga Iceland to Shakespeare's Denmark to Dirty Harry's San Francisco to his own high school in Green Bay.

How and why Miller has assumed all of these identities and gotten away with it are mysteries that he and his many fans and critics will never sort out. But if we examine his scholarly progress over the *longue durée*, clear patterns in his thought emerge, along with signs of intellectual development. Miller's *oeuvre*, like Beethoven's, falls so neatly into three stages that it can be divided into Early-Period Miller (EPM), Middle-Period Miller (MPM), and Late-Period Miller (LPM). In all three periods, Miller has relied heavily on close readings of literary and historical texts to discuss vengeance (and other ways of getting even), violence (and threats of violence), law (and norms), and emotions, as well as many other topics. But in his progression from EPM to MPM to LPM, there have been major changes in his choices of "texts" to interpret, his goals in interpreting them, the interpretive moves he has made or refused to make, the authors he has invoked to give a thin veneer of authority to views he could easily have reached on his own, and the audiences his writings have reached.

Miller's role in his own writings has changed as well. First, the self-effacing medievalist of EPM suddenly gave way to the author of MPM, who stepped into his own writings as a character, a subject, an object, and a body with bodily functions that he couldn't stop talking about. By around 2011, one could see

---

1 <https://www.law.umich.edu/FacultyBio/Pages/FacultyBio.aspx?FacID=wimiller>, accessed 27/6/2017.

2 <http://www-personal.umich.edu/~wimiller/>, accessed 27/6/2017.

that this author, too, was fading out of his writings and giving way to an older, wearier, and wiser Miller. The Miller of LPM is more interested in reading entire sagas than in analyzing individual features of Icelandic law or society. He also realizes that he is and always has been more interested in understanding saga-characters than in scrutinizing himself.

Early Period Miller consists of the sharply focused, carefully researched, boldly argued work that he published between 1983 and 1990 on "Saga Iceland." This is the term he has repeatedly used for the "honor-based" society of the period in Icelandic history that runs from the early twelfth to the late thirteenth century. Based on very close readings of thirteenth-century sagas, as interpreted in the light of the Icelandic law code called *Grágás*,[3] this early work presents what Miller described at the time as a "static picture" of "norms and social institutions."[4] After publishing a series of articles on vengeance and feud, arbitration, ordeals, gifts and other forms of exchange, sorcery, household and kinship, and violence against women and old men,[5] Miller synthesized his work on Saga Iceland in *Bloodtaking and Peacemaking: Feud, Law, and Society in Saga Iceland* (1990), which continues to be widely read nearly thirty years after its publication.[6]

Two features of EPM caught the attention of other scholars and made it highly influential. The first was the use of sagas to write the social and legal history of medieval Iceland. As Hans Jacob Orning explains below, "Miller participated in retrieving the sagas as sources that historians could use, in spite of their questionable historicity."[7] In a chapter on "Making Sense of the Sources" in *Bloodtaking and Peacemaking* that impressed Orning and many

3 Miller, *Bloodtaking and Peacemaking in Medieval Iceland: Feud, Law, and Society in Saga Iceland* (1990), 43. For full bibliographical information on this and the works of Miller cited below, see the bibliography at the end of this volume.

4 Miller, "The Historical Setting," in Theodore M. Andersson and William Ian Miller, *Law and Literature in Medieval Iceland: Ljósvetninga saga and Valla-Ljóts saga* (1989), 3–62 at 6.

5 "Choosing the Avenger: Some Aspects of the Bloodfeud in Medieval Iceland and England" (1983); "Justifying Skarpheðinn: Of Pretext and Politics in the Icelandic Bloodfeud" (1983); "Avoiding Legal Judgment: The Submission of Disputes to Arbitration in Medieval Iceland" (1984); "Dreams, Prophecy and Sorcery: Blaming the Secret Offender in Medieval Iceland" (1986); "Gift, Sale, Payment, Raid: Case Studies in the Negotiation and Classification of Exchange in Medieval Iceland" (1986); "Ordeal in Iceland" (1988); "Beating Up on Women and Old Men and Other Enormities: A Social Historical Inquiry into Literary Sources" (1988); "Some Aspects of Householding in the Medieval Icelandic Commonwealth" (1988); "Of Outlaws, Christians, Horsemeat, and Writing: Uniform Laws and Saga Iceland" (1991).

6 See also "The Historical Setting."

7 Orning, this volume, p. 202.

others, Miller wrote: "Fictionalizing dialogue, fictionalizing events, inventing characters and their psychologies might unnerve the political historian, but they need not upset the social historian at all. Even these fictions are constrained by the ranges of the possible in the culture, and hence have useful social information to reveal."[8] Unlike most of us who try to incorporate literature into history, moreover, Miller even succeeded in winning support and endorsements from leading scholars in medieval Scandinavian literature, including two eminent experts on sagas (and contributors to this volume), Carol Clover and Ted Andersson, for his project of using sagas to write social history. When Andersson and Miller edited and translated two sagas in a volume called *Law and Literature in Medieval Iceland: Ljósvetninga saga and Valla-Ljóts saga* (1989), they collaborated in making the case that sagas could be used "to write social and cultural history" and could sometimes even "surpass the quality of other, more 'historical,' sources."[9]

Another feature of EPM that attracted particular attention from other historians was Miller's success in "launching a perspective on stateless societies which was neither Hobbesian nor Rousseauian, neither determinist nor centred on (ir)rational choice."[10] Unlike the present author, Miller was never so naïve as to believe he could learn much from anthropologists. But he gracefully bowed to peer pressure by organizing his work on Saga Iceland around categories of anthropological analysis, including dispute processing, gift-exchange, and feud. He even made carefully selected references to Weber, Malinowski, Mauss, Llewellyn and Hoebel, Evans-Pritchard, Gluckman, Lévy-Strauss, Sahlins, Foucault, and Turner, although he drew the line at Geertz—and many others. Like it or not, Miller came to be associated with an anthropological or sociological view of feud in stateless Iceland that was cited approvingly by Pierre Bourdieu.[11] In the form of *Bloodtaking*, EPM traveled so well that law professors read the book, and a famous polymath federal judge *cum* legal academic even took the trouble to review it.[12]

8 Miller, *Bloodtaking*, 45.

9 Andersson and Miller, Preface, in *Law and Literature* (1989), vii–xiv at x–xi. On law and literature, see also "Beating Up on Women and Old Men" (1988).

10 Orning, this volume, p. 202.

11 Pierre Bourdieu, "Rethinking the State: Genesis and Structure of the Bureaucratic Field," translated by Loïc Wacquant and Samar Farage, in Pierre Bourdieu, *Practical Reason: On the Theory of Action* (Stanford, CA: 1998), 35–63 at 43, n. 8 (p. 61).

12 Richard A. Posner, "Medieval Iceland and Modern Legal Scholarship," *Michigan Law Review* 90 (1992), 1495–1511.

Nevertheless, since Miller had never fully embraced anthropology in MPM, he could easily divorce himself from it and take one of those "turns" that U.S. historians are always taking and attacking everyone else for not taking. The first signs of Miller's turn to MPM were evident in *Humiliation: And Other Essays on Honor, Social Discomfort and Violence* (1993), where he made a startling confession. By emphasizing "the strategic aspect of social behavior, particularly feuding behavior in saga Iceland," he wrote, he had "tended to portray people as more manipulative, more in rational control of their choices, than they were or could have been." Now, MPM would convey "a fuller picture of motive and motivation" by studying "the emotional setting of social action."[13]

Accordingly, the essays in *Humiliation* studied unwanted gifts, violence, emotions, honor, humiliation, and embarrassment, not just in sagas,[14] but in Shakespeare plays, *Sir Gawain and the Green Knight*, and cringe-making scenes from Miller's own life in order to explore "the anxieties of self-presentation, the strategies we adopt to avoid loss of face …, and the emotions which maintain us as self-respecting and respectable social actors."[15] To authorize his own authorial insights, Miller still cited anthropologists, but gave more play to Nietsche and Nozick, Rawls and Rorty, Hume and Hobbes, Swift and Smith (Adam), Elias and Elster, plus Montaigne and La Rochefoucauld. Eventually, even Lord Chesterfield would come to grace Miller's footnotes.

As MPM proceeded, its intellectual agenda took shape. In the Prologue to *The Anatomy of Disgust* (1997) Miller explained that while this book, like *Humiliation*, treated "the emotions [that] rank us in moral and social hierarchies," it did so from an opposing perspective.[16] Whereas *Humiliation* took as its starting point "the person accepting or resisting reassignment to a lower status in the social and moral ordering" as he experienced and expressed the "passions [of] shame, embarrassment, humiliation, and vengefulness," the new book examined "the emotions—disgust mostly, but also contempt—that confirm others as belonging to a lower status and thus in the zero-sum game of rank necessarily define oneself as higher."[17] By redefining class struggle as

---

13 "Emotions, Honor, and the Affective Life of the Heroic," in *Humiliation* (1993), 93–130 at 97–8, evidently alluding to Miller's approach in, e.g., "Justifying Skarpheðinn" (1983); "The Historical Setting" (1989), and *Bloodtaking* (1990).

14 See also "Sagas and Emotions" (1992); "Deep Inner Lives, Individualism and People of Honour" (1995).

15 *Humiliation* (1993), Preface, ix.

16 See also Miller's review of Alexandra Cuffel's *Gendering Disgust in Medieval Religious Polemic* (2008); "Do I disgust you? (or, rather, you me?)—Mes frères, mes sœurs, mes semblables?" (2016).

17 *The Anatomy of Disgust* (1997), x.

psychomachia, Miller did more than reject what he saw as a modernist project of citing self-interest, greed, or power-seeking to "explain most social action"; he also proposed "a more anxiety-ridden account" of social action—an account that downplayed "more offensive and assertive passions" and privileged "defensive and reactive passions, such as humiliation and disgust."[18] He also aimed to revive "a way of talking about human motivation" that combined psychology and psychiatry with "moral philosophy, literature, and history"; and he insisted that "some of our emotions generate culture as well as being generated by it."[19]

Whether or not the book's readers fully endorsed MPM's intellectual project, they must have enjoyed reading Miller on contamination, decay, feces, menstruation, semen, slime, urine, and all the smells that go with them. *Disgust* was a hit; and the hits came on coming with *The Mystery of Courage* (1997), which was largely about cowardice;[20] *Faking It* (2003), which "treats of praise and flattery, of vanity, esteem, and self-esteem, false modesty, seeming virtue and virtuous seeming, deception and self-deception";[21] *Eye for an Eye* (2006) on the Law of the Talion; and, finally, *Losing It: In Which an Aging Professor Laments His Shrinking Brain, Which He Flatters Himself Formerly Did Him Noble Service* (2011), which memorializes Miller's hypochondria, peeves, mendacity, and fears of dementia, as well as his own "death," a three-hour period in which he found himself unable to remember the immediate past and which was later diagnosed as Transient Global Amnesia. By now some of us had reason to wonder whether he was morphing for good into a public intellectual, with pieces in *Harper's*, *The Chronicle of Higher Education*, and the *London Review of Books*; the translations of his work into Spanish, Italian, Korean, and Slovenian; the glowing reviews in some of the right places; and contributions to essay collections with titles like *Facts and Fantasies about Human Cloning*, *The Philosophy of Deception*, *The Passions of Law*, *Le dégoût*, *Empire of the Senses: The Sensual Culture Reader*, and *Wicked Pleasures*.

We were wrong. The turn from the self-referential exuberance of MPM to the somber world of sagas in LPM was already in progress. In *Eye for an Eye* (2006), to be sure, Miller's concern with "the emotional side of getting even" and with "our [i.e., his] deep compulsion to rank and compare everything from quarterbacks to old loves" led him to consider the talionic subtexts of

---

18 *Disgust*, x–xi.

19 *Disgust*, xi, xiii.

20 See "Fear, Weak Legs, and Running Away: A Soldier's Story" (1999).

21 *Faking It* (2003), 5.

contemporary U.S. culture.[22] But the core of the book is "an historical and philosophical meditation on paying back and buying back [and] on retaliation and redemption"[23] that looks back to EPM's discussions of gifts, vengeance, and reciprocity in Saga Iceland and forward to LPM's discussions of these issues in the three books Miller published between 2007 and 2016, each presenting very close reading of an Icelandic saga or *þáttr*:[24] *Audun and the Polar Bear: Luck, Law, and Largesse in a Medieval Tale of Risky Business* (2008); *'Why is your axe bloody?': A Reading of Njáls saga* (2014); *Hrafnkel or the Ambiguities: Hard Cases, Hard Choices* (2017).

Late-Period Miller has affinities with MPM. However, its affinities with EPM are arguably stronger, and it takes on a character all its own by virtue of the fact that it consists of close sentence-by-sentence, chapter-by-chapter, scene-by-scene readings of entire texts, including the very short story of Audun, the very long saga of Njal, and the fairly short saga of Hrafnkel. Here, even more than in his earlier work, Miller, as Ted Andersson writes in the present volume, "has combined the analytical skills of jurisprudence and sociology with the esthetic sensibilities of a literary scholar."[25] Abandoning any pretense of reading sagas through the lens of anyone but himself and the authors, Miller puts the latter on a par with the authors of other great literature as our best guides to their own stories, which are "tales of disputes and feuds of what we might think of as the better-off sheep- and cattle-ranchers jockeying for position among others like themselves."[26] He also judges the authors of *Audun, Njáls saga*, and *Hrafnkels saga* to be at least as good as, and sometimes better than, the theorists who guided him on his earlier journeys to Saga Iceland. In Miller's eyes, the author of *Audun* is superior to Marcel Mauss as an analyst of the Gift.[27] Elsewhere he writes that "the author of *Njála* needs to be taken seriously as a political and social theorist, for he is one of consummate ability."[28] In a similar vein, he praises the author of *Hrafnkel's saga* as "an able social theorist,

22 *Eye for an Eye* (2006), 144, 161–2.

23 *Eye for an Eye*, x.

24 "Is a Gift Forever?" (2007); "Threat" (2010); "Conscience, Interest, Side-Switching, and Laxdæla Saga" (2012); "Feeling Another's Pain: Sympathy and Psychology Saga Style" (2014); (with Helle Vogt), "Finding, Sharing and Risk of Loss: Of Whales, Bees and Other Valuable Finds in Iceland, Denmark and Norway" (2015); "Where's Iceland?" (2016).

25 Andersson, this volume, p. 189.

26 *'Why is Your Axe Bloody?' A Reading of Njáls Saga* (2014), 2.

27 *Audun* (2008), 3: "The story's treatment of gift-exchange is worthy of Marcel Mauss ... and of Pierre Bourdieu."

28 *Axe*, 74; see also 193, on the same author as a "subtle ... political and social thinker" and 260–5, on the author's "critique of the law."

astute and sophisticated about disputing, about its politics and the psychology of the disputants, about strategy and tactics, about the defense of position and honor, about the difficulty of fixing the content and the ranges of the moral, about the styles of persuasion, about the sentiments, motivation, and other inner states that inform action."[29]

Yet readers who have followed Miller from EPM to MPM and on to LPM will note that "inner states" of saga characters inform their actions but don't determine them, leaving saga authors and Miller himself with the problem of how to explain fully disputes, politics, and political culture. In all three books Miller does as much as he can to treat the stories he analyzes as character-driven, in the sense that the action is to be understood, in the first instance, by reference to the characters—whose motives, Miller writes, must be inferred, as we do today, "by watching what [they] say and imputing reason or unreason, whim or calculation, passion or habit, to explain their actions."[30] In *Hrafnkel's saga*, for example, Miller finds "the impetus for action [in] a mix of desire, emotions, motives, and goals, only some of which are known or articulable by the actor or knowable by others."[31] And yet these actors skillfully engage in social actions that cannot be explained solely by reference to the passions, motives or whims that MPM analyzed and privileged. Isn't that why saga authors—and Miller, too, in his way—had to be social and political theorists? Surely they needed to understand such things as disputing and its politics, strategy and tactics, and the defense of position and honor that EPM had enabled us to understand much better than we had before, even if it overemphasized rationality and underestimated the irrationality of social action. Otherwise, how could Late-Period Miller have seen that *Njáls saga* "does not make sense unless we see that the very legal and political culture of the saga is as important to the story as are [its characters]"?[32] In Miller's reading of *Hrafnkel's saga*, "the economic, social, and geological context" is so important a character that it generates key elements of "the tale."[33] Miller also acknowledges the power of "those constraints on action that the culture generates in the form of morality, law, and social norms" in shaping the action of the story.[34] Although Miller has obviously moved a long way from the purely legal and sociological approach to feud that he used in EPM, the change from EPM to LPM had more to do with the ways in which

29 *Hrafnkel or the Ambiguities: Hard Cases, Hard Choices* (2017), 8.

30 *Audun*, 2; for more on motive, see *Axe*, 13–14.

31 *Hrafnkel*, 12.

32 *Axe*, 74.

33 *Hrafnkel*, 24.

34 *Hrafnkel*, 13.

Miller wants to explain social action in sagas than with the kinds of social action he wants to explain. And as always, the main kinds of social action to be studied all involve conflict and with it, emotion, violence, vengeance, and law.

Individually, the authors of the chapters in this volume cannot match Miller in blurring the boundaries between "historical" and "literary" texts (not to mention film), or promiscuously intermingling the volume's themes of emotion, violence, vengeance, and law in medieval Europe and beyond. Collectively, however, they have come close enough to his eclecticism to make any sequential ordering of their work seem arbitrary. For this reason, the chapters are grouped together into three categories, depending on whether they are based mainly on historical or literary medieval sources or use these or other kinds of sources to provide comparative perspectives on themes treated in the other chapters. Still, by reading the chapters through the lens of Miller's work, one can also see that they all discuss conflicts in medieval European and other "honor-based" societies. Driven by anger (Chapter 1), envy, jealousy, greed, or the impulse to avenge wrongs (Chapters 11, 13) and arising out of conflicting loyalties, personal rivalry, and competition for honor, position, property, and other limited goods, these conflicts are played out in larger or smaller arenas such as law courts (Chapters 1, 2, 3, 4, 5, 7, 8, 12), churches (Chapters 2, 3, 6), a modern city (Chapter 12), small rural settlements (Chapter 13), Saga Iceland (Chapters 7 and 8), a medieval kingdom (Chapters 9, 10, 11), an ancient empire (Chapter 14), and sitting-rooms in Jane Austen's England (Epilogue).

For our authors, as for Miller, conflict is precipitated by many forms of violence, including homicide (Chapters 1, 2, 6, 7, 8, 11), rape, attempted rape, and wild consensual sex (Chapters 5, 10, 13); war, rebellion, feud, and turf war (Chapters 4, 7, 8, 9, 10, 11, 12, 14). The conflicts discussed in this volume are also carried on, "processed," or "mediated," physically, emotionally, legally, politically, and verbally in many different ways. A very partial list includes: legal argument (Chapter 2), judicial processes (Chapters 1, 2, 3, 4, 5, 7, 8), threats (Chapter 3), insults (Chapter 5, 11), gifts and rituals of humiliation (Chapter 6), blood vengeance (Chapters 7, 10, 13), sexual vengeance (Chapter 11), mutilation, and single combat (Chapter 10), burning (Chapter 9), "The Game" (Chapter 12), severed heads (Chapter 14), and wounding words and silence (Epilogue).

•••

In Chapter 1, "Hot Anger and Just Indignation: Defensive Strategies in Early Modern German Homicide Trials," Susanne Pohl-Zucker shows how a modified form of an "honor-based" culture of provocation and angry riposte was incorporated into judicial proceedings in the courts of Reutlingen and

Württemberg. There, lawyers frequently made use of a *ius commune* concept known as *Excess*, which enabled them to defend slayers who had exceeded the requirements of self-defense due to hot anger and allowed judges to exempt these slayers from the death penalty if they had killed during a quarrel and in response to some provocation, such as physical or verbal assault. These were situations where men fought and reacted not just in defense of their physical integrity, but also in defense of their honor and reputation. The concept of *Excess* permitted lawyers to develop arguments based on a slayer's emotional state in order to reinforce the claim that the defendant had not intended to kill his opponent.

In Chapter 2, "Trial by Ordeal by Jury in Medieval England, or Saints and Sinners in Literature and Law," Elizabeth Papp Kamali makes the case for using hagiography and other ecclesiastical texts, as well as legal sources, to elucidate England's transition from using unilateral ordeals of cold water and hot iron to employing jury trials after 1215, when clerical participation in unilateral ordeals was barred by a decree of the Fourth Lateran Council. Her essay explores the hypothesis that this transition was significantly influenced by the papal interdict imposed on England by Innocent III between 1208 and 1214. Kamali examines a miracle story set during the interdict regarding a law case in which a woman accused of murder underwent an ordeal of hot iron to prove her innocence. Because the outcome of the ordeal was judged by twelve knights, the essay argues that by suspending liturgies, the interdict might have forced experimentation with alternative means of reaching verdicts in felony cases, including the involvement of juries in the issuance of ordeal verdicts; it also suggests that the shift from trial by ordeal to trial by jury may have been less a moment of rupture than a transition from one form of trial using juries to another. In making this argument, Kamali also reflects on the value to legal historians of using non-legal sources, including literary ones.

In Chapter 3, "Threats and Intimidation in Anglo-Norman Legal Disputes," William Eves draws on Miller's recent article on "Threat" (2010), which explains how characters in Icelandic sagas, among others, gain what game theorists call "threat advantage." Using monastic chronicles, charters, and hagiographical texts, Eves examines the explicit threats and subtler forms of intimidation that lay and ecclesiastical litigants used to the same effect in Anglo-Norman county courts and hundred courts, and shows how their judgments could be influenced by overbearing sheriffs and ecclesiastics who threatened their adversaries with excommunication or malediction. In other cases, litigants gained "threat advantage" by securing support from powerful people who brought their men to court, by locking opponents into a church where their case was to be heard, or by seizing the charter on which the opposing party based his case.

In this way, Eves demonstrates that in Anglo-Norman England, "extra-legal factors" could influence litigation in court.

In Chapter 4, "Courts and Rule-Making in Eleventh-Century Western France," Matthew McHaffie uses a very close analysis of a monastic charter recording a dispute over land heard in the court of Count Geoffrey the Bearded of Anjou to argue for the importance of considering the role of Angevin courts in making and promulgating rules with wider application beyond individual cases. That courts would have performed such a function, he suggests, was partially the result of the ways in which law and politics intersected during the period before this case was decided, when the counts of Anjou expanded by conquest the territories under their control. In addition to discussing these substantive issues, McHaffie also addresses the interpretive problem of reconstructing the perspective of courts and court-holders from charters that describe court-cases from the perspective of monastic disputants.

In Chapter 5, "Standing up in Court: Gender and Genitalia in Fourteenth-Century Zurich," Jamie Page examines the bizarre legal complaint of Rudolf Abdorf in the court of the Zürich city council that Heintz Wenginer had seduced Abdorf's daughter Agnes and repeatedly penetrated her with his "standing penis." Although the graphic depictions of sex and sexual organs, the jurisdictional entanglements, and the family drama of the Abdorf-Weniger case initially seem unfathomable, Page shows that by interpreting this extended law case as a tale of vengeance, he can explain why Abdorf publicly exposed his daughter's dishonor—and his own. In doing so, Page draws on the historiography of medieval law and disputing, and also finds in popular literature a broader frame of cultural reference for reading the Abdorf-Weniger case.

In Chapter 6, "How to Be Remembered: Securing the *Memoria* of a Slain Person in Medieval Denmark," Helle Vogt directly challenges Miller's contention in *Eye for an Eye* that in "honor-based" societies, the only meaningful and appropriate way of remembering a homicide victim was to take blood vengeance on the slayer himself or, failing that, on one of the slayer's associates. Noting that Miller bases this view largely on literary sources, where blood revenge is far more commonly found than it is in historical sources, Vogt uses wills and donation letters from fourteenth-century Denmark to study four cases in which slain men were memorialized and honored by gifts made to churches by the slayer and his kin for the purpose of endowing prayers for the slain men's souls, while associated rituals honored the slain man's surviving kin.

In Chapter 7, "Telling Evidence in *Njáls saga*," Carol J. Clover points out that although two important trials in this saga turn on very "murky" matters—in one case the issue of who is responsible for the plot to kill Gunnar and in the other, the issue of who is responsible for the burning of Njál and his family—the accounts of these trials barely mention evidence or proof that would clarify or resolve these matters. By examining one passage that resolves the first question and another that answers the second, Clover reveals the lengths to which the "telling" narrative goes in these two passages to identify the relevant actors and to establish every act necessary to establish their actions. By doing so, she also shows just how crucial the process of proof-by-evidence was to the makers of the sagas as well as to the legal tradition behind the text.

In Chapter 8, "Widening Horizons in *Njáls saga*," Ted Andersson closely examines the story's legal dimension as well as other issues in order to suggest that the author "almost self-consciously takes a nationalizing perspective on Icelandic history." To show how a saga "centered on the south" achieves "a supra-regional perspective," Andersson points out that "legal business is transacted almost exclusively at the Allthing" and only once at a local assembly; that legal negotiations toward the end of the saga focus on the East as much or more than the South" and involve important figures from the North and the West; and that in the famous scenes at the Allthing where Njál's party seeks support for a legal case, each chieftain they approach comes from a different region of Iceland, so that their progress takes them in turn to men from the south, the west, the northwest, the central north, and the northeast.

In Chapter 9, "Feud in the State: The Conflict between Haakon Haakonsson and Skule Baardsson," Hans Jacob Orning analyses what has generally been seen as the last serious rebellion in Norway during the high Middle Ages, Duke Skule Baardsson's uprising against his son-in-law, King Haakon Haakonsson, in 1239–40. Orning bases his study of this conflict largely on Sturla Þórðarson's *Hákonar saga Hákonarsonar* (*The Saga of Haakon Haakonsson*), which was commissioned soon after King Haakon's death in 1263 by his son and successor, King Magnus Haakonsson. Despite the saga's ideological dimensions and royalist perspective on events, Orning uses it as a relatively reliable source for reconstructing the lengthy relationship between Skule and King Haakon and argues that the conflict between them, though represented as a rebellion by a duke against a king, can now be seen as a feud that largely conforms to Miller's influential model of feud.

In Chapter 10, "*Waltharius*: Treasure, Revenge and Kingship in the Ottonian Wild West," Simon MacLean shows that the Latin poem *Waltharius*—set in a pseudo-historical version of fifth-century Europe, the Age of Attila the Hun—merits comparison with Icelandic sagas by reading it as a psychologically complicated story about greed, revenge, kingship, violence, and the conflicting loyalties of the three protagonists. Endorsing the argument that the poem was dedicated to Bishop Erchanbald of Strasbourg (965–91), MacLean asks why an Ottonian bishop of this city might have been interested in it and what associations might have been triggered by his reading it. MacLean's answer is that the poem's depictions of Frankish encounters with Huns and the author's anxieties about the reliability of kings fit comfortably into a mid-tenth-century context in regions such as Alsace, former royal heartlands whose political leaders now found themselves on the fringes of the Ottonian Empire and feared that their territories were turning into a kind of Wild West, where rulers were rarely seen and the violence of the powerful was unrestrained.

In Chapter 11, "*Braveheart* and Sexual Revenge," Robert Bartlett argues for interpreting Mel Gibson's 1995 film as tale of medieval sexual revenge, in which the attempted rape and execution of William Wallace's wife turns him into an English-slaughtering killing machine. After discussing the legendary elaborations of historical sources on which the film's story is based, Barlett argues that the film—by showing that Wallace's revenge is not to rape his enemies' women but to captivate and impregnate them—plays on the equation in both medieval and modern societies of blood with semen and the beloved country with a woman's body.

In Chapter 12, "Stringer's Saga: Njal and *The Wire*," John Hudson and Mark West follow Miller's lead in expanding the canon of stories of feuding and revenge to include the long-running American television series *The Wire*. Hudson and West's analysis of *The Wire* allows them to explore four issues that arise in *Njal's saga*, Miller's work on it, and Icelandic feud more generally: the starting point of feud, the options for escaping feud, the possibility and nature of peace in the feud, and the perceived perpetuity of feud. They also find points of comparison between characters in *The Wire* and *Njal's Saga*, notably Stringer Bell in the former and Skarphedin in the latter.

Chapter 13's *hommage* to Miller, "'An Overdeveloped Sense of Vengeance'? The Middle Ages, Vengeance and Movies" by Stuart Airlie, takes the form of a fellow-medievalist and fellow film aficionado's observations on vengeance in three films that his work illuminates even as they themselves cast light on it. The films are *The Virgin Spring* (1960), a tale of a father's vengeance for the rape and murder of his daughter in medieval Sweden, directed by Ingmar Bergman; *Harakiri* (1962), also known as *Seppuku*, a story of an avenging samurai warrior set in seventeenth-century Japan, directed by Masaki Kobayashi; and *Unforgiven* (1992), with Clint Eastwood as director and star in a bleak story of outrage and vengeance in the American West that is arguably Miller's favorite vengeance film.[35] As in much of Miller's work on vengeance, Airlie's focus is

35 "Clint Eastwood and Equity: Popular Culture's Theory of Revenge" (1998); see also the discussion of "the modern revenge" film with particular reference to *Death Wish* and *Dirty Harry* in "In Defense of Revenge" (1999).

on individual acts of revenge taken by individual avengers and on the idea of emotional satisfaction in vengeance.

By examining a number of appearances of severed and severing heads in reliefs and royal texts for the last great Neo-Assyrian king, Ashurbanipal, Chapter 14, "Getting A Head in the Neo-Assyrian Empire: Narratives of Enemy Decapitation in Ashurbanipal's Sources" by Eva Miller, shows how in these sources, as in Icelandic sagas, severed heads could be used to communicate.[36] Miller takes the narrative of the beheading of the enemy king Teumman at the Battle of Til-Tuba in 653 BCE and the subsequent ritual humiliation of his disembodied head as the starting point for examining other severed-head incidents, notably one in which Teumman's relative Urtak, wounded by arrows and lying on the battlefield, demands that his head be cut off and taken to Ashurbanipal. Miller's analysis of the narratives of Teumman and Urtak, along with several others, reframes the traditional interpretation of these episodes and shows how heads both function as markers of individual identity and deliver complex messages.

In the subtlest study of conflict in the entire volume, the Epilogue, "Silence as a Weapon of Self-Defence in *Sense and Sensibility*" by the late Nora Bartlett, listens to the "wounding words" that pass between Elinor Dashwood and her sister Marianne and to the "silences between them" in Jane Austen's novel. Calling our attention to the "words that sharpen, and the silences that sustain" the conflict between Elinor and Lucy Steele, a "cunning little vixen" who is Elinor's rival for the affections of Edward Ferrars, Bartlett brings her readers face to face with a study of female courage under fire—and possibly a hint of female vengeance.

36 On severed heads in sagas, see, e.g., Miller, "Choosing the Avenger" (1983), 159, 175–9.

Bill the Boundless

Jordan Corrente Beck

The first time I met Bill Miller I was in a crowded teacher's room in rural Japan. The two-by-two-inch video player was having a hard time containing him, the glacially slow shared connection taking his voice out of sync with the facial expressions I would later come to know so well as his student. I had heard of him, of course—that to study Icelandic sagas with a man whose listed scholarly interests included "vices and virtues" could be part of traditional legal study played no small role in determining where I would attend—but now I was *hearing* him, in that distinctive Wisconsin voice he so proudly defends. Not ready to stop listening when the video ended, I took to reading whatever was available without fee or subscription or was downloadable by e-reader—*The Anatomy of Disgust, Losing It,* a law review article on horsemeat—in all of which he criss-crossed the borders of disciplines and even of tone, at once self-reflective and bordering on the confessional and academic.

I originally proposed "On Boundaries" as the tentative title of my contribution to this Festschrift, thinking it an appropriate nod to the many facets of Bill at Michigan in the student mind—the demarcation and dispute of boundaries studied on day one of Property; the weighings and counterbalances of violence and gift in Bloodfeuds (the turns too of the shifting borders of the saga landscape); the dual roles of performer and observer in *Faking It*—in each case the focus being on the determination of the boundary line, whether it is hard or soft, and what sort of consequences follow if it is crossed. But this theme of defining, weighing, and even stepping over boundaries is equally suited to a portrait of Bill the teacher, who seems seamlessly aligned with Bill the man.

His classes draw enough students that it's a challenge to get into them, the competition less for the subject matter (though, in response to the occasional critique that they lack seriousness, all who take his courses can speak to their rigor and relevance to the law school curriculum by term's end) than for the chance to spend a few hours a week with Bill Miller being Bill Miller. But once one gains that access, his lessons are an invitation to cross the threshold and share what he loves (more often than not the sagas, and when not, his dog) or his latest outrage (just as likely to have been prompted by smartphones or pedestrian crossings as by faculty meetings). There is no pretense with Bill; or at least, whatever pretense there is he identifies quickly and very publicly outs (and then teaches another oversubscribed course on).

© KONINKLIJKE BRILL NV, LEIDEN, 2018 | DOI 10.1163/9789004366374_003

But there are other lines crossed as well. Bill's comments on student response papers step over any boundaries its writer might have tried to set up, his reactions interjected in tracked changes every few sentences to make a different reference, to slightly chide or—the kindest of interruptions—to simply write "nice." In his lectures, sentences are stopped to discuss the etymology of the word last uttered, and whole classes can be interrupted by some deliberate provocation to see how the students will react. Sometimes, when he decides he has crossed a self-imposed boundary of his own, he will send out an apology note, which of course is never necessary and so never serves as an apology proper but rather as another invitation into his psyche, drawing students closer to him.

Then there is that uncontainable Miller presence. The walls of the Hutchins' lecture halls can barely contain him, and he is larger still once outside. The nights spent out drinking with students are legendary, with apparently no limit to how much he can drink. These occasions also see no boundary between Bill and student; or for that matter, Bill and wait staff, who more often than not know him by name. On one memorable occasion after Bill had a bicycle accident, my fellow students and I received the message, "Class canceled until Weds. Miller concussed." We held class anyway, with beer, in his honor. This accident seemed to cause an increase in the number of Bill's "helmets are for sissies" diversions in lecture, despite the rumor (or was it fact?) that he taught a Property class afterward that he couldn't remember—the rumor has it he was also still bleeding; this hasn't been verified.

What I am calling a lack of boundaries, a delight in the pushing of boundaries, and the continual transcending of boundaries might better be termed "transparency," but the transparency would have no significance if what it revealed were not so rich. The lack of bounds allows an amount of intimacy that lets me hold equally dear both receiving from Bill the Christopher Smart fragment beginning *For I will consider my Cat Jeoffry* when my own cat fell ill and, after a night of exceptional drinking with some former students, receiving the quick morning-after message: "How hungover are you?"

And yet I can't even say the man's name: Bill. He knows this, of course, and I know that he knows this; of his messages received as a student and since, my favorite was signed "BILL—bet you choke trying to say that." Even though it's clearly permitted, I have yet to graduate to using the informal "Bill": except, inexplicably, in this small piece. In consequence, I have adopted the practice of not using his name at all. Given that our relationship has grown almost entirely out of writing and letter reading and exchanging notes on his books, it won't surprise him that I have taken this first bold step on the page and not to his face.

This piece could have been spun in countless themes that would be near to Bill's heart and teaching, and perhaps better than that of boundaries would have been that of gift. For just as Bill berates his classes at length for ever thinking a gift does not demand a return, he is equally candid about all the gifts he has received that he can never repay (the soul of Skarphedin chief among them). Borrowing his frequent turn of phrase, I am sure I speak for his students past, present (and I am sure, if he will have it, future) when I say that to him we owe a quite unrepayable debt, and of the nicest kind.

Bill Miller and Toby

Miller(ed) in St Andrews

Kimberley-Joy Knight and John Hudson

Over the years, staff and students at the University of St Andrews have been fortunate enough to hear some of William I. Miller's insightful, innovative and, occasionally, incendiary, research. Typical was an address given at the 'Emotions in the Courtroom' symposium, held on 3–4 May 2015, from which some of the contributions to this volume emerged. Because he had been far ahead of the recent 'emotional turn' scholarship, with his publications on emotions in the sagas and studies on disgust, humiliation and shame, Bill needed a little cajoling to revisit 'a tired-out subject, which didn't have much energy in the first place'. By the end of the symposium—and with only one enraged formal complaint about him presented to the organisers—Bill was wholly converted to the enterprise, remarking that 'there was not one bad paper' and that 'everyone's time could not have been better spent'. In his own discussion of fear and anger in high-stakes lawsuits in the Icelandic sagas, Miller explained how swelling, fainting and bleeding could all be read as expressions of vengeance and can give vital clues as to inner emotional states. These are topics that have often been covered in his papers in St Andrews, each time with a different twist, new and fascinating insights and an unfailingly captivated audience. Post paper, Bill is famed as a kind of pied piper, leading his willing audience to a nearby watering hole to continue the discussion. The time spent listening to the post-paper paper often passes so quickly and with so many drinks that the participants are known to feel rather 'Millered' the next morning.

Bill first came to St Andrews in the mid-1990s. It was just after his fiftieth birthday and he was complaining of being old, and of never previously having had a birthday that made him feel old. He came partly in search of beer, and the quest for Burton ale and latterly Timothy Taylor Landlord was undertaken with characteristic dedication (his latter-day preference for Landlord shows, in the eyes of anyone from Yorkshire, another of Bill's qualities, his willingness to modify his views when persistently confronted with clear evidence). He was also coming to visit Rob Bartlett, whom he had first met while Rob was employed at the University of Chicago. Visits recurred, as did the giving of papers which typically were loved by 95 percent of the audience and loathed by 5 percent, and which contained typical Miller aperçus: for example, that the discovery of the individual took place not in the twelfth century but during bouts of insomnia by anyone who has ever had difficulty sleeping. In the mid-2000s Bill

© KONINKLIJKE BRILL NV, LEIDEN, 2018 | DOI 10.1163/9789004366374_004

had a six-month stay in St Andrews as holder of a highly prestigious Carnegie Centenary professorship; this was just after his sixtieth birthday and he was complaining of being old, and of never previously having had a birthday that made him feel old. Since then he has been a regular visitor for three weeks each year, as an Honorary Professor in, first, the School of History and, most recently, the Institute of Legal and Constitutional Research.

Bill's activities at St Andrews have been many and various. One extraordinarily privileged class of Honours students were taught a class on Courtroom Dramas by Bill and his old friend Steve White, with the supposed teacher John Hudson as another fortunate observer. He has also offered reading groups, most often on sagas. It has often been the case that a reading group dedicated to covering several chapters of a text will only get through a few lines. One instance of this was *Hrafnkel's saga*, where Bill delighted in every detail, explaining with great understanding and wit the depths and complexities of the text. He has given numerous lectures, seminars, and other papers, always punctuated by frolics and detours, normally involving his motorcycle and his difficult relationship with speed limits.

Most of all he has talked with, talked to, and drunk beers with generations of St Andrews PhD students. For those in the 'early career' phase, Bill's St Andrews seminar papers have always been an occasion. Along with the guarantee of learning plenty about saga episodes involving exploding bodies and bloody axes, there is also the hope of a diversion into anecdote territory. The real prizes come for those who stick around after the paper and follow the speaker to the Central Bar or Whey Pat (the latter pub rivalling even Ann Arbor's Grizzly Peak in his affections), where the anecdotes fly thick and fast. Sometimes these address the early career phases of august members of the School of History, but more often than not they involve Bill's own follies and escapades.

In 2016 Bill narrated a re-enactment of the trial of the first Scottish Protestant martyr, Patrick Hamilton, before a sold-out crowd in St Andrews's Byre Theatre, an event which has recently received a prestigious national award. His contribution was the more remarkable as it came shortly after his seventieth birthday, and he was complaining of being old, and of never previously having had a birthday that made him feel old. And his activities have stretched beyond St Andrews, notably to collaborations with historians in Madrid and beyond. His official position was 'Visiting Scholar', though he functioned as much as court jester, or perhaps, as he would prefer, Lear's Fool. Only a bicycle accident in Ann Arbor prevented his 100 percent attendance record for events in appealing European locations; the symptoms that his family were told to look out for during his convalescence are reproduced below as Appendix A.

Bill is not simply a fascinating, fun and friendly annual visitor to St Andrews, but he has come to be so much part of the furniture that he is often asked to write references for younger scholars. However, as a cautionary tale for future PhD students, a Miller reference is just as full of frolics and detours as a Miller paper. Recently a hiring committee received a reference with all the colour that one could expect from Bill. It read: 'She can fight bears and shoot the eye out of moose at 30 feet with a hand gun. I recommend her to you with considerable enthusiasm'.

Appendix A

The document transcribed below was given to Bill to share with his family after he was concussed in a bicycle accident. It was intended to alert them to any personality changes. As his family rapidly realised, the document was not well suited for this purpose. However, drawing as surely it must on deep knowledge of the Miller character, writings, and conversation, it does provide a useful character sketch for inclusion in a Festschrift:

Information for Patient and Family Following Head Injury with Loss of Consciousness

Following an accident resulting in an injury to the head with loss of consciousness you may experience the following side effects:

- anger/irritability (especially in environments with multiple stimuli)
- impatience
- slow thinking
- increased mental fatigue
- depression
- sleep/wake disruption
- insomnia
- disinhibition/impulsivity
- headaches/co-ordination impairment
- impaired memory
- impaired judgement/reasoning
- impulse control problems
- aggression
- apathy
- inability to multi-task
- impaired tolerance of multiple stimuli

Please avoid alcohol. You should always wear a helmet for bicycle or motorcycle riding.

PART 1

Emotion, Violence, Vengeance, and Law in Medieval Historical Sources

CHAPTER 1

Hot Anger and Just Indignation: Justificatory Strategies in Early Modern German Homicide Trials

Susanne Pohl-Zucker

In a letter of supplication to the duke of Württemberg in 1495, Barbara Tücken, a housewife from the village of Tusslingen in the duchy of Württemberg, described her husband's killing of the village bailiff. Her account of this homicide was brief; she wrote that the bailiff and her husband had quarreled and that her husband had been "moved by anger" (mit Zorn bewegt) at his opponent's insults.[1] The dispute then turned violent and Hans Tücken killed the bailiff. Fights among men in which insults were exchanged and honor was at stake followed a culturally accepted dynamic of challenge and riposte.[2] The use of violence in the defense of honor was an expected disputing strategy in fights among men and was often punished leniently.[3]

1 Hauptstaatsarchiv Stuttgart (hereafter cited as HStA) A 602 WR 14962.

2 For a discussion of violence as a disputing strategy in fights among men in German society see, for example, Hans de Waardt, "Ehrenhändel, Gewalt und Liminalität," in *Verletzte Ehre. Ehrkonflikte in Gesellschaften des Mittelalters und der Frühen Neuzeit*, ed. Klaus Schreiner and Gerd Schwerhoff (Cologne, Weimar, Vienna: 1995), 303–19; Michael Frank, "Ehre und Gewalt im Dorf der frühen Neuzeit: Das Beispiel Heiden (Grafschaft Lippe) im 17. und 18. Jahrhundert," in *Verletzte Ehre*, 320–38. For discussions of the dynamic of "challenge and riposte" influencing disputes in honor-based societies see Pierre Bourdieu, "The Sentiment of Honor in Kabyle Society," in *Honour and Shame: The Values of Mediterranean Society*, ed. J. G. Peristiany (London: 1966), 191–241. In the past decades, anthropological analyses of dispute cultures have strongly influenced the German historiography of medieval and early modern German dispute culture. See, for example, Gerd Schwerhoff, *Köln im Kreuzverhör* (Cologne: 1991), 314–5.

3 Throughout the German Middle Ages and even during the early modern period, monetary sanctions and extrajudicial agreements were common in cases of slayings that occurred during heated quarrels. See Hans Jänichen, "Schwäbische Totschlagssühnen im 15. und 16. Jahrhundert," *Zeitschrift für Württembergische Landesgeschichte* 19 (1960), 128–40; Helga Schnabel-Schüle, *Überwachen und Strafen im Territorialstaat* (Cologne, Weimar, Vienna: 1997), 247. Such homicides were often termed "manslaughter" in opposition to "murder," which was committed in secrecy, with malice aforethought, or as the result of a reprehensible motivation. Murder was commonly punished with the death penalty. For further discussion

© KONINKLIJKE BRILL NV, LEIDEN, 2018 | DOI 10.1163/9789004366374_005

In Barbara Tücken's terse narrative, her husband's anger was therefore less central than the provocation he had suffered. While the slayer's anger was an understandable reaction to the bailiff's insult, it was the victim's attack that justified her plea for lenient treatment rather than her husband's emotional state. Tücken explicitly stressed that the bailiff had initiated the dispute.[4] During the course of the early modern period, the increasing influence of *ius commune* concepts and categories allowed lawyers to stretch and modify the references to a defendant's anger that they used as an exculpating strategy. This essay explores varying interpretations of a slayer's anger that originated in distinct legal settings: the courts of the imperial city of Reutlingen, where slayers who had killed in the heat of anger could claim asylum, and the courts of the nearby duchy of Württemberg, where angry slayers were in greater need of justification.

It is not my intention to imply that a medieval legal focus on provocation was superseded by a sudden search for slayers' "deep inner lives" in early modern courts, to use Bill Miller's expression.[5] The legal arguments focused on slayers' emotional states that German jurists used increasingly during the sixteenth and seventeenth centuries had been developed, discussed and used in legal practice by Italian jurists since the late Middle Ages. Roman-canonical concepts also influenced individual German legal codes long before the sixteenth century. The present discussion analyses how *ius commune* concepts coexisted with, contributed to and modified justificatory arguments based on provocation. The analysis of cases tried in Reutlingen and in Württemberg also illustrates that the use of these concepts was varied and uneven and dependent on existing legal parameters.

The city of Reutlingen had recieved an imperial privilege in 1495 which allowed the city council to grant asylum to slayers who had killed either in self-defense or in the heat of anger. Slayers who claimed asylum were interviewed

of the distinction between manslaughter and murder see Philipp Allfeld, *Die Entwicklung des Begriffes Mord bis zur Carolina. Ein rechtsgeschichtlicher Versuch* (Erlangen: 1877); and Gerd Schwerhoff, *Köln im Kreuzverhör* (Cologne: 1991), 275–6 and the literature cited there. It is important to note, however, that the terms "manslaughter" and "murder" could also be used interchangeably in the sources used in this essay.

4 HStA A 602 WR 14692. According to late medieval custom, it was important to prove who had provided the so-called *Anlass* (cause) of the dispute. See Eduard Osenbrüggen, *Das Alamannische Strafrecht im deutschen Mittelalter* (Aalen: 1968), 73–165; Rudolf His, *Das Strafrecht des deutschen Mittelalters. Erster Teil: Die Verbrechen und ihre Folgen im allgemeinen* (Leipzig: 1920), 209–15.

5 William Ian Miller, "Deep Inner Lives, Individualism and People of Honour," *History of Political Thought* 16 (2) (1995), 190–207.

when they arrived at the city gate. If their justifications corresponded to the privilege, they could remain in the city for life. Their claim to asylum could be challenged, however, before the court at Reutlingen. Private parties or local officials from their hometowns could initiate a trial by accusing a slayer of having committed an intentional and premeditated murder. If the accusing party could prove their case, Reutlingen would hand over the slayer to be tried by his local jurisdiction.[6] Frequently, slayers escaped to Reutlingen from the duchy of Württemberg.[7] In Württemberg, trials in homicide cases were generally initiated *ex officio* rather than by private accusation. After an investigative stage referred to as *processus informativus*, the inquisition procedure was replaced by the so-called fiscal accusation procedure, in which a local official acted as prosecutor for the duke of Württemberg. The administration of criminal justice was centralized; each verdict needed the approval of the duke and his councillors.[8]

Ius commune-trained lawyers were present at every stage in the Reutlingen trials and increasingly also at the homicide trials that took place in Württemberg courts.[9] The growing influence of the *ius commune* on early modern German criminal jurisdiction, commonly referred to as the *Rezeption des römischen Rechts* (reception of the Roman law) was promoted by the publication of the *Carolina*, the imperial criminal code from 1532, which was heavily based on Roman legal concepts and categories.[10] In Württemberg, Duke Christoph ordered his judges in the 1550s to use the *Carolina*, and if in doubt, to consult with legal experts.[11] This process, called *Aktenversendung*, was common throughout the empire. From the late sixteenth century, Württemberg's lay

6 See Ralf Reck, "Das Totschläger-Asyl der Reichsstadt Reutlingen 1495–1804," *Reutlinger Geschichtsblätter*, Neue Folge 8 (1970), 46–78. Reck has argued that the city probably had a long tradition of granting asylum to slayers reaching back to the Middle Ages. The city held on to the privilege until 1804.

7 Ibid., 80.

8 For a detailed overview of Württemberg's criminal justice system, see Schnabel-Schüle, *Überwachen und Strafen*, 76–123.

9 In Württemberg, homicides committed during disputes were frequently resolved through extrajudicial agreements during the sixteenth century. Towards the late sixteenth century, trials became more frequent, and seventeenth-century homicide cases were nearly always tried in court.

10 For an introduction to the historiography of the *Rezeption* see Schnabel-Schüle, *Überwachen und Strafen*, 216–8 and the literature cited there. The literature on the *Carolina* is extensive. For an introduction see Friedrich-Christian Schroeder, *Die Carolina. Die peinliche Gerichtsordnung Kaiser Karls V. von 1532* (Darmstadt: 1986).

11 See Schnabel-Schüle, *Überwachen und Strafen*, 81–82.

judges generally sent the records of homicide trials to the law professors of the local university in Tübingen for a *consilium*, a legal recommendation that also contained a suggested verdict. In these *consilia*, the authors supported their arguments with numerous quotations from learned jurists and contributed to the spread of *ius commune* concepts and terms. The judges of the asylum court in Reutlingen likewise commissioned *consilia* and consulted the law professors in Tübingen or other independent jurists.

Ius commune judged a slayer's guilt on the basis of his intent, which encouraged the discussion of mental and emotional states.[12] The cases discussed here show that the legal language of anger was equivocal, influenced by cultural notions of male assertive honor but also by Roman concepts of diminished capacity and a governmental discourse that valued emotional balance. The manner in which jurists and defendants employed or mixed these different concepts depended on the legal context, the circumstances of a homicide and a defendant's general reputation. The legal evaluations of the emotions of male slayers who had killed during heated disputes were located on a spectrum ranging from controlled and reasonable indignation on one side to mad and uncontrolled rage on the other side.[13]

•••

Although the *Carolina* sanctioned manslaughter committed in the heat of anger with the death penalty in article 137, article 142 allowed judges to use

12 While this article discusses legal strategies focusing on emotional states, it is important to note that jurists considered other circumstantial evidence, such as the kind of weapon a slayer used or the kind of wound he had administered during the dispute.

13 In the records discussed here the slayers are men. While women might use verbal and physical violence to defend their honor in disputes, they are generally missing from the ranks of slayers convicted of having committed manslaughter during a heated quarrel. (For an exception, see a Württemberg case from 1659: Universitätsarchiv Tübingen 84/12, fols. 198v–207v). Women appeared as defendants predominantly in cases that were judged as premeditated murder. There are, for example, a number of extant cases from Württemberg where women were judged as murderesses after having killed their husbands. An example is a case from 1688 in which the defense counsel's consideration of the defendant's mental and emotional state centered on her fear of her husband's violence and her "typically female" lack of understanding. The jurist referred to her as an *einfältig weib* (simple woman): HStA A 209 Bü 1604, *consilium* from September 1688; see Rublack, *Magd, Metz oder Möderin*, 315–25.

their discretion when a slayer exceeded the limits of self-defense.[14] According to the *ius commune*, the requirements of self-defense concerned the manner, the timing and the cause of the slayer's strike against his attacker. It was crucial to prove that a slayer lacked malicious intent. Jurists demanded that a slayer's weapon should not have been more lethal than the one used by the victim, that the strike have occurred immediately after the initial attack and that imminent danger rather than vengeance had prompted the violent response.[15] If a slayer violated these requirements in anger, judges were allowed to impose a *poena extraordinaria*, an arbitrary punishment, rather than the death penalty.[16] German jurists made frequent use of this concept, which was often referred to in Württemberg records as *Excess*, in order to save from the death penalty slayers who had killed during a heated dispute. Within the *ius commune* there were different interpretations of the nature of a slayer's anger: one which emphasized the victim's provocation and one which focused more strongly on the perturbed emotional state of the defendant.

The most frequently used interpretation of the nature of a slayer's anger was based on the writings of late medieval Italian jurists who had asserted that in order to be exculpatory, anger had to have a just cause.[17] Just anger responded to unwarranted provocations, such as verbal or physical attacks, which threatened the defendant's honor and sometimes his life. The degree of exculpation, however, depended on the nature of the provocation that the slayer had suffered. If the provocation was slight—for example, only a verbal attack—a slayer's cause could be less just and he was often more severely punished. The concept of *Excess* allowed lawyers to employ a language of honor and provocation in the slayer's defense. Take for example a Württemberg *consilium* from

14 *Die Peinliche Gerichtsordnung Kaiser Karls V. und des Heiligen Römischen Reichs von 1532 (Carolina)*, ed. Friedrich-Christian Schroeder (Stuttgart: 2014), 85–86 and 87–88.

15 See, for example, the discussion of self-defense by the fourteenth-century jurist Bartolus of Sassoferrato, which can be found in his commentary on the eighth book of Justinian's *Codex* (Unde vi, I, n. 7), quoted here from a sixteenth-century edition: "Quæero in quo consistat illud moderamen. Gl. Hic dicit, circa tria. Primo circa modum. Secundo circa tempus. Tertio circa causam." Bartolus de Saxoferrato, *Bartoli Commentaria in secundum Codicis partem* (Lyon: 1550) <http://digital.ub.uni-duesseldorf.de/ihd/content/pageview/2853209—http://digital.ub.uni-duesseldorf.de/ihd/content/pageview/2853209>, fol. 106r, accessed 13/6/2017. For further discussion of the requirements of the *moderamen* see Kenneth Pennington, "*Moderamen inculpatae tutelae*: The Jurisprudence of a Justifiable Defense," *Rivista internazionale di diritto commune* 24 (2014), 27–55.

16 Arbitrary sanctions in early modern Württemberg included, for example, monetary fines or temporary exile, but also dishonorable punishments such as public whipping.

17 See Woldemar Engelmann, *Die Schuldlehre der Postglossatoren* (Leipzig: 1895), 116–22.

1571 which considered Michael Schaich's homicide of Hans Feuer an *Excess*. Schaich had killed his unarmed victim in response to a verbal insult. In his justification of a lenient punishment, the jurist took Schaich's emotional state into account. The jurist argued that Schaich undoubtedly had become *erzürnt* (angry) when Feuer had questioned his skill as a weaver. The author of the *consilium* implied that Schaich's honor had been at stake when he wrote that Schaich must have considered his victim's insult *schmechlich* (shameful).[18]

While a slayer's anger could thus be interpreted in the context of a rhetoric of honor and provocation, lawyers also had to prove that the slayer had not intended to kill his victim. The slayer's angry response was considered a "slip"—albeit an understandable one—from the expected moderate response. Slayers and their counsel thus mostly desisted from too vehement an insistence on a customary right to avenge injured honor. Instead, they developed defensive strategies which employed a rhetoric of distancing but also conveyed that the slayer had been justly angered by his opponent's provocation.

Jurists frequently accomplished this by combining a focus on the injured honor of the defendants with an emphasis on the civic and peaceful behavior that he showed by resisting the use of violence to the last. Take, for example, the case of the slayer Paul Doll, who was tried in the asylum court in Reutlingen in 1544 after killing Hans Guckher following a tavern dispute. His lawyer, Dr. Krauss, emphasized Doll's exemplary behavior before and during the course of the dispute. Doll had conducted himself in a friendly and affable manner, Krauss said. Although Guckher insulted Doll repeatedly, Doll had tried to prevent a fight with "repeated and friendly pleas."[19] Doll had asked him to "be of good cheer and peaceful" and had even offered to buy him wine.[20] According to witness testimony, Doll had not become angry until Guckher slapped his face, which was a grave insult in early modern German dispute culture.[21] But even then, Doll had not responded in kind or tried to follow Guckher, after bystanders had forced him to leave the tavern.[22] The *Ius commune* offered jurists an additional concept of a slayer's anger that had to do less with the justness of its cause than with the resulting emotional turmoil. During the sixteenth

18 HstA A 209 Bü 141 (*consilium*, 28 April 1571).

19 Stadtarchiv Reutlingen (hereafter cited as StRT) A 910a (plea of the defense, 1 June 1545): "vilfeltig pitt unnd freunndtlich erpietten."

20 Ibid.: "guter ding unnd fridsam zůßein."

21 See ibid. and Frank, "Ehre und Gewalt," 335.

22 See StRT, A 910a (plea of the defense, 1 June 1545). Guckher waited outside, however, and attacked Doll again, when Doll left the tavern shortly afterwards to go home. During this second stage of the fight, Doll killed Guckher.

century, the French commentators Hyppolitus de Marsiliis and Andreas Tiraquellus went a step further in diminishing the responsibility of slayers who exceeded the requirements of self-defense in anger. Both jurists emphasized a kind of emotional perturbation that was independent of its provocation: it was the impulse, an impediment to the senses, rather than the provocation which constituted the mitigating circumstance. Slayers overcome by an impulse were not themselves: their senses were deranged and their capacity to form an intention was severely impeded.[23] An angry man was comparable to a madman, a *furiosus*; he was temporarily "outside of himself" (*extra se*) and not master of his mind.[24] The crucial difference between these French commentators and the Italians hinged on this point, for Hyppolitus and Tiraquellus argued that the punishment of the angry slayer could be mitigated even if his victim had not caused his anger.[25] Most contemporary jurists remained wary of this assertion and insisted that it was the provocation rather than the emotion that mitigated punishment.[26]

Yet the situation was unique in the asylum court at Reutlingen because the privilege did not specify the nature of a slayer's anger or stipulate that this anger had to have been just. It sufficed to prove that the slayer had become suddenly angry. These records therefore illustrate the variety of possible

23 Hyppolitus and Tiraquellus came closer to the doctrine of canon lawyers, many of whom assumed that impulse excluded the presence of *animus* (intention) completely; see Engelmann, *Die Schuldlehre*, 113. The canon lawyer Guilelmus Durantis wrote, for example, that a person who hurt another with words or deeds should not be condemned because "what is done in anger should not be imputed" (quod calore iracundiae fit, non imputatur) (ibid.).

24 Andreas Tiraquellus, *De poenis legum ac consuetudinem statutorumque temperandis aut etiam remittendis* (Venice: 1565), *prima causa*, no. 20.

25 Ibid., no. 10. "etiam si, qui occisus est, non dederit causam irae, quae occisorem ad maleficium impulerit, ut videlicet in hoc casu sit mitius puniendus" (even if he who is killed did not give cause for the anger which drove the slayer to the crime, one may see that in this case he should be punished more leniently); and Hyppolitus de Marsiliis, *Practica causarum criminalium* (Lugano: 1529), § *Quoniam*, no. 94: "Attamen est in potestate iudicis non condemnare homicida poena mortis quem impulit iracundia, orta etiam aliter quam ex facto offensi" (Nevertheless it is in the power of the judge not to condemn to the death penalty the slayer whom rage impels, even if it sprang from causes other than the deed of the one who was injured).

26 The influential German jurist Benedict Carpzov asserted this opinion in his treatise on criminal law in 1638. See Benedict Carpzov, *Practicae Novae Imperialis Saxonicae Rerum Criminalium. Pars I*, trans. and ed. Dietrich Oehler (Goldbach: 2000), 47–49. Jurists conceded that a *maxima iracundia* that was akin to temporary insanity could exist, but they rarely used this concept.

scenarios that jurists could develop when they discussed a slayer's emotional state. Not all lawyers appearing before the Reutlingen court interpreted the defendant's anger as Paul Doll's lawyer had done, as a reasonable and contained emotion. Other counsel sought instead to strengthen their claim that the defendant had been angry at the time of the homicide by focusing on both just cause and emotional perturbation. When in 1576 Junghans Petermann was accused in the court of Reutlingen of murderous intent in killing his victim Hentzler, the depiction of Petermann's emotional state in the *consilium* was ambiguous. According to the witness testimony, the homicide had occurred after Petermann and his friend Neuffer had been drinking with Hentzler in a tavern. But they had eventually disagreed about each of their shares for the bill. At one point, Petermann and Neuffer got up and left in protest. Hentzler yelled after them that they were *Lumpen* (ne'er-do-wells).[27] This term was a strong insult in early modern German dispute culture because it implied dishonesty.[28] In response, Neuffer and Petermann challenged Hentzler to meet them outside if he was a *biderman* (an honorable man).[29] Hentzler was swinging a hayfork; Petermann and Neuffer drew their knives.[30] The disputants circled each other, yelling insults. Hentzler eventually struck Neuffer. Petermann then told Henztler to leave his friend in peace, because whoever wanted to hit Neuffer should also try to hit him, Petermann. Hentzler took this as a challenge and immediately threatened to strike Petermann also.[31] Yet Petermann told Hentzler at this point to keep the peace and said that he would no longer run from him but stand his ground, a statement that could be interpreted both ways: as an effort to make peace, which is how the defense read it, or as defiance, which was the line taken by the lawyer for the plaintiff.[32] When Hentzler did not desist from threatening to hurt him with the hayfork, Petermann did not wait for the blow, but struck him. Hentzler died of the blow a few days afterwards.

The jurist who wrote the *consilium* in this case, Dr. Hochmann, confirmed Petermann's claim to asylum because he had committed an *Excess* in just anger. In the portrayal of Petermann's emotional state, Hochmann put this anger into

27 StRT A 919 (*consilium*, 2 November, 1587), fol. 7v.

28 For further discussion of particularly dishonoring insults in German dispute culture see Gerd Schwerhoff, *Köln im Kreuzverhör*, 312–22; and Frank, "Ehre und Gewalt," 325–27 and the literature cited there.

29 StRT A 919 (*consilium*, 2 November, 1587), fol. 7v.

30 Ibid., fols. 8r–v.

31 Ibid., fol. 8v.

32 See ibid. (plea of the plaintiff, 2 August 1587), fol. 5v and (plea of the defense, 20 August, 1587), fol. 3r.

perspective by affirming that Petermann was generally known as a man with an even emotional balance. He was known "never to have angered a child" (nie kein Kindt soll erzürnet) and had always behaved "quietly and well" (sich still und woll verhalten).[33] In contrast, his victim Hentzler had been "proud and quite defiant" and "always ready to start a fight."[34] While Hochmann thus emphasized Petermann's peaceful conduct, he also relied on a cultural acceptance of a dynamic of challenge and riposte which validated a disputant's anger in the face of insults to his honor. He argued that it was easy to believe that being called a *Lump* had moved the accused to anger.[35] Hochmann claimed that anger which had originated from a "just and legitimate cause" (ex iusta et legitima causa) deserved a mitigated punishment.[36]

Yet Hochmann subsequently added an additional twist to his discussion of Petermann's anger. He legitimated his claim that anger constituted a mitigating circumstance with quotations from the writings of the French jurist Tiraquellus, who suggested that the senses of angry men were deranged. Hochmann quoted from a passage in which Tiraquellus wrote that an angry man was like a madman, "outside of himself," and that "anger obstructs the mind, so that it can not recognize truth."[37] Although Hochmann had earlier asserted that Petermann's anger was due to a just cause—that is, the provocations of his victim—these quotations stressed the derangement of the senses over provocation and made the point that passionate anger did not necessarily need to stem from the provocations of the deceased.[38] By choosing quotations that emphasized the distressing effects of anger, Hochmann allowed for the

33 Ibid. (*consilium*, 2 November, 1587), fol. 17v.

34 Ibid., fols. 17r–v: "stoltz und fretzig gnuog"; "hab gern gehadert."

35 Ibid., fol. 14r.

36 Ibid., fol. 16v.

37 Ibid., fol. 14v: "extra se"; "impedit ira animum, ne possit cernere verum." These quotations come from Tiraquellus, *De poenis, prima causa*, nos. 20 and 21, where Tiraquellus quotes from Roman authors and Roman laws to strenghten his interpretation of anger.

38 Ibid. Tiraquellus makes this point in *De poenis prima causa*, no. 10. The case has been made by historians that early modern jurists' selections of quotations were not always the product of a deliberate choice but rather were influenced by the specific books that their university's law library possessed; see, for example, Schnabel-Schüle, *Überwachen und Strafen*, 71. Dr. Hochmann was a law professor at the University of Tübingen, which had an extensive law library. Contemporary *consilia* from Tübingen contain numerous references to the writings of jurists who privileged just cause over emotional perturbance. It can be supposed, therefore, that Hochmann deliberately chose to mention Tiraquellus because the terms of the asylum privilege gave him the freedom to substantiate his case from different angles.

possibility that anger had deranged Petermann's senses and that it was this internal state which constituted the mitigating circumstance. In order to justify Petermann's claims from these two legal perspectives, Hochmann represented the defendant as both an indignant sufferer of an unjust provocation to his honor and a raging madman who could no longer distinguish between right and wrong. According to the latter argument, anger came close to diminished intent. Hochmann obviously did not present these two characterizations of Petermann as mutually exclusive or contradictory, but rather as aspects of a complete portrait that could include several possible motivations or emotional states.

In the case of Endris Zittelmann, tried in the asylum court in 1584 for the slaying of his brother during a heated quarrel, the defense lawyer alleged both self-defense and emotional perturbation to justify Zittelmann's claim to asylum.[39] The counsel argued that if Zittelmann's claim of self-defense was not believed, he could avail himself of the other condition recognized by the privilege: slayings committed in the heat of anger.[40] Because his assertion that the anger was due to just cause was challenged by the counsel for the plaintiff, the counsel for the defense based his arguments on Tiraquellus' claim that the punishment was mitigated even if there was no just cause for anger.[41] Here the counsel for the defense pretended that this was accepted legal doctrine rather than the opinion of a minority, in order to undermine the plaintiff's claim that Zittelmann did not have a just cause for his anger. He alleged that Zittelmann was consumed with an anger that was "not a common sheep's anger" (kein gemeiner schaffs zorn) but a "heated, passionate rage" (brünstiger, hitziger entrüst).[42] In a manner similar to Tiraquellus, whom he had evoked earlier and who portrayed angry offenders as no longer in command of their senses, the lawyer stressed impulse over provocation and depicted Zittelmann as a man consumed by his rage. Previously, however, the lawyer had presented Zittelmann as a man acting in self-defense who had resisted responding to his brother's attack with "angry words" (boes wortt).[43] The counsel did not commit himself to one or the other of these characterizations but allowed them

39 StRT A 916b (plea of the counsel for the defense, 22 October, 1578); see, for example, fols. 49r–61r.

40 Ibid., fol. 55r.

41 Ibid., fols.. 58r–59r.

42 Ibid., fol. 60r. The term "sheep's anger" is not quite clear, but the lawyer probably evoked the image of a sheep to describe a meeker emotion than the passionate rage he ascribed to Zittelmann.

43 Ibid., fol. 34r. See also fol. 49r.

both equal weight.[44] Nor did he address whether it would be possible for both to be true. His concern was to develop both characterizations as vividly as he could in order to enhance Zittelmann's chances of continuing to enjoy asylum. He also used his opponent's accusation for this purpose. When the counsel for the plaintiff tried to interpret Zittelmann's wrath as a deliberate and malicious intent to kill and used the term *grimmig* (grim) to characterize his emotional state, the counsel for the defense used this claim as further proof that Zittelmann had been angry and thus deserved to stay in the asylum. He wrote that "even the ducal lawyer tried hard to charge the accused with a very great and grim anger."[45]

In the trial of Michel Pfeffer, who had killed Hans Rhein in 1546 in the Württemberg village of Genkhingen, the defense lawyer likewise claimed self-defense and alleged that his client had been angry at the time of the slaying.[46] In defense of his client, the lawyer had to undermine the portrait painted by his opponent, a lawyer representing the duke of Württemberg who challenged Pfeffer's claim to asylum. Michel Pfeffer killed Hans Rhein after a serious dispute with his children over dividing the dowry of their late mother, during which Pfeffer hit his daughter so hard that she began to bleed. His second wife, afraid that her husband would harm the children, ran into the street and screamed for help. Hans Rhein, a village constable, came running into the house with a stick in his hand. After a quick and heated exchange, Pfeffer took a sword from a corner of the room and stabbed Rhein, who then ran out of the house, only to fall dead within a few steps.

The plaintiff's lawyer was faced with a difficult challenge. In order to undermine Pfeffer's claim to asylum, he had to prove a murderous intent, although the victim's presence had been unexpected and so came as a surprise to the slayer. The lawyer solved this problem by presenting Pfeffer as a monstrous person ready to kill anyone who crossed him. In his *articulos probatoriales* (a list of articles or statements which presented the witnesses with his view of the case and asked them to agree or disagree), the counsel denied that

44 The terms of the asylum privilege, allowing the claims of both self-defense and hot anger encouraged lawyers to waver between these arguments. The judges at the Reutlingen court apparently did not ask counsel to choose between these claims.

45 Ibid. 916c (plea of the counsel for the plaintiff, 15 July, 1578), fol. 4r and ibid. 916b (plea of the counsel for the defense, 22 October, 1587), fol. 60r: "Zůdem so hatt fürstl. Anwalt in sein zwölfften unnd dreÿzehenden probatorial sich unterstanden ein sondern grossen grim unnd zorn uff beklagten zu treiben." The counsel for the defense emphasized that the counsel for the plaintiff's reasoning seemed "amusing" (*witzig*) to him, probably because this argument proved his own plea.

46 StRT A 912.

Pfeffer had any reason to deal harshly with his children and argued that he had launched into "inappropriate, mad, wild, cruel, murderous screaming,"[47] beating his innocent daughter so that the blood streamed down her face. In answer to the screams of Pfeffer's wife, Rhein advanced to make peace. But when Pfeffer saw Rhein, Pfeffer drew his sword and "attacked him, thirsting for his blood."[48] Rhein, having no weapon, was very frightened and tried to escape, but Pfeffer "with armed and blood-dripping hands bloodthirstily pursued the hard-pressed, frightened, fleeing Rhein," killing him "by stabbing him from behind, cruelly, intentionally and pitifully."[49] This barrage of colorful adjectives and adverbs served to establish a marked contrast between the murderous Pfeffer and the peaceful, frightened Rhein, who was portrayed as doing his civic duty. Rhein had acted from the purest motives, out of "duty, love and Christian faithfulness," and obeyed his sworn oath to always give assistance when the hue and cry was raised.[50] According to the counsel for the plaintiff, Pfeffer's wild madness did not indicate that he was temporarily not himself. His rage, it was claimed, was fueled by a longstanding secret hatred toward Rhein, which would make Pfeffer a murderer without any claim to the asylum.[51] The counsel argued that Pfeffer had always intended to kill Rhein and executed this intention when Rhein ran into his house.

In his contrasting interpretation of the homicide, the counsel for the defense claimed that when Rhein had charged into Pfeffer's house, Pfeffer had killed him to protect himself and his household. He thus portrayed Pfeffer as

47 Ibid. (*articulos probatoriales*, 18 March, 1557, article one): "ein ungepürlich, wuetterisch, ungestüm, grausam, mordt geschreihisch wesen." Unfortunately, the concluding speech of the counsel for the plaintiff was given orally, and no written record is extant. We must instead follow his arguments through his *articulos probatoriales*.

48 Ibid. (article nine): "hart unnd bluettdurstiglich getrungen."

49 Ibid. (article eleven): "waar disen beclagten, ime geängsten, genöttrengten, fliehenden Schützen, hefftig nachgesetzt, fur das hauß durch den hoff, mit gewerter, bluettreiwender handt, bluettgürlich, nach geiagt, am gatter des hoffs ereÿlt, unnd hinderwertz greulichen, fürsetzlich unnd jämerlich erstochen, das er Hanns Reÿn mit dem gatter, in die gassen hinauß gefallen."

50 Ibid. (article fourteen): "aus solcher schuldig pflicht, menschlich liebe unnd Christennlicher trew."

51 Ibid. (article fifteen): "It is true that such damage and murderous homicide was not committed without a longstanding secret hatred, premeditation and unlawful presumptuousness" (waar solche beschedigung, unnd wol mordmessige endtleibung nit ohne vorgeenden heimlichen neid, haß, fürsatz, unnd frewentlich muettwillen sein unnd beschehen). Secret and premeditated hatred was a typical characteristic of murder according to the law: see n. 3 above.

fulfilling his duty as the head of the family, while Rhein was the troublemaker who had attacked the peace of Pfeffer's house without cause. In addition to claiming self-defense, the lawyer also referred to Pfeffer's anger as a mitigating circumstance. The lawyer used the concept of just anger and the notion of an exculpating mad rage in order to characterize Pfeffer's emotional state. He first maintained that Pfeffer had become justly angry when his daughter insulted him during their dispute.[52] But this anger had quickly turned into a wild rage. The lawyer alleged that when Pfeffer struck at Rhein he was consumed with "a burning anger" (brennenden Zorn) and his "senses were deranged" (in Zuerrüttung seiner selbs), so that the stroke unintentionally turned out badly.[53] The lawyer dismantled his opponent's claim that Pfeffer's attack from behind indicated a murderous intent by claiming that a senseless madman was unaware of what he was doing and did not know "whether he hit, struck, knocked or stabbed."[54] In his attempt to portray Rhein both as a responsible householder and father and as a raging madman, the counsel even combined the notions of a mad anger and self-defense in the same phrase. He claimed that Pfeffer had killed Rhein in "a mad and crazy manner to reestablish peace and quiet for himself and his house."[55] The term *unbesinnt* (mad) was commonly used to refer to insane people. The counsel was arguing that Pfeffer was insane but at the same time capable of forming a clear and sensible intention, that of restoring peace and quiet to his house. These claims may appear at odds, but the counsel apparently felt that they doubled Pfeffer's chances of asylum protection.

During this legal battle over Pfeffer's emotional state, two different concepts of the relationship between trigger and emotional response emerged. According to the concept of just anger, this relationship was straightforward and easily comprehensible for an outsider. Anger was triggered in response to an insult or an attack, according to a cultural script of challenge and riposte that was easily recognized. In contrast and according to the above-mentioned French commentators' interpretation of anger, the relationship between cause and effect was less clear. Their concept of mitigating anger resembled madness and did not follow a script; it could not be foreseen when this anger would find its outlet and who might be the target. In their interrogations of the witnesses,

52 Ibid. (*articulos defensionales*, 9 April, 1557, article six).

53 Ibid. (article nineteen).

54 Ibid. (plea of the counsel of the defense, 5 July, 1557): "ob er hauw, schlag, stoß oder stech."

55 Ibid.: "auß unbesinter zorniger weiß, und ihm selbs darmit frid und rhuw ihn seinem aigen haus zueschaffen."

both lawyers made strategic use of arguments that both asserted and challenged the notion that a slayer's emotions were easily comprehensible.

The defense's question concerning article eight of the accusation employed the latter strategy, claiming that a person's emotional state was not necessarily obvious to others. In article eight, the counsel for the plaintiff had asserted that the victim Rhein was startled and frightened by the screams of Pfeffer's wife and ran toward the house with the intention of making peace. This was in contrast to the defense counsel's assertion that Rhein had been aggressive rather than frightened. In his question concerning article eight of the accusation, the defense demanded how a witness who had agreed with this article could have known that Rhein was frightened, and "whether he [the witness] had been so close by that he was able to see into his [Rhein's] heart and know his mind and recognize that he had friendly or angry, malevolent intentions."[56] The first witness answered that he saw in Rhein's face that he was frightened. Yet he also conceded that it was not possible to see into anyone's heart.[57]

With these questions, the counsel for the defense tried to confuse the witnesses and undermine any assertions that Rhein was frightened when he ran toward Pfeffer's house. He did so on the assumption that emotions and intentions were hidden in a man's heart. Yet according to jurists of the *ius commune*, external behavior provided a clue to intention. Jurists established different presumptions, *praesumptiones*, based on the behavior and comportment of

---

56 Ibid. (*Pfefferlins Interrogatoria*, article eight, no. seven): "ob er dazuemal bey [...] ihm gewesen, das er sein hertz und gemuet erkent, das er fründlicher oder zorniger neidiger mainung zuegelauffen."

57 Ibid. (testimony of Martin Entz, nos. 6 and 7). The counsel for the defense had pursued a similar strategy earlier when he tried to get the witnesses to challenge the counsel for the plaintiff's assertion in article four of the *articulos probatoriales* that Pfeffer had "intended nothing good" (nichts guetz im sinn gehapt) when he returned home and started a fight with his children (ibid., *articulos probatoriales*, 18 March, 1557, article four). The corresponding question of the counsel for the defense asked: "1.... how he [the witness] could know that he [Pfeffer] had intended nothing good. 2. Also whether it was possible to look into a man's heart and presume from the outside what his intention was. 3. Also whether a man's heart and thoughts were not hidden and unknown." (1.... woher auß was grundt ihm eigentlich wissennt das er nichts gutts ihm sinn gehaptt. 2. Item ob er einem menschen ihns hertz sechen und außwendig abnemmen und erkhennen khöndt, wie ein iegklicher ihnwendig gesinnett. 3. Item ob nit eins menschen hertzen und gedancken verborgen und unbekhant seien) (ibid. *Pfefferlins interrogatoria*, article four, nos. 1–3). The counsel for the defense was successful with these questions. The witnesses either agreed that it was impossible to determine the inner state of another human being, or they appeared to be completely baffled by the question, not having given heed at all to Pfeffer's behavior, and thus had nothing to say.

disputants, which could be a guide to inner thoughts.[58] The defense counsel ignored this maxim and asserted instead a sort of popular wisdom that no one could see into another person's heart. This the witnesses were not prepared to deny.

But two could play at this game. The counsel for the plaintiff composed questions to be put to the witnesses concerning each of the articles of the defense. With these questions, he sought to strike the defense with his own weapons. In articles seventeen and nineteen, the counsel for the defense had described Pfeffer's emotions. The defense counsel asserted in article seventeen that Pfeffer was startled and frightened when Rhein charged into the house with his stick. According to article nineteen, Pfeffer was also moved by anger which had been incited by the dispute with his children.[59] In his questions to the witnesses concerning this article, the counsel for the plaintiff tried to establish a contradiction between these claims. He appealed to the psychological insight of the witnesses just as his adversary had done before, and he asked them whether it was "humanly possible to be both angry and frightened at the same time."[60] The lawyer wanted to challenge Pfeffer's claim to asylum by disputing that Pfeffer had been angry. He therefore asked the witnesses whether Pfeffer's fright did not rather indicate that he was no longer angry and had therefore struck Rhein intentionally.[61]

The lawyer apparently assumed that popular opinion held a "simple" view of human emotions and that the witnesses would only consider it possible to have one emotion at a time. This view contrasted with the notion that slayers were capable of multiple and overlapping emotions, motivated both by a desire for peace and by just anger; or both indignantly resisting an insult and deranged by wrath.[62] In the characterizations of a slayer's mindset before the asylum court, cultural views concerning the relationship between anger and provocation were thus overlaid and mixed with concepts which both reinforced and subtly undermined the concept that anger in response to provocation had to be reasonable and just in order to be mitigating.

---

58 For a discussion of the importance of *praesumptiones* in early modern German trials, see Alexander Jendorff, *Der Tod des Tyrannen. Geschichte und Rezeption der Causa Barthold von Wintzingerode* (Munich: 2012), 134.

59 See StRT A 912 (*articulos defensionales*, 9 April, 1557, articles 17 and 19).

60 StRT A 912 (*Fragstück*, counsel for the plaintiff, 14 April, 1557, questions concerning article nineteen, no. 1): "Ob menschlich und müglich zuemal zornig sein … und erschrockhen."

61 Ibid. (questions concerning article eighteen, no. 1).

62 It was also in contrast to *ius commune* interpretations of a slayer's state of mind when he exceeded the requirements of self-defense in the heat of the moment. In the writings of late medieval jurists, a slayer's anger could be accompanied by pain or even fear.

In the courts of Württemberg, outside of the legal context of asylum, lawyers' options were more limited when they described a slayer's emotional state. In their pleas and *consilia* for homicides tried under ducal jurisdiction, lawyers adhered to the standard legal opinion that anger had to be just in order to mitigate a slayer's criminal responsibility. In Württemberg, the judgement of a slayer, who was also a ducal subject, was negotiated with concepts of *gute policey* (good police). *Gute policey* was an important governmental maxim which sought to promote the "common good" through a series of legislative measures. These decrees regulated community life and matters of economy, but also the behavior of subjects according to virtues such as industry, lawfulness and modesty.[63] A defendant who had a good reputation and who was a "useful subject" (*nützlicher Untertan*) was frequently treated more leniently in early modern Germany.[64] In 1627, the Württemberg duke even issued an edict which specifically encouraged judges to refrain from imposing dishonorable corporal punishments if there was hope for correction. The purpose of this edict was to ensure that such "useful" defendants should not incur lasting shame and thus be prevented from practicing their professions.[65]

When lawyers in the courts of Württemberg justified lenient sanctions, they took care to connect the character and prior conduct of defendants with this civic discourse. They generally avoided portraying a slayer as caught in the grip of a burning rage, in order to maintain a sharp distinction between unintentional just anger and intentional murderous rage. A *consilium* from 1649 is a good example of this latter representation. This homicide lacked a just cause: Konrad Hauser had killed a tavern apprentice merely because he had not responded to his jokes. The jurists writing the *consilium* for this case emphasized that Hauser was guilty not just of homicide, but also of violating rules of conduct prescribed both by the law of the land and by religion. Hauser

---

63 For an introductory discussion of the concept of *gute policey* and its importance to early modern German government and political thought, see Andrea Iseli, *Gute Policey. Öffentliche Ordnung in der Frühen Neuzeit* (Stuttgart: 2009) and the literature cited there.

64 For a discussion of the utilitarian aspects of *gute policey*, see, for example, Karl Härter, "Social Control and the Enforcement of Police-Ordinances in Early Modern Criminal Procedure of Criminal Justice in Early Modern Criminal Procedure," in *Institutions, Instruments and Agents of Social Control and Discipline in Early Modern Europe*, ed. Heinz Schilling and Lars Behrisch (Frankfurt am Main: 1999), 39–64 at 61.

65 See August Heeger, *Die praktische Thätigkeit der Juristenfakultäten des 17. und 18. Jahrhunderts in ihrem Einfluss auf die Entwicklung des deutschen Strafrechts von Carpzov ab* (Tübingen: 1899), 88. The shame of suffering a dishonorable punishment could result in the exclusion of artisans from their guilds.

had "profaned the Sunday by playing skittles in a tavern" rather than attending church.[66] Hauser's anger was not just, but rather was unnecessary and had sprung "aus aigenem unfug" (from his own mischief).[67] The jurists implied that Hauser had wilfully given in to his anger; therefore, emotional turmoil did not mitigate Hauser's guilt but rather increased it. The jurists claimed that if this kind of anger was accepted as a mitigating circumstance, this was a "recipe for encouraging misdeeds and terrible manslaughter."[68] Hauser was executed.

While such murderous rage was also an indication of a bad character, a defendant's just anger could also be represented as a sign of his overall worth. In a *consilium* from 1650, for example, the author presented his client Martin Erckenweiler's anger as the just indignation of a virtuous citizen who had opposed an unruly troublemaker. The law professor suggested the lenient sanction of a fine, in part because the defendant had a good reputation and should not be kept from continuing his work as a baker by a dishonorable punishment.[69] The jurist described Erckenweiler's offense as an *Excess* and explained how his anger had been incited by his adversaries. Erckenweiler had been roused from his sleep when three apprentices banged on his window shutters at night. After a heated exchange with Erckenweiler, who demanded peace and quiet, one of the apprentices challenged him to meet them outside. Armed with a wooden crowbar, Erckenweiler accepted the challenge and opened his door, where he found that one of the apprentices had drawn his epée. Erckenweiler hit him with his crowbar and then struck the butcher's apprentice Georg Seitz, who stood close by. Seitz died instantly. It was an aggravating circumstance that mortal danger had not been imminent in this case: Erckenweiler could have stayed in his house rather than responding to the apprentices' challenge.[70]

Erckenweiler had acted in accordance with a cultural script of challenge and riposte. He had insulted the apprentices in his turn (he had called them "dog's cunt," *hundsfött*) and accepted the challenge to meet them outside.[71] The author of the *consilium*, however, represented Erckenweiler as a peaceful citizen in need of a night's rest, who had become legitimately angry at

66 HStA A 209 Bü 1906 (*consilium* 25 June 1649): "das angeclagter denn sontag prophaniert mit kegel spiehl." This *consilium* was written by two independent jurists, rather than by the law professors from the University of Tübingen.

67 Ibid.

68 Ibid. "würde thür und thor geöffnet zue der gleichen unthaten und erschröckenlichen todtschlägen."

69 See Universitätsarchiv Tübingen, 84/8, fol. 788r.

70 See ibid.

71 Ibid., fol. 782r.

the unwarranted disturbance of the apprentices. The jurist's choice of words implied that Erckenweiler's emotion had intensified in proportion to the justness of its cause. Erckenweiler first became "angry and displeased" (zu zorn und unwillen bewegt) when the noise woke him.[72] This "displeasure" escalated as he became "irritated and ... provoked to just anger" (irritiert und ... ad iustam iram provoziert) when none of the three apprentices answered him after he asked who they were.[73] When he found himself face to face with the armed apprentice, this just anger had increased to a "most just anger" (iustissima ira).[74] But the jurist also downplayed the effects of anger on Erckenweiler's mind. He claimed that his judgement had mainly been impaired by the confusing situation and the dark of the night. While Erckenweiler had exceeded the requirements of self-defense, his anger was comprehensible and reasonable. The jurist's language almost implies that Erckenweiler's action displayed his good sense. The repetitions and degrees of comparison of the term "just" seem to reinforce the characterization of Erckenweiler as a deserving subject.

In a *consilium* from 1688, utilitarian considerations also prompted a lenient sentence in a case of *Excess*. According to its author, the reputation of the defendant Samuel Thierer was *nicht bös* (not bad), and he was also a peasant who had to provide for a wife and small children.[75] A harsh punishment might have endangered his ability to provide for them, a pragmatic concern that often influenced criminal verdicts in early modern Württemberg. The author of the *consilium* accepted that Thierer had become angry when his victim Hanold, who had misplaced his gloves, insulted him by calling him a *Handschuhdieb*, a "glove-thief."[76] Yet Thierer had killed his victim an hour after the initial dispute, and he was also known for his occasionally quarrelsome behaviour. Thierer's general character was therefore not as faultless as Erckenweiler's, and his anger was also a bit less just. While the jurist accepted Thierer's anger as a mitigating circumstance, he also wrote that Thierer should not have allowed the *gächheit* (heat) of his anger to master him to such an extent.[77] While he thus acknowledged to a greater degree than the jurist who had composed Erckenweiler's *consilium* that the defendant's reason had been affected by his emotions, he

72 Ibid., fol. 783v.

73 Ibid., fol. 783r. For further discussion of these cases see Susanne Pohl-Zucker, *Making Manslaughter: Process, Restitution and Punishment in Württemberg and Zurich, 1376–1700* (Leiden and London: 2017).

74 Ibid., fol. 784r.

75 HStA A 209 Bü 1164 (*consilium* from 5 January 1688).

76 Ibid.

77 Ibid.

also qualified the exculpatory nature of this mental state. When he later suggested that Thierer should be punished more leniently because there was still hope for correction, he might have been implying that this correction would include Thierer's learning to moderate his anger in the future.

Thierer's defense lawyer, on the other hand, was willing to push further the claim that Thierer had not been completely in control of his senses. He complemented the concept of just anger with the additional claim of drunkenness. He argued that Thierer had been moved to "anger and impatience" (zorn und ungeduld) by his opponent's insults. But he also claimed in the same sentence that Thierer had been drunk at the time and therefore could not remember threatening Hanold, as one of the witnesses had alleged.[78] Although drunkenness was not mentioned in the *Carolina*, it was an accepted mitigating circumstance according to the *ius commune*.[79]

Although the law professor who wrote the *consilium* in Thierer's case did not pick up the excuse of drunkenness, drunk anger was occasionally used to justify the imposition of a *poena extraordinaria* in cases where the slayer's violation of the requirements of self-defense was more severe.[80] Drunken anger that was also just may have been an acceptable compromise for Württemberg jurists negotiating concepts of mitigating anger with governmental ideals of *gute policey*. It saved the slayer from the death penalty but justified greater chastisement and correction. Thierer was sentenced to a year of forced labor, a punishment that had been explicitly introduced to correct offenders who could be reintegrated into the community.[81]

78 Ibid. The plea of the defense is not extant, but the lawyer's arguments were summarized in the *consilium*.

79 Social and legal attitudes towards drunkenness were ambiguous, however. Drinking was an important and accepted part of male sociability, and occasional drunkenness did not necessarily indicate a character flaw. At the same time, territorial ordinances frowned on bawdy drinking customs and contemporary morality condemned drunkards as irresponsible householders. At court, arguments based on drunkenness were used in two ways: either to incriminate a defendant or to exculpate him. For a nuanced discussion of cultural and legal attitudes towards drinking in early modern Germany, see Ann Tlusty, *Bacchus and Civic Order: The Culture of Drink in Early Modern Germany* (Charlottesville and London: 2001), for example, 80–102.

80 See, for example, Universitätsarchiv Tübingen 84/8, fol. 257v, 1634 or HStA A 309 Bü 117, 1657.

81 See August Ludwig Reyscher, ed., *Vollständige, historisch und kritisch bearbeitete Sammlung der württembergischen Gesetze*, vol. 5 (Stuttgart and Tübingen: 1832), 380. The Edict that introduced forced labor specifically mentions that this sanction should be used

When slayers addressed the duke and local officials with pleas for lenient sanctions in letters of supplication (probably often advised by counsel or supporters who knew some law), in order to prove the absence of intent they also made use of available legal concepts to describe their state of mind.[82] When Endres Erhard claimed drunk anger in a letter of supplication from 1590, he both stressed his right to avenge his opponent's insults and claimed that his judgment had been clouded.[83] He wrote that his victim Geßler had insulted him by saying such "unjust things" that he "was shamed in front of the many persons who sat in the room and who might have heard this."[84] At the same time, he qualified the reasonableness of his anger by alleging that he had been "overcome with wine and moved to anger and struck [*Geßler*] with a drawn weapon."[85] In addition, he adopted a humble stance typical of the rhetoric of letters of supplication, admitting that he had acted badly and regretted his deed but hoped for divine forgiveness, and promising to conduct himself honourably and well in the future.[86]

---

when "there was hope that a sinner might perhaps change his ways" (alßdann auch eine Hoffnung seyn koennte, es moechte ein solcher Suender sich etwan bessern): ibid., 380.

82 Unfortunately, few such letters are extant; the examples mentioned above thus provide only a glimpse of how defendants made use of concepts of anger and provocation.

83 Erhard had claimed asylum in Reutlingen. In the meantime, his family negotiated an agreement with the victim's family, which compensated them financially for the loss of their son and husband. As soon as Erhard learned of the successful negotiations, he sent a letter of supplication to the duke of Württemberg. In his letter, Erhard appealed to the duke to allow him safe passage into Württemberg without arrest and a subsequent trial. According to the law, the duke could impose a monetary fine without a trial, if the slayer had reconciled with the victim's family. Theoretically, only slayers who had killed in self-defense and by negligence or accident could atone for their deed in this manner. Yet the duke and his councillors generally permitted slayers who had committed homicides that might be characterized as *Excess* to atone for their offense with a monetary fine and a negotiated agreement. While such extrajudicial agreements often replaced trials in homicide cases during the sixteenth century, trials increased during the last decades of the century. During the seventeenth century, slayers were almost always tried in court, although extrajudicial agreements with the victim's family might still be negotiated.

84 HstA A 209 Bü 652, letter of supplication of Endres Erhard, dated 5 November 1590: "unbillicher sachen ... als das ich mich vor vilen in der stůben geseßenen personen, die solches gehört, schämen müeßen."

85 Ibid. "dardůrch ich dann, als vom wein uberwůnden, zů zorn bewegt, und ihme mit gefasster wöhr einen Straich geben." One of the witnesses testified that Erhard had used his epée. See ibid., witness testimony from 25 February 1590.

86 See ibid., letter of supplication of Endres Erhard, dated 5 November 1590.

While Erhard used a rhetoric of both distancing and provocation, the slayer Eustachius von Buchholtz insisted more forcefully on his injured honor. Von Buchholtz, a local noble, had killed Johann von Thumb in 1641 after von Thumb had insulted his wife and struck him during a dispute.[87] The circumstances were aggravated because the homicide happened sometime after their quarrel, when von Buchholtz left to obtain a set of pistols and then pursued and shot von Thumb. Von Buchholtz used the concept of just anger in his letter of supplication to the duke of Württemberg. He emphasized the "various gross defamations" and "most atrocious injuries" to his honor as well as the "violent insult" he had innocently suffered.[88] At the same time he acknowledged that he had acted in "*ÿberÿltem zorn*," which might be translated as "rash" or "precipitate" anger, and because he had feared for his life.[89] In his letter, von Buchholtz ignored the passage of time between the quarrel and the homicide, which constituted a severe violation of the requirements of self-defense. In another letter of supplication, written by von Buchholtz's supporters, the authors emphasized his emotional perturbation more strongly in order to mitigate this incriminating circumstance. They stressed that the slayer's anger had been just, particularly since von Buchholtz and his wife were "vom urahltem adenlichen geschlecht" (of an old and noble family) and had been insulted in a manner that was *ehrenrührig* (injurious to their honor). These insults had prompted emotions such as "unwillen, eifer und zorn" (indignation, fervor and anger), which von Buchholtz had not been able to get "aus seinem Kopf"(out of his head).[90] This comment implied that the slayer's judgement had remained clouded after the quarrel, thus accounting for the lapse of time. The jurist who wrote the *consilium* in this case did not accept anger as a mitigating circumstance, however, but emphasized that von Buchholtz's *furi* (fury) indicated a murderous intent and should be punished with the death penalty.[91] The duke and his councillors chose a lenient punishment, however, in response to the numerous letters of supplication in von Buchholtz's support and in consideration of his noble status. While they did not mention von Buchholtz's emotional state in their justification of a mild sentence or consider whether his senses had been clouded, a slayer's anger could be a justificatory argument if

87 HStA A 209 Bü 1546.

88 Ibid., letter of supplication from Eustachius von Bucholtz, 16 December 1641: "... underschidlichen, hohen diffamationibus ... atrocissimis iniuriis ... gewaltsame insultation ...".

89 Ibid.

90 Ibid., letter of supplication from Enndris Döner, Alexander Österlin, Hannß Manngolt, Hannß Jerg Weingartner and other citizens of the town of Marbach, 9 July 1642.

91 Ibid., *consilium* from 28 June 1642.

the ducal councillors disagreed with the verdict suggested by the *consilium*. In a case from 1676, the slayer had killed his unarmed victim with an axe after what the author of the *consilium* considered to be only a slight verbal insult. In response to his wife's supplication, however, the councillors mitigated the suggested death penalty and argued that the victim's threat to take away his tobacco prompted the defendant's anger. They therefore implied that this anger had been at least somewhat just.[92]

In early modern Württemberg, *ius commune* concepts of mitigating anger were not exploited to the same degree as in the Reutlingen trials, but the concept of just anger was still flexible enough to allow variations in the depictions of slayers' emotional states. These flexible representations of anger also helped legitimate the distinctions lawyers made among various slayings considered *Excess*. The indeterminacy of *ius commune* terms and categories thus allowed jurists and defendants to develop different shades of meaning in considering a slayer's anger, alternately diminishing or reinforcing a slayer's responsibility for his action in varying degrees. These portraits of emotional states were shaped by legal and political parameters of judging which both reinforced and modified entrenched notions of male honor and provocation. As Jonas Liliequist has argued, cultural norms regarding violent responses to provocations are historically contingent and shift over time, although "not uniformly in the direction of the civilisation of violence."[93] The cases described here illustrate how varying legal attitudes towards a slayer's mindset coexisted in time, in part because of the differing legal parameters that shaped justice in Reutlingen and in Württemberg, but also because the adaptability of legal concepts allowed lawyers to adjust their arguments within a specific legal setting. In both courts, lawyers could strategically draw on, adjust and modify cultural notions of self-restraint, diminished intent and righteous anger depending on the context of a case.

Works Cited

Manuscript Sources

Hauptstaatsarchiv Stuttgart:

Oberrat: Kriminalakten (A 209 Bü 100, 141, 652, 1164, 1546, 1604, 1906)

Württembergische Regesten (A 602 WR 14962)

92 HStA A 209 Bü 100, letter from the ducal councillors, 26 April 1676.

93 Jonas Liliequist, "From Honour to Virtue: The Shifting Social Logics of Masculinity and Honour in Early Modern Sweden," in *Honour, Violence and Emotions in History*, ed. Carolyn Strange, Robert Cribb and Christopher E. Forth (Bloomsbury: 2014), 45–68 at 66.

Stadtarchiv Reutlingen:
Akten aus der Reichsstadtzeit (A 910, 912, 916, 919)
Universitätsarchiv Tübingen:
Konsilien (84/8, 12)

Printed Sources

Allfeld, Philipp. *Die Entwicklung des Begriffes Mord bis zur Carolina. Ein rechtsgeschichtlicher Versuch*. Erlangen: 1877.

Bartolus de Saxoferrato. *Bartoli Commentaria in secundum Codicis partem*. Lyon: 1550.

Bourdieu, Pierre. "The Sentiment of Honor in Kabyle Society." In *Honour and Shame: The Values of Mediterranean Society*, edited by J. G. Peristiany, 191–241. London: 1966.

Carpzov, Benedict. *Practicae Novae Imperialis Saxonicae Rerum Criminalium. Pars I.* Translated and edited by Dietrich Oehler. Goldbach: 2000.

Engelmann, Woldemar. *Die Schuldlehre der Postglossatoren*. Leipzig: 1895.

Frank, Michael. "Ehre und Gewalt im Dorf der frühen Neuzeit: Das Beispiel Heiden (Grafschaft Lippe) im 17. und 18. Jahrhundert." In *Verletzte Ehre. Ehrkonflikte in Gesellschaften des Mittelalters und der Frühen Neuzeit*, edited by Klaus Schreiner and Gerd Schwerhoff, 320–38. Cologne, Weimar, Vienna: 1995.

Härter, Karl. "Social Control and the Enforcement of Police-Ordinances in Early Modern Criminal Procedure of Criminal Justice in Early Modern Criminal Procedure." In *Institutions, Instruments and Agents of Social Control and Discipline in Early Modern Europe*, edited by Heinz Schilling and Lars Behrisch, 39–64. Frankfurt am Main: 1999.

Heeger, August. *Die praktische Thätigkeit der Juristenfakultäten des 17. und 18. Jahrhunderts in ihrem Einfluss auf die Entwicklung des deutschen Strafrechts von Carpzov ab*. Tübingen: 1899.

Hyppolitus de Marsiliis. *Practica causarum criminalium*. Lugano: 1529.

His, Rudolph. *Das Strafrecht des deutschen Mittelalters. Erster Teil: Die Verbrechen und ihre Folgen im allgemeinen*. Leipzig: 1920.

Iseli, Andrea. *Gute Policey. Öffentliche Ordnung in der Frühen Neuzeit*. Stuttgart: 2009.

Jänichen, Hans. "Schwäbische Totschlagssühnen im 15. und 16. Jahrhundert." *Zeitschrift für Württembergische Landesgeschichte* 19 (1960): 128–40.

Jendorff, Alexander. *Der Tod des Tyrannen. Geschichte und Rezeption der Causa Barthold von Wintzingerode*. Munich: 2012.

Liliequist, Jonas. "From Honour to Virtue: The Shifting Social Logics of Masculinity and Honour in Early Modern Sweden." In *Honour, Violence and Emotions in History*, edited by Carolyn Strange, Robert Cribb, and Christopher E. Forth, 45–68. Bloomsbury: 2014.

Miller, William Ian. "Deep Inner Lives, Individualism and People of Honour." *History of Political Thought* 16 (2) (1995): 190–207.

Osenbrüggen, Eduard. *Das Alamannische Strafrecht im deutschen Mittelalter*. Aalen: 1968.

Pennington, Kenneth. "*Moderamen inculpatae tutelae*: The Jurisprudence of a Justifiable Defense." *Rivista internazionale di diritto commune* 24 (2014): 27–55.

Pohl-Zucker, Susanne. *Making Manslaughter: Process, Restitution and Punishment in Württemberg and Zurich, 1376–1700*. Leiden and Boston: 2017.

Reck, Ralf. "Das Totschläger-Asyl der Reichsstadt Reutlingen 1495–1804." *Reutlinger Geschichtsblätter*, Neue Folge 8 (1970): 46–78.

Reyscher, August Ludwig, ed. *Vollständige, historisch und kritisch bearbeitete Sammlung der württembergischen Gesetze*. Vol. 5. Stuttgart and Tübingen: 1832.

Schnabel-Schüle, Helga. *Überwachen und Strafen im Territorialstaat*. Cologne, Weimar, Vienna: 1997.

Schroeder, Friedrich-Christian. *Die Carolina. Die peinliche Gerichtsordnung Kaiser Karls V. von 1532*. Darmstadt: 1986.

Schroeder, Friedrich-Christian, ed. *Die Peinliche Gerichtsordnung Kaiser Karls V. und des Heiligen Römischen Reichs von 1532* (Carolina). Stuttgart: 2014.

Schwerhoff, Gerd. *Köln im Kreuzverhör*. Cologne: 1991.

Tlusty, Ann. *Bacchus and Civic Order: The Culture of Drink in Early Modern Germany*. Charlottesville and London: 2001.

Tiraquellus, Andreas. *De poenis legum ac consuetudinem statutorumque temperandis aut etiam remittendis*. Venice: 1560.

de Waardt, Hans. "Ehrenhändel, Gewalt und Liminalität." In *Verletzte Ehre. Ehrkonflikte in Gesellschaften des Mittelalters und der Frühen Neuzeit*, edited by Klaus Schreiner and Gerd Schwerhoff, 303–19. Cologne, Weimar, Vienna: 1995.

CHAPTER 2

Trial by Ordeal by Jury in Medieval England, or Saints and Sinners in Literature and Law

Elizabeth Papp Kamali[1]

With a vacancy in the coveted archbishopric of York in 1140, several candidates, Henry de Sully and William Fitzherbert included, vied for the title. Henry's election was quashed, due in part to his conflicting duties as Abbot of Fécamp. A lengthy and bitter contest ensued, with accusations of impropriety lodged against the remaining candidate, William, by the Cistercian luminary Bernard of Clairvaux, in correspondence with successive popes.[2] Among other things, Bernard accused William of simony and unchaste living. When Bernard died in August 1153, the cloud over William's candidacy lifted, and in December, he finally secured his archiepiscopal title. As fate would have it, less than a month after his triumphal return to York, William himself died, reputedly from poison in his chalice.[3]

---

1 I offer my thanks to the participants in the Medieval Studies Seminar at Harvard, especially Sean Gilsdorf, Piotr Górecki, Intisar Rabb, and Daniel Lord Smail, as well as Rabia Belt, Glenn Cohen, Andrew Crespo, Christine Desan, Charles Donahue, John Goldberg, Thomas Green, Richard Helmholz, Genevieve Lakier, Adriaan Lanni, Thomas McSweeney, John Rappaport, Daphna Renan, Jocelyn Simonson, Henry Smith, and my research assistant, Michael Reiterman. Sincere gratitude is owed as well to the participants in the Harvard Law School Faculty Workshop, and to Dr. Bruce Barker-Benfield, Senior Assistant Librarian in the Department of Special Collections and Western Manuscripts at the Bodleian Library, who examined MS Dodsworth 125 on my behalf.

2 On the controversy surrounding William's election as archbishop, see David Knowles, "The Case of Saint William of York," *The Cambridge Historical Journal* 5, no. 2 (1936), 162–77, 212–4; Reginald L. Poole, "The Appointment and Deprivation of St. William, Archbishop of York," *The English Historical Review* 45, no. 178 (1930), 273–81; C. H. Talbot, "New Documents in the Case of Saint William of York," *The Cambridge Historical Journal* 10, no. 1 (1950), 1–15; Watkin Williams, *Saint Bernard of Clairvaux* (Manchester: 1935), 167–76.

3 For an account of William's life by the fourteenth-century Dominican friar Thomas Stubbs, see *The Historians of the Church of York and Its Archbishops*, ed. James Raine, vol. 2 (London: 1886), 396–7. For a brief biography, see Janet Burton, "William of York (*d.* 1154)," in *Oxford Dictionary of National Biography* (Oxford: 2004). For a chronology of William's death and canonization and an introduction to the later Whitsuntide Commemorations in his memory, see Nigel K. Tringham, "The Whitsuntide Commemoration of St William of York: A Note,"

© KONINKLIJKE BRILL NV, LEIDEN, 2018 | DOI 10.1163/9789004366374_006

William's death marked a new beginning for York Minster, with regard to both its physical footprint and its reputation vis-à-vis its great rival to the south, Canterbury. During the tenure of William's successor, Roger de Pont L'Évêque, York Minster was rebuilt. Roger, however, caught the ire of Canterbury's Thomas Becket after having the audacity to crown Henry the Young King, heir apparent to Henry II, in York in 1170, a privilege normally reserved for Canterbury.[4] Becket, in turn, excommunicated Roger, but soon after met his own earthly end. By 1173, Becket was canonized—a rival saint for a rival city—as was William's old nemesis, Bernard of Clairvaux, a year later. Perhaps not coincidentally, within a few years miracles began to be reported in York, centered around the tomb of the now Blessed William, a site of popular veneration by the 1170s.[5] From 1177 onwards, miracles at William's tomb gathered pace.[6] According to one such miracle story, the focal point of this essay, William healed the hand of a woman condemned to death after undergoing trial by hot iron. In some instances by means of holy oil oozing from his tomb, William reportedly healed the blind and deaf, the crippled and maimed, and even a woman experiencing digestive difficulties after inadvertently swallowing a frog baked into Eucharistic bread (*panem vitae*)—an ordeal, no doubt, all its own, albeit of the amphibian variety.[7] By 1180, toward the end of Roger's time as archbishop, a cult had formed around William's memory as York consciously developed a new civic order, visually represented in the city's infrastructure by a chapel dedicated to William on a new bridge over the river Ouse, the site of his first miracle in 1154.[8]

Records of Early English Drama 14, no. 2 (1989), 10–12. On the trial of Osbert of Bayeux for the alleged poisoning of William, see R. H. Helmholz, "The Early History of the Grand Jury and the Canon Law," *The University of Chicago Law Review* 50, no. 2 (1983), 618–9; Adrian Morey, "Canonist Evidence in the Case of St. William of York," *The Cambridge Historical Journal* 10, no. 3 (1952), 352–3. For letters to Pope Adrian IV regarding Osbert's pending case, see *The Letters and Charters of Gilbert Foliot* (Cambridge: 1967), ed. Z. N. Brooke, Adrian Morey, and C. N. L. Brooke, 164–5; *The Letters of John of Salisbury*, ed. W. J. Millor and H. E. Butler, vol. 1 (London: 1955), 26–27.

4 Rosalind M. T. Hill and Christopher N. L. Brooke, "From 627 until the Early Thirteenth Century," in *A History of York Minster*, ed. G. E. Aylmer and Reginald Cant (Oxford: 1977), 38–40.

5 Christopher Norton, *St William of York* (York: 2006), 150 ff.

6 See ibid., 165–6; Ellen K. Rentz, "Castles for St. William: The Late Medieval Commemoration of York's Local Saint," *Viator* 43, no. 2 (2012), 115.

7 For the Latin accounts of these miracles and others, see Raine, *Historians*, vol. 2, 531–43.

8 On the development of William's cult, see Sarah Rees Jones, "Cities and Their Saints in England, circa 1150–1300: The Development of Bourgeois Values in the Cults of Saint William

Long after the deaths of Roger de Pont L'Évêque and Thomas Becket, rivalry persisted between York and Canterbury—a rivalry over local saints, souls, and seniority within the English church.[9] In the early thirteenth century, another building campaign took place at York Minster under Archbishop Walter de Gray (r. 1215–1255), just as William's candidacy for canonization accelerated.[10] York would soon have its own saint to rival Canterbury's. In April 1223, Pope Honorius III issued mandates to several English bishops and abbots to take depositions related to William's reported miracles, and the York saint was canonized in 1226.[11] This essay will focus on one of the miracle stories presented

---

of York and Saint Kenelm of Winchcombe," in *Cities, Texts and Social Networks, 400–1500: Experiences and Perceptions of Medieval Urban Space*, ed. Caroline Goodson, Anne E. Lester, and Carol Symes (Farnham: 2010), 205–9. In 1154, William was said to have rescued people who were drowning in the river Ouse following a bridge collapse.

9 More localized competition existed as well with the cults of St John at Beverley and St Cuthbert at Durham. Jane E. Sayers, *Papal Government and England during the Pontificate of Honorius III (1216–1227)* (Cambridge: 1984), 180. Local saints drew pilgrims and their purses. One particularly colorful miracle story played up the comparative efficacy of cures at Canterbury and York. Albreda of Gisburne found no relief for her urinary tract ailments in a pilgrimage to the shrine of Thomas Becket in Canterbury. Hearing of William's reputation for healing, she subsequently made a trip to York and found immediate relief. See Raine, *Historians*, vol. 2, 537.

10 On the rebuilding, see Lawrence Hoey, "The 13th-Century Transepts of York Minster," *Gesta* 25, no. 2 (1986), 227–8. See also Roy Martin Haines, "Walter de Gray (*d.* 1255)," in *Oxford Dictionary of National Biography* (Oxford: 2004).

11 For Pope Honorius's 1223 mandate for "diligent enquiry as to alleged miracles at the tomb of William," and for the deposition of witnesses a year later, see *Calendar of Entries in the Papal Registers: Papal Letters*, ed. W. B. Bliss, vol. 1 (Nendeln: 1971), 90–91, 96. The pope specifically requested assistance from the bishop of Ely (who, incidentally, had previously served as abbot of Fountains) and the abbots of Fountains and Rievaulx. Given the opposition of these two Cistercian abbeys to William's appointment as archbishop, the selection smacks more of devil's advocates than of promoters of William's canonization, suggesting that the pope wished to have a rigorous review of the evidence for and against William's candidacy. On the abbeys' opposition to William's appointment, see Talbot, "New Documents," 1. The bishop of Ely from 1220 to 1225 was John of Fountains, who had also examined the miracles of Hugh of Lincoln in 1219. See Dorothy M. Owen, "Fountains, John of (*d.* 1225)," in *Oxford Dictionary of National Biography* (Oxford: 2004). At the time of the interdict, Cistercian Matthew of Rievaulx wrote from York that the interdict was God's retribution upon England for her sins, particularly the appointment of unworthy men to high ecclesiastical positions, a charge reminiscent of the earlier critique issued from Fountains and Rievaulx in response to William's appointment as archbishop. See Peter D. Clarke, *The Interdict in the Thirteenth Century: A Question of Collective Guilt* (Oxford: 2007), 134. When announcing William's canonization in April 1226, Honorius III

as evidence of William's sanctity—a tale of trial by ordeal—to speak in part about the transition in England to trial by jury, and in part about the value of what, for lack of a better term, I might call "extra-legal" sources, in this instance hagiography, for the writing of legal history. The essay will juxtapose the canonization of William, a worldly man before his accession as archbishop, with the equally unlikely commutation of the death sentence of a convicted felon following a miracle at William's tomb. This is that female felon's story, translated in full:

> Two women accused of homicide were arrested and incarcerated according to the custom of the realm; one died a natural death with the passage of time, while the other woman, still living, remained in prison. At last, with the arrival of the justices of the lord king, she was produced and accused of the said homicide. And because she denied having been present at that homicide, she was adjudged to the purgation of hot iron,[12] according to the custom of the realm as it then was, so that it might be seen whether she was guilty of the homicide or not. When she had carried [the iron], there was found on the woman's hand a blister the size of half a walnut, for which reason she was judged to death by twelve knights sent for this purpose, as one guilty of the aforesaid homicide, and she was [sentenced] to be burned by fire. When these things were announced to the principal justices, the said woman, having been extended license to pray, approached the tomb of Blessed William. As soon as she entered the enclosure which was around the tomb, the blister vanished, so that no vestige or blister remained.[13] When this deed was announced to the

promised a reprieve of forty days' penance for visitors to York Minster on William's feast day. By 1291, this benefit had grown to a year and forty days. Ibid., 109, 540. See also "A Decree of Honorius III Authorising the Beatification of William Archbishop of York," in *Historians of the Church of York*, vol. 3, ed. James Raine (London: 1894), 127–30.

12 There is some evidence that women endured trial by hot iron more often than trial by water. See Margaret H. Kerr, Richard D. Forsyth, and Michael J. Plyley, "Cold Water and Hot Iron: Trial by Ordeal in England," *Journal of Interdisciplinary History* 22, no. 4 (1992), 581 ff. See also the burglary claim brought by a man named Wulward at the 1201 Cornish eyre, in which six male suspects, including one Bill Miller (i.e., Willelmus Molendinarius), were ordered to purge themselves by water, while a female suspect was instead sent to the judgment of iron. JUST1/1171 AALT 0012 (1201), <http://aalt.law.uh.edu/AALT4/JUST1/JUST1no1171/IMG_0012.htm>, accessed 20/6/2017 (incipit "Wulwardus de Ponte Gode burgatus fuit").

13 Dodsworth's transcription reads "nullum vestigium v.... vesica remansit," indicating a lacuna in the original manuscript. The "v" may be the beginning of "vel." My thanks to Kate Gilbert.

justices, they sent for the twelve knights to inspect the woman's hand; it being the case that she appeared to be without any lesion and vestige of the said blister, [nor] of any other infirmity whatsoever, they [i.e., the knights] reported this to the aforesaid principal justices, who, judging the same woman absolved and innocent, sent her forth free, saying, "As God and Blessed [William] have absolved her, so we do not wish to condemn her"; and the said knights, who condemned her, were adjudged in the mercy of the lord king, because they presented false testimony, and produced an iniquitous judgment. But indeed, the woman carried the glowing iron in the cathedral church of York before the altar of Blessed Michael;[14] and the aforesaid twelve knights who observed her and the hand itself, wished to drag her from the church as one guilty of homicide, but the priest and custodian of the tomb would not permit her to be abducted, because she had been cured by a miracle of Blessed William.[15]

14 This sentence marks a curious chronological break with the preceding narrative, as it returns to the moment of trial, which had already concluded earlier in the text. The author may be trying to comment on the episode, highlighting the intransigence of the knights in refusing to accept the miracle. This may also be a later interpolation. Significantly, the altar of St Michael was reputedly the most important altar in medieval York Minster, located in the center of the ambulatory east aisle. Archbishop Gray was buried there, at an altar of his founding, in 1255. Eric A. Gee, "Architectural History until 1290," in *History of York Minster*, 128, 131, 145. It is unclear whether there had been a preexisting altar dedicated to St Michael; if not, the ordeal tale's authorship would not likely antedate Gray's tenure as archbishop. Gray might have refurbished an existing altar, given the fact that St. Michael, known as the weigher of souls, would seem a fitting choice for an altar used in ordeal procedure. See Norton, *William of York*, 168. St Peter's was the main altar in York Minster. Eric Gee, "The Topography of Altars, Chantries and Shrines in York Minster," *The Antiquaries Journal* 64, no. 2 (1984), 340.

15 Raine, *Historians*, vol. 2, 542–3 (my translation). "Duæ mulieres accusatæ super homicidio captæ fuerunt secundum consuetudinem regni et incarceratæ; quarum altera processu temporis naturali morte defuncta, reliqua mulier viva in carcere remansit. Tandem in adventu justitiariorum domini regis producta et accusata fuit super dicto homicidio. Et cum negaret se interfuisse illi homicidio, adjudicata fuit et purgatio ferri candentis, secundum consuetudinem regni quæ tunc fuit, ut appareret utrum esset rea ejus homicidii vel non. Quod cum tulisset, reperta fuit in manu mulieris vesica quædam ad quantitatem medietatis unius juglandis, quare fuit adjudicate morti a xii. militibus ad hoc missis, tanquam rea prædicti homicidii, et igni concremanda. Quæ dum nuntiarentur justitiariis principalibus, dicta mulier extenta licentia orandi accessit ad tumbam Beati Willelmi. Statim ut intravit clausuram, quæ est circa tumbam, evanuit vesica, ita quod nullum vestigium v [....] vesica remansit. Quo facto nuntiato justitiariis, missi fuerunt xii. milites ad manum ipsius mulieris inspiciendam; quæ cum appareret sine omni læsione et vestigio dictæ vesicæ, et cujuslibet alius infirmitatis, reportaverunt hoc justitiariis prædictis principalibus, qui, eandem mulierem absolutam et innoxiam judicantes, dimiserunt liberam, dicentes:

The tale is a curious one, for a variety of reasons. First, the judges condemned the knights for a wrongful judgment when only omniscience—predicting a miraculous healing—could conceivably have led them to a different initial verdict. Second, the story leaves unanswered the question that to the modern reader would seem most pressing: did the woman commit the homicide or not? The author leaves us guessing as to whether the initial verdict of guilt was wrong, or whether instead the miraculous intervention of William was perceived to be a grant of mercy freely given, a grace perhaps not entirely deserved. Third, and most remarkably, the guilty verdict was handed down by a group of twelve knights summoned to York Minster to issue an ordeal verdict. Essentially, this was a trial by ordeal by jury! Procedurally speaking, the text describes a curious mélange of a pre-Lateran IV (pre-1215) *iudicium dei* and trial by jury, typically associated with the post-Lateran IV period in England.[16] As such, the story threatens to upset the tidy distinction English legal historians tend to draw between the era of trial by ordeal and the latter-day use of jury trial.[17]

'Ex quo Deus et Beatus [Willelmus] absolverunt, tam nolumus eam condemnare'; et dictos milites, qui eam condemnaverunt, in misericordia domini regis adjudicantes, quia falsum perhibuerunt testimonium, et iniquum judicium tulerunt. Quæ vero ferrum candens portavit in ecclesia cathedrali Eboracensi coram altare Beati Michaelis; et prædicti xii. milites qui eam observabant et manum ipsius, eandem mulierem, tanquam ream homicidii, voluerunt extrahere ab ecclesia, sed noluit sacerdos custos tumbæ permittere eam abduci, quæ curata fuit per miraculum Beati Willemi." Raine relied on Dodsworth's handwritten copy of the *Miracula*, which he criticized as "very carelessly transcribed." Ibid., xxxi. Examination of an image of MS Dodsworth 125, fol. 142v, suggests that Raine, in the final sentence, may have substituted *noluit* for *voluit* (particularly when the word is compared with *voluerunt* in the preceding line) and *permittere* for *promittere*, but Raine's word choices make sense in the context of the story and may therefore be credible emendations of Dodsworth's transcription. In the penultimate sentence, I replaced the *idem* of Raine's version with *tam* after examining the same folium. Another translation may be found in *English Lawsuits from William I to Richard I*, ed. R. C. van Caenegem, vol. 2 (London: 1991), 558–9. This tale is discussed briefly in Elizabeth Papp Kamali and Thomas A. Green, "A Crossroads in Criminal Procedure: The Assumptions Underlying England's Adoption of Trial by Jury for Crime," in *Law and Society in Later Medieval England and Ireland: Essays in Honour of Paul Brand*, ed. Travis Baker (New York: 2018), 51–81.

16 Whereas England moved to trial by jury after 1215, jurisdictions in continental Europe adopted inquisitorial procedure as an ordeal substitute.

17 I refer throughout to unilateral ordeals, as opposed to bilateral ordeals (i.e., trial by battle), which continued after Lateran IV.

Hagiography in the Service of Legal History

As should be clear on first reading, this is not a trial record from the plea rolls, the official records of the royal courts. Rather, it is a miracle tale, written for the purpose of advancing the claim that York's late archbishop, once demonized by Bernard of Clairvaux, should be canonized. As Theodore Andersson and Bill Miller have written about the use of sagas for writing social and cultural history, historians "need to acquire the skills of the literary critic and literary historian in order to read them well."[18] To my mind, this advice also applies to hagiography, which raises complex issues of authorship, narrative and audience.[19] To start with the obvious, miracle tales may report historical events, but they may also contain wholesale inventions of events; even with actual historical events, details may be fabricated. Furthermore, hagiography can prove particularly resistant to precise dating. This story appears in a miracle collection, *Miracula quaedam Sancti Willelmi*, and was copied down in the seventeenth century by antiquarian Roger Dodsworth from a late fourteenth-century parchment-adorned tryptich in York Minster.[20] James Raine included the *Miracula* in his multi-volume *Historians of the Church of York* in the late nineteenth century.[21] The tryptich relayed historical tidbits from the cathedral archives alongside heroic tales of York's ancient roots within the context of a *slightly* broader history of the entire world since Creation. Although the tale cannot be dated with certainty, it appears to reference events occurring in the late twelfth or early thirteenth century, late in the era of trial by ordeal.[22]

18 Theodore M. Andersson and William Ian Miller, *Law and Literature in Medieval Iceland* (Stanford: 1989), xii.

19 For a discussion of the genre and cautions about mining it for historical facts, see Kathleen Ashley and Pamela Sheingorn, *Writing Faith: Text, Sign, and History in the Miracles of Sainte Foy* (Chicago: 1999), 1–21.

20 For a description and dating of the York tables, see J. S. Purvis, "The Tables of the York Vicars Choral," *The Yorkshire Archaeological Journal* 41 (Wakefield: 1966), 741–8.

21 See Raine, *Historians*, vol. 2, xxxi, in which he identifies the transcription as [Bodleian] MS Dodsworth 125, fol. 131. <http://www.bodley.ox.ac.uk/dept/scwmss/wmss/online/1500-1900/dodsworthCLD/dodsworthCLD.html>, accessed 17/5/2017. This tale appears on fols. 141v–142r.

22 The event itself, inasmuch as it involves an ordeal, suggests a *terminus ad quem* of c. 1215, when England responded swiftly to Lateran IV's effective abolition of the ordeal, adopting trial by jury for felony cases within a few years. Of course, the miracle could have been invented by a hagiographer looking back and imagining, from a post-Lateran IV perspective, what trial by hot iron must have looked like. On the dating of the various miracles attributed to William, see Norton, *William of York*, 165–6.

William of York's most recent biographer, Christopher Norton, proposes 1208 or 1210 as likely candidates for the trial episode's date, again assuming that the miracle tale presents, even in dramatically modified form, an actual historical event.[23] Regrettably I could find no reference to a woman tried for homicide in the spotty surviving trial records of early thirteenth-century York.[24] Internal evidence supports the notion that the authorship may be later than the date of the events themselves: namely, the author's reference to "the custom of the realm as it then was" suggests either that the custom of trial by hot iron had changed by the time the miracle was recorded, or else that ordeals were no longer used. There is reason to believe the miracle tale was initially recorded in the early thirteenth century, and later amended when miracle accounts were compiled to promote William's candidacy for canonization circa 1223–4.[25]

To what extent can historians, particularly those interested in the history of law and legal institutions, rely on the fantastical genre of hagiography for historical insight? Such reliance is not without great risk due to the interpretive difficulties presented by the genre and its reliance on distinct rhetorical strategies.[26] Here, for example, the author of the miracle story wished to

23 Norton bases this on the timing of two visits of King John's justices in eyre. Ibid., 169.

24 For pleas of the crown from York in 1208, see *Pleas before the King or His Justices, 1198–1212*, vol. 4, ed. Doris Mary Stenton (London: 1967), 94–117, which includes two references to trial by water; *Three Yorkshire Assize Rolls*, ed. Charles Travis Clay (Leeds: 1911), 25–42.

25 I believe the ordeal miracle can be grouped authorially with the exoculation narrative (discussed infra), which Norton has dated with some certainty to an actual duel fought c. 1207/8. See Norton, *William of York*, 178. Both tales employ legal settings, express doubt about the efficacy of a form of proof, refer to William as "*beatus*" (not "*sanctus*"), and describe the supplicant approaching the "*tumbam*," whereas earlier stories in the collection tend to refer to William's resting place as either a "*sepulchrum*" or "*tumulum*." Note that the use of "*beatus*" versus "*sanctus*" is not dispositive in this period of an individual's stage in the canonization process, although in this case the use of the same term might offer a minor clue as to common authorship. See Eric Waldram Kemp, *Canonization and Authority in the Western Church* (Westport, CT: 1979), 116 (describing the two terms as interchangeable in the later Middle Ages). My suspicion is that the tale was recopied during the tenure of Archbishop Walter de Gray (r. 1215–1255) in the lead-up to William's canonization, which would explain the reference to past custom as well as what appears to be a break in the narrative flow (from the phrase "but indeed" (quae vero) forward). This apparent addendum references the altar of St. Michael, a place of special significance to Walter de Gray. See supra, n. 14.

26 See, e.g., Stephen D. White, "Garsinde v. Sainte Foy: Argument, Threat, and Vengeance in Eleventh-Century Monastic Litigation," in *Religious and Laity in Western Europe, 1000–1400: Interaction, Negotiation, and Power*, ed. Emilia Jamroziak and Janet Burton (Turnhout: 2006), 171–3.

promote William's case for canonization, not to record the procedure of trial by hot iron. Nevertheless, this does not mean that a legal historian may not exploit the story for an end never envisioned by the hagiographer.[27] In fact, tales of this sort, as well as other forms of non-hagiographical imaginative literature, can offer insight to legal historians precisely because the legal information appears incidentally, not formulaically as in the plea rolls, and, in this instance, not as part of the overall propagandistic agenda of the hagiographer. Rather, such sources offer bits of legalistic color designed to help the author situate the tale in realistic, real time, and to boost the plausibility of the story.[28] John Baldwin, puzzled that legal historians have not relied more on ordeal accounts in vernacular literature, aptly refers to such scene-setting as "touches of authenticating realism."[29] One might contrast this with the authorial work of the legal scribes of the plea rolls, who were trained to drain out the incidentals to produce a tidy administrative record. Baldwin argues that literary depictions of the ordeal, which admittedly tend to focus more on bilateral than unilateral trials, are trustworthy as historical accounts, and that there is in fact "little significant distinction between the portrayal of ordeals in fictional accounts and what we know about them from other historical documentation."[30] In other words, literary accounts, including hagiography, can sometimes furnish evidence of actual ordeal practice.

---

27 Andersson and Miller make a similar observation about sagas. *Law and Literature*, xii.

28 Too great a deviation from actual ordeal practice, for example, might have piqued the attention of the examiners in William's canonization investigation, who likely had at least some familiarity with ordeal procedure.

29 John W. Baldwin, "The Crisis of the Ordeal: Literature, Law, and Religion Around 1200," *Journal of Medieval and Renaissance Studies* 24, no. 3 (1994), 328, 333. On legal procedures in literature, see also R. Howard Bloch, *Medieval French Literature and Law* (Berkeley: 1977); Ralph J. Hexter, *Equivocal Oaths and Ordeals in Medieval Literature* (Cambridge: 1975).

30 Baldwin, "Crisis," 329, 333. Baldwin argues that authors carefully placed ordeals in settings that mirror what can be found in chronicles and charters. For instance, clergy were typically present. Paul Hyams makes a similar claim in describing a late tenth-century trial by hot iron found in a monastic chronicle. Hyams, "Trial by Ordeal," in *On the Laws and Customs of England*, ed. Morris S. Arnold et al. (Chapel Hill: 1981), 94. See also Andersson and Miller, *Law and Literature*, 4 (briefly describing the use of sagas for insight into ordeal procedure). Of course, our own experience with popular depictions of twenty-first-century legal settings, whether in novels or television dramas, might encourage a healthy dose of skepticism in applying an interpretive lens to medieval texts describing trial procedure.

Ordeal Procedure

What do we know about unilateral ordeals, and more specifically about trial by hot iron? Plea roll evidence regarding English ordeal procedure is scant; most entries regarding the *iudicium dei* indicate only that an individual was ordered to undergo trial by hot iron or trial by cold water.[31] Surviving liturgies provide some sense of the ritually complex lead-up to the moment of trial, but do not tend to elucidate precisely how the outcome of the ordeal itself was determined, or by whom.[32] In fact, historians describing ordeal practice often employ the passive voice in depicting the moment of judgment, indicating, for example, that the "hand was examined."[33] In most cases, we simply do not know who determined whether a proband had passed or failed. This gap in our knowledge is striking, as it leaves a mystery at the very heart of ordeal procedure. In its later English form, trial by hot iron appears to have involved a period of fasting and prayer by the accused; a special liturgy celebrated by a priest who would bless and heat the iron; the swearing of a solemn oath by the

---

31 See, for example, the 1207 case of Margery, wife of Hugh Dobin, an alleged adultress and suspect in Hugh's untimely death. The record merely tells us that she was ordered to purge herself by hot iron. At the same court session, two men suspected as accomplices went to trial by water, while a third, aptly for the purposes of this Festschrift named Bill Miller (Willelmus Molendinarius), wisely fled the vicinity. *Curia Regis Rolls, 8–10 John* (Nendeln: 1971), 64–65. Occasionally the plea rolls include a verdict, as in the case of Walter Trenchebof, who was hanged after failing the ordeal of water. *Curia Regis Rolls, 15–16 John* (Nendeln: 1971), 247. In England at the turn of the twelfth to thirteenth century, "trial by water" seems to refer to cold water, not immersion of one's hand in boiling water. See, e.g., Robert Bartlett, *Trial by Fire and Water* (Oxford: 1986), 25.

32 See, e.g., *Ordeals, Compurgation, Excommunication and Interdict*, ed. Arthur C. Howland (Philadelphia: 1898), 7–18. For ordeal liturgies, see also *Die Gesetze der Angelsachsen*, ed. F. Liebermann, vol. 1 (Halle: 1903), 401–31. For Merovingian and Carolingian antecedents, see K. Zeumer, *Formulae Merovingici et Karolini Aevi* (Hanover: 1886).

33 See, e.g., H. L. Ho, "The Legitimacy of Medieval Proof," *Journal of Law and Religion* 19 (2003–2004), 261; Ian Pilarczyk, "Between a Rock and a Hot Place: The Role of Subjectivity in the Medieval Ordeal by Hot Iron," *Anglo-American Law Review* 25 (1996), 90; Kerr, Forsyth, and Plyley, "Cold Water," 589; Bartlett, *Trial*, 1. Peter T. Leeson more confidently asserts that priests were tasked with examining the hand, but he bases this on a 1901 translation of Aethelstan's dooms regarding trial by hot iron, which describes the priest's role in preparing the iron but is vague as to who should inspect the hand. See Howland, *Ordeals*, 12. Leeson observes that in West Frisian law the community might pronounce the outcome of an ordeal. See Leeson, "Ordeals," *Journal of Law and Economics* 55, no. 3 (2012), 698, n. 22, citing Rebecca V. Colman, "Reason and Unreason in Early Medieval Law," *Journal of Interdisciplinary History* 4, no. 4 (1974), 590.

accused, who would then carry the hot iron a prescribed number of paces; occlusion of the burned hand, most likely for a period of three days; followed by the unveiling of the hand and examination for signs of healing or putrefaction, leading to the pronouncement of judgment and, if convicted, sentence.[34]

Liturgical manuals can help us envision what the process might have looked like in finer detail. A Norman-era English liturgical rite describes the procedure that followed a legitimately made accusation.[35] Trial by ordeal was preceded by three days of penance and prayer, presumably by the accused and perhaps also the accuser. On the day of the ordeal, a priest in sacred vestments carried the iron with forceps before the altar and called upon God to bless the space and all those in it. Next, the priest prayed over the iron itself, asking God to "illuminate our hearts and our minds" (illumina corda nostra et sensus nostros). After this, the priest placed the iron into the fire and sprinkled water to bless it, no doubt a sizzling spectacle. The iron heated while Mass was celebrated, during which the accused received the Eucharist. Later, a lengthy litany was recited. In addition to beseeching the saints, the litany included requests for deliverance "from the devil's snares" (ab insidiis diaboli), "from eternal damnation" (ab dampnacione perpetua) and, in phrasing redolent with immediate and long-term import, "on the day of Judgment" (in die Iudicii).[36] Calling upon God as the "just judge" (iudex iustus), the priest then asked God to "guide our judgment" (dirige iudicium nostrum), an acknowledgment that human discernment was not entirely avoided by reliance on the *iudicium dei*. The iron was removed from the fire and placed "on the wood [*lignum*, a word that could also signify the gallows or the cross]," while the priest uttered a prayer, asking that the innocent be absolved and the guilty exposed. Finally, the accused carried the iron "nine measured feet" (novem pedum mensuram), after which the hand was occluded and sealed to prevent tampering. When the hand was uncovered later, the accused was pronounced guilty if discharge was discovered, demonstrating the hand's unclean state of healing; if otherwise, an acquittal followed, and God was glorified and praised. The liturgical rite suggests a solemn, ritualistically charged spectacle, culminating in the moment of judgment.

34 On ordeal procedure, see John Hudson, *The Formation of the English Common Law* (London: 1996), 72–73; Dominique Barthélemy, "Diversité des ordalies médiévales," *Revue Historique* 280, no. 1 (1988), 3–25; Hyams, "Trial by Ordeal," 106–11. On trial by hot iron specifically, see Henry Charles Lea, *The Ordeal* (Philadelphia: 1973), 40–56.

35 For this liturgical rite, dated to 1067–c.1210, see Liebermann, *Gesetze*, vol. 1, 427–9.

36 Charles Donahue (personal communication, 6/6/17) points out that these deliverance requests were not unique to ordeal liturgies.

England under Interdict

But was such an elaborate procedure followed in the trial of the woman in York Minster? The miracle tale mentions no liturgy, nor does it identify the woman's accuser or describe her oath. Ordeal procedure, although often presented as static and monolithic by historians, likely varied regionally and across time in response to changing social pressures and power dynamics. The trial story here betrays few procedural details, but what little it does provide allows for some speculation in the broader context of the city of York during the late ordeal period. If Norton is correct in dating the events to 1208 or 1210 during one of York's eyres, then the trial occurred at a time of papal interdict (1208–1214) shortly before Lateran IV. Most liturgies and sacraments were suspended during the interdict, which was imposed upon England by Pope Innocent III after King John refused to accept the appointment of Stephen Langton as archbishop of Canterbury. This, incidentally, made shrines like that of William of York all the more crucial to the faithful who could no longer participate in the Mass.[37] Moreover, York had further disorder all its own: at the time the interdict was announced, the see was under the administration of royal custodians because of conflict between York's archbishop, Geoffrey Plantagenet, and his half-brother, King John; Geoffrey went into exile in France in 1207, where he died five years later.[38]

Insofar as ordeals involved liturgies, the interdict might seem to preclude such trials altogether. Infant baptism and confession of the dying were treated as exceptions to the interdict's liturgical and sacramental ban, but no explicit exception seems to have been made for ordeal liturgies.[39] As a result, the interdict may have pushed England prematurely toward experimentation with alternative trial procedures when access to liturgies narrowed. To further complicate matters, there is some evidence of local variation in how the terms of the interdict were understood.[40]

---

37 Norton, *William of York*, 179.

38 On Geoffrey's tumultuous tenure, see Marie Lovatt, "Geoffrey (1151?–1212), archbishop of York," in *Oxford Dictionary of National Biography* (Oxford: 2004); Decima L. Douie, *Archbishop Geoffrey Plantagenet and the Chapter of York* (York: 1960). On the assignment of royal custodians to administer the archbishopric of York through 1213, see C. R. Cheney, "King John's Reaction to the Interdict on England," *Transactions of the Royal Historical Society* 31 (1949), 140.

39 Even these exceptions to the liturgical ban were not available at the interdict's outset. See Clarke, *Interdict*, 131.

40 See ibid., 130–2.

A York assize roll dated to September–October 1208, several months after the interdict went into effect, included an order from the justices that a certain William Staikebutter, suspected of his wife's death, should purge himself through trial by water.[41] This lends itself to a few interpretations, including the possibilities that: York had not yet learned of the interdict, an unlikely scenario given the passage of time since the announcement; the terms of the interdict, including which liturgies were banned outright and which might be performed in exigent circumstances, were not yet understood locally in York, although one would assume that itinerant royal justices would know whether ordeals could be administered during the interdict; the assize justices wrongly assumed the interdict would be short-lived and therefore did not hesitate to order trial by ordeal despite the immediate unavailability of a liturgy; York continued to administer ordeals with liturgies during the interdict, a possibility bolstered by the fact that York Minster's royal custodians, presumptively partisans of King John, may have been less inclined than others to respect the interdict's prohibitions;[42] ordeal liturgies had become perfunctory or even fallen away by this time, perhaps replaced by a streamlined priestly procedure or a simple blessing, such that the ban on liturgies did not affect the operation of the ordeal; or the ordeal liturgy was curtailed or dropped in response to the interdict, with justices improvising procedurally until they received further guidance. Indeed, the justices in York might have decided to continue administering the ordeal sans liturgy during the interdict. This could explain why our ordeal story mentions justices and knights but not priests, aside from the custodian at William's tomb, an omission all the more curious in light of the

41 Stenton, *Pleas*, vol. 4, 101. See also ibid., 116, for a second suspect ordered to undergo trial by water in autumn 1208. William Staikebutter never had to serve as the local York test subject for the interdict's prohibition on liturgies, since he escaped from the locality after coming under suspicion of felony. A cursory search of the Curia Regis rolls from 1207 to 1215 unearthed a couple of ordeals in 1208, around the time the interdict was imposed, and a couple of ordeals in 1214, around the time the interdict was lifted. The one mention I found of an ordeal in the interim involved a person who had abjured the realm after failing the ordeal, and who wished to return to England; the ordeal itself could have happened years earlier, before the interdict. See *Curia Regis Rolls, 8–10 John*, 64, 65; *Curia Regis Rolls, 11–14 John* (Nendeln: 1971), 256; *Curia Regis Rolls 15–16 John*, 241, 247. I need to complete a more thorough search of the Curia Regis rolls as well as any other surviving criminal trial records of the period to confirm my hypothesis that the ordeal may have been interrupted by the interdict.

42 There is some evidence that ecclesiastical courts continued trying cases during the interdict, but with trials held in cemeteries or priests' homes rather than within churches. Clarke, *Interdict*, 166–67.

tale's hagiographical purpose.[43] The delegation of the verdict to twelve knights might reflect accommodation of the interdict, during which the justices might have tried to distance themselves from direct administration of the normally liturgically rich event. In fact, the absence of a liturgy at the center of the ordeal procedure could have created the opportunity and need for William's miraculous intercession. Presumably, had there been a preceding liturgy, the woman might have sought divine intercession earlier.[44] The ordeal itself, after all, involved the miraculous in its normal operation, insofar as it was predicated upon God's direct involvement in the outcome.[45] Without a liturgy to summon God's assistance, the woman might have been compelled to invoke the aid of the local saint after the ordeal failed to go her way.

Doubting the Iudicium Dei

The campaign for William's canonization coincided with the transitional period from ordeal to jury trial. He was finally declared a saint in 1226, not long after jury trial replaced the ordeal in England. Other scholars have already documented growing doubt in the twelfth century within clerical élites about the efficacy of trial by ordeal and concern about priestly participation in blood judgments more generally.[46] What this ordeal tale adds is evidence that discomfort with the ordeal was not confined to the high-level theologians whose writings influenced Pope Innocent III and informed the eventual Lateran IV

43 Of course, the hagiographer could have deliberately removed priests from administration of the woman's ordeal, knowing that the story would call the procedure's efficacy into doubt.

44 It is not, of course, uncommon in medieval sources for miraculous interventions to occur after conviction, and sometimes during or after execution. See, e.g., Robert Bartlett, *The Hanged Man: A Story of Miracle, Memory, and Colonialism in the Middle Ages* (Princeton: 2006).

45 See Peter Brown, "Society and the Supernatural: A Medieval Change," *Daedalus* 104, no. 2 (1975), 135–6 (describing the ordeal as a "controlled miracle"). But see Finbarr McAuley, "Canon Law and the End of the Ordeal," *Oxford Journal of Legal Studies* 26, no. 3 (2006), 483 (arguing that the ordeal was not viewed as a miracle by theologians like Peter the Chanter, who found in it instead an illicit testing of God).

46 See John Baldwin, "The Intellectual Preparation for the Canon of 1215 against Ordeals," *Speculum* 36, no. 4 (1961), 613–36; McAuley, "Canon Law," 473–513. But see Bartlett, *Trial*, 42–53, for the argument that ordeals were still flourishing and even spreading during the years leading up to the 1215 prohibition.

pronouncements.[47] Rather, skepticism about the ordeal also penetrated the comparably plebeian level of hagiography aimed at promoting the canonization of a local York figure. While not necessarily written for the purpose of disavowing the ordeal, the woman's story called into question the reliability of ordeal outcomes in revealing who should die and who should live. The story takes what appears to be a straightforward ordeal verdict based on a manifestly blistered hand and throws it into doubt when William intercedes with instantaneous healing. Of course, it is not clear that the author intended to imply that the knights initially got their verdict wrong, compelling the soon-to-be-saint William to correct the erroneous outcome. Nowhere does our narrator tell us that this was all a case of mistaken identity, or that the woman had not, in fact, committed the homicide. Whether this means that the woman was innocent *ab initio*, and wrongfully convicted of homicide, or whether instead it means that the woman was guilty of the underlying charge, but nevertheless was rescued by the soon-to-be saint, possibly due to her piety, later repentance, or out of grace generously granted regardless of her desert, is left entirely ambiguous by the author.[48] Yet at the core of the tale is an ordeal verdict called into doubt by later evidence, placing the story in a larger tradition of ordeal-questioning narratives. After all, the woman would have been executed were it not for the fortuity that she asked for and was granted permission to visit William's tomb, a but-for scenario easily recognizable by the story's audience.

---

47 Concern with the ordeal's reliability was neither new nor confined to English felony cases. For example, Stephen D. White argues that litigants strategically tried to avoid the uncertainties of ordeals in eleventh-century western French property disputes. White, "Proposing the Ordeal and Avoiding It: Strategy and Power in Western French Litigation, 1050–1110," in *Cultures of Power: Lordship, Status, and Process in Twelfth-Century Europe*, ed. Thomas N. Bisson (Philadelphia: 1995), 89–123. Yet White also argues that twelfth- and thirteenth-century vernacular authors writing about imaginary trials were not engaged in the kinds of legal and theological argument common in clerical critique of the ordeal. White, "Imaginary Justice: The End of the Ordeal and the Survival of the Duel," *Medieval Perspectives* 13 (1998), 32–55 at 34, 36.

48 In sermon *exempla*, repentance and sincere confession sometimes ensured a favorable ordeal outcome or even erased ordeal-inflicted wounds. See John W. Baldwin, "From the Ordeal to Confession: In Search of Lay Religion in Early Thirteenth-Century France," in *Handling Sin: Confession in the Middle Ages*, ed. Peter Biller and A.J. Minnis (York: 1998), 205–6. See also Lea, *Ordeal*, 51 (describing how a heretic in Cambrai c. 1215 was sentenced to death at the stake after an ordeal by hot iron, but was encouraged to confess and repent by a priest as he walked to his execution; his hand duly began to heal, and he was pronounced innocent and released).

Another miracle attributed to William similarly cast doubt on the efficacy of a different form of proof, trial by battle, also a target of criticism at Lateran IV. That tale recounts:

> A certain man, named Ralph, appealed [i.e., privately prosecuted] for breaking the king's peace, was convicted in a duel, and was deprived of one of his eyes by his adversary, who was named Besing; the other eye was put out afterwards because he had been vanquished. He was handed over to the executor of justice, who took out the other eye, and a certain boy named Hugo collected both extracted eyes, and carried them in his hand; and after another day passed, the same Ralph, approaching the tomb of Blessed William, fasting and praying, regained two other eyes smaller than the previous ones, and with clear and acute sight, but his previous eyes were a different color, namely, like woad.[49]

This version of the tale, like the ordeal story, is ambiguous as to the defeated person's guilt with regard to the underlying offense. Also like the ordeal story, William intervened to undo the sentence after judgment had been passed. Unlike the ordeal tale, the exoculation story has a parallel version in another text, the anonymous *Vita Sancti Willelmi*, as well as in the miracles of Sainte Foy and Thomas Becket, suggesting the possibility of a hagiographical trope.[50] The version from the *Vita* drops some details, most notably the names of the parties, but fleshes out the story considerably, even clarifying that the accused man was indeed innocent. The accuser, "a certain rustic, robust and full of envy" (quidam rusticus robustus et livore plenus), contrived a plan to subject his neighbor to a false accusation of arson. According to the narrator, "The accuser loosened his poisonous tongue toward perjury; anger led to blows, envy to sorrow, cruelty to bloodshed."[51] The neighbor, a physically weaker man, fell

49 For the original Latin, see "Miracula quaedam Sancti Willelmi," in Raine, *Historians*, vol. 2, 539. For an analysis of this miracle story, see Norton, *William of York*, 169–80 (remarkably connecting the tale to an actual duel fought c. 1207–1208). For the observation that literary accounts sometimes depict trial by battle producing a just outcome, see White, "Imaginary Justice," 35–37.

50 See "Vita Sancti Willelmi, Auctore Anonymo," in Raine, *Historians*, vol. 2, 289–90; Pamela Sheingorn, *The Book of Sainte Foy* (Philadelphia: 1995), 53–55; van Caenegem, *Lawsuits*, 507–14, and Hudson, *Formation*, 159–60. The Becket miracle also involved "a certain rustic" and the restoration of eyesight and genitals after trial by ordeal. My thanks to Steve White for the Sainte Foy reference.

51 "Venenatam linguam suam relaxat accusator ad perjuria; prosolit ad ictus ira; livor ad luctum; crudelitas ad cruorem." Raine, *Historians*, vol. 2, 289 (my translation).

in battle; his opponent proceeded to cut out his eyes and emasculate him, throwing the severed body parts to the crowd. The narrator reports that the judges, horrified by the spectacle, tolerated the envious man's actions although they did not approve of them.[52] Like the woman in the ordeal tale, the dismembered man beseeched the help of William of York, who restored both his genitals and his eyes; the latter were changed in color. In these stories geared toward offering evidence for William's canonization case, doubt was cast upon the efficacy of the forms of proof relied upon in adjudicating disputes in the king's courts and also upon the competence of judges in administering royal justice.[53]

In fact, the procedure for canonization underwent reform at the same time that the *iudicium dei* came under heightened scrutiny by theologians. Before the twelfth century, popular acclaim might suffice for declaring a new saint. From the twelfth century forward, the church introduced stringent investigatory procedures and centralized canonization more firmly in the papacy.[54] Having been subjected to the newly elaborated and papal-centric procedures for canonization introduced by Pope Alexander III (r. 1159–1181), William emerged victorious from his own posthumous trial, in which grave doubts about his reputation were ultimately quashed as his biography was purged and transformed into hagiography in the run-up to Honorius III's decree authorizing his canonization. William, like the woman he reportedly saved from death by burning, was granted a second chance despite his chequered reputation as a worldly man who had acquired his archbishopric by questionable means. His sanctity having been tested and proved, William could stand shoulder-to-shoulder alongside Bernard of Clairvaux and Thomas Becket in the revised litany of saints.

---

52 Van Caenegem translates this passage as follows: "the judges [were] filled with horror at this enormity, which they permitted in the exercise of their official duties rather than being in agreement with it." *Lawsuits*, 557.

53 An alternative reading of the ordeal miracle suggests that juries fared no better: the story also casts doubt upon the reliability of jury verdicts.

54 See Norton, *William of York*, 192–201; E.W. Kemp, "Pope Alexander III and the Canonization of Saints: The Alexander Prize Essay," *Transactions of the Royal Historical Society* 27 (1945), 13–28. But see Stephan Kuttner, "La réserve papale du droit de canonisation," *Revue Historique de Droit Français et Étranger* (1938), 172–228 (attributing the definitive shift toward papal reservation of the right to canonize to the papacy of Gregory IX (r. 1227–1241) instead of Alexander III).

Expanding Use of Juries

The miracle story, therefore, reveals something about the kinds of proof marshalled in support of canonization in the early thirteenth century. Methods of proof were changing in the secular world as well, and the ordeal tale adds credence to an already well-supported theory that England's transition to trial by jury was swift in part due to the expanding use of juries in the decades leading up to Lateran IV. Particularly from the reign of Henry II (r. 1154–1189) forward, juries were used extensively in criminal and civil cases alike—most notably in the grand assize, by means of which a jury of twelve knights determined the outcome of possessory actions. In the criminal law area, juries of presentment, ancestors of the grand jury, brought initial accusations against individuals suspected of crime, while juries were also tasked with responding to writs *de odio et atia*, through which a defendant alleged that he or she had been accused of felony out of hate and spite.[55] Juries assisted justices in sorting between cases that should be dismissed outright, and those for which ordeal was appropriate. For example, the treatise *Glanvill* (c. 1187–1189) observes that, when a person was accused on the basis of public notoriety, "the truth of the matter shall be investigated by many and varied inquests and interrogations before the justices, and arrived at by considering the probable facts and possible conjectures both for and against the accused, who must as a result be either absolved entirely or made to purge himself by the ordeal."[56] The woman of York's ordeal tale tantalizingly suggests that juries might have sometimes been used to issue verdicts in trial by ordeal, which could further explain why England made such a quick transition from ordeal to jury trial after Lateran IV.

Although we have no plea roll accounts to support the idea that juries of knights ever issued ordeal verdicts, the plausibility of our ordeal tale is bolstered by the fact that juries of knights were doing all sorts of things in the late twelfth and early thirteenth centuries. It is far from unimaginable that juries might have issued the occasional ordeal verdict during a time when clerics, and perhaps non-clerical justices, were looking to distance themselves from a dubious criminal procedure.[57] It is also worth acknowledging the uncertainty that

55 On these two uses of the jury in pre-1215 criminal cases, see Roger D. Groot, "The Jury in Private Criminal Prosecutions before 1215," *American Journal of Legal History* 27, no. 2 (1983), 113–41.

56 *The Treatise on the Laws and Customs of the Realm of England Commonly Called Glanvill*, ed. and trans. G. D. G. Hall (Oxford: 1993), 171.

57 Pushing against this possibility are the fits and starts in the adoption of final jury verdicts as an ordeal replacement post-1215. In other words, while jury trial soon emerged

persists in accounts of ordeal procedure with regard to who actually viewed the burned hand and pronounced whether it was healing. Although historians often speak of trial by hot iron or other ordeals as if they may be reduced to a single procedural template, the reality is more complicated. While there is evidence that priests celebrated pre-ordeal liturgies and that justices or other officials often presided over ordeals, it is not easy to ascertain who pronounced God's judgment, a responsibility that might have been borne by different parties over time and in various geographic locales.

In recounting the late tenth-century trial by hot iron of a slave, for example, Paul Hyams indicates that many were present when the slave's hand was unwrapped, including the reeve tasked with adjudicating the case.[58] The reeve was further obligated to prepare the fire, a job often assigned to a priest in other accounts of ordeal procedure. Also present at the unwrapping of the hand were the reeve's "cronies," as Hyams describes them, and unspecified onlookers who saw decay where the reeve and his cronies saw instead a healed hand. The difference between Hyams's account of trial by ordeal, with procedure dominated by a reeve, and other accounts involving priests more squarely in the procedure, may reflect local variations and also change over time, as the ordeal perhaps became increasingly sacralized, although never a sacrament, sometime after the late tenth century. Our ordeal tale, in which the royal justices never appeared to enter York Minster themselves, while the knights tried to pry the acquitted woman out of the sanctuary space, suggests that the *iudicium dei* may have been taking a secular turn in York prior to its abolition, possibly in response to the interdict's restriction on liturgies. This, in turn, could explain the convicted woman's appeal to William, who stepped in to play an intercessory role when the initial *iudicium dei*, mediated by twelve knights, proved unfavorable.

Justices administering the ordeal might have been especially eager to foist this burden upon juries by the late twelfth or early thirteenth century, a time when increasingly intellectualized rumblings of concern about the ordeal were emanating from Paris and other theological centers toward distant dioceses and parishes. The interdict could have accelerated this change if justices

as the solution to the post-Lateran-IV crisis, it did so after some experimentation and hesitation in granting the authority to convict, rather than merely acquit, to jurors. See Roger D. Groot, "The Early-Thirteenth-Century Criminal Jury," in *Twelve Good Men and True: The Criminal Trial Jury in England, 1200–1800*, ed. J. S. Cockburn and Thomas A. Green (Princeton: 1988), 10–33; Thomas J. McSweeney, "Magna Carta and the Right to Trial by Jury," in *Magna Carta: Muse and Mentor*, ed. Randy J. Holland (Eagan, MN: 2014), 150–52.

58 Hyams, "Trial by Ordeal," 93–94.

found they could no longer rely as heavily on priests, who were compelled to scale back their liturgical commitments. Moreover, juries or jury-like groups may never have been entirely absent from English ordeal procedure. Collective judgments, after all, were used elsewhere in trial by ordeal.[59] The *Leges Edwardi Confessoris* (a twelfth-century text purporting to relay eleventh-century law) alludes to the presence of *legales homines*, a phrase later associated with juries, at the administration of ordeals. The *Leges* prescribed that the bishop's official and other clergy should attend the ordeal, in addition to "the king's justices, with lawful men of that district" (iusticia regis cum legalibus hominibus provincie illius), in order to "see and hear that all things are done justly" (ut uideant et audient quod eque omnia fiant).[60] The knights in our tale may represent something like the *legales homines* alluded to in this text, although their responsibility in this instance involved pronouncing the woman's guilt or innocence, not merely standing by as witnesses to the procedure. If groups of "lawful men" helped administer late ordeal procedure, then discussing a clear break from trial by ordeal to trial by jury may obscure the role played by juries before 1215 in determining the outcome of felony cases. Without further evidence about who typically judged whether a hand had healed or a person had sunk, it would be unwise to assume that the use of twelve knights was a literary invention by William's hagiographer. Rather, recourse to juries to issue ordeal verdicts, or at least to assist in the issuance of verdicts, could simply be another example of the expanding use of juries in royal judicial processes prior to 1215. It was a jury, after all, which determined who should face the ordeal in the first place.

Justice and Jury Dynamics

The ordeal tale provides insight as well into the dynamics of the relationship between justices and jurors in the criminal law context during the transitional period from ordeal to jury trial. A few aspects of the story merit further

59 Eleventh- or twelfth-century Frisian law regarding trial by hot iron, for example, required two groups to examine the hand: the priest and three royal witnesses on the one side, and the magistrate, lawsayer, and another royal witness on the other. In case of disagreement, the priest's group was to prevail if inclined toward acquittal, thereby favoring acquittals over convictions. Sydney Fairbanks, *The Old West Frisian Skeltana Riucht* (Cambridge: 1939), 56, 89.

60 See *Leges Edwardi Confessoris*, §9: <http://www.earlyenglishlaws.ac.uk/laws/texts/ecf1/view/#edition,1/edition,1_0_c_9>, accessed 19/5/2017.

consideration: the reliance by the justices on twelve knights to examine the hand and issue an initial verdict, and to reexamine the hand later after the reported healing; the justices' decision to punish the knights for their initial verdict; the justices' willingness to hand down the revised judgment saving the woman from the death penalty; and the knights' continued insistence on the woman's actual guilt.

With regard to the first point, the royal justices appeared to be reluctant to get too deeply involved in proclaiming the woman innocent or guilty. Instead, they delegated examination of the hand to the knights, who initially declared her guilty. This placed some distance between the justices, representatives of the crown in a distant northern circuit, and the local populace, which might have resented royal intrusion into York affairs. Relatedly, the justices may have felt that a local crime might best be judged by local actors, although it is unclear just how local the knights were.[61] This concern could also have been at play in the exoculation narrative, in which the justices were described as horrified by the false accuser's violence toward the defendant, yet reluctant to intervene in the resolution of a local private prosecution.

At the same time, the distancing tactic may reflect a concern with the greater perils at play in capital cases, namely the peril to one's soul in judging others and potentially condemning an innocent person to death.[62] Even after hearing that the woman's hand had suddenly healed, the justices summoned the knights to examine her instead of viewing her hand directly. Only then did the justices confidently hand down the new judgment, freeing the woman and crediting God and Blessed William with her fortunate fate. The justices may have feared for their own souls in judging a doubtful capital case, a fear that was relieved when the only judgment possible was acquittal after a miraculous healing. As the *Leges Henrici Primi* cautioned in the early twelfth century, the "danger is so much the greater to the judge than to the person who is being judged to the extent that we know, from the words of the Lord, that any judgment we pass on others is held in store for ourselves."[63] The justices' willingness to announce the revised verdict suggests that they could have, but chose not to, proclaim the initial verdict as well, foisting this burden instead upon

61 The text says only that the knights were sent to participate in the ordeal, which leaves open the question of whether the knights were from York or farther afield. Presumably they were more local than the itinerant royal justices, and in fact they could have comprised a presenting jury that initially accused the woman of homicide.

62 On this theme, see James Q. Whitman, *The Origins of Reasonable Doubt* (New Haven: 2008).

63 *Leges Henrici Primi*, ed. and trans. L. J. Downer (Oxford: 1972), 130–1.

knights who, by virtue of their occupation, were already tainted by blood. In reexamining the hand, the knights appeared to be demoted to mere eyewitnesses of the state of healing, in contrast to their earlier role in pronouncing the actual verdict.[64] The hagiographer, in fact, makes clear that the knights stood by their earlier declaration of guilt despite the justices' decision to overturn the conviction.

Why did the knights continue to insist on the woman's guilt? Perhaps they were skeptical of the sudden spate of saintly healings emanating from York Minster; the justices, possibly but not likely clerics, may have been more inclined to credit the miracle.[65] Relatedly, this could be a plot device introduced by the hagiographer, dramatically pitting unbelieving knights against pious justices, who were more willing to give credence to the healing miracle.[66] Alternatively, the knights might have accepted the miracle but felt that the verdict, as announced, should nevertheless stand. Foreshadowing later jury practice in felony cases, maybe the knights saw their role as broader than

64 This is not unlike the role played by knights in cases of mayhem, or maiming, during the era of trial by ordeal. Namely, knights were sometimes charged with examining an accuser's wounds and determining whether the accused should proceed to trial by ordeal. See, e.g., *Pleas before the King or His Justices, 1198–1212*, vol. 2, ed. Doris Mary Stenton (London: 1952), 80 (knights sent to view appellor's wounds, finding him unharmed), 81 (knights sent to view appellor's wounds, after which the accused was sent to trial by hot iron).

65 On the clerical status of royal justices at this time, see Ralph Turner, "Clerical Judges in English Secular Courts: The Ideal Versus the Reality," in *Medievalia et Humanistica* 3, ed. Paul Maurice Clogan (Cleveland: 1972), 75–98. Turner initially argued that the late twelfth century was the "peak period for clerical justices." Ibid., 92. However, Turner later revised his view, observing that during the reign of King John only four out of fifteen royal justices were clerics, and arguing that it could no longer credibly be held that clerics dominated the royal judiciary until Edward I's time. Turner, "The Judges of King John: Their Background and Training," *Speculum* 51, no. 3 (1976), 454. Royal justices were perhaps less likely to be clerics during the interdict, when service to the king was at odds with loyalty to mother church. Some bishops, for example, went into exile. See W. L. Warren, *King John* (London: 1961), 163–73.

66 On the other hand, if the justices were men willing to serve King John during the interdict, the knights might have been engaged in resistance to royal justice. Stephen Langton, after all, from his safe perch in continental exile, had reminded knights of their obligation to defend the church and oppose King John's sins. See Clarke, *Interdict*, 42, 170. For Langton's letter to the English people, see *Acta Stephani Langton, Cantuariensis Archiepiscopi, A.D. 1207–1228*, ed. Kathleen Major (Oxford: 1950), 2–7. This does not, however, help explain why the knights would have resisted changing a verdict in response to a miracle. It is also worth noting that some clerics and laity alike may have felt more loyalty to King John than to a distant pope. See Clarke, *Interdict*, 169.

simply declaring whether or not the hand had healed, and going instead to the more profound question of the woman's actual guilt or innocence of the alleged crime. The knights' continued insistence on the woman's guilt suggests that their initial verdict may have been based on more than the state of her blistered hand.

For example, the woman might have been known as a bad actor locally, a fact that the knights could have been privy to, either directly or through rumor and gossip, but which the itinerant royal justices, who were likely more at home in Westminster than York, would not.[67] The ordeal tale highlights the difficulty of assessing culpability in those cases where all one could rely upon was outward signs, most notably the state of healing of a burned hand, but also circumstantial evidence connecting the accused to the homicide, as well as the accused's comportment and reputation. Only the most formalist account of ordeal procedure would presume that there was no room for interpretation in determining whether a person's hand was festering or healing, or whether a person subjected to trial by water had sunk or floated.[68] The fact-finder's inclination toward one interpretation or the other was very likely influenced by familiarity with any known facts about the alleged crime—whether acquired firsthand or, more likely, through rumor—as well as familiarity with the accused herself, both in terms of prior reputation (if she were a known local actor) and with regard to her self-presentation at the time of trial. Where a defendant's culpability remained in doubt, the tendency would have been toward acquittal. As the author of the *Mirror of Justices* would later write, "in case of doubt one should rather save than condemn."[69] An acquittal might also have seemed appropriate when the exigencies of pre-trial detention, the administration of the ordeal itself, and possibly an out-of-court settlement appeared to have satisfied any retributive desire for adequate punishment. Evidence suggests that acquittal rates were high both under trial by ordeal and later under jury trial, offering further support for the idea that doubt about an individual's guilt or about the appropriateness of the death penalty would have inclined

67 There is evidence in the late ordeal period that juries tasked with determining whether a person should face the ordeal were, on average, well informed about facts related to alleged crimes. See Kerr, Forsyth, and Plyley, "Cold Water," 576.

68 For two accounts emphasizing the manipulation of the process or the verdict, see Leeson, "Ordeals," 691–714; Ho, "Legitimacy of Medieval Proof," 259–98. See also Brown, "Society and the Supernatural," 139 (describing examination of the hand as the equivalent of a Rorschach test). Moreover, juries were already engaged in sorting when they determined who should proceed to trial by ordeal in the first place. See Roger D. Groot, "The Jury of Presentment before 1215," *American Journal of Legal History* 26, no. 1 (1982), 1–24.

69 See *The Mirror of Justices*, ed. William Joseph Whittaker (London: 1895), 167.

jurors and justices toward acquittal or pardon.[70] Remarkably, however, the knights in this tale were so convinced of the woman's guilt that they tried to drag her out of York Minster.

One possible explanation is that the knights simply believed she deserved to die. Medieval English literature, while steeped in calls for mercy and cautions against judging, also acknowledged that some individuals deserved the death penalty, and that in fact there was a special place in hell for those condemned to death. By this account, had she truly been guilty and proceeded to execution, the woman would have experienced torments after death far exceeding the pain of the searing iron on her hand. "Thereunder is a wall of iron that is all filled with souls," commented an old English poem. "Upon it is bound many in iron that is hotter than the brand. Therein are the souls brought of those who were beheaded or hanged."[71] Executed criminals not only deserved their grisly death, but also merited eternal damnation. The knights could have felt justified in condemning the woman if she seemed to fit the paradigm of the hell-bound, irredeemable wrongdoer in their estimation, particularly if they were not persuaded by the alleged miracle. The disparity in the elevated status of the knights and the presumptively lesser status of the woman compelled to undergo trial by hot iron—a disparity that also existed between her and the justices, admittedly—could have further influenced the knights' perception of her unworthiness for mercy, as could doubt about the reliability of a woman's oath in general.[72]

Furthermore, the knights' comfort level with the task of judging a felony case—and with standing stubbornly by their judgment despite the risk of condemnation and amercement by the justices—might be attributed in part to the moral comfort inherent in juries, which submerged the identity of individual

---

70 On the high acquittal rate in ordeals, see Kerr, Forsyth, and Plyley, "Cold Water," 580, 588–9. On acquittal rates in jury trials, see John G. Bellamy, *The Criminal Trial in Later Medieval England* (Toronto: 1998); Barbara A. Hanawalt, *Crime in East Anglia in the Fourteenth Century* (Norfolk: 1976), 20.

71 "The XI Pains of Hell," in *An Old English Miscellany*, ed. Richard Morris (London: 1872), 154 (my translation). "Her-vnder is of iren a wal / Þat is of saulen ifuld al. / On heom is mony yrene beond / Þat is hatture þen þe brond. / Þer-inne beoþ þe saulen i-don / Þat weren biheaueded oþer an-hon."

72 For the suggestion that only persons of low social status may have been subject to trial by ordeal in some settings, see Baldwin, "Intellectual Preparation," 620. Medieval romances, admittedly, frequently feature high-born individuals as participants in ordeals. See Bloch, *Medieval French Literature and Law*, 21–22; Hexter, *Equivocal Oaths*, 16–37. On the credibility of women's oaths, see White, "Imaginary Justice," 46–47.

jurors within a collective decision.[73] Being one of twelve men bringing accusations against a neighbor must have lightened the psychological burden of serving on a jury of presentment, the ancestor of our grand jury. Safety in numbers may also help explain the facility with which juries adjudicated writs *de odio et atia*, determining whether a felony defendant had been accused out of hate and spite; the knights' response could result in the defendant walking free, but it could also lead instead to the ordeal. Knights accustomed to serving on these kinds of juries would have similarly experienced some moral comfort in collectively declaring a verdict in trial by hot iron. This may have given the knights the confidence needed to stand by their assessment of the woman's guilt, even to the point of trying to drag her from the cathedral.

Conclusion

In leaning so heavily on this ordeal tale, I do not mean to suggest that legal historians have comparatively little to glean from the legal record itself. However, I do contend that delving into other narrative sources offers further credible evidence and helps us pose new questions. For example, was ordeal procedure undergoing transformation in England prior to its abandonment after Lateran IV? How was trial by ordeal affected by the imposition of a papal interdict on England in the early thirteenth century? Such questions would be impossible to answer on the basis of legal records alone, particularly given the scant documentation of ordeals in the English plea rolls. Reliance on extra-legal sources also fosters strategies for reading legal sources, going beyond the basic issues of paleography and translation and focusing instead on matters of exegesis. After all, litigants, too, were crafting narratives. These narratives were then curated and mediated by scribes, who translated them into the Latinate legal jargon of the plea rolls. Just as I assume literary license in the ordeal tale I recounted earlier, I must also assume some measure of literary license in medieval English legal sources, not taking them entirely at face value. Furthermore, I must notice not only the words on the parchment, but also the lacunae, the things left unsaid by scribes, such as who exactly pronounced the outcome in any given ordeal.

In closing, I stake one final claim about the value of leaning on literature in producing legal scholarship: it is a medieval practice in and of itself, a practice engaged in by theologians, chroniclers, and the authors of legal treatises, who

73 On moral comfort in criminal procedures, see Whitman, *Origins of Reasonable Doubt*, 10–25.

might borrow from literary sources or invent tales all their own in furtherance of their objectives.[74] To take one example, in arguing against the use of ordeals in twelfth-century Paris, theologian Peter the Chanter relied on compelling stories about ordeals gone wrong, most notably the tale of a pilgrim falsely accused and convicted of murdering his traveling companion, who returned home shortly after the pilgrim's execution; the story is remarkably reminiscent of a tale from the writings of Seneca.[75] In light of this genre-bending practice, medieval legal historians must be on guard against overweening confidence in our capacity to separate neatly the legal from the literary, fact from fiction, and the historical from the fantastical, a confidence that is woefully misplaced in dealing with sources whose authors may not have assumed such distinctions could or should be drawn. This is not to suggest that genre is a modern innovation: certainly literate men and women distinguished among romances, saints' lives, legal records, and theological tracts in the age of ordeal just as we do today in trying to make sense of ordeals. Yet where they were comfortable with permeability between genres, we are much less so, and therefore have to cultivate a tolerance for ambiguity, messiness, and blurred lines in order to understand our sources fully. This, in turn, brings us back full circle to our perplexing ordeal story, in which Blessed William forced the hand of a jury of knights by healing the hand of a dubious character. Was this fact, fiction, or something else entirely? Did the woman do it, did she not, and does it matter in the end?

Just as Peter the Chanter drew upon a tragic tale to make a normative argument about the efficacy of trial by ordeal, I have relied here on a miracle story to make claims about the nature of ordeals and jury trials in England at the turn of the thirteenth century. This has taken me into speculative terrain, an admittedly uncomfortable locale for a legal historian! Yet medieval legal historians, if too wedded to seemingly objective legal sources and to the range of questions they allow historians to ask, also run the risk of engaging in under-speculative legal-historical analysis and failing to acknowledge the mysteries

74 Most memorable in the context of legal treatises is the literary license taken by the author of the *Mirror of Justices*, who invented scores of fictitious judges with whimsical Anglo-Saxon names in reporting King Alfred's harsh response to bad judging. See Whittaker, *Mirror of Justices*, 166–71. See also David J. Seipp, "The Mirror of Justices," in *Learning the Law: Teaching and the Transmission of English Law, 1150–1900*, ed. Jonathan A. Bush and Alain Wijffels (London: 1999), 104–6.

75 Petrus Cantor Parisiensis, *Verbum Adbreviatum: Textus Conflatus*, ed. Monique Boutry (Turnhout: 2004), 507. For a discussion of the Senecan tale, see Elizabeth Papp Kamali, "A Felonious State of Mind: Mens Rea in Thirteenth- and Fourteenth-Century England," (PhD dissertation, University of Michigan, 2015), 420–1 <https://deepblue.lib.umich.edu/handle/2027.42/113574>, accessed 10/12/2017.

hidden behind scribal formulae, mysteries that might only shed their secrets once we venture into the unsteady landscape of tales like that of the woman with a half-walnut-sized wound. This is a lesson, of course, that Bill Miller has been preaching by example throughout his career, masterfully unwrapping the layers of mystery surrounding medieval Iceland's complex legal world through tales of berserkers, polar bears, and bloodied shirts waved by vengeance-seeking women. Where the English plea rolls are silent as to late ordeal procedure, this miracle tale of sinners and saints whispers volumes about the hesitancy of royal justices in administering the ordeal, the convergence of concerns about proof in canonical and secular procedure, and the use of a procedural hybrid, trial by ordeal by jury, possibly in the historical context of York Minster and most certainly in one hagiographer's imagination.

Works Cited

Manuscript Sources

Oxford Bodleian MS Dodsworth 125. <http://www.bodley.ox.ac.uk/dept/scwmss/wmss/online/1500-1900/dodsworthCLD/dodsworthCLD.html>, accessed 17/5/2017.

The National Archives of the UK (TNA): JUST 1/1171. JUST1/1171 AALT 0012 (1201), <http://aalt.law.uh.edu/AALT4/JUST1/JUST1no1171/IMG_0012.htm>, accessed 20/6/2017.

Printed Sources

Andersson, Theodore M. and William Ian Miller. *Law and Literature in Medieval Iceland*. Stanford: 1989.

Ashley, Kathleen and Pamela Sheingorn. *Writing Faith: Text, Sign, and History in the Miracles of Sainte Foy*. Chicago: 1999.

Baldwin, John W. "The Crisis of the Ordeal: Literature, Law, and Religion Around 1200." *Journal of Medieval and Renaissance Studies* 24, no. 3 (1994): 327–53.

Baldwin, John W. "From the Ordeal to Confession: In Search of Lay Religion in Early Thirteenth-Century France." In *Handling Sin: Confession in the Middle Ages*, edited by Peter Biller and A. J. Minnis, 191–209. York: 1998.

Baldwin, John W. "The Intellectual Preparation for the Canon of 1215 against Ordeals." *Speculum* 36, no. 4 (1961): 613–36

Barthélemy, Dominique. "Diversité des ordalies médiévales." *Revue Historique* 280, no. 1 (1988): 3–25.

Bartlett, Robert. *The Hanged Man: A Story of Miracle, Memory, and Colonialism in the Middle Ages*. Princeton: 2006.

Bartlett, Robert. *Trial by Fire and Water*. Oxford: 1986.

Bellamy, John G. *The Criminal Trial in Later Medieval England*. Toronto: 1998.

Bliss, W. B. *Calendar of Entries in the Papal Registers: Papal Letters*. Vol. 1. Nendeln: 1971.
Bloch, R. Howard. *Medieval French Literature and Law*. Berkeley: 1977.
Boutry, Monique, ed. *Petrus Cantor Parisiensis. Verbum Adbreviatum: Textus Conflatus*. Turnhout: 2004.
Brooke, Z. N., Adrian Morey, and C. N. L. Brooke, eds. *The Letters and Charters of Gilbert Foliot*. Cambridge: 1967.
Brown, Peter. "Society and the Supernatural: A Medieval Change." *Daedalus* 104, no. 2 (1975): 133–51.
Burton, Janet. "William of York (d. 1154)." In *Oxford Dictionary of National Biography*. Oxford: 2004.
Cheney, C. R. "King John's Reaction to the Interdict on England." *Transactions of the Royal Historical Society* 31 (1949): 129–50.
Clarke, Peter D. *The Interdict in the Thirteenth Century: A Question of Collective Guilt*. Oxford: 2007.
Clay, Charles Travis, ed. *Three Yorkshire Assize Rolls*. Leeds: 1911.
Coleman, Rebecca V. "Reason and Unreason in Early Medieval Law." *Journal of Interdisciplinary History* 4, no. 4 (1974): 571–91.
Curia Regis Rolls, 8–10 John. Nendeln: 1971.
Curia Regis Rolls, 11–14 John. Nendeln: 1971.
Curia Regis Rolls, 15–16 John. Nendeln: 1971.
Douie, Decima L. *Archbishop Geoffrey Plantagenet and the Chapter of York*. York: 1960.
Downer, L. J., ed. and trans. *Leges Henrici Primi*. Oxford: 1972.
Fairbanks, Sydney. *The Old West Frisian Skeltana Riucht*. Cambridge: 1939.
Gee, Eric A. "Architectural History until 1290." In *A History of York Minster*, edited by G. E. Aylmer and Reginald Cant, 111–48. Oxford: 1977.
Gee, Eric A. "The Topography of Altars, Chantries and Shrines in York Minster." *The Antiquaries Journal* 64, no. 2 (1984): 337–50.
Groot, Roger D. "The Early-Thirteenth-Century Criminal Jury." In *Twelve Good Men and True: The Criminal Trial Jury in England, 1200–1800*, edited by J. S. Cockburn and Thomas A. Green, 3–35. Princeton: 1988.
Groot, Roger D. "The Jury in Private Criminal Prosecutions before 1215." *American Journal of Legal History* 27, no. 2 (1983): 113–41.
Groot, Roger D. "The Jury of Presentment before 1215." *American Journal of Legal History* 26, no. 1 (1982): 1–24.
Haines, Roy Martin. "Walter de Gray (d. 1255)." In *Oxford Dictionary of National Biography*. Oxford: 2004.
Hall, G. D. G., ed. and trans. *The Treatise on the Laws and Customs of the Realm of England Commonly Called Glanvill*. Oxford: 1993.
Hanawalt, Barbara A. *Crime in East Anglia in the Fourteenth Century*. Norfolk: 1976.

Helmholz, R. H. "The Early History of the Grand Jury and the Canon Law." *The University of Chicago Law Review* 50, no. 2 (1983): 613–27.

Hexter, Ralph J. *Equivocal Oaths and Ordeals in Medieval Literature*. Cambridge: 1975.

Hill, Rosalind M. T. and Christopher N. L. Brooke. "From 627 until the Early Thirteenth Century." In *A History of York Minster*, edited by G. E. Aylmer and Reginald Cant, 1–43. Oxford: 1977.

Ho, H. L. "The Legitimacy of Medieval Proof." *Journal of Law and Religion* 19 (2003–2004): 259–98.

Hoey, Lawrence. "The 13th-Century Transepts of York Minster." *Gesta* 25, no. 2 (1986): 227–44.

Howland, Arthur C., ed. *Ordeals, Compurgation, Excommunication and Interdict*. Philadelphia: 1898.

Hudson, John. *The Formation of the English Common Law*. London: 1996.

Hyams, Paul. "Trial by Ordeal." In *On the Laws and Customs of England*, edited by Morris S. Arnold et al., 90–126. Chapel Hill: 1981.

Jones, Sarah Rees. "Cities and Their Saints in England, circa 1150–1300: The Development of Bourgeois Values in the Cults of Saint William of York and Saint Kenelm of Winchcombe." In *Cities, Texts and Social Networks, 400–1500: Experiences and Perceptions of Medieval Urban Space*, edited by Caroline Goodson, Anne E. Lester, and Carol Symes, 192–213. Farnham: 2010.

Kamali, Elizabeth Papp. "A Felonious State of Mind: Mens Rea in Thirteenth- and Fourteenth-Century England." PhD dissertation, University of Michigan: 2015. <https://deepblue.lib.umich.edu/handle/2027.42/113574>, accessed 10/12/2017.

Kamali, Elizabeth Papp and Thomas A. Green. "A Crossroads in Criminal Procedure: The Assumptions Underlying England's Adoption of Trial by Jury for Crime." In *Law and Society in Later Medieval England and Ireland: Essays in Honour of Paul Brand*, edited by Travis Baker, 51–81. New York: 2018.

Kemp, Eric Waldram. *Canonization and Authority in the Western Church*. Westport, CT: 1979.

Kemp, Eric Waldram. "Pope Alexander III and the Canonization of Saints: The Alexander Prize Essay." *Transactions of the Royal Historical Society* 27 (1945): 13–28.

Kerr, Margaret H., Richard D. Forsyth, and Michael J. Plyley. "Cold Water and Hot Iron: Trial by Ordeal in England." *Journal of Interdisciplinary History* 22, no. 4 (1992): 573–95.

Knowles, David. "The Case of Saint William of York." *The Cambridge Historical Journal* 5, no. 2 (1936): 162–77.

Kuttner, Stephan. "La réserve papale du droit de canonisation." *Revue Historique de Droit Français et Étranger* (1938): 172–228.

Lea, Henry Charles. *The Ordeal*. Philadelphia: 1973.

Leeson, Peter. "Ordeals." *Journal of Law and Economics* 55, no. 3 (2012): 691–714.

Liebermann, F., ed. *Die Gesetze der Angelsachsen.* Vol. 1. Halle: 1903.

Lovatt, Marie. "Geoffrey (1151?–1212), archbishop of York." In *Oxford Dictionary of National Biography*. Oxford: 2004.

Major, Kathleen, ed. *Acta Stephani Langton, Cantuariensis Archiepiscopi, A.D. 1207–1228.* Oxford: 1950.

McAuley, Finbarr. "Canon Law and the End of the Ordeal." *Oxford Journal of Legal Studies* 26, no. 3 (2006): 473–513.

McSweeney, Thomas J. "Magna Carta and the Right to Trial by Jury." In *Magna Carta: Muse and Mentor*, edited by Randy J. Holland, 139–57. Eagan, MN: 2014.

Millor, W. J. and H. E. Butler, eds. *The Letters of John of Salisbury*. Vol. 1. London: 1955.

Morey, Adrian. "Canonist Evidence in the Case of St. William of York." *The Cambridge Historical Journal* 10, no. 3 (1952): 352–3.

Morris, Richard, ed. *An Old English Miscellany*. London: 1872.

Norton, Christopher. *St William of York*. York: 2006.

Owen, Dorothy M. "Fountains, John of (d. 1225)." *In Oxford Dictionary of National Biography*. Oxford: 2004.

Pilarczyk, Ian. "Between a Rock and a Hot Place: The Role of Subjectivity in the Medieval Ordeal by Hot Iron." *Anglo-American Law Review* 25 (1996): 87–112.

Poole, Reginald. "The Appointment and Deprivation of St. William, Archbishop of York." *The English Historical Review* 45, no. 178 (1930): 273–81.

Purvis, J. S. "The Tables of the York Vicars Choral." *The Yorkshire Archaeological Journal* 41 (1966): 741–8.

Raine, James, ed. *The Historians of the Church of York and Its Archbishops*. Vol. 2. London: 1886.

Raine, James, ed. *The Historians of the Church of York and Its Archbishops*. Vol. 3. London: 1894.

Rentz, Ellen K. "Castles for St. William: The Late Medieval Commemoration of York's Local Saint." *Viator* 43, no. 2 (2012): 111–30.

Sayers, Jane E. *Papal Government and England during the Pontificate of Honorius III (1216–1227)*. Cambridge: 1984.

Seipp, David J. "The Mirror of Justices." In *Learning the Law: Teaching and the Transmission of English Law, 1150–1900*, edited by Jonathan A. Bush and Alain Wijffels, 85–112. London: 1999.

Sheingorn, Pamela. *The Book of Sainte Foy*. Philadelphia: 1995.

Stenton, Doris Mary, ed. *Pleas before the King or His Justices, 1198–1212*. Vol. 2. London: 1952.

Stenton, Doris Mary, ed. *Pleas before the King or His Justices, 1198–1212*. Vol. 4. London: 1967.

Talbot, C. H. "New Documents in the Case of Saint William of York." *The Cambridge Historical Journal* 10, no. 1 (1950): 1–15.

Tringham, Nigel K. "The Whitsuntide Commemoration of St William of York: A Note." *Records of Early English Drama* 14, no. 2 (1989): 10–12.

Turner, Ralph. "Clerical Judges in English Secular Courts: The Ideal Versus the Reality." In *Medievalia et Humanistica* 3, edited by Paul Maurice Clogan, 75–98. Cleveland: 1972.

Turner, Ralph. "The Judges of King John: Their Background and Training." *Speculum* 51, no. 3 (1976): 447–61.

Van Caenegem, R. C., ed. *English Lawsuits from William I to Richard I*. Vol. 2. London: 1991.

Warren, W. L. *King John*. London: 1961.

White, Stephen D. "Garsinde v. Sainte Foy: Argument, Threat, and Vengeance in Eleventh-Century Monastic Litigation." In *Religious and Laity in Western Europe, 1000–1400: Interaction, Negotiation, and Power*, edited by Emilia Jamroziak and Janet Burton, 169–82. Turnhout: 2006.

White, Stephen D. "Imaginary Justice: The End of the Ordeal and the Survival of the Duel." *Medieval Perspectives* 13 (1998): 32–55.

White, Stephen D. "Proposing the Ordeal and Avoiding It: Strategy and Power in Western French Litigation, 1050–1110." In *Cultures of Power: Lordship, Status, and Process in Twelfth-Century Europe*, edited by Thomas N. Bisson, 89–123. Philadelphia: 1995.

Whitman, James Q. *The Origins of Reasonable Doubt*. New Haven: 2008.

Whittaker, William Joseph, ed. *The Mirror of Justices*. London: 1895.

Williams, Watkin. *Saint Bernard of Clairvaux*. Manchester: 1935.

Zeumer, K. *Formulae Merovingici et Karolini Aevi*. Hanover: 1886.

Online Sources

Leges Edwardi Confessoris, §9: <http://www.earlyenglishlaws.ac.uk/laws/texts/ecf1/view/#edition,1/edition,1_0_c_9>, accessed 19/5/2017.

CHAPTER 3

Threats and Intimidation in Anglo-Norman Legal Disputes

William Eves

English justice during the Anglo-Norman period lacked the administrative centralisation and widespread procedural regularity of the later English common law. Compared to subsequent periods, a greater number of disputes may have been conducted and resolved without being brought before a court, with the parties instead preferring extra-curial negotiation or low-level violence to settle the matter. Disputes which did follow a more formal legal process could be heard in a number of different courts, some pre-dating the Conquest and others introduced by the Normans, and cases could proceed with a certain amount of procedural flexibility. A number of factors, including a potential lack of clarity concerning legal norms, or power differences between the parties, meant that 'extra-legal' tactics are likely to have influenced the outcome of a significant number of these cases.[1]

This essay, drawing on William I. Miller's work on the psychology of medieval disputing, examines the use of threats as one such extra-legal tactic.[2] It focusses on disputes which came before secular courts, and on cases which might later be termed 'civil' rather than criminal. It thus avoids the particularly inflammatory situations which are likely to have occurred in homicide cases or other disputes arising from allegations of inter-personal violence. Likewise, cases from the period 1066–1135 are considered, but Stephen's reign is excluded so that our picture is not distorted by the exceptional circumstances of the Anarchy.

The most obvious types of threats are those made explicitly, whereby an opponent is promised unpleasant consequences if they act, or refrain from

1 For an overview of disputing in this period, see J. G. H. Hudson, *The Formation of the English Common Law: Law and Society in England from the Norman Conquest to Magna Carta* (London: 1996), 8–16; and J. G. H. Hudson, *The Oxford History of the Laws of England, Volume II, 871–1216* (Oxford: 2012), 4–9. I would like to thank John Hudson, Joanna Thornborough, and Sarah White for their helpful comments on drafts of this essay.

2 See in particular W. I. Miller, 'Threat', in *Feud, Violence and Practice: Essays in Medieval Studies in Honor of Stephen D. White*, ed. B. Tuten and T. Billado (Farnham: 2010), 9–27.

© KONINKLIJKE BRILL NV, LEIDEN, 2018 | DOI 10.1163/9789004366374_007

acting, in a certain way. Nevertheless, as Miller explains, many threats are implicit; 'they are simply in the air because of certain talents or blessings, or "suggestivenesses" that cause the other to fear you'.[3] The use of both types of threat in Anglo-Norman lawsuits is therefore considered.

•••

Some of the most important lay courts in Anglo-Norman England are mentioned in a writ issued by Henry I in 1108:

> Know that I grant and order that henceforth my shire courts and hundred courts shall meet in the same places and at the same terms as they were wont to do in the time of King Edward.... And if in the future there should arise a dispute concerning the allotment of land, or concerning its seizure, let this be tried in my own court if it be between my tenants-in-chief. But if the dispute be between the vassals of any baron of my honour let the plea be held in the court of their common lord. But if the dispute be between the vassals of two different lords let the plea be held in the shire court.[4]

Henry's writ thus highlights the operation of the king's own court, the county (shire) and hundred courts, and the seigniorial courts of lords.

The role of the king in hearing pleas was well established before the Conquest. Medieval kings were frequently called upon to dispense justice, and English kings and Norman dukes certainly heard pleas before 1066.[5] The king's court also heard a wider range of disputes than those outlined in Henry's writ. As John Hudson points out, the fact that the king was regarded as the fount of justice meant that his court was 'potentially omnicompetent'.[6] Pleas might be heard as the king travelled around the country, although if he was unavailable royal administrators would sometimes hear a case. Likewise, if the king was out of the country, a family member or royal official would be designated to deal with judicial matters.[7]

---

3 Miller, 'Threat', 9.

4 'Charter of Henry I concerning the holding of courts shire and hundred (26 July 1108–August 1111)', in *English Historical Documents*, vol. 2, *1042–1189*, ed. D. C. Douglas and G. W. Greenaway (2nd ed., London: 1981), no. 43, at 474–5.

5 Hudson, *Formation*, 27.

6 Ibid., 28.

7 Ibid., 30.

As Henry's writ suggests, county and hundred courts were also part of the English legal landscape before 1066. County courts seem to have met twice a year at around the time of the Conquest, although by the thirteenth century many seem to have met every four weeks.[8] The legal treatise known as the *Leges Henrici Primi* (written c. 1116) explains that 'bishops, earls, sheriffs, deputies, hundredmen, aldermen, stewards, reeves, barons, vavassours, village reeves and other lords of lands' were expected to attend.[9] County courts could meet in a variety of locations, sometimes outdoors but also in castles, halls, houses, and monasteries. Hearings, over which the sheriff would preside, could concern a variety of pleas, from land disputes to cases of theft or violence.[10] Occasionally individuals could be instructed by the king to act as royal justices and preside over meetings of the county when they dealt with certain matters which pertained to the king in some way.[11]

Hundreds (known as 'wapentakes' in former Danelaw regions) were administrative areas smaller than a shire. At the time of the Conquest, hundred courts met about once every month, although by the thirteenth century they seem to have met every fortnight.[12] The greater lords and landholders of the hundred were expected to attend, and a bailiff appointed by the sheriff, or by a lord if the hundred was in seigniorial hands, usually presided.[13] The court could meet at local landmarks, or at a certain landowner's property.[14] Hundred courts dealt with matters ranging from land disputes to cases of theft or violence, although serious cases which might involve the death penalty were perhaps heard in the county court. In other matters, the jurisdictional relationship between the shire and hundred courts is somewhat obscure, and royal writs from the period sometimes regard either as an appropriate court in which a particular land dispute could be heard.[15]

Honorial courts, where lords heard disputes between their knightly or more important tenants, appear to have emerged in England after the Conquest.[16]

---

8 Hudson, *Oxford History*, 276.

9 *Leges Henrici Primi*, ed. and trans. L. J. Downer (Oxford: 1972) (hereafter cited as *LHP*), ch. 7.2 (Downer, 99–101).

10 Hudson, *Oxford History*, 278–9.

11 P. A. Brand, *Origins of the English Legal Profession* (Oxford: 1992), 7.

12 Hudson, *Formation*, 38. See also A. Harding, *The Law Courts of Medieval England* (London: 1973), 17–18.

13 Hudson, *Oxford History*, 281.

14 See Hudson, *Formation*, 38, suggesting that graveyards or thorn bushes may have also been used as meeting places.

15 Hudson, *Oxford History*, 282.

16 Hudson, *Formation*, 41.

Lords could hear disputes between their men as and when they arose, but they also held special sessions to hear pleas. These hearings could take place in the lord's castle or hall, although ecclesiastics who were secular lords might, if they did not possess a castle, hold their court in their cathedral or monastery, or even a house of one of their tenants.[17] We cannot be sure how frequently honorial courts met, although it is possible they did so only periodically.[18] The lord presided over the court and his tenants were expected to attend, but others who did not hold land of the lord, or were not his men, might also come to court.[19] Lords also held courts for their peasant tenants, known as manor courts or 'hallmoots', over which one of the lord's reeves, or sometimes his steward, might preside.[20] These were perhaps the most important type of court for unfree tenants, where the manor's agricultural matters might be discussed or complaints about the lord's officials heard.[21]

In practice, the composition of courts sometimes varied and the distinction between one type of court and another may not always have been obvious. Royal justices, for example, might be welcomed into a lord's court, and the presence of county landholders who were not the lord's men could also obscure the court's seigniorial origins.[22] Furthermore, the jurisdictional boundaries between Anglo-Norman courts were somewhat flexible, and competition between court-holders to hear pleas, or an agreement between the parties, might bring a case before a court other than that stipulated in Henry's writ. Nevertheless, Hudson suggests that it would be wrong to consider these types of court as interchangeable and their business wholly negotiable.[23] Henry's writ shows that jurisdictional considerations mattered, at least to some, and arguments could be raised by litigants about the proper court before which their dispute ought to be heard.[24]

Court proceedings began with the plaintiff stating his or her claim. The plaintiff's opponent would then make their defence through a formal denial of the claim. Further pleading might then follow.[25] If the parties did not reach a settlement, or if the truth of the matter was not common knowledge, the

---

17 Hudson, *Oxford History*, 285.

18 Brand, *Legal Profession*, 5.

19 Hudson, *Oxford History*, 286.

20 Ibid., 288–9. See also Brand, *Legal Profession*, 5–6.

21 Hudson, *Oxford History*, 289.

22 Hudson, *Formation*, 25–26.

23 Ibid., 26.

24 Ibid., 26–27. See also the case discussed below at n. 79 and accompanying text.

25 For a detailed examination of procedure, see Hudson, *Oxford History*, 303–32. See also Brand, *Legal Profession*, 4–5.

court would make a 'mesne' judgment on who should provide proof, and the type of proof that was required. This could be documentary evidence, such as charters, or the use of oaths and sworn testimony. If there was no other way to resolve the dispute, recourse might be had to the unilateral ordeal of hot iron, or hot or cold water. Trial by battle could also be used in such circumstances. Final judgment would then be awarded on the basis of this proof.[26]

Judgments were generally made by the 'suitors', that is, those who had a duty to attend hearings, although the president of the court may have exerted some influence over the decision. The *Leges Henrici Primi* thus explains that county court judgments were made by the 'barons of the county', probably drawn from the landholders, nobles, and public officials who were expected to attend court.[27] These suitors also made judgments when royal justices presided over the court.[28] The judgments of the hundred court were likewise made by at least some of the landholders of the hundred who were in attendance, and the judgments of honorial courts were made by the lord's tenants, sometimes with other individuals added to the court with the lord's permission.[29] The king could make judgments when hearing pleas, but in general the decisions of the king's court often seem to have been made by his tenants-in-chief.[30]

Although the president and suitors of the court were not legal experts (in the sense that we understand the term today), pleading in court could involve recourse to legal norms. Hudson has shown that reference to such norms was, however, sometimes implicit rather than explicit. Arguments could, for example, concern the veracity of 'legally charged' facts, rather than a clear statement of a norm followed by an assertion that the facts of the case required the norm to be followed. A litigant may have argued, for instance, that an individual could not sell land because it was held in alms, invoking (although not explicitly stating) the norm that land held in alms was inalienable.[31]

Nevertheless, legal argument was only one factor which could influence the outcome of a dispute.[32] Some cases, for example, could lack clear norms for

---

26 Trial by battle was probably introduced by the Normans following the Conquest. See Hudson, *Oxford History*, 84–85 and 303.

27 *LHP* ch. 29, 1 and 1a (Downer, 131). See Brand, *Legal Profession*, 6–7.

28 Brand, *Legal Profession*, 7.

29 Ibid., 5–6.

30 Ibid., 6.

31 J. G. H. Hudson, 'Court Cases and Legal Arguments in England, c.1066–1166', *Transactions of the Royal Historical Society*, ser. 6, vol. 10 (2000), 91–115 at 100–2 and 104. See also P. R. Hyams, 'Norms and Legal Argument before 1150', in *Law and History*, ed. A. D. Lewis and M. Lobban, Current Legal Issues 6 (Oxford: 2004), 41–61.

32 Hudson, *Formation*, 11.

guidance as to how the dispute should be resolved.[33] These lawsuits, if they were not settled, may have been decided by arguments based upon moral and social considerations, or simply by the power, wealth, or influence of the parties.[34] Even cases underpinned by clear legal norms could be affected by extra-legal factors, which probably had a greater impact on lawsuits of the period than they do in modern law.[35]

The power, wealth, or influence of the parties could be brought to bear on a dispute in a number of ways. Much depended on the circumstances of the case and the particular advantages held by the litigant in question. Some litigants were able to secure the assistance of prominent individuals, maybe even the king himself, who might intervene in proceedings on their behalf. The *Liber Eliensis*, for example, mentions that Simeon, abbot of Ely, was able to quash various claims through not just legitimate argument, but also royal favour.[36] Some wealthy individuals also made payments, perhaps to the king, to obtain favourable treatment in court.[37] Litigants could also use threats to influence the outcome of the case.

•••

A study of the way in which threats were used in lawsuits is restricted somewhat by the nature of the surviving sources. Evidence is limited because proceedings were largely oral, and courts of the period do not appear to have kept any formal written records of hearings. We can glean some information about litigation from treatises such as the *Leges Henrici Primi*, although these texts generally describe what the author thought should be done in court, and do

---

33 Hudson, 'Court Cases', 109. See also Hyams, 'Norms and Legal Argument', 52–53.

34 Hudson, 'Court Cases', 109. For studies of disputing in France from the eleventh century onwards which emphasise the centrality of social and moral arguments, political pressure and the importance of settlements, see S. D. White, '"*Pactum ... Legem Vincit et Amor Iudicium*": The Settlement of Disputes by Compromise in Eleventh-Century Western France', *American Journal of Legal History* 22 (1978), 281–308; and F. L. Cheyette, '*Suum Cuique Tribuere*', *French Historical Studies* 6 (1970), 287–99. On norms and their role in legal arguments in French courts, see S. D. White, 'Inheritances and Legal Arguments in Western France, 1050–1150', *Traditio* 43 (1986), 55–103.

35 Hudson, 'Court Cases and Legal Arguments', 112–3.

36 *Liber Eliensis*, ed. E. O. Blake, Camden Third Series 92 (London: 1962), book ii: 119 at p. 203. For an English translation, see *Liber Eliensis: A History of the Isle of Ely from the Seventh Century to the Twelfth*, trans. J. Fairweather (Woodbridge: 2005), 241.

37 Hudson, *Oxford History*, 9.

not provide detailed information about individual cases.[38] The provisions contained in such treatises can nevertheless shed light upon certain patterns of litigant behaviour which the courts, or others involved in the administration of justice, were attempting to encourage or prohibit.

Information about individual cases can be found in sources such as charters, Domesday Book *clamores*, letters, hagiographical texts, and monastic chronicles. The number of recorded cases available to us is nevertheless quite small. R. C. van Caenegem's largely comprehensive collection of material relating to Anglo-Norman lawsuits contains accounts of fewer than 'ten cases per decade in 1071–1080, between ten and twenty in 1081–1090, between twenty and thirty in 1091–1110, between thirty and forty per decade in 1111–1120 and 1131–1150, [and] between forty and fifty in 1121–1130'.[39] Narrative accounts of cases, found in sources such as hagiographies and chronicles, are the most useful for discovering information about the use of threats in the period. However, these accounts are particularly scarce, comprising only about thirty percent of the material collected by van Caenegem.[40]

Some of these narratives may be accurate accounts of what was said in court—the *ipsissima verba* of the parties.[41] However, caution is required as it is possible that some reported speech was invented by the scribe. Furthermore, these accounts are often Latin descriptions of vernacular proceedings, which raises the possibility that the words of the parties have been distorted in translation.[42] Accounts of litigation which do not report direct speech may also portray events inaccurately. As Hudson points out, most narrative accounts of cases are recorded in monastic chronicles, often to record the successful claims of the house. They are not, therefore, impartial records and may seek to present the opposing party in as poor a light as possible. This also means that in most cases at least one of the parties belonged to the clergy, and cases involving only laymen are rare.[43] As Hudson also suggests, some narratives have a tendency to sensationalise, possibly exaggerating the actions of litigants in court. Likewise, unusual or particularly problematic cases may have been accorded the most detailed treatment, potentially giving a false impression of the general nature

38 See Hudson, *Formation*, 249–50.

39 *English Lawsuits from William I to Richard I*, ed. R. C. van Caenegem, 2 vols, Selden Society 106 and 107 (London: 1990 and 1991) (hereafter cited as *Lawsuits*), I, xxiv.

40 *Lawsuits*, I, xxiii.

41 Ibid., xv–xvi.

42 Hudson, 'Court Cases', 93.

43 Ibid., 94. See also *Lawsuits*, I, xxiv.

of cases in the period.[44] It must also be noted that, as the authors of these accounts were not writing specifically for a legal audience, information that a legal historian may wish to know is sometimes omitted. The status of the parties, for example, is not always clear and we cannot tell on every occasion whether a litigant is a knight or an ordinary freeman.[45] Likewise, the type of court before which the case was heard cannot always be discerned, although as discussed above there may not always have been a clear distinction between certain types of court in the period.[46] The scarcity and nature of the sources thus prevents any kind of quantitative analysis of case material. Nevertheless, even with our limited sample, and bearing in mind the above caveats, the surviving records of cases offer a revealing insight into the way threats were used in Anglo-Norman lawsuits.

Threats could take many different forms. Individuals with sufficient worldly power could, for example, threaten their opponent with consequences such as inter-personal violence, imprisonment, loss of land, or the loss or destruction of possessions. Even the threat of homicidal violence was not unknown. According to the *Liber Eliensis*, two noble families, the Richards and the Giffards, had made it unsafe 'for anyone at all from among the magnates to compete with them over the reception of guests or the conduct of lawsuits, since frequent killings were carried out at court by their hands and on many occasions they had struck terror into the king's majesty'.[47] Churchmen too could resort to physical violence, although perhaps not to such extremes. The *Abingdon Chronicle* recounts that Abbot Adelelm once used a stick to beat a royal reeve who had demanded transport services for the king and wood from the abbey and, the next time they met, terrified him to such an extent that he fled on horseback and then waded through a river in an attempt to get away.[48]

A case described in the *Textus Roffensis* between Gundulf, bishop of Rochester and Picot, the sheriff of Cambridgeshire, provides a striking example of how such threats could be delivered, and the way in which they

44 Hudson, 'Court Cases', 94–95.

45 *Lawsuits*, I, xxiv.

46 Ibid., xxv.

47 *Liber Eliensis*, book ii: 142 (Blake, 226; Fairweather, 273).

48 *Historia Ecclesie Abbendonensis: The History of the Church of Abingdon*, ed. and trans. J. G. H. Hudson, 2 vols (Oxford: 2002–2007), II, 15. This case is *Lawsuits*, I, no. 12. Note that van Caenegem's translation in *Lawsuits* is based on Stevenson's earlier edition of the text: *Chronicon monasterii de Abingdon*, ed. J. Stevenson, Rolls Series 2, 2 vols. (London: 1858). This essay uses Hudson's translation of material from the *Abingdon Chronicle* throughout.

could influence a dispute.[49] As Robin Fleming notes, it provides an insight into the 'real-world, hard-ball politics that must have operated at every court in the tenth and eleventh centuries'.[50] Gundulf brought a claim for certain land in Isleham, Cambridgeshire, arguing that the land, an appurtenance of Freckenham in Suffolk, belonged to Rochester Cathedral. Picot, who had granted it to a certain king's serjeant, said that the land belonged to the king. The case came before the county court of Suffolk, with Odo of Bayeux presiding. It seems that the court comprised not just Suffolk landholders, but also men from Staploe, the Cambridgeshire hundred in which Isleham was located.[51] When the matter came to judgment, we are told that the suitors, because they feared the sheriff, affirmed that the land belonged to the king ('Illi autem congregati, terram illam regis esse pocius quam Beati Andree timore vicecomitis affirmaverunt'). As the malign influence of Picot was suspected, twelve of the suitors were assembled to confirm on oath that what they had just said was true. At least five of those selected were from Staploe, and it is possible that all twelve came from this hundred.[52] However, when these twelve had withdrawn to consider their oath, 'they were utterly terrified by a message [or messenger] from the sheriff' (a vicecomite per internuncium conteriti fuissent). On returning, they 'swore to be true that which they had said before'.[53] The matter was eventually rectified when a monk, formerly a reeve of Freckenham, heard about the case and told the bishop that he knew for a fact that Isleham belonged to the cathedral. The bishop informed Odo of Bayeux, who summoned two of the twelve jurors who had sworn the oath at the county court to appear before him. These two jurors confessed their perjury. Odo then ordered Picot to send the remaining ten jurors to London, along with another twelve of the suitors of the county court who were tasked with confirming the oath of the former twelve.[54] An assembly was convened with many of the greater barons of England in attendance, and the men who had sworn the original oath were convicted of perjury. The second twelve then wished to assert that

---

49 The Latin text is provided in *Registrum Roffense*, ed. J. Thorpe (London: 1769), 31–32. For a translation, see *Lawsuits*, I, no. 19.

50 R. Fleming, 'Oral Testimony and the Domesday Inquest', in *Anglo-Norman Studies* 17, ed. Christopher Harper-Bill (Martlesham: 1995), 108. For a similar perspective on this case, see A. Cooper, 'Protestations of Ignorance in Domesday Book', in *The Experience of Power in Medieval Europe, 950–1350*, ed. R. F. Berkhofer, A. Cooper and A. J. Kosto (Aldershot: 2005), 169–182, at 178–179.

51 Fleming, 'Domesday Inquest', 107–8.

52 Ibid., 108.

53 *Lawsuits*, I, no. 19, p. 51. This is a slightly modified version of van Caenegem's translation.

54 Ibid.

they had not been in agreement with those who had sworn the first oath and promised to undergo the ordeal of hot iron to prove this. However, they either reneged on this promise or failed the ordeal ('se facturos promiserunt, et facere non potuerunt') and were fined a total of three hundred pounds.[55] As Fleming points out, Picot appears to have escaped punishment, despite the fact that his threats caused the whole controversy.[56]

As this account is written from Rochester's perspective, it may attempt to portray Picot as a thuggish oppressor to give more credence to the cathedral's own claim to the land. However, the *Textus Roffensis* is not alone in suggesting that the sheriff was a formidable opponent, and one who would readily employ such tactics. The *Liber Eliensis*, for example, complains about his frequent vexations of Ely Abbey and refers to him as 'the most vile man in the populace'.[57] The same source also mentions his 'Gaetulian temperament', most likely a reference to Sallust's description of North African Gaetuli tribesmen as people controlled 'neither by customs, laws, nor the authority of any ruler'.[58]

Though we do not know the exact content of the message, Picot's threat was clearly effective for a number of reasons. First, it was communicated to the jurors with impeccably sinister timing, reaching them whilst they were still considering the oath that they were about to swear. The fact that it was apparently delivered by a messenger, rather than in person, would have added to their terror as they were left to dwell on its implications without any opportunity to plead with the sheriff or determine whether he was bluffing. The force of the threat would have been further intensified if the messenger was himself intimidating, especially if he was tasked with delivering the threat orally. However, additional factors also determined the effectiveness of the threat. The case was heard in Suffolk, a county in which Picot, as sheriff of neighbouring Cambridgeshire, probably had considerable influence. Furthermore, a number of the suitors came from Cambridgeshire, including at least some of those selected to swear the oath, and were thus particularly susceptible to Picot's influence. It was therefore not simply the content of the threat and the manner in which it was delivered that made it effective. The location of the hearing and the composition of the court also played a large part in determining its effectiveness.

---

55 Ibid.

56 Fleming, 'Domesday Inquest', 108.

57 *Liber Eliensis*, book ii: 132 (Blake, 212; Fairweather, 251).

58 *Liber Eliensis*, book ii: 131 (Blake, 211; Fairweather, 250); Sallust, *Bellum Iugurthinum*, ch. 18, in *The Conspiracy of Catiline and the Jugurthine War*, trans. Rev. J. S. Watson (Philadelphia: 1896), 146.

The dispute between Gundulf and Picot thus shows how threats backed up by worldly force could have a dramatic effect on the course of litigation. Nevertheless, threats were not confined to the secular world. Some litigants, for example, attempted to strike fear into their opponents with warnings of excommunication or malediction. Here, the success of the threat would depend upon the perceived spiritual authority of the individual making it, and how seriously the recipient treated such warnings of spiritual peril.[59] Litigants could also make threats which had both religious and secular force, and the combined pressure of this two-pronged approach could be particularly effective.

The *Chronicle of the Archbishops of York* describes a dispute between Ealdred, archbishop of York, and the sheriff of Yorkshire which provides a good illustration of how such threats could work in practice. The part of the *Chronicle* containing this account was written in the early twelfth century to emphasise the importance of the archbishopric of York and its independence from the See of Canterbury.[60] We should therefore be aware that it is likely to have exaggerated, and perhaps fictionalised, aspects of the dispute in an attempt to portray Ealdred as a masterful guardian of the rights of his archbishopric. Nevertheless, it is a powerful example, and at the very least it illustrates how individuals in the early twelfth century were aware of the way in which such threats could be delivered for maximum effect.

We are told that the dispute began just outside York when the sheriff encountered a number of horses and carts carrying wheat and other foodstuffs intended for the archbishop.[61] Ealdred's servants explained that what they were carrying was necessary for his sustenance. However, the sheriff, 'having no respect for the archbishop and his servants ... ordered his underlings to

59 In addition to what follows, for a good later twelfth-century example of the potential uses of excommunication see T. Walsingham, *Gesta Abbatum Monasterii Sancti Albani*, 3 vols, ed. H. T. Riley, Rolls Series 28.4 (London: 1867–9), I, 159–66. For a translation of this St Albans case, see *Lawsuits*, II, no. 396. Disputes from the Anglo-Saxon period also show how excommunication could be used against an opposing party. See, for example, *Liber Eliensis*, book ii: 96 (Blake 165–6; Fairweather, 196–7). Limitations of space prevent a discussion of whether depictions of saintly vengeance, as found in hagiographic texts, might also be used as a basis for threats during the course of a dispute. For examples of disputes involving the vengeance of saints, and a discussion of religious attitudes towards this type of vengeance in the Anglo-Norman period, see P. R. Hyams, *Rancor and Reconciliation in Medieval England* (New York: 2003), 119–28.

60 *Historians of the Church of York and Its Archbishops: Volume II*, ed. J. Raine, Rolls Series 71 (London: 1886), x–xii.

61 Raine, *Historians*, 350–3. For a translation, see *Lawsuits*, I, no. 1.

divert all the supplies to the castle of York'.[62] The source, obviously sympathetic to the archbishop, implies that the sheriff unjustly and opportunistically seized goods intended for the archbishop. It is possible, however, that the real cause of the confrontation was a dispute over the right of the sheriff to certain exactions.

When the archbishop heard that his carts had been seized, 'he at once sent messengers, with clerics and citizens' to the sheriff, ordering him 'to restore to him what was his and to give satisfaction to St Peter and himself, his vicar, otherwise he should know that afterwards he would take pontifical action'.[63] The sheriff was indignant and 'proudly answered with several grave threats, treating the messengers with injuries and contumelies'.[64] The messengers retreated and told the archbishop what had happened. Ealdred immediately travelled to London, where he was met by the bishop of London and a large gathering of clergy and laymen. The bishop accompanied Ealdred to worship at St Paul's church, and then at St Peter's church at Westminster. It was here that the archbishop, wearing his pall and carrying his episcopal staff, encountered King William. The king was kneeling, perhaps in prayer or perhaps ready to receive a customary blessing. Before he could get to his feet, Ealdred stood before him and, 'without any fear of the king's majesty or the impudence of the leading men who were standing around', said:

> Listen ... King William. When you, a foreigner, had, because God allowed it and punished the pride of our people, obtained the kingdom of Britain, albeit with much bloodshed, I consecrated you as king and placed the crown on your head with my blessing. Now, however, because you have deserved it, instead of my benediction I shall pronounce my malediction against you as a persecutor of God's church, an oppressor of his servants, and a transgressor of the promises and oaths which you swore to me before the altar of St Peter.[65]

62 Raine, *Historians*. 351. (*Lawsuits*, I, no. 1, p. 1).

63 Ibid.

64 Ibid.

65 Ibid., 352 (*Lawsuits*, I, no. 1, pp. 1–2): 'Audi ... Willelme Rex, cum esses alienigena, et, Deo permittente nostraeque gentis superbiam puniente, regnum Britanniae, quamvis multo cum sanguine, obtinuisses, ego te in regem consecravi, et coronam capiti tuo cum benedictione imposui. Nunc autem, quia ita meruisti, pro benedictione maledictionem tibi imponam, sicut ecclesiae Dei persecutori, et ministrorum Ejus oppressori, et promissionum atque juramentorum quae mihi coram altare Sancti Petri jurasti transgressori'. The English translation is a modified version of van Caenegem's translation in *Lawsuits*.

According to the *Chronicle*, the king was frightened by these words and threw himself at the archbishop's feet, imploring him to explain what he had done to deserve such a threat. The magnates who were standing around were shocked and, suggesting that the archbishop should be exiled, urged him to let the king get to his feet. Ealdred simply replied, 'let him lie, for he is not lying at the feet of Ealdred, but at Peter's feet. He who has not feared to cause the vicar of Peter injury must undergo Peter's power'.[66] He then took hold of the king's hand, helped him to his feet, and explained the reason for his visit. The king listened gravely and 'begged him to change the malediction, with which he had been threatened, into a benediction'.[67] The matter was decided in favour of the archbishop, who was rewarded with honours and gifts. The king sent one of his most trusted magnates to Yorkshire with a letter to the sheriff ordering that everything be restored to the archbishop, even down to the ropes that had been on the sacks.[68]

Ealdred's threat was almost certainly different to that made by Picot in the latter's case against Gundulf of Rochester. It was also delivered in a different manner: openly and dramatically rather than slyly and by proxy. However, as in Picot's case, its success owed much to its timing and the place in which it was made. Ealdred approached the king in a church, wearing his archiepiscopal garb and carrying his staff, which emphasised his religious authority to the fullest extent. The fact that the meeting took place at Westminster, where William had sworn his coronation oath and where Ealdred himself had placed the crown on his head, also helped remind the king of the archbishop's importance and spiritual authority. Furthermore, William did not have time to stand up but remained kneeling in a position of subservience while the archbishop addressed him. Ealdred's speech, although probably embellished by the author of the *Chronicle*, was also finely crafted and deserves attention. The archbishop began forcefully ('Audi, Willelme Rex'), and used the circumstances of William's coronation to his advantage. By pointing out that God had allowed William ('a foreigner') to obtain the crown in order to punish the pride of the English, he implied that God might also punish the new king's pride. Furthermore, Ealdred reminded William that he had been crowned with his blessing, making his threatened malediction all the more significant. The archbishop continued to emphasise his spiritual authority when challenged by William's magnates, explaining that the king had offended not simply Ealdred the man, but Ealdred the vicar of St Peter.

66 Ibid.

67 Ibid.

68 Ibid., 353 (*Lawsuits*, I, no. 1, p. 2).

The impact of Ealdred's threat was also amplified by its immediate real-world implications. Whilst attempting to consolidate his conquest of England, William could not afford to lose the support of the English Church. The support of the archbishop of York was especially important as the legitimacy of Stigand, the archbishop of Canterbury, was in doubt. Stigand's appointment in 1052 had been subject to papal disapproval, as he had obtained the archbishopric from the exiled Robert of Jumièges and had failed to relinquish the See of Winchester upon doing so. As a result, he had not travelled to Rome to receive his pallium from Pope Leo IX, instead wearing the one which had been abandoned by Robert. He eventually received his own pallium from Benedict X, but the latter's legitimacy as Pope was also in doubt.[69] It was because of this concern over Stigand's position that Ealdred oversaw the coronation of William, and the king would have been well aware that if he displeased the archbishop he risked losing the support of the most powerful religious voice in England at that time.

The political influence of Ealdred amongst the English magnates further added to the potency of the threat. In the years preceding the Conquest, the archbishop had been a strong supporter of the Godwin family. Following Harold Godwinson's defeat at Hastings, he joined with the earls Eadwine and Morcar in an attempt to rally support for Edgar the Aetheling's claim to the English throne before submitting to William at Berkhamsted in December 1066.[70] Ealdred's threatened malediction thus had purely secular connotations. It carried the message that, in a period in which William was attempting to retain the support of the remaining English magnates, it would be unwise for the king to lose the support of one of his most powerful native-English supporters.

•••

Explicit threats could therefore take various forms and have a significant impact on the outcome of a dispute. However, parties could also manipulate lawsuits without voicing their threats directly. Implicit threats, communicated by an individual's conduct or demeanour, could play a large part in proceedings. Litigants often, for example, sought to intimidate their opponents by arriving at a hearing backed by powerful supporters. Such individuals might, of course,

69 H. E. J. Cowdrey, 'Stigand (*d.* 1072)', in *Oxford Dictionary of National Biography*, vol. 52, ed. H. C. G. Matthew and Brian Harrison (Oxford: 2004), 774–7.

70 M. K. Lawson, 'Ealdred (*d.* 1069)', rev. Vanessa King, in *Oxford Dictionary of National Biography*, vol. 17, ed. H. C. G. Matthew and Brian Harrison (Oxford: 2004), 552–4.

make their own explicit threats, but their mere presence at court could speak volumes in itself.

A number of abbeys secured, or attempted to secure, the assistance of powerful figures by making grants of land on the condition that the grantee would support them in lawsuits.[71] For example, Nigel d'Oylly, baron of Hook Norton, constable of Oxford castle, and constable of Henry I, held land in the fee of Abingdon on the condition that he would support the abbot in any pleas heard in the king's court unless the abbey's opponent was the king himself. The abbot brought a lawsuit against Nigel to do homage for his lands and acknowledge the services he owed in which it was made clear that this support was not simply general encouragement, but Nigel was to be 'present on the abbot's side' at court (ipsius abbatis parti idem aderit).[72] Other examples, noted by Paul Brand, include Hamo *dapifer*, the sheriff of Kent and steward to the king, who had an obligation to 'advise, help and succour' the abbot of St Augustine's, Canterbury, and his church in pleas in the county court and king's court.[73] A certain Colswain, lord of the Brattleby barony, also had an obligation to 'maintain' the property of the abbey of Peterborough and the men of the abbey in the county court and elsewhere.[74] These men, as Brand notes, were 'friends' well worth having.[75]

Whilst having one powerful supporter could be valuable, some litigants attempted to secure the assistance of as many as possible. As Miller points out, a group of men 'is rarely a benign phenomenon', and a large gathering of supporters would have been particularly intimidating.[76] According to the *Liber Eliensis*, for example, it was not just the Richards and Giffards families' reputation for violence that scared people, but the fact that, 'whenever a meeting of nobles took place, their procession was supported by a huge entourage which was terrifying'.[77]

71 For the following, see P. A. Brand, 'The Origins of the English Legal Profession', *Law and History Review* 5, no. 1 (1987), 31–50 at 33–34.

72 *Historia Ecclesie Abbendonensis* (Hudson, II, 195). This case is *Lawsuits*, I, no. 206.

73 *The Register of St Augustine's Canterbury, Commonly Called the Black Book*, ed. G. J. Turner and H. E. Salter, vol. II (London: 1924), 462–3.

74 E. King, 'The Peterborough *Descriptio Militum* (Henry I)', *English Historical Review* 84, no. 330 (1969), 84–101 at 100.

75 Brand, 'Origins', 33–34.

76 As Miller notes, the word 'threat' is of Anglo-Saxon origin (*þréat*) and, at its core, meant simply a group or press of men. It was the fact that a group of men was 'rarely a benign phenomenon' that gave the word its pejorative sense. Miller, 'Threat', 12.

77 *Liber Eliensis*, book ii: 142 (Blake, 226; Fairweather, 273).

The advantage of appearing in court with supporters is also recognised by the *Leges Henrici Primi*, which explains that it was sometimes better, if possible, to postpone or defer a case 'depending on the presence or absence of friends or opponents'.[78] This also hints at the manoeuvring which could take place as each side attempted to maximise their own support and proceed with the case at the moment when their opponent was weakest. A case from the *Chronicle of Battle Abbey* illustrates how these manoeuvres could play out in practice, and shows how such tactics could be combined with other indirect attempts to intimidate an opponent.

We are told that, while the abbey was in the custodianship of Geoffrey de St Calais in the early twelfth century, its manor of Wye was found to be in a state of neglect. Robert de Chilton, the reeve of Wye, was summoned to the manor court to answer for his actions.[79] However, Robert arrived 'backed by the force of the county nobles' and refused to accept the accusations or even come to an equitable agreement.[80] We have no record of any explicit threats being made, but the threat advantage Robert obtained by arriving with a throng of powerful county nobles is clear.

Following Robert's refusal to answer the accusation laid against him, Geoffrey summoned him to appear at the court of Battle Abbey. At first, he and his supporters refused to accept the summons. Eventually, however, Robert and 'many other barons' (aliique barones quamplurimi) came to the court. We are told that they were brought 'by the power and terror of the royal name' (vi ac terrore regii nominis), which may imply that Geoffrey had obtained a royal writ.[81] As it was late in the afternoon, the custodian adjourned proceedings until the morning so that young members of the abbey could be present. The *Chronicle* reports that this was done 'by conviction, albeit regretfully', and the postponement accords with the Rule of St Benedict's stipulation that if anything important is to be done in the monastery 'the abbot shall call the whole community together ... [as] the Lord often reveals what is better to the younger [brothers]'.[82] Nevertheless, the postponement was to the abbey's advantage. Geoffrey's opponents, now his guests, were treated to lavish hospitality, which

78 *LHP*, 49, 2a (Downer, 163).

79 *The Chronicle of Battle Abbey*, ed. and trans. E. Searle (Oxford: 1980), 108–12. This case is *Lawsuits*, I, no. 174.

80 *Chronicle of Battle Abbey* (Searle, 109–11; *Lawsuits*, I, no. 174, p. 145).

81 *Chronicle of Battle Abbey* (Searle, 109–11; *Lawsuits*, I, no. 174, p. 146). See also van Caenegem's comments at n. 7, p. 146.

82 *Chronicle of Battle Abbey* (Searle, 111; Lawsuits, I, no. 174, p. 146). *Regula*, ch. 3. See T. Fry, *The Rule of St Benedict in English* (Collegeville, MN: 1982), 25.

created the opportunity for discussion about the case in a situation where, as his opponent's host, Geoffrey was in a dominant position. Furthermore, the parties reconvened the next morning in Battle Abbey church with Geoffrey's monastic brothers seated around him. The threat advantage gained by Robert in the manorial court had been lessened, if not nullified. The *Chronicle*'s assertion that the postponement was made regretfully, but by conviction perhaps reveals an understanding of how advantageous the delay actually was.

Opening the morning's proceedings, the custodian asked his opponents whether they would accept the justice of the abbey's court. They replied that they were bound to the justice done in their own county court, but not the abbey's court. There was argument on this point until Geoffrey asked whether they would consider themselves bound by the judgment of a royal court. They answered that they would. 'Well then', Geoffrey replied, 'you cannot on that ground resist this court, for it is the king's'.[83] The custodian's argument was that Battle Abbey was so closely connected to the king that its honorial court was, in effect, a royal court.[84] It appears that Robert and his supporters had no answer to this. Finding themselves trapped by Geoffrey's argument, they got up and attempted to walk out. However, the custodian immediately ordered the doors to be locked, 'vowing that each of them would be reported to the king if they would not subject themselves to the rights of a royal court'.[85]

Geoffrey now possessed several advantages. He had the support of all his monks, who were carefully assembled in his own abbey, and a compelling argument backed up by the threat of royal sanctions. He also had his opponents in the humiliating position of being locked in court, showing that he was not intimidated by Robert's powerful supporters. It is also significant that the hearing took place in the abbey's church. Here, Robert and his supporters were surrounded by religious architecture and imagery, reminding them of the influence the Church had over the fate of their souls. Few explicit threats had been made, but Geoffrey was clearly in control of the proceedings. We are told that once his opponents had 'thought over the courage of this man and the fairness of the royal distraint, finally the timid tyrants [pavidi tiranni] subsided and declared that they would both do and receive justice there'.[86] Judgement was then passed against Robert, who was fined ten pounds of silver and ten measures of wheat. Geoffrey closed the proceedings by asking those present if anyone had any complaint against him, although we may suspect that this was

83 *Chronicle of Battle Abbey* (Searle, 111–13; *Lawsuits*, I, no. 174, p. 146).

84 Hudson, *Formation*, 26–27.

85 *Chronicle of Battle Abbey* (Searle, 113; *Lawsuits*, I, no. 174, p. 146).

86 Ibid. Note that here Searle translates '*pavidi … tiranni*' as 'timid bullies'.

less of a question and more of a slightly threatening statement that no more should be said on the matter. When no one spoke up, the court was dismissed. Perhaps only at this point were the doors unlocked.

The dispute between Geoffrey and Robert de Chilton may be compared to a case in the *Abingdon Chronicle* which shows what could happen if a party appeared in court without supporters.[87] During the vacancy of Abingdon following the death of Abbot Faritius in 1117, a number of people desired to get hold of some of the abbey's land.[88] They turned to a certain Benedict, a man 'of extremely crafty nature' (plurimum callenti ingenio) who frequently acted as counsellor to the earl of Chester.[89] Benedict began to demand unaccustomed dues from the land and, when these were not delivered, carried off whatever could be found there. The abbey sent an envoy to the earl of Chester's court, carrying a charter which bore witness 'to the earl's own authority regarding the freedom from all exaction of that land'.[90] The envoy entered the earl's court and made his complaint 'in the presence of the greater of the suitors'.[91] He produced the charter and read it to the court. Benedict, who was also in court, then asked for it to be handed over to him as he did not quite understand it. However, as soon as he took hold of the charter he hid it away in his tunic. The *Abingdon Chronicle* records that the envoy was 'amazed at his action, and at first stood stunned. Then when he sought back the letters, he received nothing from that predator except laughter [*risum*]'.[92] The suitors of the earl's court 'whom justice pleased' were indignant, but others joined in the mockery of the envoy, who returned to the abbey 'defeated and worn out by his toils and despondency'.[93] Fortunately for Abingdon, Benedict eventually fell out of favour with the earl and was expelled from his service. He left the charter behind, presumably with the earl, and it was subsequently recovered by the abbey.

It is unlikely that the envoy would have been openly mocked, nor the charter he was carrying stolen, if he had been accompanied by a group of powerful supporters such as those who accompanied Robert de Chilton to Battle Abbey's court. In the latter case, the presence of Robert's supporters meant that the

87 *Historia Ecclesie Abbendonensis* (Hudson, II, 105–7). This case is *Lawsuits*, I, no. 217.

88 The source describes these individuals as 'greedy-minded men' (quidam cupide mentis homines), which serves to remind us that the account is written from the monks' perspective. *Historia Ecclesie Abbendonensis* (Hudson, II, 104; *Lawsuits*, I, no. 217, p. 183).

89 Ibid., 105 (*Lawsuits*, I, no. 217, p. 183).

90 Ibid., 106–7 (*Lawsuits*, I, no. 217, p. 183).

91 Ibid. (*Lawsuits*, I, no. 217, p. 184).

92 Ibid. For another example of mockery in court, see *Liber Eliensis*, book ii: 33 (Blake, 266–9; Fairweather, 320–5). This latter case is *Lawsuits*, I, no. 204.

93 *Historia Ecclesie Abbendonensis* (Hudson, II, 107; *Lawsuits*, I, no. 217, p. 184).

custodian of the abbey had to manoeuvre very carefully in order to defeat his powerful adversaries. In contrast, Benedict, who enjoyed the friendship of the earl of Chester and the support of at least some of the suitors, was faced with no such constraints. Indeed, the latter's behaviour conveyed a certain threat of its own as it sent the monks a message that the earl's man could do as he liked without fear of repercussions, and that they should be wary of pursuing the matter further. It is also significant that the dispute occurred while the abbey was without an abbot who might muster support and act as a powerful figure in his own right to back up the abbey's claims.[94]

A comparison of these cases also highlights the advantages which could be obtained by having a dispute heard in one's own court, or the court of a close ally. Like the custodian of Battle Abbey, who overcame his opponents when the case was heard at the abbey, Benedict could derive confidence not just from the presence of supporters, but from the familiarity of the surroundings. Shame and some loss of authority might, of course, follow a defeat on home territory, but this would itself work to a litigant's advantage if the fear of such a defeat provided them with additional motivation to emerge victorious. Custodian Geoffrey would not have wished to lose his case against Robert de Chilton in front of his monastic brethren, especially not the junior members of the community whom he had ensured were present. Benedict, too, would have been wary of losing face before the earl's men, especially once he had made the bold move of stealing the charter from the envoy in front of the whole court.

•••

The cases discussed here illustrate a variety of ways in which threats could be used in lawsuits. They also allow some comments to be made on the attitudes displayed towards threats, and the relationship between threats and legal norms. Although the scarcity of sources means that we cannot draw wide-ranging conclusions, some points stand out. The surviving accounts of lawsuits do not always discuss threats negatively. Threats were sometimes regarded, at least by the side making them, as praiseworthy attempts to ensure that justice prevailed against a nefarious oppressor. The way Ealdred handled his case and terrified the king, for example, showed 'how steadfast that man

94 The *Abingdon Chronicle* also reveals that during the vacancy of the abbey, Simon the dispenser of Henry I obtained possession of Marcham church through a royal order because 'there was no one there to provide resistance', *Historia Ecclesie Abbendonensis* (Hudson, II, 235). This part of the *Abingdon Chronicle* is reproduced in *Lawsuits*, I, no. 222.

was'.[95] In contrast, threats made by an opponent were regarded with distaste. The account of the dispute between Bishop Gundulf of Rochester and Picot the sheriff undoubtedly presents Picot's actions as improper. Likewise, the author of the *Battle Chronicle*, writing about Robert de Chilton's case, makes his feelings about Robert and his supporters clear when he describes them as 'timid tyrants'. As one might expect, these accounts reveal a flexible attitude amongst litigants and their supporters as to what was considered acceptable, depending on whether they or their opponents made the threat. This is similar to the way in which some litigants justified the use of money or gifts to influence a case. The party making (or receiving) a gift or payment could explain it as a measure to ensure that justice was not obstructed or delayed. The same individuals might, however, criticise an opponent who made a similar payment or gift for attempting to pervert the course of justice through bribery.[96]

Parties might use threats instead of invoking legal norms, but threats could also be used alongside legal argument. The exact stage of proceedings at which they were used depended on the circumstances. Archbishop Ealdred threatened King William and then afterwards laid out his case whilst, according to the York *Chronicle*, the terrified king listened anxiously. Geoffrey, the custodian of Battle Abbey, gathered his monastic brethren to oppose Robert de Chiltern's supporters and then raised a legal argument about the jurisdiction of the court. When this was rejected he locked his opponents inside the church, thus bookending his legal argument with behaviours designed to intimidate his opponents.

The importance of legal argument should therefore not be ignored. Indeed, litigants who could invoke clear norms and argue their cases eloquently may sometimes have been able to overcome even powerful opponents without threats. The *Abingdon Chronicle*, for example, records a time when several English pleaders (*causidici*) were retained at the abbey, 'whose arguments

95 Raine, *Historians*, 350 (Lawsuits, I, no. 1, p. 1).

96 For an attempt by a twelfth-century royal official to explain that justice was not sold when such payments were accepted by the treasury, but merely hastened, see Richard fitz Nigel, *Dialogus de Scaccario, and Constitutio Domus Regis / The Dialogue of the Exchequer, and The Establishment of the Royal Household*, ed. and trans. E. Amt and S. D. Church (Oxford: 2007), II, 23 (Amt and Church, 178–80). See also Hudson, *Oxford History*, 9. For an account critical of the use of money to influence a case, see *The Vita Wulfstani of William of Malmsbury*, ed. R. R. Darlington, Camden Society 3rd Series, 40 (London: 1928), 24–26 (reproduced in *Lawsuits*, I, no. 3). Cf. *Historia Ecclesie Abbendonensis* (Hudson, II, 51–53; *Lawsuits*, I, no. 146) for a case before the king in which both sides bid against each other to receive a favourable judgement.

no wise man opposed' (quorum collationi nemo sapiens refragabatur).[97] According to the *Chronicle*, whilst these men were protecting the abbey's public affairs, 'its opponents became tongue-tied' (eius oblocutores elingues fiebant).[98] This also suggests that threats were of little use against individuals who could argue their case with particular adroitness, although the abbey's experience may not have been typical.

•••

This essay has illustrated the variety of ways in which litigants in the Anglo-Norman period used threats to influence the outcome of lawsuits. These threats could have a secular or religious character, sometimes combining elements of both worldly and spiritual intimidation. They could be made, explicitly or implicitly, against either the court or an opposing party. It is possible that some litigants used threats as their sole means of influencing the outcome of a lawsuit. However, threats could also be used alongside legal arguments, and might form part of a wider disputing strategy which incorporated a variety of legal and extra-legal factors.

The surviving accounts of lawsuits perhaps do not record every instance of threatening behaviour in the cases they describe, whilst some may instead invent or embellish threats. Nevertheless, the instances of threatening behaviour in the accounts available to us suggest that litigants often thought carefully about how they could bring threats, explicit or implicit, to bear upon a dispute. Although the success of such threats could vary, the cases which have been discussed also show that some litigants were able to develop and use their threat advantage very skilfully. Bill Miller, focussing in particular on legal disputes in Icelandic sagas, suggested that medieval people 'were masters of threat', with many spending 'a good portion of their social lives cultivating threat advantage, or undermining that of their opponents and competitors'.[99] The evidence found in the surviving accounts of Anglo-Norman lawsuits does much to support this statement.

97 *Historia Ecclesie Abbendonensis* (Hudson, II, 5). This case is *Lawsuits*, I, no. 4.

98 Ibid. (*Lawsuits*, I, no. 4, p. 7).

99 Miller, 'Threat', 14.

Works Cited

Brand, P. A. 'The Origins of the English Legal Profession', *Law and History Review* 5, no. 1. (1987): 31–50.

Brand, P. A. *Origins of the English Legal Profession*. Oxford: 1992.

Cheyette, F. L. 'Suum Cuique Tribuere', *French Historical Studies* 6 (1970): 287–99.

Chronicon monasterii de Abingdon. Edited by J. Stevenson. 2 vols. Rolls Series 2. London: 1858.

Cooper, A. 'Protestations of Ignorance in Domesday Book'. In *The Experience of Power in Medieval Europe, 950–1350.*, edited by R. F. Berkhofer, A. Cooper and A. J. Kosto, 169–182. Aldershot: 2005.

Douglas, D. C. and G. W. Greenaway, eds. *English Historical Documents*, vol. 2, *1042–1189*. 2nd ed. London: 1981.

Fairweather, J., trans. *Liber Eliensis: A History of the Isle of Ely from the Seventh Century to the Twelfth*. Woodbridge: 2005.

fitz Nigel, Richard. *Dialogus de Scaccario, and Constitutio Domus Regis / The Dialogue of the Exchequer, and The Establishment of the Royal Household*. Edited and translated by E. Amt and S. D. Church. Oxford: 2007.

Fleming, R. 'Oral Testimony and the Domesday Inquest'. In *Anglo-Norman Studies* 17, edited by Christopher Harper-Bill. Martlesham: 1995.

Harding, A. *The Law Courts of Medieval England*. London: 1973.

Historia Ecclesie Abbendonensis: The History of the Church of Abingdon. Edited and translated by J. G. H. Hudson. 2 vols. Oxford: 2002–2007.

Hudson, J. G. H. 'Court Cases and Legal Arguments in England, c. 1066–1166', *Transactions of the Royal Historical Society*, ser. 6, vol. 10 (2000): 91–115.

Hudson, J. G. H. *The Formation of the English Common Law: Law and Society in England from the Norman Conquest to Magna Carta*. London: 1996.

Hudson, J. G. H. *The Oxford History of the Laws of England, Volume II, 871–1216*. Oxford: 2012.

Hyams, P. R. 'Norms and Legal Argument before 1150'. In *Law and History*, edited by A. D. Lewis and M. Lobban, 41–61. Current Legal Issues 6 Oxford: 2004.

Hyams, P. R. *Rancor and Reconciliation in Medieval England*. New York: 2003.

King, E. 'The Peterborough Descriptio Militum (Henry I)'. *English Historical Review* 84, no. 330 (1969): 84–101.

Leges Henrici Primi. Edited and translated by L. J. Downer. Oxford: 1972.

Liber Eliensis. Edited by E. O. Blake. Camden Third Series 92. London: 1962.

Miller, W. I. 'Threat'. In *Feud, Violence and Practice: Essays in Medieval Studies in Honor of Stephen D. White*, edited by B. Tuten and T. Billado, 9–27. Farnham: 2010.

Oxford Dictionary of National Biography. Edited by H. C. G. Matthew and Brian Harrison. Oxford: 2004.

Raine, J., ed. *Historians of the Church of York and Its Archbishops: Volume II*. Rolls Series 71. London: 1886.

Registrum Roffense. Edited by J. Thorpe. London: 1769.

Sallust. *Bellum Iugurthinum*. In *The Conspiracy of Catiline and the Jugurthine War*, translated by Rev. J. S. Watson. Philadelphia: 1896.

Searle, E., ed. and trans. *The Chronicle of Battle Abbey*. Oxford: 1980.

Turner, G. J. and H. E. Salter, eds. *The Register of St Augustine's Canterbury, Commonly Called the Black Book*. Vol. 2. London: 1924.

van Caenegem, R. C., ed. *English Lawsuits from William I to Richard I*. 2 vols, Selden Society 106 and 107. London: 1990 and 1991.

William of Malmsbury. *The* Vita Wulfstani *of William of Malmsbury*. Edited by R. R. Darlington. Camden Society 3rd ser. 40. London: 1928.

Walsingham, T. *Gesta Abbatum Monasterii Sancti Albani*. Edited by H. T. Riley. 3 vols. Rolls Series 28.4. London: 1867–9.

White, S. D. 'Inheritances and Legal Arguments in Western France, 1050–1150'. *Traditio* 43 (1986): 55–103.

White, S. D. '"*Pactum … Legem Vincit et Amor Iudicium*": The Settlement of Disputes by Compromise in Eleventh-Century Western France'. *American Journal of Legal History* 22 (1978): 281–308.

CHAPTER 4

Courts and Rule-Making in Eleventh-Century Western France

M. W. McHaffie[1]

I want to begin with a story.[2] It took place at some point between late 1061 and 1062, and is recorded in an original charter produced by the monks of Saint-Florent de Saumur.[3] At a court presided over by Count Geoffrey le Barbu of Anjou (1060–1067/1068), Abbot Sigo of Saint-Florent (1055–1070) and Geoffrey son of Bérard (whom I shall refer to simply as Bérard) gathered for judgment over Bérard's challenge.[4] His claim was this: Bérard's father had held 'land of Saint-Florent' at rent from Abbot Frédéric of Saint-Florent, but lost it in 1026 when Fulk Nerra, count of Anjou, conquered Saumur amidst the longstanding conflict between the counts of Anjou and counts of Blois.[5] A 'great change' of inhabitants then took place when Fulk Nerra gave Saumur to his son Geoffrey Martel, whereupon, according to the monks of Saint-Florent, Martel seized lands there from some to give to others, howsoever he pleased. Bérard's father was one of those thus dispossessed, when Martel made a gift of his land to one

1 I thank the Leverhulme Trust for generously funding my research for the past three years. An especial thanks to Tegan Currie, for her assistance—both practical and impractical—and her ceaseless support.

2 What follows is a summary rather than a translation of the text of the charter, with additional details to clarify the context. The Latin text can be followed in the footnotes.

3 Archives départementales de Maine-et-Loire (hereafter cited as ADML) H 2117, no. 3. I follow the transcript of this charter in *Chartes originales antérieures à 1121 conservées en France*, ed. Cédric Giraud, Jean-Baptiste Renault and Benoît-Michel Tock (Nancy and Orléans: 2010), no. 3365, online at <www.cn-telma.fr/originaux/charte3365/>, accessed 14/6/2017. For an accurate cartulary copy see Bibliothèque nationale de France NAL 1930, 'Livre noir de Saint-Florent de Saumur' (hereafter cited as 'Livre noir'), fols. 108v–109r, which is the earliest of the monks' four extant cartularies, and was probably compiled in c. 1070. Marc Saché, *Inventaire sommaire des archives départementales antérieures à 1790, série H*, vol. 2, *Abbaye Saint-Florent-de-Saumur* (Angers: 1926), 103–4 summarizes the charter, but omits several details noted below.

4 Since there are at least four further men named Geoffrey in this dispute, I refer to Geoffrey son of Bérard simply as Bérard, to distinguish this Geoffrey clearly from all the others.

5 The narrative is covered in Louis Halphen, *Le comté d'Anjou au XIe siècle* (Paris: 1906), 38–45; and Bernard Bachrach, *Fulk Nerra, the Neo-Roman Consul, 987–1040* (Berkeley: 1993), 180–3.

© KONINKLIJKE BRILL NV, LEIDEN, 2018 | DOI 10.1163/9789004366374_008

Joscelin Roonard.[6] Abbot Frédéric then made an agreement with Joscelin: in return for 10*l*., Joscelin abandoned this land to the abbot—with the consent of Geoffrey Martel—and the monks thereafter held it 'for twenty years or more without lawful challenge'.[7] This then was Bérard's challenge: he claimed the right to inherit land once held at rent by his father from Saint-Florent.

The disputing parties gathered before Count Geoffrey le Barbu for judgment, in the second year of Geoffrey's rule as count after succeeding his uncle Geoffrey Martel in November 1060.[8] We know very little about how Bérard and Abbot Sigo came to court—all the charter says is that they decided to take their case before the count—nor do we know much about the composition of this court, whether it was gathered specifically for this case, or even where it took place (though presumably it was in Saumur).[9] What we do have, though, is the text of the decision, as represented in the charter:

> After judgment, it was confirmed that if the count and abbot wished, they would never have to answer to him [i.e. Bérard] over this matter, in accordance with custom. Otherwise, it would be necessary to return other properties of this sort to their former possessors, which, as had been decided, could not reasonably be done.[10]

---

6 ADML H 2117, no. 3: 'Tempore quo Fulco Andegavensis castrum salvum murum coepit, erga ipsius loci habitatores mutatio magna facta fuit. Comes nanque Gosfridus ejus filius in cujus manum dono patris venit, prout sibi placuit aliis abstulit, aliis dedit. Hac ergo de causa Berardus, pater Gosfridi, cognomine Berardi, terram Sancti Florentii quam ad censum tenebat perdidit, et Goscelinus cognomento Rotundator eam dono comitis habuit'.

7 Ibid.: 'Qua in re abbas Fredericus qui tunc temporis erat, dampnum suum non minimum cognoscens, cum eo sic convenit ut de suo acciperet, et terram sibi omnino dimitteret. Quod et ita illi placuit. Acceptis itaque decem nummorum libris, annuente Gosfrido comite terram abbati dimisit quam postea Sanctus Florentius annis XX aut eo amplius legali calumnia absolutam habuit'.

8 Ibid.: 'Mortuo vero Gosfrido comite, item nepos ejus Gosfridus successit in honore. Quo jam secundo anno comitatum exercente, et Sigone tunc abbate, predictus Gosfridus Berardi filius, terram quam diximus monachis Sancti Florentii calumniatus fuit, in tantum ut abbas et ipse inde causam statuerent, quatinus ante comitem ad judicium venirent'. This court case cannot be dated more precisely than to the second year of Geoffrey le Barbu's reign, so, between November 1061 and November 1062.

9 Although the charter does not use the word 'court' when describing the 1062 events, because Bérard and Abbot Sigo decided to submit to a powerful third-party expressly to receive a judgment (*judicium*), this can fairly be described as a court case.

10 ADML H 2117, no. 3: 'Habito vero judicio, approbatum fuit, quod si comes et abbas vellent, nunquam ei de hac re secundum consuetudinem responderent. Alioquin alias res hujus

The court made two decisions. The first was the judgment delivered against Bérard's specific inheritance claim—though we do not know who pronounced judgment, nor how it was reached. The second was a broader statement articulating a generalized rule, framed 'in accordance with custom', that might be expressed as follows: neither the count nor the abbot was required to answer a challenge concerning landed property lost because of the conquest of Saumur and the subsequent changeover in landholders there, because to do so would have brought too many problems in its wake.[11] The effect of this rule was to transform the conquest of Saumur in 1026 into a period of legal prescription, barring claims that might be connected to specific losses following the conquest. Much of the present study will work outwards from this decision (as opposed to the specific judgment delivered against Bérard), exploring its significance and asking what we can learn from it. First, however, let us consider the rest of the case.

Bérard remained undeterred. His inheritance claim defeated in judgment, he tried a second line of argument, alleging that in return for the service Bérard had performed to him, Geoffrey Martel had promised to intervene on Bérard's behalf with the abbot of Saint-Florent by asking him to let Bérard have the land as his father had held it, the only condition being that Bérard pay 10*l.* to the abbot of Saint-Florent to compensate him for the sum paid earlier to Joscelin Roonard.[12] In support of his claim, Bérard named two witnesses to his prior agreement (*conventio*) with Martel: Geoffrey Fuel from his own party, and Geoffrey the Fat on behalf of the count—presumably Martel.[13] While one of the witnesses was delayed in coming to court, however, Bérard began 'to think over the weakness of his case', according to the monks, and consequently

---

modi ad priores possessores necesse esset redire, quod sancitum fuerat rationabiliter fieri non posse'.

11 Olivier Guillot, *Le comte d'Anjou et son entourage au XIe siècle*, 2 vols. (Paris: 1972), I, 326 briefly discusses the decision in relation to the Angevin counts' right of conquest.

12 ADML H 2117, no. 3: 'Verbi igitur hujus oppositione repulsus, vertit se ad aliud, dicens Gosfridum comitem dum adhuc viveret, apud quoddam castrum Pontem Andegavensium, pro servicio quod sibi fecerat convenisse, quod abbatem rogaret uti terram istam sicut pater suus habuerat sibi habendam permitteret, ita tamen ut abbati pecuniam quam Goscelino dederat redderet'. It is unclear whether this alleged promise had been made during the abbacy of Frédéric or Sigo. For dates of the abbacies of Saint-Florent's eleventh-century abbots, see William Ziezulewicz, 'La chronologie des abbés de Saint-Florent de Saumur au XIe siècle', *Revue bénédictine* 108 (1998), 282–97.

13 Ibid.: 'Hujusque conventionis, sibi testes nominavit unum de parte sua scilicet Gauzfridum Fualdum, alterum de parte comitis, Gauxfridum Crassum'.

threatened to plunder the abbey's land.[14] The threat spurred the abbot into action, anxious lest his community suffer loss, but also, apparently, concerned lest Bérard endanger his soul by attacking monastic property.[15] Abbot Sigo therefore, in response to Bérard's threat, and acting on the counsel of Count Geoffrey le Barbu, gave Bérard 4*l.* and the spiritual benefits (societatem in elemosinis et orationibus) of the abbey, and named Vivian Brochard as his surety to this agreement, with Geoffrey Fuel and Bouchard de l'Ile-Bouchard acting as witnesses.[16] The following day, Bérard entered Saint-Florent's chapterhouse

14 Ibid.: 'Sed quia alter eorum aberat, causa remansit indefinita. Interea Gosfridus peticionis sue infirmitatem secum reputans, testem expectare noluit, sed terram Sancti Florentii predari minatus fuit'. The copy in the 'Livre noir', fols. 108v–109r adds 'Berard[us]' as an interlinear gloss above Geoffrey's name at this point in the text. The charter does not specify which of the two witnesses caused the delay, but given that Geoffrey Fuel witnessed the final settlement to the dispute, it seems reasonable to conclude that Geoffrey the Fat was the absentee witness. On the tactical use of the threat of violence, William Ian Miller's 'Threat', in *Feud, Violence and Practice: Essays in Medieval Studies in Honor of Stephen D. White*, ed. Belle S. Tuten and Tracey L. Billado (Farnham: 2010), 9–27 is destined to become a classic, not least for managing to refer to Glaswegian 'neds' in an academic paper. For discussion of the tactical use of threat in eleventh-century Angevin disputing see Stephen D. White, 'Proposing the Ordeal and Avoiding It: Strategy and Power in Western French Litigation, 1050–1110', in *Cultures of Power: Lordship, Status, and Process in Twelfth-Century Europe*, ed. Thomas Bisson (Philadelphia: 1995), 89–123.

15 ADML H 2117, no. 3: 'Quod abbas audiens, omnia pacificari quam conturbari malens, consilium coepit quo suis dampnum non veniret, et ille animam suam non perderet'. The motif that the monks of Saint-Florent sought to minimize the dangers to their lay adversaries' souls incurred by their actions appears in other cases as well, such as an early charter produced by these monks concerning 'unjust customs' imposed upon one of their priories by Aubrey, a fidelis of Count Fulk Nerra. For the text, see Halphen, *Le comté d'Anjou*, 346–7 (pièce justificative no. 2); for commentary, see Tracey L. Billado, 'Rhetorical Strategies and Legal Arguments: "Evil Customs" and Saint-Florent de Saumur, 979–1011', in *Oral History of the Middle Ages: The Spoken Word in Context*, ed. Gerhard Jaritz and Michael Richter (Krems: 2001), 128–41.

16 ADML H 2117, no. 3: 'Fecit itaque finem hujus calumnie per Vivianum Brocardum, testem et vadem conventionis sue, dans ei quatuor libras denariorum, et promittens societatem in elemosinis et orationibus fratrum. Hoc autem cum consilio comitis factum est, testibus Gauzfrido Fualdo, et Burcardo de Insula, et aliis pluribus testimonium hujus rei perferentibus'. The copy in 'Livre noir', fols. 108v–109r erroneously adds 'filio Arnaldi' after Bouchard's name; Guillot, *Le comte d'Anjou*, I, 331, n. 233 highlights this error as well. Although Saché's summary in *Inventaire*, 103 omits the reference to Vivien Brochard, the text states that the settlement was reached 'per Vivianum', whose designation as a witness and a surety (testem et vadem) indicates that he guaranteed the sum of 4*l.* the abbot promised Bérard.

to receive the gift of the abbey's spiritual benefits (donum societatis); and there, before the abbot and the brothers, he fully relinquished his challenge (*calumnia*) to the land and promised to free the disputed land from any outside challenge for the rest of his life. Then, before six named lay witnesses, he made a surrender of his claim upon an altar, presumably having moved to the abbey church.[17] The charter concludes with nine signatures, including those of Bérard, Joscelin Roonard, Geoffrey Fuel, Bouchard de l'Ile-Bouchard, and Abbot Sigo—but not, it seems, Count Geoffrey le Barbu.

Historiographical Perspectives

Bérard's case encapsulates a phenomenon typical of disputing in eleventh-century western France.[18] On the one hand, a dispute over conflicting property claims was taken to a court presided over by a figure of political authority, in this case the count of Anjou, to receive a judicial decision that could be formulated in ways revealing a sophisticated normative rationale. The importance of 'formal judicial processes' in contributing to wider patterns of dispute settlement might indeed have been a distinctive feature of western post-Carolingian France in contrast to other regions such as the Languedoc.[19] Yet on the other

---

17 ADML H 2117, no. 3: 'Sequenti autem die quo hec acta sunt, ad recipiendum societatis donum quod abbas promiserat in capitulum venit, ibique coram abbate et fratribus terre calumniam quam fecerat omnino dimisit, et si aliquis in tota vita sua illam calumniaret, manu sua absolvendum promisit, et deinde hujus dimissionis donum super altare posuit, videntibus et audientibus hoc Gausfrido filio Salconis, et famulis nostris, Popelino, Girardo Vitrario, Stabili, Frotgerio, Landrico Bersagio'. Saché, *Inventaire*, 103 mistakenly represents Bérard as renouncing his 'injustes prétensions' and omits his promise to help the abbey in the event of future challenges.

18 The starting-point for studying courts and disputing in this region is Louis Halphen, 'La justice en France au XIe siècle. Région angevine', *Revue historique* 77 (1901), 279–307. Yvonne Bongert, *Recherches sur les cours laïques du Xe au XIIIe siècle* (Paris: 1949), makes good use of the evidence from this region, though her conclusions have largely been superseded by subsequent scholarship. The essays collected in Stephen D. White, *Feuding and Peace-Making in Eleventh-Century France* (Aldershot: 2005), written between the late 1970s and the early 2000s, have shaped modern approaches to disputing in the region (and many others besides). Henk Teunis, *The Appeal to the Original Status: Social Justice in Anjou in the Eleventh Century* (Hilversum: 2006); and Bruno Lemesle, *Conflits et justice au Moyen Âge. Normes, loi et résolution des conflits en Anjou aux XIe et XIIe siècles* (Paris: 2008), present two recent (though very different) studies on Angevin courts and disputing.

19 On the distinctiveness of western France see Stephen D. White, '"*Pactum ... Legem Vincit et Amor Judicium*": The Settlement of Disputes by Compromise in Eleventh-Century

hand, as Bérard's case well shows, judgments were often ineffective in terminating a dispute. 'Formal judicial processes' broke down quickly when Bérard threatened predation upon Saint-Florent's lands, thereby inducing his adversary, it would appear, to agree to a compromise favourable to Bérard, who received pecuniary and spiritual payments. Judgments were seldom enforced, and after any such judgment, a litigant could refuse to accept it, reach a compromise with his or her adversary, and secure payments and gifts in return for giving up his or her claim.[20] Any wider evaluation of the nature of eleventh-century courts must start from these apparently contradictory and empirically grounded observations, which we might refer to as the 'problem of non-enforcement'.[21]

Whilst an older generation of historians viewed the lack of routine enforcement of judicial decisions as indicating the failure of eleventh-century courts to settle disputes effectively—which Georges Duby then integrated into his vision of abrupt social, political, and legal change in c. 1000—scholarship since the 1970s has approached the study of courts in this period through the lens of 'dispute processing'.[22] 'Dispute processing' scholarship varies considerably

Western France', *The American Journal of Legal History* 22, no. 4 (1978), 281–308, esp. 307; see too Jane Martindale, '"His Special Friend"? The Settlement of Disputes and Political Power in the Kingdom of the French (Tenth to Mid-Twelfth Century)', *Transactions of the Royal Historical Society* 5, sixth series (1995), 21–57. For a recent introduction to the history of France during the central Middle Ages see Florian Mazel, *Féodalités, 888–1180* (Paris: 2010).

20 See White, '"*Pactum ... legem*"', esp. 295–8; Dominique Barthélemy, *La société dans le comté de Vendôme de l'an mil au XIVe siècle* (Paris: 1993), 653, 662–5.

21 This phrase takes inspiration from Alice Taylor, '*Lex Scripta* and the Problem of Enforcement: Anglo-Saxon, Welsh and Scottish Law Compared', in *Legalism*, vol. 2: *Community and Justice*, ed. Fernanda Pirie and Judith Scheele (Oxford: 2014), 47–75.

22 Halphen, 'La justice', 279–307; Marc Bloch, *Feudal Society*, trans. L. A. Manyon (London: 1962), 359–74; and Bongert, *Recherches sur les cours laïques*. See Georges Duby, 'The Evolution of Judicial Institutions: Burgundy in the Tenth and Eleventh Centuries', in Duby, *The Chivalrous Society*, trans. Cynthia Postan (Berkeley: 1977), 15–58 for Duby's early arguments about a radical transformation in the exercise of justice around the year 1000. For discussions from various perspectives of the broader debate on whether there was a *mutation féodale* or 'feudal revolution', see Dominique Barthélemy, *La mutation féodale de l'an mil a-t-elle eu lieu? Servage et chevalerie dans la France des Xe et XIe siècles* (Paris: 1997); Christian Lauranson-Rosaz, 'Le débat sur la "mutation féodale": État de la question', in *Europe around the Year 1000*, ed. Przemyslaw Urbancyzk (Warsaw: 2001), 11–40; Stephen D. White, 'Tenth-Century Courts at Mâcon and the Perils of Structuralist History: Re-reading Burgundian Judicial Institutions', in *Conflict in Medieval Europe: Changing Perspectives on Society and Culture*, ed. Warren C. Brown and Piotr Górecki

in the claims advanced by its different practitioners, but takes inspiration to greater or lesser degrees from the works of anthropologists working mostly on regional political communities without strong, centralized States.[23] Such an approach does not take an argument about the failure of courts to settle disputes effectively as its goal, but rather considers questions such as how disputes *were* settled, if not routinely through 'formal judicial processes', and why compromise—where neither party left empty-handed—might have been a more desirable way of halting, at least temporarily, most conflicts.[24]

Historians have not reached a consensus on how these above questions are answered. Nevertheless, at a general level, a 'dispute processing' approach involves a reorientation away from courts and towards disputants themselves, whereby those same courts are viewed from the perspective of the litigants. From this perspective, courts, in addition to being centres for adjudication, were privileged arenas of negotiation where disputants worked out their disagreements in a public, ritualized sphere. The judgments that such courts sometimes pronounced might thus have served to produce a moment of clarity during a dispute, offering a snapshot of where public opinion might have lain, and perhaps inducing one party to admit publicly his or her guilt

---

(Aldershot: 2003), 37–68; Florian Mazel, 'Pouvoir aristocratique et Église aux Xe–XIe siècles. Retour sur la "Révolution féodale" dans l'œuvre de Georges Duby', *Médiévales* 54 (2008), 137–52; Charles West, *Reframing the Feudal Revolution: Political and Social Transformation between Marne and Moselle, c. 800–c. 1100* (Cambridge: 2013), esp. 1–9.

23 See Stephen D. White, 'From Peace to Power: The Study of Disputes in Medieval France', in *Medieval Transformations: Texts, Power, and Gifts in Context*, ed. Esther Cohen and Mayke B. de Jong (Leiden: 2001), 203–18 for an overview of the historiography concerning eleventh-century France. Studies exploring 'dispute processing' include: *Le règlement des conflits au moyen âge* (Paris: 2001); *Conflict in Medieval Europe*, ed. Brown and Górecki; Chris Wickham, *Courts and Conflict in Twelfth-Century Tuscany* (Oxford: 2003); Lemesle, *Conflits*; and *Disputing Strategies in Medieval Scandinavia*, ed. Kim Esmark et al. (Leiden: 2013). *Disputes and Settlements: Law and Human Relations in the West*, ed. John Bossy (Cambridge: 1983); and *The Settlement of Disputes in Early Medieval Europe*, ed. Wendy Davies and Paul Fouracre (Cambridge: 1986) both remain foundational contributions to the subject.

24 For three now-classic articles that take different positions on these questions in eleventh-century France, see Fredric L. Cheyette, 'Suum cuique tribuere', *French Historical Studies* 6, no. 3 (1970), 287–299; White, '"*Pactum ... legem*"', 281–308; and Patrick J. Geary, 'Living with Conflicts in a Stateless France: A Typology of Conflict Management Mechanisms, 1050–1200', in Geary, *Living with the Dead in the Middle Ages* (Ithaca and London: 1994), 125–60.

or simply back down.[25] Judgment, accordingly, may have been nothing other than a privileged moment when the transactions costs of disputes were made clear for all those involved in them. What I have termed the 'problem of non-enforcement' is not so contradictory, therefore: by viewing courts as arenas for negotiation, disputants might have approached courts with the specific aim of reaching a compromise and restoring amicable ties, rather than obtaining a unilateral judgment pronounced in favour of one party or another.[26]

The shift to the disputants' perspective is an approach partially dictated by the nature of our sources. Evidence for eleventh-century courts survives almost exclusively in monastic charters.[27] The interpretative challenges posed by this corpus of material are considerable, and extend far beyond the obvious point that in recording disputes, such texts are *ex parte*, preserving only the perspective of the monastic party. More structurally, the perspective of monastic charters remains not just that of one of the disputants, but that of dispute itself. Such accounts were often retrospective compositions, almost invariably produced after a settlement (of whatever form) had been reached; in constructing narratives of eleventh-century disputes, monastic scribes—though utilizing formulaic phraseology and narrative conventions—exercised much more freedom than their predecessors had done to tell stories, into which they

25 Barthélemy, *La société*, 665; and Bruno Lemesle, '"Ils donnèrent leur accord à ce jugement". Réflexions sur la contrainte judiciaire (Anjou, XIe–XIIe siècle)', in *La justice en l'an mil*, Collection Histoire de la justice 15 (Paris: 2003), 123–47.

26 White, '"*Pactum ... legem*"', esp. 298–307; see also Richard E. Barton, *Lordship in the County of Maine, c. 890–1160* (Woodbridge: 2004), 174–96, esp. 175. Both deal primarily with disputes between parties of relatively equal status. Barton, *Lordship*, 190 notes that a differential in power between disputants might, conversely, mean judgment, rather than compromise, was more likely. White, 'From Peace to Power', esp. 213–14 stresses the need to look at disputes cutting across social strata, a point echoed in John Hudson, 'Legal History and the History of Disputes', in Esmark et al., *Disputing Strategies*, 333–4.

27 For eleventh-century monastic charters in this region see Barthélemy, *La société*, esp. 19–83; Dominique Barthélemy, 'Une crise de l'écrit? Observations sur des actes de Saint-Aubin d'Angers (XIe siècle)', *Bibliothèque de l'École des Chartes* 155 (1997), 95–117; and Olivier Guyotjeannin, '"*Penuria scriptorum*": Le mythe de l'anarchie documentaire dans la France du Nord (X^{e}–première moitié du XIe siècle)', in ibid., 11–44. Lemesle, *Conflits*, 19–32 reflects on Angevin dispute charters, and Jean Vezin, *Les scriptoria d'Angers au XIe siècle* (Paris: 1974) covers the intellectual environment in which monastic scribes were working. For an overview of charter studies in France, see Nicolas Ruffini-Ronzani and Jean-François Nieus, 'Société seigneuriale, réformes ecclésiales: Les enjeux documentaires d'une révision historiographique', in Ecclesia in medio nationis: *Reflections on the Study of Monasticism in the Central Middle Ages/Réflexions sur l'étude du monachisme au Moyen Âge central*, ed. Steven Vanderputten and Brigitte Meijns (Leuven: 2011), 77–100.

could incorporate (or not) as they saw fit selected elements of the pre-history of the dispute and its wider social context, and the alleged motivations leading disputants to the re-formation of peace and amicable ties. Eleventh-century monastic charters are thus extremely well suited to reconstructing the social history of disputing, at least from a monastic perspective, but they remain opaque when it comes to exploring courts themselves. Our sources thus reflect the interests of monastic disputants in narrating how disputes were settled: the picture of courts preserved in charters is pre-conditioned to approach them from the perspective of whether they effectively terminated disputes—that is, questions concerning the 'problem of non-enforcement'.

One of the key interpretative challenges in working with eleventh-century monastic charters, therefore, lies in transcending the viewpoint of the monastic disputant to approach that of the court and court-holder itself. If it is possible to say something about the perspective of the court, might this help us to re-think the broader contribution of courts to 'dispute processing', perhaps even identifying roles that go beyond the termination of individual cases? Bérard's case, as narrated above, provides the occasion for reflection on this issue. I want to consider the possible relationship between at least this eleventh-century court and the formulation of a legal rule aimed at general applicability, a relationship Bérard's case certainly suggests. Whilst a case study alone can only be suggestive, it can be used to frame some larger questions that may merit further research.

A final preliminary note on courts, and what I mean by this term. Courts in eleventh-century western France were not fixed institutions in the sense that they had a routine schedule of meetings, in a fixed place.[28] They lacked regular composition, nor were they staffed by professional lawyers and judges—if by 'professional' we mean individuals whose living derived principally from the practice of law.[29] They had instead an 'ephemeral and contextual nature', according to Richard Barton, and might better be viewed as meetings, or occasions.[30] This does not mean, however, that courts were not conceptually set apart from the hubbub of normal life; through their rituals, and probably also the patterns of speech such occasions demanded, they had a distinctive legal identity, albeit one defined in terms of function and behaviours, rather

28 In addition to Halphen, 'La justice', who identified many of these features, see also Stephen D. White, 'Inheritances and Legal Arguments in Western France, 1050–1150', *Traditio* 43 (1987), 55–103, esp. 65–70.

29 See here especially Susan Reynolds, 'The Emergence of Professional Law in the Long Twelfth Century', *Law and History Review* 21, no. 2 (2003), 347–66.

30 Barton *Lordship*, 188.

than institutions.[31] Under the presidency of often important and powerful aristocratic lords, including counts, courts were also public events.[32] Public events were likewise political events, or at least political in the sense that courtholders, as well as the people attending the court, might all have had stakes to varying degrees in the dispute, either on substantive grounds or because of pre-existing relations with one or more of the disputing parties. Courts were thus seldom neutral, apolitical affairs.

The 1062 Court and the Construction of a Legal Rule

Let us return to Bérard's case, and refresh our memories of the judicial decision, which reads as follows:

> After judgment, it was confirmed that if the count and abbot wished, they would never have to answer to him over this matter, in accordance with custom. Otherwise, it would be necessary to return other properties of this sort to their former possessors, which as had been decided, could not reasonably be done.[33]

The decision attempted to forestall Bérard's claim, and others like it, by affirming that neither the count nor the abbot was obligated to respond to his challenges 'in accordance with custom'. The text of the decision centred around a basic rule about prescription: by invalidating the claims of Bérard and/or others like him, the court put forward a rule that the claims that litigants might have brought to lands they had lost during the conquest of Saumur in 1026 and its aftermath were null and void. To see why this is the case, we need to examine the issue of prescription more closely, and to consider in what ways the 1062 decision should be seen as an expression of a legal rule.

The charters of Anjou illustrate that prescription periods could be constructed in several different ways. Thirty- or forty-year prescription periods, informed by canon law, represented one means of setting legal time limits, though as Bruno Lemesle has noted, the earliest reference to a thirty- or forty-year prescription period survives in a charter from 1074, and explicit references

31 Chris Wickham, 'Conclusion', in *The Moral World of the Law*, ed. Peter Coss (Cambridge: 2000), 240–49, esp. 241–2.

32 Lemesle, *Conflits*, 35–81 is now the definitive statement on this point for the Angevin region.

33 ADML H 2117, no. 3.

to canonical prescription only become slightly more common from the first third of the twelfth century.[34] In other instances, prescription might be limited to twenty years, as Abbot Sigo appears to have argued in response to Bérard's challenge.[35] Prescription might, alternatively, be understood as a period of ten years. During a case heard in the abbey of Saint-Aubin's own court (*curia*), for instance, judgment went against a lay claimant, 'in accordance with human laws', because he had waited more than ten years to make a challenge.[36] In yet other charters, prescription is presented by monastic scribes as a period of one year and one day, as in a case from c. 1050 × c. 1055 when the nuns of Le Ronceray offered a witness to testify that they had enjoyed possession of a disputed mill for a year and a day 'without challenge'.[37] And in at least one example, after a man named Bodin abandoned a challenge he was making to his brother's gift to the community of Fontevraud in 1101 × 1116, Gautier de Montsoreau declared that 'whoever wished to challenge this gift should make his challenge within eight days, because otherwise his challenge will not be heard'.[38]

What the above examples illustrate is that some period of prescription likely featured as a basic principle of eleventh-century customary law, but that the length of the period might vary considerably. Geoffrey le Barbu's court in 1062 thus articulated a rule that attempted to promote a specific understanding of prescription, one in which prescription was identified with the 'great change' (magna mutatio) in the Saumurois following the Angevin conquest and Martel's subsequent redistribution of lands there. The basis for such a conclusion lies in the fact that the decision explicitly singled out 'other properties of this sort'—that is, properties lost in a similar way to how Bérard's father had

34 Lemesle, *Conflits*, 140, citing *Cartulaire de l'abbaye de Saint-Aubin d'Angers*, ed. Bertrand de Broussillon, 3 vols. (Paris: 1903) (hereafter cited as SAA), I, no. 106 (1074). For examples from the first third of the twelfth century, see Lemesle, *Conflits*, 140, n. 4.

35 ADML H 2117 no. 3. See also *Premier et Second livres des Cartulaires de l'abbaye Saint-Serge et Saint-Bach d'Angers (XIe et XIIe siècles)*, ed. Yves Chauvin, 2 vols. (Angers: 1997), (hereafter cited as SSE), I, no. 371 (c. 1150) for a later example of the invocation of a twenty-year prescription period when a Saint-Serge scribe noted that his abbey had held disputed land for more than twenty years.

36 SAA, II, no. 421 (c. 1100), which is discussed briefly in Lemesle, *Conflits*, 141. See also SAA, II, no. 485 (1171) for a later example where the abbey of Saint-Aubin sought to defend its right to property by arguing that the original donor from whom they received it had held it 'for ten years in peace, without challenge' (decem annos in pace et sine calumnia).

37 'Cartularium monasterii Beatae Mariae Andegavensis', in *Archives d'Anjou*, ed. Paul Marchegay, vol. 3 (Angers: 1854) (hereafter cited as RA), no. 240.

38 *Grand cartulaire de Fontevraud*, ed. Jean-Marc Bienvenu, Robert Favreau, and Georges Pons, vol. 1 (Poitiers: 2000), no. 281 (1101 × 1106).

lost his land—as the types of claim affected by the rule. Barring claims made for 'other properties of this sort' can only refer to lands lost in the 'great change' of 1026 and the following years, which means that the 1062 court effectively transformed the circumstances surrounding past conquest into a measure of legal time to serve as a *terminus a quo* invalidating subsequent challenges. Whilst the court in 1062 did not identify the conquest of Saumur in 1026 specifically as this measure of legal time—an ambiguity I shall come back to shortly—it did, all the same, attempt to forestall any claims that would arise concerning lands lost through conquest.

How did 'prescription by conquest' relate to the monks' own claim that they had held the disputed land for 'twenty years or more without lawful challenge'? At a very basic level, the monks' own claim presented an alternative prescription period, this one based on a fixed duration of twenty years rather than in reference to past events. The two forms of prescription at play in the 1062 case need not be incompatible nor contradictory, however. Abbot Sigo and his monks, in answering Bérard's initial challenge, advanced an argument for long possession of the contested land, expressed as a period of twenty years 'or more'. Whilst such a statement may imply that the abbey's re-acquisition of their property from Joscelin Roonard took place in 1042, the monks' argument here may equally have served to express a general principle of long and peaceful possession—albeit a principle that could be expressed several different ways—rather than a precise reckoning of time. But the court offered its own definition of prescription in its generalized decision, whereby the past event of conquest was transformed into a measure of legal time and served as an alternative way of constructing prescription. The 1062 decision thus effectively re-defined prescription. Since the 1062 charter presents multiple measures of legal time, and since that of the monks differed from that of the court in an important, but not contradictory way, this may be one example of how the 1062 charter opens a window onto the perspective of the court itself, rather than just that of the monastic disputant. Prescription by conquest might then have been the court's own viewpoint.

It is possible to consider the decision made in 1062 as the expression of a legal rule, if by legal rule one follows the recent definition of 'legalism' given by Hannah Skoda:

> By this [legalism], we mean rules that are distinct from practice (rules that are "formulated," in other words) and rules characterized by the claim to be more than simply spontaneous improvisations, but in some sense often systematic. Rules we might describe as legal are general statements that often organize generalizing concepts ... or relate such concepts to

each other. These rules need not even be regulatory, and certainly need not be coercive.[39]

The decision articulated in Geoffrey le Barbu's court in 1062 appears to have distilled a series of complex events and claims arising out of Fulk's conquest of Saumur and the subsequent tenurial re-arrangements down to two such 'generalizing concepts'. The first was that there existed measures of time that determined whether an individual could legitimately make a challenge. Abbot Sigo appears to have argued that twenty years was a sound unit of measurement for prescription, and the court itself seems to have expressed that some period of prescription was a basic tenet of customary law: such a view is at least suggested by the phrase 'according to custom' recorded in the text. The second was that there was a conceptual category of land claims for properties lost through processes of conquest that could be and should be viewed by courts and litigants alike as a coherent group. The court's pronouncement in the 1062 decision brought these two concepts together when it transformed the event of conquest into a measure of legal time against which prescription can be measured. The 1062 decision thus created a legal rule—in the sense given above by Skoda—whereby territorial conquest could work as a frame of reference for understanding prescription.

If identifying the 1062 decision formulated in response to Bérard's case as a legal rule is a relatively straightforward task, more complex is the question of why such a rule might have been expressed in this way by the court at all—especially when, presumably, it could simply have used Abbot Sigo's argument of twenty-year prescription to justify its own decision. It is to this question that I now turn.

Law and Politics

The 1062 court provided an answer to the question of why it formulated its rule about prescription: were the count and abbot to answer Bérard's challenge at law, then other potential claimants who had lost lands as Bérard's father did would have good grounds for seeking the restitution of their own properties. Olivier Guillot described the 1062 decision as 'extremely prudent'.[40] Since Bérard's claim implicitly called into question the legitimacy of Angevin

39 Hannah Skoda, 'A Historian's Perspective on the Present Volume', in *Legalism: Anthropology and History*, ed. Paul Dresch and Hannah Skoda (Oxford: 2012), 39.

40 Guillot, *Le comte d'Anjou*, I, 326.

expansion into the Saumurois, that the court's decision—which, as Guillot pointed out, did not go so far as to legitimate conquest, affirming instead that practical reasons made it too difficult to deal with Bérard's claim—sought to transform conquest into prescription was 'extremely prudent' indeed.[41] Moreover, given the 'great change' in inhabitants that followed the conquest of 1026, it is possible that such a decision aimed at barring a series of potential claims that a hypothetical group of dispossessed men might have brought following Angevin expansion into the Saumurois.[42] To explore, therefore, the rationale offered by the 1062 court in justifying the rule it articulated, it is necessary to situate this rule amidst four layers of interests: that of Abbot Sigo; that of Bérard; that of Geoffrey Fuel and Bouchard de l'Ile-Bouchard; and that of Count Geoffrey le Barbu.

In a straightforward way, the rule articulated by the 1062 court sought to forestall any future claims Bérard might have brought against Abbot Sigo and his monks, which would have been useful for the monks following what had likely been an acrimonious dispute. Not only had the case been taken to court—implying that alternative out-of-court methods of resolution had failed—but Bérard had also threatened to use force against the abbey's land. Just how serious a threat this was is impossible to know, but the fact that Abbot Sigo offered 4*l.*—no small sum—and the equally valuable 'society of the alms and prayers of the brothers' suggests that Bérard's threat was taken seriously enough to justify valuable material and spiritual payments.[43] Further, part of the settlement saw Bérard promise Abbot Sigo that should this property become subject to another challenge, he would help the monks defend it.[44] Promises of this sort were sometimes given by individuals when abandoning challenges upon monastic property, and constituted the commitment to future good behaviour made by a former adversary.[45] Monks might have been particularly keen to

41 Ibid.

42 The disruptions might have been less severe amongst lower status landholders, as William Ziezulewicz, 'An Argument for Historical Continuity: Low and Middle Vassal Families in the Eleventh-Century Saumurois', *Medieval Prosopography* 8, no. 1 (1987), 93–110 argues.

43 Stephen D. White, *Custom, Kinship, and Gifts to Saints: The* Laudatio parentum *in Western France, 1050–1150* (Chapel Hill: 1988), esp. 153–76 remains essential for understanding the gifts of spiritual benefits that monks sometimes made to laymen (including their adversaries); see also Bruno Lemesle, 'Les querelles avaient-elles une vocation sociale? Le cas des transferts fonciers en Anjou au XIe siècle', *Le Moyen Âge* 115 (2009), 337–64, who stresses the economic value of spiritual benefits.

44 ADML H 2117, no. 3.

45 See 'Livre noir', fols. 55r–v (1060 × 1070), 71v–72r (1076 × 1096), 103v–104r (c. 1058), and 107r–v (1064 × 1070) for similar types of promise made by quitclaimants recorded in the

receive such promises, sometimes delivered on oath, as part of the resolution to particularly tense disputes. So, set amidst the context of a heated dispute between Sigo and Bérard—one in which violence had been threatened—the formulation of a rule that stated categorically that Abbot Sigo did not have to answer his opponent's claims at all must have been an attractive one for the abbot and his monks to receive.

But something does not quite add up. Bérard does not appear to have had significant interests in the Saumurois, and is found instead in the orbit of the castle of l'Ile-Bouchard in the lower Touraine. His earliest appearance in documents from this region comes in a charter dated 1062 × 1064–1068, where he witnessed the gift of an oven made to the monks of Noyers.[46] Bérard, from the 1060s onwards, appears in roughly a dozen charters from the abbey of Noyers. From c. 1070, he held rights in a *bourg* located near the castle of l'Ile-Bouchard; and in a charter unfortunately only datable to 1080 × 1111, an individual described Bérard as 'my lord' (dominus meus), implying that by the later eleventh century Bérard was exercising some form of lordship over others.[47] His interests were focalised around his *bourg* and the castle of l'Ile-Bouchard, since he often appears as a witness to transactions that were expressly taken to the castle to be confirmed by the lords of l'Ile-Bouchard.[48] A further connection with l'Ile-Bouchard is that in the 1062 case with Saint-Florent, Geoffrey Fuel and Bouchard—the lords of the castle of l'Ile-Bouchard—witnessed Bérard's settlement.[49] Given that Bérard's landed interests lay in the Touraine, rather

---

charters of Saint-Florent. On how such promises could create new social ties between former adversaries, see White, '"*Pactum … legem*"', 296.

46 *Cartulaire de l'abbaye de Noyers*, ed. Casamir de Chevalier (Tours: 1872) (hereafter cited as *Noyers*), no. 42; for the date, I follow Chantal Senséby, 'Une notice fausse du cartulaire de l'abbaye tourangelle de Noyers?', *Bibliothèque de l'École des chartes* 155 (1997), 82, n. 97, in preference to the editor's date of c. 1065. Archives départementales de Indre-et-Loire (hereafter cited as ADIL) H 332, no. 1 (1020) records a gift of customs by Bouchard I de l'Ile-Bouchard, where one of the signatories to the relevant charter was a man named Bérard: if this Bérard is the father of our Bérard, it suggests the connection between this family and the lords of l'Ile-Bouchard extended earlier than 1026, and may imply that the family origins were in the Touraine, rather than the Saumurois.

47 For the former: *Noyers*, nos. 62 and 318 (c.1103) for more on Bérard's rights in this *bourg*; for the latter: *Noyers*, no. 329. On *bourgs* in this region, see Chantal Senséby, 'Un aspect de la croissance: Le développement des bourgs aux confins du Poitou, de l'Anjou et de la Touraine (XIe et XIIe siècles)', *Journal des savants* 1, no. 1 (1997), 59–98.

48 *Noyers*, nos. 77 (c. 1080), 98 (c. 1082), 147 (c. 1087), 315 (c. 1103).

49 ADML H 2117, no. 3.

than the Saumurois, it is unclear just how likely it was that he would renew at a later date his challenge against the monks of Saint-Florent.

Bérard's connection with l'Ile-Bouchard leads us to consider the presence of Geoffrey Fuel and Bouchard de l'Ile-Bouchard, who both witnessed the 1062 decision and added their signatures to the charter. Geoffrey Fuel and Bouchard de l'Ile-Bouchard were kinsmen (the former was the latter's uncle), and had a longstanding dispute over the inheritance of the castle of l'Ile-Bouchard similar in substance to Bérard's challenge.[50] Put briefly, when Bouchard's father died (sometime before 1037), guardianship over the young Bouchard and his castle was given to his uncle Aimeri and then, on this latter's death, to Geoffrey Fuel.[51] In 1044, after Geoffrey Martel conquered the Touraine, Geoffrey Fuel, then in possession of l'Ile-Bouchard, was first dispossessed by Geoffrey Martel and then later re-granted control of the castle by the Angevin count. Geoffrey Fuel's continued possession seems to have extended beyond the agreed-upon duration of Bouchard's minority, however. After receiving his arms from the count of Blois, Bouchard waged a 'very great war' (werram maximam) against his uncle to recover his inheritance, during which Marmoutier's priory at Tavant was attacked and put to the torch.[52] The chronology of events in the charter recording this werra is confused, but a date sometime around 1060—so, prior to Bérard's case—seems likely.[53] At any rate, the two parties secured a measure of peace, since from around 1060—after the werra—a period of 'cohabitation' followed in which both Geoffrey and Bouchard appear together in

50 This dispute features in Jacques Boussard, 'L'éviction des tenants de Thibaud de Blois par Geoffroy Martel, comte d'Anjou, en 1044', *Le Moyen Âge* 69 (1963), 141–9, which is superseded now by Dominique Barthélemy, 'Les comtes, les sires, et les "nobles de châteaux" dans la Touraine du XIe siècle', in *Campagnes médiévales: L'homme et son espace. Études offertes à Robert Fossier*, ed. Elisabeth Mornet (Paris: 1995), 439–53.

51 The details are recorded in a charter written by the monks of Marmoutier, ADIL H 332 no. 3 (c. 1071), no. 1499 in Giraud, Renault, and Tock, *Chartes originales* (see n. 3 above) and online at <http://www.cn-telma.fr/originaux/charte1499/>, accessed 16/6/2017.

52 Two charters recount the 'werra': Giraud, Renault, and Tock, *Chartes originales* no. 1499, as cited in preceding note; and ADIL H 332 no. 5 (c. 1071), a damaged charter that provides much more detail on the 'werra' itself. Barthélemy, 'Les comtes', 440–42 discusses the different details preserved in these two texts, using complete transcriptions made in the seventeenth and eighteenth centuries, now at the Bibliothèque nationale de France, details of which are provided in ibid., 442, n. 16. For 'werra' in the Touraine during this period, see Stephen D. White, 'Feuding and Peace-Making in the Touraine around the Year 1100', *Traditio* 42 (1986), 195–263.

53 Barthélemy, 'Les comtes', 446.

charters.[54] Most charters, though, list Geoffrey as the lord of l'Ile-Bouchard.[55] It is only after 1067/1068—i.e. with the accession of Fulk le Réchin to the countship of Anjou—that Bouchard, perhaps by throwing in his lot with the young Angevin count, emerges as the sole lord of the castle.[56]

The essence of this dispute hinged on the ways in which territorial conquest (that of 1044) influenced competing inheritance claims: Fuel's position seems to have been that his right in the property was in some sense bound up with Martel's favour, after having received the castle as a gift from the Angevin count.[57] Conversely, Bouchard's position was that of the 'natural heir' (naturalis heres), the son who, as a matter of law and principle, ought to succeed to his father's possessions.[58] The nub of the matter was the legitimacy of right derived from conquest and a gift from a count.

Given the structural similarities between Bérard's case and the ongoing dispute between Geoffrey Fuel and Bouchard, the fact that these latter two were present at the 1062 court case hardly seems accidental, not least since, as we have seen, Bérard's landed interests lay near l'Ile-Bouchard. Geoffrey Fuel and Bouchard must have had an especial interest in the outcome of Bérard's case, since whatever decision he received might have had implications for the status of their own respective claims against each other and against the Angevin count. Since, moreover, Bérard's landed interests in the Saumurois were limited by 1062, it is tempting to ask whether the impetus to bring a claim against the abbot originated with Bérard at all. Might the two men competing for lordship

---

54 Ibid., 445; and Guillot, *Le comte d'Anjou*, 331. On the co-habitation of Geoffrey Fuel and Bouchard, see also *Noyers*, nos. 26 (c. 1062), 41 (c. 1065), and 42 (c. 1065), which are all cited in Barthélemy, 'Les comtes', 446, n. 26.

55 See for example *Livre des serfs de Marmoutier*, ed. André Salmon (Tours: 1864), no. A 22 (1064) for the following: 'unde cum apud Insulam [l'Ile-Bouchard] in curia Gausfredi Foelli carta hec recitata fuisset'. The charter itself was witnessed by Bouchard de l'Ile-Bouchard. See also Guillot, *Le comte d'Anjou*, I, 331, n. 232.

56 Barthélemy, 'Les comtes', 446 emphasises the Angevin succession in explaining Bouchard's emergence as sole lord.

57 A charter dated 1056 × 1059 lists Geoffrey Fuel as a member of Geoffrey Martel's *masnadia*, or household, suggesting a degree of personal service and patronage on the part of the Angevin count towards Fuel: see SAA, I, no. 178 and Guillot, *Le comte d'Anjou*, II, no. 179, who rectifies the date supplied by the editor of the cartulary of Saint-Aubin. Boussard, 'L'éviction', 147 noted how Geoffrey Fuel tied himself to the lot of the Angevins.

58 According to Barthélemy, 'Les comtes', 448–50, the persistence of Marmoutier's scribes in describing Bouchard as the 'natural heir' may hide genuine debate over the rules of succession at l'Ile-Bouchard between principles of collateral inheritance (favouring Geoffrey Fuel) and primogeniture (favouring Bouchard).

over l'Ile-Bouchard have encouraged a man of l'Ile-Bouchard to press a claim that was so structurally similar to the substance of their own dispute, simply to see what the result would be? Whilst this last point can only be speculative, the underlying observation seems less so: implicit in Bérard's challenge about the status of his heritable right to property following the Angevin conquest of Saumur in 1026 were questions about the status of more recent Angevin conquests in the Touraine after 1044. Bérard's challenge raised as a topic of discussion the legitimacy of Angevin territorial expansion itself.

The interests most threatened by such an issue were those of the count of Anjou; and accordingly, the individual with the highest stakes in the dispute was Geoffrey le Barbu himself. Count Geoffrey had recently succeeded his uncle Geoffrey Martel, who died in November 1060.[59] Bérard's claim, like Geoffrey Fuel's and Bouchard's, was thus made at a moment of political transition, early in the new count's reign. Whether Geoffrey Fuel and Bouchard (and Bérard) sought to exploit a potential moment of political insecurity by making their challenge so early in the new Count Geoffrey's reign must remain a speculative point, but the timing of the challenge was unlikely to have been random. Geoffrey le Barbu has been perceived by historians as a weak count, with his reign ending in the 'Angevin civil war' of 1067–1068 that led to his capture and lifelong imprisonment at the hands of his brother, Fulk le Réchin.[60] Whilst it is difficult to identify a precise moment when things started to go wrong, when Bérard made his challenge 'in the second year of Geoffrey's rule', it is doubtful that Geoffrey le Barbu occupied a position of strength, certainly when compared to his predecessor.

The nature of the different arguments raised in the course of Bérard's challenge galvanized the interests of various parties, and pressured Count Geoffrey le Barbu from multiple directions. Bouchard de l'Ile-Bouchard's own interest in a son's rights of inheritance was mirrored very closely by Bérard's first argument against Abbot Sigo, which perhaps gave Bouchard the basis for raising questions about the legitimacy of Angevin expansion into the Touraine. Additional problems came in Bérard's second argument concerning the agreement he had made with Geoffrey Martel: namely that in return for his service,

59 Halphen, *Le comté d'Anjou*, 133–51; and Guillot, *Le comte d'Anjou*, I, 102–111 both provide the narrative of Geoffrey's reign.

60 Guillot, *Le comte d'Anjou*, I, 104–5. On the 'civil war' see W. Scott Jessee, 'The Angevin Civil War and the Norman Conquest of 1066', *The Haskins Society Journal: Studies in Medieval History* 3 (1991), 101–9; and W. Scott Jessee 'Urban Violence and the *Coup d'état* of Fulk le Rechin in Angers, 1067', *The Haskins Society Journal: Studies in Medieval History* 7 (1995), 75–82.

the late count had promised to intervene on his behalf with the abbot of Saint-Florent whereby, it was hoped, Bérard could recover his father's property. Geoffrey Fuel, whose own claim to right in the castle of l'Ile-Bouchard had marked parallels to Bérard's second argument, might have expected—or hoped—that the new Angevin count would affirm the principle at work here: i.e. that political favour and patronage was a secure basis to right in land. But Abbot Sigo objected to Bérard's argument—such an objection, may in fact, lie behind the charter's statement that Bérard thought about 'the weakness of his case', referring here specifically to Bérard's second argument. Moreover, since Abbot Sigo in the early years of Geoffrey le Barbu's reign had brought a number of challenges against the new count seeking the confirmation of an apparent deathbed remission of 'evil customs' (malae consuetudines) made by Geoffrey Martel, the new count might have found himself under additional pressure to take Saint-Florent's side.[61] But if Count Geoffrey had in consequence affirmed, explicitly, Abbot Sigo's rights against Bérard's second argument, he might have implicitly undermined the position of Geoffrey Fuel himself. Count Geoffrey found himself in an immensely delicate political situation.

Just such a context helps then to explain the sense of urgency underlying the 1062 rule as formulated in Geoffrey le Barbu's court. There seem to have been two goals underlying this decision. First, it re-defined prescription in terms of territorial conquest, whereby the event of conquest was transformed into a measure of legal time. The vagueness regarding which conquest specifically the 1062 rule envisaged as the basis of prescription—1026 or 1044—may, considering the preceding argument, have been deliberate: it was the generalized phenomenon of conquest, rather than a specific act of conquest, that mattered. Second, the 1062 rule explicitly sought to avoid the creation of a quasi-precedent, betraying an awareness that however Geoffrey le Barbu's court decided with respect to Bérard's claim would have implications for other, similar types of challenge. It seems probable that the potential similar challenges were those of Geoffrey Fuel and Bouchard de l'Ile-Bouchard. If this interpretation is correct, it suggests at the very least a degree of political nous on the part of Geoffrey le Barbu. Regardless, when articulating its rule about prescription in 1062, Geoffrey le Barbu's court effectively stated that the Angevin count was not required to pronounce decisions in land claims arising from the

61 See Tracey L. Billado, 'The Politics of "Evil Customs" in Eleventh-Century Anjou' (PhD dissertation, Emory University: 2006), 48–57, 65–70. Geoffrey le Barbu's poor reputation extends to disastrous relations with the church, on which see Halphen, *Le comté d'Anjou*, 138–42; Guillot, *Le comte d'Anjou*, I, 106–9.

conquests of his predecessors, nor was he accountable for the consequences of such conquests.

When Olivier Guillot characterized the 1062 decision as 'extremely prudent', he had in mind the ramifications of the Angevin conquest into the Saumurois in the mid-to-late 1020s.[62] The preceding argument suggests that the rule was formulated just as much, if not more so, with Angevin expansion into the Touraine in mind, and the practical and very live problems concerning right in land that the conquest brought in its wake. If this interpretation is correct, then it also tempers Jacques Boussard's claims for the 'éviction brutale' conducted by Geoffrey Martel following the battle of Nouy in 1044, and his assertions about the relative ease of Martel's defeat of his rival, Thibaud III de Blois, and the permanence (*pérennité*) of the conquest.[63] If the articulation of a legal rule in 1062 was aimed just as much towards the fallout from 1044 as it was towards the conquest of 1026, then this implies that the legitimacy of Angevin expansion into the Touraine was still very much a hot topic in the early 1060s.[64]

More structurally, Bérard's case effectively blurs the line between politics and law. As Stephen White has stressed, the relationship between political conflict and legal dispute merits further exploration in attempting to understand further the processes of disputing in eleventh-century France.[65] One possible consequence of the intersection between politics and law might be the formulation of explicit legal rules, aiming to resolve, mask, or avoid the political dimensions of conflict. When it came to working out the politics of conquest, law—or at least the formulation of legal rules aimed at a level of generalized applicability—might have operated as a language and register for political practice. The stakes in framing rights in property following conquest might have incentivized courts like that which gathered in 1062 to develop a

---

62 Guillot, *Le comté d'Anjou*, I, 326.

63 Boussard, 'L'éviction', 148. Guillot, *Le comte d'Anjou*, I, 327–33 already nuanced Boussard's arguments by showing that most examples of confiscation identified by Boussard saw the seized properties move to a collateral branch of the same family, not to a complete outsider (as indeed may have been the case in the Saumurois).

64 Abbot Sigo (and Frédéric before him) had been a monk at the abbey of Marmoutier, near Tours, and retained close ties with the abbey of Marmoutier during his abbacy. Since Marmoutier's extensive holdings had been affected by the Angevin-Blésois conflicts, it is likely that Abbot Sigo was familiar with possible debates about the legitimacy of Angevin expansion into the Touraine through these ties. On the connection between Marmoutier and Saint-Florent, see William Ziezulewicz, 'Abbatial Elections at Saint Florent-de-Saumur (Ca. 950–1118)', *Church History* 57, no. 3 (1988), 289–97.

65 White, 'From Peace to Power', esp. 213, 215.

keen interest in the promulgation of rules, and to set benchmarks for disputing and legal practice more widely.

Bérard's case thus opens a window looking onto the perspective of a mid-eleventh-century court. It is essential to qualify this immediately by stating that we only see this perspective here because the expression of the court's rule was beneficial to the monks of Saint-Florent as well: it is, in effect, serendipitous that the interests of the monks and the activities of the court and its court-holder overlapped so neatly in this case. On one level, the rule was of course formulated to protect the interests of Abbot Sigo and the monks of Saint-Florent. But crucially, the rule was also articulated with the interests of the Angevin count—that is, the court-holder—firmly in mind, and with an eye towards a much wider political context that had little direct bearing on the interests of the monks of Saint-Florent as affected in this specific case. Whilst our perspective in this case—as in all eleventh-century cases—is constrained by the monastic disputants' point of view, we also therefore have a trace of the perspective of the court itself. The ability to point to privileged documentary moments where we can plausibly reconstruct the perspective of courts, independent of the disputants' view, is thus of prime importance.

In Guise of a Conclusion

Although a case study cannot be used to offer more general conclusions, the discussion of this essay can usefully frame some larger questions that would benefit from further research. One suggestion raised by Bérard's case is that the decisions made in courts, and the arguments court-holders or their judges made in order to rationalize those decisions, might have formed an important source of law and legal rules in eleventh-century western France. Why does it matter that courts might have operated as sources of law and legal rules? For a start, it helps to approach the function of courts differently from the immediate perspective of 'dispute processing', where the role of courts is to terminate disputes. Marc Galanter, in an article of 1981, distinguished between centripetal and centrifugal perspectives on courts.[66] 'Centripetal perspectives', for Galanter, refers to the idea that the court's function is to pull in disputes for settlement, to apply rules to cases and terminate disputes. A 'centrifugal perspective', conversely, draws attention to the ways courts diffuse information: 'Courts produce not only decisions, but messages [...] These messages

66 Marc Galanter, 'Justice in Many Rooms: Courts, Private Ordering, and Indigenous Law', *Journal of Legal Pluralism* 19, no. 1 (1981), 1–47.

are resources which parties and others use in envisioning, devising, pursuing, negotiating and vindicating claims (and in avoiding, defending and defeating them)'.[67] Such a statement is wholly consistent with the view sketched earlier that courts in eleventh-century western France served as privileged arenas of negotiation for disputants. The advantage of Galanter's centrifugal view of courts, however, is that it re-fixes our attention on those courts themselves, rather than exclusively on the disputants.[68] Courts, in this view, might be envisaged as legal broadcast towers, disseminating rules and information, in addition to serving as sites of dispute settlement (or negotiation).

The key issues here are agency and power; and how to reconstruct the agency of court-holders and the political community that gathered for the occasion of a court; and how to understand the interests of both court-holder and curial community. Viewing courts as sources of law helps us envisage this agency beyond the capacity to terminate disputes effectively—that is, beyond what I earlier termed the 'problem of non-enforcement'. The stakes of court-holders in the wider arena of disputing may have been to ensure control over the definition of rules, along with the categories and generalizing concepts that structured dispute itself.[69] From this perspective, the particular forms of settlement might have mattered less to court-holders than control over the conceptual framework in which settlement took place. Accordingly, the enforcement (or not) of judgment may be a less reliable indicator of the importance of eleventh-century courts and their contribution to the wider world of disputing. If the role of courts is approached, at least partially, in terms of their ability to articulate legal rules and to organize generalizing concepts, then we may have a way of re-thinking the longstanding and problematic question about the relationship between justice and the exercise of power, a relationship which could be characterised as control over the symbolic and normative field of dispute.[70] Not only might the legal rules formulated in these eleventh-century

---

67 Galanter, 'Justice', 13.

68 Galanter also outlined how his centrifugal view of courts can help us better understand disputant behaviour, particularly differences across status, class, and knowledge in how well disputants understand the messages emanating from courts. See also Galanter, 'Why the "Haves" Come Out Ahead: Speculations on the Limits of Social Change', *Law and Society Review* 9 (1974), 95–160.

69 This point owes much to Alice Taylor, 'Crime without Punishment: Medieval Scottish Law in Comparative Perspective', *Anglo-Norman Studies* 35 (2013), 287–304.

70 On power as an emerging topic in dispute studies (or rather, re-emerging), see White, 'From Peace to Power'; Warren C. Brown and Piotr Górecki, 'Where Conflict Leads: On the Present and the Future of Conflict Studies in the United States', in Brown and Górecki, *Conflicts in Medieval Europe*, 265–85; and Florian Mazel, 'Justice, société et pouvoir à

courts have served to enable the exercise of power, but, intriguingly, perhaps they also served as a focal point for resistance to the exercise of power.[71] Seeing courts as a source of law may help us then approach the vexed question of how political and legal authority during this period was structured, legitimated, and operated, and, most vexed of all, how it all changed.[72]

Works Cited

Manuscript Sources

Archives départementales de Indre-et-Loire H 332, no. 1.
Archives départementales de Indre-et-Loire H 332, no. 3.
Archives départementales de Indre-et-Loire H 332, no. 5.
Archives départementales de Maine-et-Loire H 2117, no. 3.
Bibliothèque nationale de France NAL 1930, 'Livre noir de Saint-Florent de Saumur'.

Printed Sources

Bachrach, Bernard. *Fulk Nerra, The Neo-Roman Consul, 987–1040*. Berkeley: 1993.

Barthélemy, Dominique. 'Les comtes, les sires, et les "nobles de châteaux" dans la Touraine du XIe siècle'. In *Campagnes médiévales: L'homme et son espace. Études offertes à Robert Fossier*, edited by Elisabeth Mornet, 439–53. Paris: 1995.

Barthélemy, Dominique. 'Une crise de l'écrit? Observations sur des actes de Saint-Aubin d'Angers (XIe siècle)'. *Bibliothèque de l'École des Chartes* 155 (1997): 95–117.

Barthélemy, Dominique. *La mutation féodale de l'an mil a-t-elle eu lieu? Servage et chevalerie dans la France des Xe et XIe siècles*. Paris: 1997.

Barthélemy, Dominique. *La société dans le comté de Vendôme de l'an mil au XIVe siècle*. Paris: 1993.

Barton, Richard E. *Lordship in the County of Maine, c. 890–1160*. Woodbridge: 2004.

Billado, Tracey L. 'The Politics of "Evil Customs" in Eleventh-Century Anjou'. PhD dissertation. Emory University: 2006.

Billado, Tracey L. 'Rhetorical Strategies and Legal Arguments: "Evil Customs" and Saint-Florent de Saumur, 979–1011'. In *Oral History of the Middle Ages: The Spoken*

l'époque féodale: Nouvelles perspectives. À propos de deux ouvrages récents', *Revue historique* 662, no. 2 (2012), 477–91.

71 Note here John Hudson, *The Oxford History of the Laws of England, Volume II: 871–1216* (Oxford: 2012), 4–5; and Hudson, 'Legal History', esp. 338–41.

72 See Chris Wickham, 'Public Court Practice: The Eighth and Twelfth Centuries Compared', in *Rechtsverständnis und Konfliktbewältigung: Gerichtliche und außergerichtliche Strategien im Mittelalter*, ed. Stefan Esders (Cologne: 2007), 17–30.

Word in Context, edited by Gerhard Jaritz and Michael Richter, 128–41. Krems: 2001.

Bloch, Marc. *Feudal Society*. Translated by L. A. Manyon. London: 1962.

Bongert, Yvonne. *Recherches sur les cours laïques du Xe au XIIIe siècle*. Paris: 1949.

Bossy, John, ed. *Disputes and Settlements: Law and Human Relations in the West*. Cambridge: 1983.

Boussard, Jacques. 'L'éviction des tenants de Thibaud de Blois par Geoffroy Martel, comte d'Anjou, en 1044'. *Le Moyen Âge* 69 (1963): 141–9.

Brown, Warren C. and Piotr Górecki, eds. *Conflict in Medieval Europe: Changing Perspectives on Society and Culture*. Aldershot: 2003.

Brown, Warren C. and Piotr Górecki. 'Where Conflict Leads: On the Present and the Future of Conflict Studies in the United States'. In *Conflict in Medieval Europe: Changing Perspectives on Society and Culture*, edited by Warren C. Brown and Piotr Górecki, 265–85. Aldershot: 2003.

Cartulaire de l'abbaye de Noyers. Edited by Casamir de Chevalier. Tours: 1872.

Cartulaire de l'abbaye de Saint-Aubin d'Angers. 3 vols. Edited by Bertrand de Broussillon. Paris: 1903.

'Cartularium monasterii Beatae Mariae Andegavensis'. In *Archives d'Anjou*, vol. 3. Edited by Paul Marchegay. Angers: 1854.

Chartes originales antérieures à 1121 conservées en France. Edited by Cédric Giraud, Jean-Baptiste Renault, and Benoît-Michel Tock. Nancy and Orléans: 2010. Online at <http://www.cn-telma.fr/originaux/index/>, accessed 26/6/2017.

Cheyette, Fredric L. 'Suum cuique tribuere'. *French Historical Studies* 6, no. 3 (1970): 287–299.

Davis, Wendy and Paul Fouracre, eds. *The Settlement of Disputes in Early Medieval Europe*. Cambridge: 1986.

Duby, Georges. 'The Evolution of Judicial Institutions: Burgundy in the Tenth and Eleventh Centuries'. In Georges Duby, *The Chivalrous Society*, trans. Cynthia Postan, 15–58. Berkeley: 1977.

Esmark, Kim et al., eds. *Disputing Strategies in Medieval Scandinavia*. Leiden and Boston: 2013.

Galanter, Marc. 'Justice in Many Rooms: Courts, Private Ordering, and Indigenous Law'. *Journal of Legal Pluralism* 19, no. 1 (1981): 1–47.

Galanter, Marc. 'Why the "Haves" Come Out Ahead: Speculations on the Limits of Social Change'. *Law and Society Review* 9 (1974): 95–160.

Geary, Patrick J. 'Living with Conflicts in a Stateless France: A Typology of Conflict Management Mechanisms, 1050–1200'. In Patrick J. Geary, *Living with the Dead in the Middle Ages*, 125–60. Ithaca and London: 1994.

Grand cartulaire de Fontevraud, vol. 1. Edited by Jean-Marc Bienvenu, Robert Favreau, and Georges Pons. Poitiers: 2000.

Guillot, Olivier. *Le comte d'Anjou et son entourage au XIe siècle*, 2 vols. Paris: 1972.

Guyotjeannin, Olivier. '"*Penuria scriptorum*": Le mythe de l'anarchie documentaire dans la France du Nord (X^e–première moitié du XIe siècle)'. *Bibliothèque de l'École des Chartes* 155 (1997): 11–44.

Halphen, Louis. *Le comté d'Anjou au XIe siècle*. Paris: 1906.

Halphen, Louis. 'La justice en France au XIe siècle. Région angevine'. *Revue historique* 77 (1901): 279–307.

Hudson, John. 'Legal History and the History of Disputes'. In *Disputing Strategies in Medieval Scandinavia*, edited by Kim Esmark et al., 333–41. Leiden and Boston: 2013.

Hudson, John. *The Oxford History of the Laws of England, Volume II: 871–1216*. Oxford: 2012.

Jessee, W. Scott. 'The Angevin Civil War and the Norman Conquest of 1066'. *The Haskins Society Journal: Studies in Medieval History* 3 (1991): 101–9.

Jessee, W. Scott. 'Urban Violence and the *Coup d'état* of Fulk le Rechin in Angers, 1067'. *The Haskins Society Journal: Studies in Medieval History* 7 (1995): 75–82.

Lauranson-Rosaz, Christian. 'Le débat sur la "mutation féodale": État de la question'. In *Europe around the Year 1000*, edited by Przemyslaw Urbancyzk, 11–40. Warsaw: 2001.

Lemesle, Bruno. *Conflits et justice au Moyen Âge. Normes, loi et résolution des conflits en Anjou aux XIe et XIIe siècles*. Paris: 2008.

Lemesle, Bruno. '"Ils donnèrent leur accord à ce jugement". Réflexions sur la contrainte judiciaire (Anjou, XIe–XIIe siècle)'. In *La justice en l'an mil*, Collection Histoire de la justice 15, 123–47. Paris: 2003.

Lemesle, Bruno. 'Les querelles avaient-elles une vocation sociale? Le cas des transferts fonciers en Anjou au XIe siècle'. *Le Moyen Âge* 115 (2009): 337–64.

Livre des serfs de Marmoutier. Edited by André Salmon. Tours: 1864.

Martindale, Jane. '"His Special Friend"? The Settlement of Disputes and Political Power in the Kingdom of the French (Tenth to Mid-Twelfth Century)'. *Transactions of the Royal Historical Society* 5, sixth series (1995): 21–57.

Mazel, Florian. *Féodalités, 888–1180*. Paris: 2010.

Mazel, Florian. 'Justice, société et pouvoir à l'époque féodale: Nouvelles perspectives. À propos de deux ouvrages récents'. *Revue historique* 662, no. 2 (2012): 477–91.

Mazel, Florian. 'Pouvoir aristocratique et Église aux Xe–XIe siècles. Retour sur la "Révolution féodale" dans l'œuvre de Georges Duby'. *Médiévales* 54 (2008): 137–52.

Miller, William Ian. 'Threat'. In *Feud, Violence and Practice: Essays in Medieval Studies in Honor of Stephen D. White*, edited by Belle S. Tuten and Tracey L. Billado, 9–27. Farnham: 2010.

Premier et second livres des cartulaires de l'abbaye Saint-Serge et Saint-Bach d'Angers (XIe et XIIe siècles). 2 vols. Edited by Yves Chauvin. Angers: 1997.

Le règlement des conflits au moyen âge. Actes des congrès de la Société des historiens médiévistes de l'enseignement supérieur public, 31e congrès, Angers, 2000. Paris: 2001.

Reynolds, Susan. 'The Emergence of Professional Law in the Long Twelfth Century'. *Law and History Review* 21, no. 2 (2003): 347–66.

Ruffini-Ronzani, Nicolas, and Jean-François Nieus. 'Société seigneuriale, réformes ecclésiales: Les enjeux documentaires d'une révision historiographique'. In Ecclesia in medio nationis: *Reflections on the Study of Monasticism in the Central Middle Ages/Réflexions sur l'étude du monachisme au Moyen Âge central*, edited by Steven Vanderputten and Brigitte Meijns, 77–100. Leuven: 2011.

Saché, Marc. *Inventaire sommaire des archives départementales antérieures à 1790, série H*, vol. 2, *Abbaye Saint-Florent-de-Saumur*. Angers: 1926.

Senséby, Chantal. 'Un aspect de la croissance: Le développement des bourgs aux confins du Poitou, de l'Anjou et de la Touraine (XIe et XIIe siècles)'. *Journal des savants* 1, no. 1 (1997): 59–98.

Senséby, Chantal. 'Une notice fausse du cartulaire de l'abbaye tourangelle de Noyers?'. *Bibliothèque de l'École des chartes* 155 (1997): 61–94.

Skoda, Hannah. 'A Historian's Perspective on the Present Volume'. In *Legalism: Anthropology and History*, edited by Paul Dresch and Hannah Skoda, 39–54. Oxford: 2012.

Taylor, Alice. 'Crime without Punishment: Medieval Scottish Law in Comparative Perspective'. *Anglo-Norman Studies* 35 (2013): 287–304.

Taylor, Alice. '*Lex Scripta* and the Problem of Enforcement: Anglo-Saxon, Welsh and Scottish Law Compared'. In *Legalism*, vol. 2: *Community and Justice*, edited by Fernanda Pirie and Judith Scheele, 47–74. Oxford: 2014.

Teunis, Henk. *The Appeal to the Original Status: Social Justice in Anjou in the Eleventh Century*. Hilversum: 2006.

Vezin, Jean. *Les scriptoria d'Angers au XIe siècle*. Paris: 1974.

West, Charles. *Reframing the Feudal Revolution: Political and Social Transformation between Marne and Moselle, c. 800–c. 1100*. Cambridge: 2013.

White, Stephen D. *Custom, Kinship, and Gifts to Saints: The* Laudatio parentum *in Western France, 1050–1150*. Chapel Hill: 1988.

White, Stephen D. *Feuding and Peace-Making in Eleventh-Century France*. Aldershot: 2005.

White, Stephen D. 'Feuding and Peace-Making in the Touraine around the Year 1100'. *Traditio* 42 (1986): 195–263.

White, Stephen D. 'From Peace to Power: The Study of Disputes in Medieval France'. In *Medieval Transformations: Texts, Power, and Gifts in Context*, edited by Esther Cohen and Mayke B. de Jong, 203–18. Leiden: 2001.

White, Stephen D. "Inheritances and Legal Arguments in Western France, 1050–1150'. *Traditio* 43 (1987): 55–103.

White, Stephen D. '"*Pactum … Legem Vincit et Amor Judicium*": The Settlement of Disputes by Compromise in Eleventh-Century Western France'. *The American Journal of Legal History* 22, no. 4 (1978): 281–308.

White, Stephen D. 'Proposing the Ordeal and Avoiding It: Strategy and Power in Western French Litigation, 1050–1110'. In *Cultures of Power: Lordship, Status, and Process in Twelfth-Century Europe*, edited by Thomas Bisson, 89–123. Philadelphia: 1995.

White, Stephen D. 'Tenth-Century Courts at Mâcon and the Perils of Structuralist History: Re-reading Burgundian Judicial Institutions'. In *Conflict in Medieval Europe: Changing Perspectives on Society and Culture*, edited by Warren C. Brown and Piotr Górecki, 37–68. Aldershot: 2003.

Wickham, Chris. 'Conclusion'. In *The Moral World of the Law*, edited by Peter Coss, 240–9. Cambridge: 2000.

Wickham, Chris. *Courts and Conflict in Twelfth-Century Tuscany*. Oxford: 2003.

Wickham, Chris. 'Public Court Practice: The Eighth and Twelfth Centuries Compared'. In *Rechtsverständnis und Konfliktbewältigung: Gerichtliche und außergerichtliche Strategien im Mittelalter*, edited by Stefan Esders, 17–30. Cologne: 2007.

Ziezulewicz, William. 'Abbatial Elections at Saint Florent-de-Saumur (Ca. 950–1118)'. *Church History* 57, no. 3 (1988): 289–97.

Ziezulewicz, William. 'An Argument for Historical Continuity: Low and Middle Vassal Families in the Eleventh-Century Saumurois'. *Medieval Prosopography* 8, no. 1 (1987): 93–110.

Ziezulewicz, William. 'La chronologie des abbés de Saint-Florent de Saumur au XIe siècle'. *Revue bénédictine* 108 (1998): 282–97.

CHAPTER 5

Standing up in Court: Gender and Genitalia in Fourteenth-Century Zurich

Jamie Page

Introduction: Strange Cases

In the introduction to her 1998 monograph *Fallen Bodies*, celebrated for its pathbreaking analyses of the medieval body in a variety of discursive registers, Dyan Elliot channels Carlo Ginzburg to reflect upon the notion that 'the superficially marginal is often imaginatively (and hence ideologically) central'. According to Elliot (and indeed Ginzburg), 'it is precisely in the anecdotal, the incidental, the idiosyncratic, that we often find the keys to unlocking much larger issues'.[1] For scholars accustomed to long days combing through registers of court records, the occasional idiosyncratic or 'strange' case—whether 'strange' because it reveals some procedural oddity, shows up a distinctive scribal feature, or, more often, offers a story of unusual behaviour—can exert a powerful attraction.[2] Strange cases are also largely to thank for the emergence of a distinct genre in the form of microhistory, though the latter's fascination with eccentricities and oddities has supplied ammunition to its critics, too.[3]

1 Dyan Elliot, *Fallen Bodies: Pollution, Sexuality & Demonology in the Middle Ages* (Philadelphia: 1999), 11.

2 This, of course, is a more general issue of interpretation affecting sources pertaining to deviancy. From one perspective, all such sources might be considered 'strange cases', because they concern behaviour which resulted in a court case precisely because it was not 'normal'.

3 See the summary and accompanying references in Elizabeth A. Clark, *History, Theory, Text: Historians and the Linguistic Turn* (Cambridge, MA and London: 2004), 75–79; and on microhistory, most recently, see *Journal of Medieval and Early Modern History* 47: 1 (January, 2017) *Special Issue: Microhistory and the Historical Imagination: New Frontiers*, ed. Thomas Robisheaux and Thomas V. Cohen, with István M. Szijártó. The use of atypical cases as an explanatory mechanism is certainly not restricted to microhistory, of course. In a chapter on gender and community in late medieval Europe, a major new overview of the period is explicit in its use of the 'wildly atypical' examples of Catherine of Siena and Margery Kempe to explore broad themes; see Chris Wickham, *Medieval Europe* (New Haven and London: 2016), 186–90 (and see, too, Wickham's comments on the 'fascination of the strange' in reference to microhistory, ibid., 7).

© KONINKLIJKE BRILL NV, LEIDEN, 2018 | DOI 10.1163/9789004366374_009

In what follows, focussing upon the specific environment of the late medieval German-speaking urban world, I would like to present a somewhat strange case from the free imperial city of Zurich, one which concerns the body and speaks to one of the key themes of the present volume: vengeance. In my interpretation of the case, whose strangeness lies partly in its procedural features and partly in the behaviour of at least one of the actors involved, I draw brief comparisons with ecclesiastical court cases concerning marriage and sexuality before proceeding to engage at greater length with evidence from popular fiction (a realm not short of oddities, either). On the same theme, it is worth noting at the outset that in legal historical circles Zurich is, itself, something of a strange case. When compared with other regions of medieval Europe famous for their rich legal archives, such as northern Italy or southern France, the cities of the German-speaking Empire are nearly devoid of surviving sets of criminal court records. Zurich, however, is an exception. There, within the canton archives, can be found a near-immaculate series of registers holding case records produced by the city council court (or *Ratsgericht*) running from 1376 until well into the sixteenth century. Although the archive remains only modestly exploited, it offers an unparalleled view of late medieval urban life and the practice of justice in a German-speaking city.[4] And it is in this archive that the record of the following dispute can be found:

In the first half of 1379, a certain Rudolf Abdorf made a complaint to the *Ratsgericht* about his neighbour, Heintz Wenginer.[5] In the record of the resulting investigation, Abdorf stated that Wenginer had claimed to have taken

4 Although not the earliest study of the Zurich *Ratsgericht*, the most important to date is certainly Susanna Burghartz's *Leib, Ehre und Gut. Delinquenz in Zürich Ende des 14. Jahrhunderts* (Zurich: 1990). Burghartz is also the author of an important article which explores the judicial function of the court and places it in the context of late medieval justice; see 'Disziplinierung oder Konfliktregelung? Zur Funktion städtischer Gerichte im Mittelalter: Das Zürcher Ratsgericht', *Zeitschrift für Historische Forschung* 16:4 (1989), 385–407. See also, more recently, Sibylle Malamud, *Die Ächtung des "Bösen". Frauen vor dem Zürcher Ratsgericht im späten Mittelalter (1400–1500)* (Zurich: 2003); and Susanne Pohl-Zucker, *Making Manslaughter: Process, Punishment and Restitution in Württemberg and Zurich, 1376–1700*. Medieval Law and Its Practice 22 (Leiden and Boston: 2017).

5 The relevant sections of the case record can be found at Staatsarchiv Zürich (hereafter StaZH), B VI 190, fols 175v, 194r/v, 195r/v, 241v, 242r. The small council which oversaw the daily business of city government was elected twice yearly, forming the so-called *Natalrat* and the *Baptismalrat*. The records of cases handled in any given year show only which sitting of the council dealt with them, making it possible to place them only within an approximate six-month date range.

his daughter Agnes in marriage—in other words, to have exchanged words of consent with her, followed by sexual intercourse. This seems to have been an unwise move on Wenginer's part, not least because his prospective father-in-law evidently had no liking for him, but also because Abdorf was a member of the city council. As such, he held a rotating seat on the judicial bench of the *Ratsgericht*. As the investigation record notes, the court decided to fine Wenginer 10 marks for having claimed to have married Abdorf's daughter, although leafing a little further into the register reveals that a significantly larger backstory lay behind this judgment.

In a series of complaints (*Klagen*) submitted to the court by Abdorf at some point in the first half of 1379 (unfortunately no more precise dates can be attached to these actions), he claimed that Wenginer had sought to have his marriage to Agnes recognised by the ecclesiastical court in Constance, within whose jurisdiction Zurich fell. In the attempt to prove that the couple had had sex, and thus that they were legally married, Wenginer had allegedly described their sexual encounters before the judges in Constance, details of which, Abdorf said, were now set down in a sealed letter from Constance which held Wenginer's testimony. In no fewer than six consecutive complaints, each apparently submitted individually to the Zurich *Ratsgericht*, Abdorf gave his own, astonishingly vivid account of the sexual relationship between his daughter and Wenginer. In this testimony, Abdorf stated baldly that Wenginer had 'fucked' his daughter (*sie ... geminnt*) on numerous occasions and in various locations, almost always in the dark, and once even on a Sunday.[6] On each such occasion, Abdorf claimed, he had penetrated her repeatedly with his 'standing penis' (*stendem zagel*) so often and so hard that his 'semen had flowed into her vagina' (*in ir fut sinen samen liess*), the full 'shame and unchastity' (*schand und unkischheit*) of which had been revealed to the court in Constance.[7]

Following these complaints, in addition to fining Wenginer for his behaviour, the city council created a new law in 1379 which forbade marriages contracted against the will of parents, on pain of a fine of 20 marks (a remarkably

6 *Minne* is usually translated in Middle and Early New High German as 'love', specifically in a courtly context. By the later period, however, the verb *minnen* could be used in the vulgar sense of 'to fuck', whereby Grimm's dictionary offers the Latin translation *futare*; *Deutsches Wörterbuch von Jacob Grimm und Wilhelm Grimm*, s.v. *minnen*, <www.woerterbuchnetz.de/DWB?lemma=minnen>, accessed 18/5/2015.

7 Whilst the term *fut* (an ancestor of the modern German *Fotze*) is commonly used in records of the *Ratsgericht* as a vulgar expression, and hence might be translated into English as 'cunt', I have chosen here to translate it as 'vagina' because of the technical sense in which it was used by Abdorf throughout the case in specific references to sexual penetration.

high sum, which was twice that for manslaughter)[8]—an action which illustrates the apparent influence of Abdorf within the council and the sympathy of its members to his situation.[9] But this was not the end of the matter. In the second half of 1379, Abdorf resumed his legal campaign against Wenginer with a new series of complaints to the *Ratsgericht*. In the intervening period, Abdorf seems to have changed his mind about what had really happened between Wenginer and his daughter, and now seemed to doubt whether they had actually had sex—or, perhaps, sought merely to cast doubt on it in the forum of the court. Now, Abdorf's chief grievance centred on the fact that because of Wenginer's claims of sex with Agnes, the court in Constance had ordered her to undergo a physical examination to ascertain whether or not she was a virgin.[10] Abdorf described how three women had examined her and decided that she was, indeed, a virgin. In another tortuous twist in the ongoing dispute, Abdorf said that Wenginer had responded to this setback by claiming that a certain Rudolf Brentschink had administered medicine to Agnes which had closed up her vagina, with the result that the women in Constance had been unable to see that she had had sex with him. Further to this, Wenginer had allegedly asked a judge that Agnes be taken away from Brentschink and his sister, as well as her own father, and placed in a house with honourable people to be watched over and bathed until she could be examined once again by seven women. This second examination had apparently taken place, and when it was confirmed once and for all that Agnes was 'innocent of all men' (*aller manne unschuldig*), she received permission from the court in Constance to enter an appropriate religious order (*orden*).

A final act to the case pays testament to Wenginer's persistence in his attempts to marry Agnes Abdorf. Following an unsuccessful request to have his case heard by the court of the Archbishop of Mainz, in the first half of 1380 he was the subject of one more complaint by her father, in which the latter claimed that an unnamed nun had knocked on Abdorf's door, asking for a light. When Agnes looked out, Wenginer was in the street, saying 'Nessli! Nessli! Let me in!'[11]

---

8 Burghartz, *Leib, Ehre und Gut*, 172.

9 The influence of another case, involving the proposed marriage of a daughter from the wealthy Kilchmater family in 1378, can also be traced in the creation of the new law; for a discussion of the case see Burghartz, *Leib, Ehre und Gut*, 174–6.

10 On medical examinations in the context of marriage cases see Ludwig Schmugge, *Ehen vor Gericht. Paare der Renaissance vor dem Papst* (Berlin: 2008), 165–6.

11 'Nessli' is a diminutive form of 'Agnes', and appears here to have been a nickname.

Honour and Vengeance

Abdorf v. Wenginer, as we might label it, is like no other case in the records of the Zurich *Ratsgericht* from this period. Given its focus upon marital issues, we might wonder immediately why the Zurich city council court saw the putative marriage of Wenginer and Agnes Abdorf as a matter for its attention; after all, the matter had previously been handled in the proper judicial forum of the ecclesiastical court in Constance.[12] Municipal courts did, in fact, sometimes become involved in marriage disputes in this period, although the majority of the evidence for their doing so can be found from the 1400s. Secular judges could not determine the fundamental status of a marriage, but could intervene in other ways to discipline behaviour which threatened or undermined one.[13] Domestic violence was one such issue, although it was rarely seen as a matter for the courts unless it was exceptionally serious; Sibylle Malamud even points towards fifteenth-century cases from Zurich in which men seemed to reject the right of the council to intervene in their private affairs when it tried to protect wives whom they had beaten.[14] A more common scenario saw courts intervene to encourage individuals who did not fulfil marital obligations to do so, for example in scenarios where one party reneged upon a promise of marriage. In Zurich this behaviour could earn a fine of 10 marks.[15] Such cases tended overwhelmingly to be brought by women who had been abandoned by a male partner after a promise of marriage, wherein lies the suspicion that such promises were used to persuade women to engage in sex. The case of Agnes Abdorf and Heintz Wenginer, however, seems to turn this common scenario on its head, whereby the putative husband sought to have a marriage confirmed after sex had allegedly taken place between the couple.

12 On marriage law and courts, see the essays in *Regional Variations in Matrimonial Law and Custom in Europe, 1150–1600*, ed. Mia Korpiola (Leiden and Boston: 2011), particularly the survey of research and discussion of methodology in Charles Donohue Jr.'s contribution to the volume, 'Comparative Approaches to Marriage in the Later Middle Ages', 289–316. More recently, see also Ruth Mazo Karras, *Unmarriages: Women, Men, and Sexual Unions in the Middle Ages* (Philadelphia: 2012), especially chapter 4, 'On the Margins of Marriage', 165–208.

13 Schmugge, *Ehen vor Gericht*, 183.

14 We can also assume, as does Malamud in the case of fifteenth-century Zurich, that many marital disputes were settled by private mediation amongst families; see Malamud, *Die Ächtung des "Bösen"*, 216–7.

15 Arthur Bauhofer, 'Zürich und die geistliche Gerichtsbarkeit', *Zeitschrift für schweizerische Geschichte / Revue d'histoire suisse* 16:1 (1936), 1–35 at 20.

More remarkable, however, is the depiction of sex in the case, a factor which distinguishes it from every other I have been able to find in the archive. References to sex are by no means unknown in the registers of the Zurich *Ratsgericht*, even if the city council did not become seriously interested in prosecuting immoral sexual behaviour (under the general heading of *Unzucht*) until well into the 1400s, but for the late fourteenth and early fifteenth centuries no other case survives in which sexual intercourse between a couple is portrayed in such close detail.[16] Commenting on the case, Susanna Burghartz points out that Abdorf's behaviour seems to go entirely against his interests.[17] Why, if he objected to Wenginer as a potential son-in-law, did he choose to describe in such painstaking detail a series of acts which could have created a binding marriage between his daughter and Wenginer? Moreover, was it not deeply shameful for Abdorf to lay bare the intimate details of his daughter's sexual behaviour before a chamber of his peers, men whom he knew well, and upon whose esteem his own honour depended?

If, as seems probable, Heintz Wenginer was both a younger man and one lacking in the kind of political and social clout to make him a suitable son-in-law, then his going behind Abdorf's back to marry his daughter would have constituted a serious infringement of the senior man's honour. As is often true of legal cases involving women, Agnes Abdorf's own position is obscured because of the mediating influence of a male relative.[18] Although she did not initiate judicial action as an independent party (which women could certainly do in the *Ratsgericht*, so long as they had a male supporter for their testimony), she is named alongside her father as a complainant, and may thus have been present in court when the descriptions of her relationship with Wenginer were read out. Whether or not she was in court, we can only imagine what she thought of the affair, and how she reacted to the damage to her own honour.

Honour, indeed, together with class and gender, was at the heart of this conflict. Honour (*ere*, as it appears in fourteenth- and fifteenth-century sources)

---

16 *Unzucht* (literally, 'undiscipline') is a general term which could be applied to a range of sexually transgressive behaviours, though especially to adultery and clandestine prostitution (suspected or actual), which increasingly attracted the attention of the *Ratsgericht* throughout the fifteenth century; see Malamud, *Die Ächtung des "Bösen"*, 285–96.

17 Burghartz, *Leib, Ehre und Gut*, 177 and 294, n. 44.

18 On the problems of recovering women's voices from the archives, see Jeremy Goldberg, 'Echoes, Whispers, Ventriloquisms: On Recovering Women's Voices from the Court of York in the Later Middle Ages', in *Women, Agency and the Law, 1300–1700*, ed. Bronach Kane and Fiona Williamson (London: 2013), 31–41.

was at the heart of social relations in late medieval urban life,[19] an unwritten code which, in close conjunction with the concept of city peace (*Stadtfrieden*), formed the basis of the legal community (*Rechtsgemeinschaft*) of the city.[20] In Zurich, the *Ratsgericht* was one of a number of courts which sought to uphold the city peace and letter of the town law (the so-called *Richtebrief*, whose earliest version survives from 1304).[21] Its role has been characterised as a forum for the resolution of honour disputes between members of the urban population, and it was not unheard-of for members of the social and political elite, and even members of the city council, to appear in cases themselves. In this instance, Heintz Wenginer seems to have tried to keep the matter of his alleged marriage to Agnes Abdorf firmly within the jurisdiction of the Constance church court, and does not appear to have been present himself in the *Ratsgericht* when the details of his relationship with Agnes were revealed. This can be inferred from the fact that he made no complaint (*Klage*) of his own to counter the claims made by Abdorf, a common response between disputing parties in the *Ratsgericht*. It was Abdorf who was instrumental in making this a personal dispute between himself and his aspiring son-in-law, one negotiated on home

19 There exists a very considerable body of historical and anthropological literature on honour, whilst the concept has also had an important role in the study of premodern Germany and Switzerland, in which Zurich has also played a significant part. Important contributions include Martin Dinges, 'Die Ehre als Thema der Stadtgeschichte. Eine Semantik im Übergang vom Ancien Régime zur Moderne', *Zeitschrift für Historische Forschung* 16 (1989), 409–40; Katharina Simon-Muscheid, 'Gewalt und Ehre im spätmittelalterlichen Handwerk am Beispiel Basels', *Zeitschrift für Historische Forschung* 18 (1991), 1–31; Burghartz, *Leib, Ehre, und Gut*; *Verletzte Ehre*; *Ehrkonflikte in Gesellschaften des Mittelalters und der frühen Neuzeit*, ed. Klaus Schreiner and Gerd Schwerhoff (Cologne: 1995); Hillay Zmora, *State and Nobility in Early Modern Germany: The Knightly Feud in Franconia, 1440–1567* (Cambridge: 1998); *Ehre und Recht. Ehrkonzepte, Ehrverletzungen und Ehrverteidigungen vom späten Mittelalter bis zur Moderne*, ed. Sylvia Kesper-Biermann, Ulrike Ludwig and Alexandra Ortmann (Magdeburg: 2011). See also Pohl-Zucker, *Making Manslaughter*.

20 On notions of 'legal community' in Zurich, see Burghartz, *Leib, Ehre und Gut*, 47–51. For the broader context of urban law in German-speaking regions, see the relevant sections of Eberhard Isenmann's encyclopaedic *Die deutsche Stadt im Mittelalter: Stadtgestalt, Recht, Verfassung, Stadtregiment, Kirche, Gesellschaft, Wirtschaft* (Cologne, 2nd rev. ed: 2014), 133–278.

21 On the *Richtebrief*, and for an edition of the text, see *Zürcher Richtebrief*. Die Rechtsquellen des Kantons Zürich. Neue Folge. Erster Teil, erste Reihe, erster Band, ed. Daniel Bitterli (Basel: 2011). On the legal and constitutional basis of the city see Hans-Jörg Gilomen, 'Innere Verhältnisse der Stadt Zürich 1300–1500', in *Geschichte des Kantons Zürich*, ed. Niklaus Flüeler and Marianne Flüeler-Grauwiler, vol 1: *Frühzeit bis Spätmittelalter* (Zurich: 1995), 336–89 at 377–86.

turf in Zurich, and in a court in which he had acted as a judge. In doing so, given the apparent weakness of his position at the outset of the case, he seems to have had vengeance foremost in mind: seemingly having accepted the fact that Wenginer and his daughter had already had sex, and had thus undermined his honour, he sought through his actions to reciprocate the damage with whatever weapons were at his disposal.

Vengeance, then, is key to the reading of the first round of litigation in the Abdorf-Wenginer case, which will form the focus of my discussion. As an act of vengeance, Abdorf's actions can be seen in strategic terms as a means of damaging the honour of an opponent who had undermined his own, thereby making the best of a bad hand at a point in time at which he seems to have accepted that an ideal outcome—the prevention of a marriage between Wenginer and his daughter—was increasingly unlikely, if not impossible.

This reading depends on two assumptions: firstly, that Abdorf was acting of his own free will in pursuing his case—in other words, he was under no external pressure or coercion—and secondly, that he did so with a good understanding of the court and the likely response to his testifying strategy. The court evidently offered a sympathetic forum for Abdorf's complaint, not least because its judges (his own colleagues) found in his favour—an outcome he probably anticipated—but also because the council moved swiftly in the aftermath of the case to pass a new law hindering individuals from marrying against the will of their parents. The court thus seems to have acknowledged not only that Abdorf had a legitimate complaint, but also that his experience highlighted a pressing need to introduce new legislation. Moreover, as a judge in the court himself, Abdorf might well have known precisely what he was doing and how his actions would be perceived. In the absence of a body of professional advocates in Zurich, a feature of the *Ratsgericht* which becomes evident only in the mid- to late 1400s, Abdorf and his fellow judges were probably the closest thing to expert litigators to be found in Zurich at the time; Abdorf could thus plan and execute a strategy which he assumed had a good chance of success.

If Abdorf was acting strategically, then how was his strategy intended to work, and what did he hope to achieve? Unfortunately, the lack of a surviving set of procedural rules for the Zurich *Ratsgericht* for this period means that we cannot say much about the procedural context in which he presented his case, although in any event the case itself appears to be unique within the records of the court, and was enough of a novelty to result in the creation of a new law. Moreover, judicial practice in the *Ratsgericht* was grounded to a large extent in social conventions of honour, and saw judges acting upon their discretion to determine whether an injury to the honour of a complainant (or of the city itself) had taken place, and where punishment might justifiably be administered.[22] Given the fundamental importance of honour in everyday life, we can thus look to a wider frame of reference in trying to interpret Abdorf's behaviour. Here, evidence from popular fiction offers one such frame.

We have long become accustomed to the notion of fictionality within premodern witness narratives. As Natalie Zemon Davis's now-classic work on the subject has been instrumental in demonstrating, the ability to tell believable stories in court depended partly upon a litigant's ability to appeal to established forms of storytelling that could transmit the effect of truth.[23] In a recent and important book, Frances Dolan reaffirms the force of Davis's now nearly thirty-year-old insights in a stridently argued chapter on premodern depositions and historical practice, concluding, 'If there is fiction in the archives, literary criticism needs to be there as well'.[24] The kind of reading practices proposed by Davis and reaffirmed by Dolan, ones with an awareness of fictional contexts, have also been associated with the 'textualist' approach that characterised the New Historicist movement.[25] Such an approach does not collapse the distinction between fictional and non-fictional narratives, but rather regards both as products of a shared environment, and thus as representative of a shared set of meanings.[26]

These approaches shape my own interpretation of the Abdorf case, whose meanings are concerned primarily with honour and gender. I argue that at the

22 Rumour of a crime committed where no witness came forward, which could be interpreted as an injury to the honour of the city, could trigger an investigation launched by the council known as a *Nachgang* (from *nachgehen*, 'to pursue'), which bore similarities to the process of inquisition in its use of witness testimony. See Burghartz, *Leib, Ehre und Gut*, 61–66.

23 See Natalie Zemon Davis, *Fiction in the Archives: Pardon Tales and their Tellers in Sixteenth-Century France* (Stanford: 1987).

24 Frances Dolan, *True Relations: Reading, Literature, and Evidence in Seventeenth-Century England* (Philadelphia: 2013), 153.

25 On the 'textualist' approach see the remarks of Louise A. Montrose in 'Professing the Renaissance: The Poetics and Politics of Culture', in *The New Historicism*, ed. H. Aram Veeser (London and New York: 1989), 15–36, at 20; and Hayden White, 'New Historicism: A Comment', in the same volume, 293–302, at 295. Indispensable in this context is Stephen Greenblatt, *Renaissance Self-Fashioning: From More to Shakespeare* (Chicago, 2nd ed: 2005); and one of Greenblatt's signature essays, in which he discusses what he terms the 'conditions of representation' which are the object of the textualist approach discussed above: see 'Fiction and Friction', in *Reconstructing Individualism: Autonomy, Individuality, and the Self in Western Thought*, ed. Thomas C. Heller, Morton Sosna, and David E. Wellbery (Stanford: 1986), 30–52, at 46.

26 Stephen Greenblatt also calls this by the more elegant name of 'cultural poetics'; see *Renaissance Self-Fashioning*, 4–5.

moment in the case when Abdorf related the details of his daughter's sexual relationship with Wenginer to the court, he was seeking primarily to denigrate the honour (and with it, the masculinity) of his putative son-in-law, a means of 'winning' in the *Ratsgericht*. His focus on the younger man's penis in this part of his testimony can be seen as an act of sexual objectification, one which upset a normative model of sex that positioned men as sexual agents, and that violated a set of gendered expectations for the political elite in which excessive lust in men was frowned upon. To suggest how Wenginer's penis could have signified in such a way (or rather, have been *made* to signify), I draw upon a Middle High German comic narrative (*Märe*) known as 'The Nuns' Tournament' ('Das Nonnenturnier'). The story, whose plot is discussed in more depth below, focusses heavily upon the fate of a sentient penis which becomes detached from its owner, with riotous consequences when it makes an appearance in a nunnery. Edith Wenzel sees this story and others like it as part of a late medieval discourse about the relationships between person, sexuality, and gender relations, and about correct and incorrect love (*Minne*).[27] This, as I aim to show, was a discourse also determined in courtrooms like that of the Zurich *Ratsgericht*.

'With His Manly, Stiff Penis'

Figure 5.1 shows a page within the case record in which Abdorf laid out in detail how Wenginer had, on a number of occasions, visited and *geminnt* (fucked) his daughter Agnes. The visual impact of the record (each break in the text denotes a separate complaint describing an act, or series of acts) pays testament to the wantonness and persistence of Wenginer's behaviour, and seems, almost in a performative sense, to mimic the repeated penetrations of Agnes by Wenginer's own penis. The latter is is described on several occasions as a '*mannlichen ragenden zagel*' (manly, stiff penis), with which he '*die fut uff tett also ver er mocht*' (opened up the vagina as much as he wished), and from which '*sin manlichen samen in si liess*' (he let his manly seed into her).[28]

27 Edith Wenzel, '*Zers* und *fud* als literarische Helden. Zum "Eigenleben" von Geschlechtsteilen in mittelalterlicher Literatur', in *Körperteile. Eine kulturelle Anatomie*, ed. Claudia Benthien and Christoph Wulf (Reinbek bei Hamburg: 2001), 274–93, at 287.

28 *Zagel*, here, is translated similarly to *fut* above in a technical sense as 'penis' rather than a vulgar slang equivalent such as 'cock' or 'dick'. *Zagel* is used relatively less often in the records of the Ratsgericht than *zers* to mean 'penis' (though note the use of both *zers* and *zagel* in 'Das Nonnenturnier' below). Like the modern German *Schwanz*, probably the most common colloquial term for 'penis', *zagel* also means 'tail'.

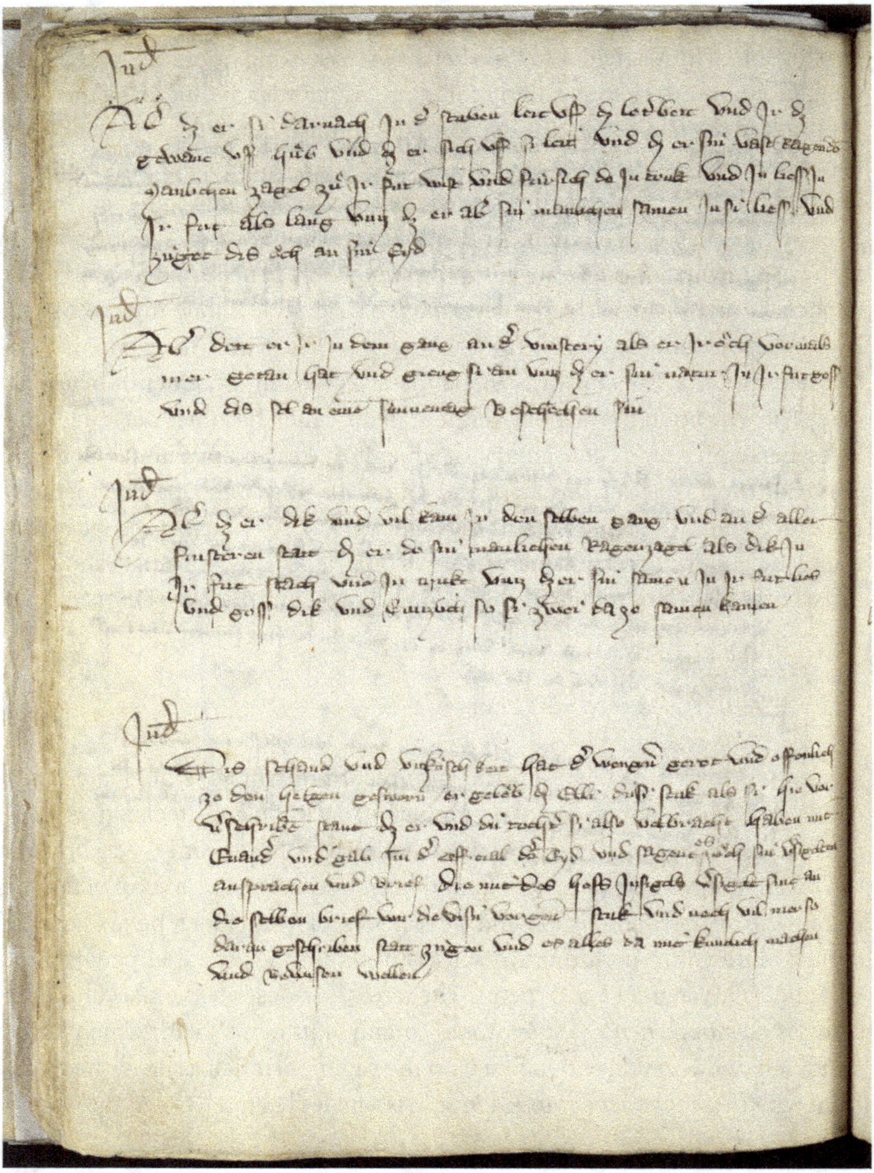

FIGURE 5.1 *Rudolf Abdorf's complaints to the Zurich Ratsgericht. Staatsarchiv Zürich B VI 190, f. 194 v.*

PHOTO CREDIT: JAMIE PAGE.

The word *ragend* stands out in particular: like *stendem* ('standing', which also appears), it can be used to mean 'protruding' (in modern German, *ragen* can also mean 'to loom' or 'to tower over'), but also has the more physical connotation of 'becoming stiff'.[29] Wenginer himself is described as having '*stach und in truckt*' (stabbed/pricked and penetrated) Agnes with it, and his semen as having '*goss*' (gushed) into her, '*dik und gantzlich*' (greatly and completely).

How Abdorf knew about any of this, or how he knew enough to describe his daughter's relationship with Wenginer in such detail, is quite difficult to say. His testimony was certainly not an attempt to document every single time his daughter had had sex with Wenginer. Although he pointed to a few specific occasions on which the pair had done so (including on a Sunday), and several different locations, including in a dark corridor and in a bed, he also said that Wenginer had come to her in the same dark corridor 'a great deal' (*dik und vil*).[30] He also described a range of actions on Wenginer's part, including opening Agnes's vagina (*die fut uff tett*) with his penis, pushing his penis towards her (*zu ir fut wist*), pushing his penis into her (*in ir fut trukt*), and ejaculating inside her (*in ir fut sinen samen liess*).[31] Again, however, this does not seem to have been an attempt to catalogue every type of sexual act between the pair. Rather, the impression is of Abdorf trying to create a scene (or, in fact, a series of scenes) of overwhelmingly gratuitous lust on Wenginer's part in order to communicate the fullest possible sense of the 'shame and unchastity' of his actions, actions which, he believed, had already been recounted before the ecclesiastical court of Constance.[32] Nor was Agnes Abdorf spared responsibility for this shameful behaviour. Although her reported behaviour conforms to gendered models of sex which constructed men as the active partners and placed women in a passive role, her own willing participation is implied in references to her placing her arms around Wenginer's neck and hanging on to him (*vieng si im den hals mit beiden armen und hanget im also an dem hals*).[33] Did she have a role in shaping Abdorf's narrative by relating to him what had happened? If so, what were the circumstances in which she revealed to her father what had happened?

29 See *Schweizerisches Idiotikon Digital* vol. VI, 716, col. 717: <https://digital.idiotikon.ch/idtkn/id6.htm#!page/60715/mode/2up>, accessed 18/5/2017.

30 StaZH, B VI 190, 194v.

31 StaZH, B VI 190, 194r/v. Note: these actions do not occur in the case record in the escalating sense given above; this reflects my own ordering of the terms.

32 StaZH, B VI 190, 194v.

33 StaZH, B VI 190, 194r. On gendered models of sex, see Ruth Mazo Karras, *Sexuality in Medieval Europe: Doing Unto Others* (New York: 2005), 3–4.

None of these questions is fully answerable, but nor do I want to push them much further than this. Rather, I am interested in the qualities of the narrative constructed by Abdorf in court, particularly in its positioning of subject and object, and how this created a certain viewpoint upon the scenes being narrated. Here, a useful comparison may be made with cases from a court whose records are more familiar to Anglophone scholars writing on the history of crime and deviancy, namely the ecclesiastical court of York.[34] One such case concerns a certain John Skathelok, who found himself the object of the court's attention in 1432 when his wife initiated legal action to annul their marriage on grounds of impotence. To establish proof that Skathelok was unable to achieve an erection, he was required to undergo what can only have been the excruciating experience of semi-public examination (the venue was a room above a pub) by a group of women identified by Jeremy Goldberg as prostitutes.[35] Their task was to incite him to sexual arousal by fondling his penis and testicles, exposing their breasts, and talking dirty.[36] Their efforts were a resounding failure: according to the record, John's penis remained little more than 'an empty intestine of mottled skin'. A second man in a similar predicament was John Marche. He, too, underwent a physical examination for impotence at the behest of the York church court, this time in 1441, and in the guildhall of the fraternity of St John the Baptist. Like Skathelok, Marche was unable to produce more than the appearance of 'white, dead, empty skin' despite the best efforts of a certain Joan Savage to excite him.[37]

In cases such as these, Goldberg suggests that judicial narratives could take on a voyeuristic, even pornographic quality—that is, they had the effect of reducing sexual subjects to the status of objects for the gratification of viewers.[38] In the instance he describes, the reduction of the scene to a form

---

34 On cases of impotence in marriage cases brought to the papal court, see Schmugge, *Ehen vor Gericht*, 157–66. See too F. J. G. Pedersen, 'Privates on Parade: Impotence Cases as Evidence for Medieval Gender', in *Law and Private Life in the Middle Ages: Proceedings of the Sixth Carlsberg Academy Conference on Medieval Legal History 2009*, ed. P. Andersen, M. Münster-Swendsen and H. Vogt (Copenhagen: 2011), 81–103.

35 See Jeremy Goldberg, 'John Skathelok's Dick: Voyeurism and "Pornography" in Late Medieval England', in *Medieval Obscenities*, ed. Nicola F. McDonald (York: 2006), 105–23.

36 Although most discussions of Skathelok do not acknowledge him as a victim of sexual violation, it is certainly possible to see him in this way (as it is, indeed, for Agnes Abdorf, who also underwent a sexual examination possibly against her will). I am grateful to Jana Hunter for alerting me to this reading of Skathelok's case.

37 Bronach Kane, *Impotence and Virginity in the Late Medieval Ecclesiastical Court of York*, Borthwick Papers 114 (York: 2008), 5, 9–10.

38 Goldberg, 'John Skathelok's Dick', 106.

of pornography depends upon the particular circumstances of the case and the involvement of sex workers, who drew on vocational skills in the attempt to arouse Skathelok.[39] In Goldberg's reading, 'the women, in this sense, were providing another professional, because paid, service, offering the court the vicarious pleasure of pornography rather than the actual carnal pleasures otherwise purchased by their clients'.[40] The scenes described were, moreover, in Bronach Kane's words, 'an apparent affront to [...] masculinity',[41] in which each man failed manifestly to respond to the demands to 'show his manhood if he were a man'.[42]

In seeking to draw comparisons with these English cases I do not mean to imply that Abdorf's strategy was an attempt to create sexual gratification for his audience; rather, from the analyses of Goldberg and Kane I take the idea that judicial narratives could create particular configurations of subject and object, and that these had implications for gender. In these instances, the narrative positioning of John Skathelok and John Marche as objects of voyeurism underlined the failure of masculinity which was linked to impotence. The court, like the settings in which each man originally underwent examination, thus became a testing-ground for manhood, in which the loss of sexual subjectivity resulted, for each individual, from a failure to 'prove himself a man'. To explore further the implications of this loss of sexual subjectivity, I now turn to the evidence of fiction.

Symbolic Castration, Grotesque Symbolism

The southern German-speaking cities of the Empire saw a boom in manuscript ownership and the production and circulation of texts from a wide variety of genres in the late Middle Ages, including fictional genres.[43] One common vehicle for transmission of popular literature amongst political and economic elites was the compilation manuscript (*Sammelhandschrift*), whose examples

39 In contrast, Ludwig Schmugge suggests that procurators in marriage courts often had difficulty in describing in precise anatomical terms physical impediments to women's ability to consummate a marriage, the reason for which he suggests lay in their fear of becoming 'too pornographic'; see Schmugge, *Ehen vor Gericht*, 164.

40 Goldberg, 'John Skathelok's Dick', 119.

41 Kane, 'Impotence and Virginity', 5.

42 Goldberg, 'John Skathelok's Dick', 119.

43 Hugo Kuhn, *Entwürfe zu einer Literatursystematik des Spätmittelalters* (Tübingen: 1980), 83. See also the discussion in Thomas Cramer, *Geschichte der deutschen Literatur im Spätmittelalter* (Munich: 1990), 11–12.

typically contained a range of texts of different types, from comic or didactic verse tales grouped under the heading of *Mären* to exempla, assorted lyrics, and other, longer narratives with their roots in classical stories.[44] In southern German-speaking regions of the Empire, a number of well-known surviving compilation manuscripts are associated with larger cities such as Augsburg and Nuremberg, where ownership by wealthy families has helped to preserve them. Zurich was also a centre of literary culture, albeit not on the same scale, though it was the location for the production in the early fourteenth century of the famous and richly illustrated Manesse Codex, the most comprehensive surviving collection of Middle High German ballads and epigrammatic poetry.[45]

For urban audiences, the consumption of popular literature through reading or public performance offered entertainment as well as the opportunity for reflection upon pressing issues, which were often presented in an explicitly urban setting. Within the surviving corpus of *Mären*, the themes of marriage and sexuality are represented especially strongly. One such story, which has become well-known and survives in an early fifteenth-century manuscript, is known as 'Das Nonnenturnier', 'The Nuns' Tournament'.[46] Alongside several other texts the tale has been placed by Hanns Fischer within a sub-genre of so-called *Priapeia*, stories in which genitalia feature centrally within the narrative, sometimes as literary characters themselves.[47] These stories have also been grouped into a subcategory of stories which feature the phenomenon of

44 These generic boundaries are not as discrete as I present them here; the term *Märe*, in particular, has been defined in a number of ways. The classic work on the latter is Hanns Fischer, *Studien zur deutschen Märendichtung* (Tübingen: 1968); issues of genre are discussed at 29–92. For a more recent extended analysis of short fictional genres, see Klaus Grubmüller, *Die Ordnung, der Witz und das Chaos. Eine Geschichte der europäischen Novellistik im Mittelalter: Fabliau—Märe—Novelle* (Tübingen: 2006).

45 On the Codex Manesse, so named for the Manesse family from the city, see Cramer, *Geschichte der deutschen Literatur*, 22–24.

46 An original handwritten heading refers to it as '*Der turney von dem czers*' 'The Tournament of the Penis'. The manuscript in question is Karlsruhe, Landesbibl., Cod. K 408. For a full description and list of critical literature, see its online entry in *Handschriftencensus* here: <http://www.handschriftencensus.de/4208>, accessed 18/5/2017. For an edition of the text and facing modern German translation, see *Novellistik des Mittelalters, Märendichtung*, ed. Klaus Grubmüller (Frankfurt am Main: 1996), 944–77.

47 On *Priapeia* see Fischer, *Studien zur deutschen Märendichtung*, 97 and, at greater length (and specifically on 'Das Nonnenturnier'), Gerd Dicke, 'Mären-Priapeia. Deutungsgehalte des Obszönen im 'Nonnenturnier' und seinen europäischen Motivverwandten', *Beiträge zur Geschichte der deutschen Sprache und Literatur* 124 (2002), 261–301.

wandering genitalia (one also seen in art).[48] Two other such stories appear in the same manuscript which holds 'Das Nonnenturnier': 'Gold und Zers' ('Gold and Penis') and 'Der verklagte Zwetzler' ('The Penis on Trial').[49]

'Das Nonnenturnier' opens with an encounter between a knight, famed for his prowess at the tournament and in the arts of courtly love, and a lady, who has been pursuing him for some time. After spending the night together, the lady asks him to remain with her, only to be rebuffed when he claims that he never spends more than a single night with a particular lady. In fury, the lady threatens to ruin the knight's sexual reputation by claiming that he is impotent; to this, she adds that only by castrating himself will he make himself truly loved by women. Later, the knight's own penis (*zagel*) pipes up and—claiming that it, not he, is primarily responsible for the knight's success in love—persuades him to castrate himself. After presenting himself to his former lady, minus one *zagel*, the knight is rejected by her and driven out of town by a horde of women to live out the rest of his life as a hermit.

In the second part of the story the penis assumes the role of protagonist. Finding its way to a nunnery, it spends a year there hiding beneath a stairwell.[50] Finally, seeking death, the penis suddenly appears in the cloister. Its appearance drives the nuns into fierce competition to possess it, many of them taking it back to their chambers to pleasure themselves with it. To solve the resulting arguments, the abbess decides to hold a tournament between the nuns to

---

48 See Ann Marie Rasmussen, 'Wandering Genitalia: Sexuality & the Body in German Culture between the Late Middle Ages & Early Modernity', KCLMS Occasional Publications 2 (2009), 1–28; and Wenzel, 'Zers und fud'.

49 In 'Gold und Zers', a penis and a pile of gold stage a debate about which of them is desired more by women. Gold wins the debate according to the judgement of a noblewoman asked to preside over the matter; afterwards the penis runs away in a huff. Soon after, the women begin to miss it, and discard the Gold, until finally the penis is found and returned, where it is mutilated by having its 'eyes' (the testicles) cut off to keep it from wandering. In 'Der verklagte Zwetzler', a young woman rejects the advances of a suitor until she discovers what he keeps under his tunic: the eponymous *Zwetzler*. Here, comedy ensues from the girl's naïveté after she experiences the *Zwetzler's* pleasurable qualities without fully realising what it actually is. The next day, she and her lover are taken to court by her enraged father, who threatens to have the offending member sliced off, though the young man narrowly escapes punishment. A comparison might also be drawn with the twelfth-century story of the nun of Watton, recounted by Aelred of Rievaulx, in which a Gilbertine nun of Watton Priory conceived a child with a male member of the order before being savagely attacked by her sisters and made to castrate her lover prior to the miraculous disposal of the unborn child.

50 A number of scholars have pointed out that this can be read as a parody of the legend of Alexius; see, for one example, Rasmussen, 'Wandering Genitalia', 8.

determine ownership once and for all. While the penis is placed on a silken cushion to overlook the spectacle, the nuns stage a brutal contest which descends into chaos, at the end of which it turns out that the penis has been stolen away by an unknown hand.

Picking up the earlier thread of 'strange cases', it is worth noting that 'Das Nonnenturnier' has attracted a similar description from critics. Although many are in agreement about the story's meaning as a warning about the dangers of uncontrolled lust, both male and female,[51] similarly to Burghartz's appraisal of the Abdorf affair, both Ann Marie Ramussen and Jutta Eming describe the role of the penis in the story as odd in various ways.[52] Critical attention has focussed heavily upon the second part of the narrative, and upon two aspects in particular: the prominence of the phallus, and the grotesque. The latter can be defined along Bakhtinian lines as a process by which a cultural code is reversed or deformed,[53] and is expressed in the story's use of reversals and subversions of stock figures, most prominently, the virile knight who castrates himself, and the (theoretically) peaceable nuns who beat one another half to death in a savage tournament.[54] Both critical focal points suggest ways in which the body, specifically the penis, could signify in late medieval culture, and thus are helpful in exploring how Rudolf Abdorf's litigating behaviour can be seen as a strategy to dishonour his opponent in court.

With regard to the phallus, the status of desired object and the cultural hegemony with which the phallus has been associated in critical thought is recognisable at several points in the story, most notably (if we take the penis's own word for it) as the source of the knight's sexual and martial prowess, and later as the tournament prize for the nuns driven wild by the sight of it.[55] Without attempting an in-depth psychoanalytic reading of the text, I want to think here about the two bodies produced by the act of castration, and the issues of

51 Wenzel, '*Zers* und *fud*', 286: 'eine Warnung vor ungezügelter weiblicher/männlicher Triebhaftigkeit'.

52 See Rasmussen, 'Wandering Genitalia', 14; and Jutta Eming, 'Der Kampf um den Phallus: Körperfragmentierung, Textbegehren und groteske Ästhetik im "Nonnenturnier"', *The German Quarterly* 85: 4 (Fall, 2012), 380–400 at 382; see here too several further bibliographic references to the story's oddness.

53 See Robert Duggan, *The Grotesque in Contemporary British Fiction* (Manchester: 2013), 110: 'The grotesque deforms through reversing or inverting a literary genre or cultural code'.

54 See Klaus Grubmüller, 'Das Groteske im Märe als Element seiner Geschichte. Skizzen einer historischen Gattungspoetik', in *Kleinere Erzählformen des 15. und 16. Jahrhunderts ed. Walter Haug and Burghart Wachinger* (Tübingen: 1993), 37–54; Dicke, 'Mären-Priapeia'; Eming, 'Der Kampf um den Phallus'.

55 On the phallus, see Eming, 'Der Kampf um den Phallus', 386.

control and mastery which the story invites its audience to imagine. Ann Marie Rasmussen sees the knight's self-castration as a process of 'de-sexing' (similarly, Edith Wenzel calls this *Ent-Sexualisierung*), one which recurs in 'wandering genitalia' stories, and is also seen in 'Gold und Zers'.[56] For Rasmussen, in 'Das Nonnenturnier' and other stories, 'without his penis, [the knight] becomes an outcast and is shunned by the world ... 'de-sexed' human characters lose their position and power in society: their loss of their 'sex' translates into a loss of 'gender' (that is to say, the social construction of sexual difference) as well.'[57]

If we choose to read the transcript of the Abdorf case like a work of fiction—in other words, as a text in which a symbolic order of sexual subject and object is present—then Abdorf's actions in narrating the sexual relationship of his daughter and her would-be husband can be seen as a kind of symbolic castration of the younger man in which he takes possession of the phallus. Wenginer, of course, seems to retain subjectivity, allowing him to remain in the narrative, unlike the 'de-sexed' knight who vanishes from the story.[58] But he does so only at the behest of the narrator, Abdorf, in whose narrative he and his genitalia come to occupy the status of an object, in a manner comparable to the impotent men exposed to the judicial gaze of the York ecclesiastical court (though, as I shall go on to explore below, the symbolism of the penis was quite different). In all of this, Wenginer's role in the narrative contrasts with that of Abdorf, 'expert' litigator and puppet-master of the performance in court. For although Wenginer features in Abdorf's testimony as a vigorous sexual actor, it is Abdorf who imbues him with agency, and who keeps the focus relentlessly upon his penis.

We can thus interpret this scene on a symbolic level, based upon possession and non-possession of the phallus, as a contrast between mastery and powerlessness whose effect is the objectification of the weaker party. But Abdorf's performance can also be seen to resonate in more concrete terms. Here its grotesque symbolism, a second key critical focal point for 'Das Nonnenturnier', comes into play. In the story, the castrated and newly ambulant penis comes to wreak disorder in the nunnery; its mere presence is sufficient to upset social and gendered conventions, as the formerly peaceable community of nuns descends into anarchy by participating in the masculine activity of the

56 Wenzel, '*Zers* und *fud*', 284.

57 Rasmussen, 'Wandering Genitalia', 12.

58 On subjectivity in the context of late medieval German literature, see Ann Marie Rasmussen, 'Gender und Subjektivität im Märe *Die zwei Beichten* (A und B)', in *Inszenierungen von Subjektivität in der Literatur des Mittelalters*, ed. Martin Baisch et al. (Königstein im Taunus: 2005), 271–87.

tournament. The result is the production of a grotesque spectacle, a reversal not just of gendered order, but, as Edith Wenzel points out, of the rules of the tournament itself, which were intended (though not always successfully) to set limits upon participants' violence.[59]

In Abdorf's narrative, too, the gratuitous depiction of the penis pushes the spectacle in the courtroom into a grotesque violation of social and gendered norms. In much of continental Europe, late medieval urban culture certainly made allowance for the (hetero-) sexual activity of young men outside of marriage through visits to prostitutes, an activity which came under official supervision throughout the fourteenth and fifteenth centuries via the institution of the civic brothel. Brothels were intended explicitly as a measure to steer these young men away from 'honourable' women who might otherwise be endangered by their lust.[60] Wenginer's sexual relationship with Agnes Abdorf was thus a violation of this moral standard, which came increasingly to be seen as critical to the maintenance of social order.

If Wenginer was both a younger man and more junior figure in the city's social and political hierarchies, his violation may also have violated norms associated with class. Increasingly throughout the later Middle Ages, older and more senior men involved in the politics of urban government were also expected to exercise moderation in their sexual behaviour, so as to be able to govern the polity effectively.[61] Wenginer's behaviour is portrayed in Abdorf's narrative as anything but moderate; rather, the emphasis is upon uncontrolled, overwhelming lust, disqualifying Wenginer from membership in the social circle he perhaps hoped to inhabit by marrying Abdorf's daughter. If the miserable hermit knight of 'Das Nonnenturnier' finds himself 'de-sexed', then as the focus of Abdorf's narrative, Wenginer is arguably *hyper*-sexed. And although he seems to have the opposite experience to the unfortunate impotent men discussed by Goldberg and Kane, his transgressive behaviour places him similarly outside the boundaries of acceptable masculine sexual performance.[62]

---

59 Wenzel, '*Zers* und *fud*', 286.

60 On the 'lesser evil' argument in relation to civic prostitution see Peter Schuster, *Das Frauenhaus. Städtische Bordelle in Deutschland, 1350 bis 1600* (Paderborn: 1992), 19, 40–51.

61 Stephanie Tarbin discusses this ethos in the context of 'civic manliness' in late medieval London; see 'Civic Manliness in London, c. 1380–1550', in *Governing Masculinities in the Early Modern Period: Regulating Selves and Others*, ed. Susan Broomhall and Jacqueline Van Gent (Farnam and Burlington VA, 2011), 23–45.

62 In the alternate reading of the case discussed at n. 68, Wenginer's sexual failure might be seen to lie in his failure to live up to masculine standards by successfully deflowering Abdorf's daughter.

To be sure, this kind of critical language and the terms I have employed to explore this case take us some distance from the original documents. Rudolf Abdorf certainly entertained no thoughts about 'cultural hegemony' or 'symbolic castration', nor, indeed, can we be sure that he ever heard a story about a group of nuns who stage a tournament to win control of a knight's disembodied penis.[63] At the same time, it is worth bearing in mind that the kind of symbolic violence found in the story was woven into the cultural codes of late medieval urban life, and in ways which had major implications for masculinity.[64] In the high Middle Ages, as Stefan Meysman has recently shown in the case of the Low Countries, symbolic or real violence practiced against the genitalia was a highly recognisable means of degrading and dishonouring male opponents in the context of elite political culture.[65] As he observes, 'in broader high-medieval society, and especially among the chivalric elite, attacks on male private parts were more usually associated with subordinate weakness, abasement and the loss of manly functionalities and honour'.[66] Whilst these comments are directed at an earlier period than that inhabited by Abdorf, chivalric culture could certainly provide an aspirational model for the late medieval urban nobility.

Moreover, as noted, by the later Middle Ages, elite civic masculinity demanded of its political figureheads the ability to exercise moderation. Portraying Wenginer as a victim of uncontrollable lust was thus a way to emphasise his failure to live up to this standard of manhood, and to impugn his honour. In the immediate context of the case, an attack upon the genitalia could offer an explicit rebuke of Wenginer's attempt to encroach upon Abdorf's right to arrange the marriage of his daughter. As Meysman further explains (this time citing Danielle Westerhof), 'in aristocratic circles mutilation of the body and especially of its most intimate parts, was meant specifically for "destroying aristocratic identity" [in Westerhof's phrase], the body being closely linked to the *natura* of noblemen, namely character, comportment and lineage'.[67] This last point has a particular relevance for Abdorf's scenario, given the attempt

63 Though nor is this wholly unlikely; although the story only survives in a single manuscript from the first half of the fifteenth century, it certainly had older roots.

64 On symbolic violence see Valentin Groebner, *Defaced: The Visual Culture of Violence in the Late Middle Ages*, trans. Pamela Selwyn (New York: 2008).

65 See Stefan Meysman, 'Degrading the Male Body: Manhood and Conflict in the High-medieval Low Countries', *Gender & History* 28: 2 (August, 2016), 367–86.

66 Ibid., 370.

67 Ibid., 371.

of Wenginer to insert himself into Abdorf's own family line—an attempt that Abdorf sought manifestly to prevent.

'Das Nonnenturnier' thus offers us two characters whose actions signify in ways which help suggest how Abdorf's behaviour in the Zurich *Ratsgericht* worked to undermine the honour of his opponent, enabling him to take revenge upon him. In the 'de-sexed' knight, we might make a comparison with the hyper-sexed Wenginer; both can be seen to violate masculine sexual norms in distinct ways. And to the frenzied response to the castrated penis we might compare the violation of social norms perpetrated upon Abdorf and his family: both signify through grotesque spectacles focussing upon the penis. In both cases, the apparent 'strangeness' of the narrative can be seen as central to the meaning of each text: they are deliberate subversions of existing cultural codes, rendered grotesque to generate specific meanings.[68]

Conclusion

In this essay I have offered some quite abstract interpretations of a legal document, which depend upon our accepting that court cases might sometimes be read like literary narratives in which a symbolically significant order of subjects and objects is present.[69] The appeal to literary evidence means that this is very much a cultural-historical reading, although one which is also aligned with a more traditional history of crime concerned with topics of honour, vengeance, and feuding. In this regard, Rudolf Abdorf's behaviour is especially suggestive of a model of honour and vengeance, here cited in relation to a quite different world, whereby, 'when the lesser did confront the greater—the slave the master, the small farmer the chieftain, the child the adult—the response was either to ignore the affront as unworthy of notice or to respond by disciplining

68 Here it is worth acknowledging a possible interpretation of the second part of the case, namely that Abdorf's later performance in court was intended to insult Wenginer—and his penis—in a new way. By demonstrating that despite having sex with Agnes on numerous occasions, Wenginer had in fact *failed* to deflower her, leaving her 'innocent of all men', Abdorf implied that Wenginer himself was not a real man. Such an interpretation might also draw on a combination of legal and literary analysis, using different combinations of texts to those discussed above. I offer thanks to Stephen White for suggesting this possibility.

69 For a further extended discussion of the reading of historical texts through the lens of literary and critical theory, see Paul Strohm, *Theory and the Premodern Text* (Minneapolis: 2000).

and "instructing" the offender'.[70] If Wenginer had hoped to gain access to a higher social circle by marrying into the Abdorf family (or if Abdorf had suspected such a motive), then in being slapped down, he may have learned a harsh lesson about the boundaries of that circle. And maybe there was also a message here for Abdorf's colleagues in the city council, one which helped to speed through the law of 1379 giving protection to parents against children's marriages undertaken against their will: *this could happen to you, too.*

What happened afterwards? This is unclear, partly because it is difficult to know much about the state of the relationship between Agnes Abdorf and Wenginer by the time the whole affair found its way into court. We are left only with an ambiguous account of their final contact with one another, which saw Wenginer come to Agnes's house and call out 'Nessli! Nessli! Let me in!' Assuming this report is accurate (the narrator is of course still Abdorf), was this a poignant scene, as Agnes's former lover sought desperately to reach her? Or was Wenginer an unwanted presence by this point, a plague on Agnes as well as her father? We hear no more of him following his attempts to have the case elevated to the court of the Archbishop of Mainz, whilst we have only a faint clue about what happened to Agnes herself. Following the note in the case record that she had received permission to enter an approved religious order, we can connect her to a reference made between the late fourteenth and early fifteenth centuries to a daughter of the Abdorf family in the Cistercian convent of Selnau, a common destination for female members of the old Zurich nobility, albeit a less popular one than the larger and more prestigious convent of Oetenbach.[71]

Strange cases: the tales of Rudolf Abdorf's family and 'Das Nonnenturnier' have both been placed in this category by scholars who have encountered them. Whilst I acknowledge that they do, indeed, seem strange, at least from the distance of six-odd centuries, and that I have sought to mitigate their strangeness through the act of interpretation, as a final question we might stop to wonder about the urge to interpret, and thus to demystify. In doing so, do we seek to close down the spaces in which the anecdotal, the incidental, and the idiosyncratic reside? I certainly make no claims to have solved any particular problems of evidence by bringing court records into conversation with fiction, nor, to return to Elliott's phrase, to have 'unlocked' definitive meanings for either text. Rather, in the spirit of collaboration and inspiration which

70 William Ian Miller, *Bloodtaking and Peacemaking: Feud, Law, and Society in Saga Iceland* (Chicago: 1990), 32.

71 Gerald Dörner, *Kirche, Klerus und kirchliches Leben in Zürich von der Brunschen Revolution (1336) bis zur Reformation (1523)* (Würzburg: 1996), 73.

underpins the present volume, I have done so predominantly to suggest ways in which we might produce mutually enriching readings across boundaries of genre, commensurate with the idea of the study of the past as a collective and unfinished—indeed unfinishable—enterprise.[72]

Works Cited

Manuscript Source

Staatsarchiv Zürich, B VI 190.

Printed Sources

Bauhofer, Arthur. 'Zürich und die geistliche Gerichtsbarkeit'. *Zeitschrift für schweizerische Geschichte / Revue d'histoire suisse* 16:1 (1936): 1–35.

Bitterli, Daniel, ed. *Zürcher Richtebrief.* Die Rechtsquellen des Kantons Zürich. Neue Folge. Erster Teil, erste Reihe, erster Band. Basel: 2011.

Burghartz, Susanna. 'Disziplinierung oder Konfliktregelung? Zur Funktion städtischer Gerichte im Mittelalter: das Zürcher Ratsgericht'. *Zeitschrift für Historische Forschung* 16:4 (1989): 385–407.

Burghartz, Susanna. *Leib, Ehre und Gut. Delinquenz in Zürich Ende des 14. Jahrhunderts.* Zurich: 1990.

Bynum, Caroline Walker. *Fragmentation and Redemption: Essays on Gender and the Human Body in Medieval Religion.* New York and Cambridge, MA: 1991.

Clark, Elizabeth A. *History, Theory, Text: Historians and the Linguistic Turn.* Cambridge, MA and London: 2004.

Cramer, Thomas. *Geschichte der deutschen Literatur im Spätmittelalter.* Munich: 1990.

Davis, Natalie Zemon. *Fiction in the Archives: Pardon Tales and their Tellers in Sixteenth-Century France.* Stanford: 1987.

Dicke, Gerd. 'Mären-Priapeia. Deutungsgehalte des Obszönen im 'Nonnenturnier' und seinen europäischen Motivverwandten'. *Beiträge zur Geschichte der deutschen Sprache und Literatur* 124 (2002): 261–301.

Dinges, Martin. 'Die Ehre als Thema der Stadtgeschichte. Eine Semantik im Übergang vom Ancien Régime zur Moderne'. *Zeitschrift für Historische Forschung* 16 (1989): 409–40.

Dolan, Frances. *True Relations: Reading, Literature, and Evidence in Seventeenth-Century England.* Philadelphia: 2013.

---

72 See, too, the essays contained in Caroline Walker Bynum, *Fragmentation and Redemption: Essays on Gender and the Human Body in Medieval Religion* (New York and Cambridge, MA: 1991), particularly 'In Praise of Fragments: History in the Comic Mode', 11–26.

Donohue, Charles. 'Comparative Approaches to Marriage in the Later Middle Ages'. In *Regional Variations in Matrimonial Law and Custom in Europe, 1150–1600*, edited by Mia Korpiola, 289–316. Leiden and Boston: 2011.

Dörner, Gerald. *Kirche, Klerus und kirchliches Leben in Zürich von der Brunschen Revolution (1336) bis zur Reformation (1523)*. Würzburg: 1996.

Duggan, Robert. *The Grotesque in Contemporary British Fiction*. Manchester: 2013.

Elliot, Dyan. *Fallen Bodies: Pollution, Sexuality & Demonology in the Middle Ages*. Philadelphia: 1999.

Eming, Jutta. 'Der Kampf um den Phallus: Körperfragmentierung, Textbegehren und groteske Ästhetik im "Nonnenturnier"'. *The German Quarterly* 85: 4 (Fall, 2012): 380–400.

Fischer, Hanns. *Studien zur deutschen Märendichtung*. Tübingen: 1968.

Goldberg, Jeremy. 'Echoes, Whispers, Ventriloquisms: on Recovering Women's Voices from the Court of York in the Later Middle Ages'. In *Women, Agency and the Law, 1300–1700*, edited by Bronach Kane and Fiona Williamson, 31–41. London: 2013.

Goldberg, Jeremy. 'John Skathelok's Dick: Voyeurism and 'Pornography' in Late Medieval England'. In *Medieval Obscenities*, edited by Nicola F. McDonald, 105–123. York: 2006.

Gilomen, Hans-Jörg. 'Innere Verhältnisse der Stadt Zürich 1300–1500'. In *Geschichte des Kantons Zürich*, vol. 1: *Frühzeit bis Spätmittelalter*, edited by Niklaus Flüeler and Marianne Flüeler-Grauwiler. Zurich: 1995, 336–89.

Greenblatt, Stephen. 'Fiction and Friction'. In *Reconstructing Individualism: Autonomy, Individuality, and the Self in Western Thought*, edited by Thomas C. Heller, Morton Sosna, and David E. Wellbery, 30–52. Stanford: 1986.

Greenblatt, Stephen. *Renaissance Self-Fashioning: From More to Shakespeare*, 2nd ed. Chicago: 2005.

Groebner, Valentin. *Defaced: The Visual Culture of Violence in the Late Middle Ages*. Translated by Pamela Selwyn. New York: 2008.

Grubmüller, Klaus, ed. *Novellistik des Mittelalters, Märendichtung*. Frankfurt am Main: 1996.

Grubmüller, Klaus. 'Das Groteske im Märe als Element seiner Geschichte. Skizzen einer historischen Gattungspoetik'. In *Kleinere Erzählformen des 15. und 16. Jahrhunderts*, edited by Walter Haug and Burghart Wachinger, 37–54. Tübingen: 1993.

Grubmüller, Klaus. *Die Ordnung, der Witz und das Chaos. Eine Geschichte der europäischen Novellistik im Mittelalter: Fabliau—Märe—Novelle*. Tübingen: 2006.

Isenmann, Eberhard. *Die deutsche Stadt im Mittelalter: Stadtgestalt, Recht, Verfassung, Stadtregiment, Kirche, Gesellschaft, Wirtschaft*, 2nd rev. ed. Cologne: 2014.

Kane, Bronach. *Impotence and Virginity in the Late Medieval Ecclesiastical Court of York*. Borthwick Papers 114. York: 2008.

Karras, Ruth Mazo. *Sexuality in Medieval Europe: Doing Unto Others*. New York: 2005.

Kesper-Biermann, Sylvia, Ulrike Ludwig and Alexandra Ortmann, eds. *Ehre und Recht. Ehrkonzepte, Ehrverletzungen und Ehrverteidigungen vom späten Mittelalter bis zur Moderne*. Magdeburg: 2011.

Kuhn, Hugo. *Entwürfe zu einer Literatursystematik des Spätmittelalters*. Tübingen: 1980.

Malamud, Sibylle. *Die Ächtung des "Bösen". Frauen vor dem Zürcher Ratsgericht im späten Mittelalter (1400–1500)*. Zurich: 2003.

Meysman, Stefan. 'Degrading the Male Body: Manhood and Conflict in the High-Medieval Low Countries'. *Gender & History* 28: 2 (August, 2016): 367–86

Miller, William Ian. *Bloodtaking and Peacemaking: Feud, Law, and Society in Saga Iceland*. Chicago: 1990.

Montrose, Louise A. 'Professing the Renaissance: The Poetics and Politics of Culture'. In *The New Historicism*, edited by H. Aram Veeser. London and New York: 1989.

Pedersen, F. J. G. 'Privates on Parade: Impotence Cases as Evidence for Medieval Gender'. In *Law and Private Life in the Middle Ages: Proceedings of the Sixth Carlsberg Academy Conference on Medieval Legal History 2009*, edited by P. Andersen, M. Münster-Swendsen and H. Vogt, 81–103. Copenhagen: 2011.

Pohl-Zucker, Susanne. *Making Manslaughter: Process, Punishment and Restitution in Württemberg and Zurich, 1376–1700*. Medieval Law and its Practice 22. Leiden and Boston: 2017.

Rasmussen, Ann Marie. 'Gender und Subjektivität im Märe *Die zwei Beichten* (A und B)'. In *Inszenierungen von Subjektivität in der Literatur des Mittelalters*, edited by Martin Baisch et al., 271–87. Königstein im Taunus: 2005.

Rasmussen, Ann Marie. 'Wandering Genitalia: Sexuality & the Body in German Culture between the Late Middle Ages & Early Modernity'. *KCLMS Occasional Publications* 2 (2009), 1–28.

Schmugge, Ludwig. *Ehen vor Gericht. Paare der Renaissance vor dem Papst*. Berlin: 2008.

Scott, Joan. 'The Evidence of Experience', *Critical Inquiry*, 17:4 (Summer, 1991): 773–97.

Schreiner, Klaus and Gerd Schwerhoff, eds. *Verletzte Ehre. Ehrkonflikte in Gesellschaften des Mittelalters und der frühen Neuzeit* (Cologne: 1995)

Schuster, Peter. *Das Frauenhaus. Städtische Bordelle in Deutschland, 1350 bis 1600*. Paderborn, 1992.

Simon-Muscheid, Katharina. 'Gewalt und Ehre im spätmittelalterlichen Handwerk am Beispiel Basels'. *Zeitschrift für historische Forschung* 18 (1991): 1–31.

Strohm, Paul. *Theory and the Premodern Text*. Minneapolis: 2000.

Tarbin, Stephanie. 'Civic Manliness in London, c. 1380–1550'. In *Governing Masculinities in the Early Modern Period: Regulating Selves and Others*, edited by Susan Broomhall and Jacqueline Van Gent. Farnam and Burlington VA: 2011, 23–45.

Wenzel, Edith. '*Zers* und *fud* als literarische Helden. Zum "Eigenleben" von Geschlechtsteilen in mittelalterlicher Literatur', in *Körperteile. Eine kulturelle*

Anatomie, edited by Claudia Benthien and Christoph Wulf, 274–93. Reinbek bei Hamburg: 2001.

White, Hayden. 'New Historicism: A Comment'. In *The New Historicism*, edited by H. Aram Veeser, 293–302. London and New York: 1989.

Wickham, Chris. *Medieval Europe*. New Haven and London: 2016.

Zmora, Hillay. *State and Nobility in Early Modern Germany: The Knightly Feud in Franconia, 1440–1567*. Cambridge: 1998.

Online Sources

Deutsches Wörterbuch von Jacob Grimm und Wilhelm Grimm: <www.woerterbuchnetz.de/DWB?lemma=minnen>, accessed 18/5/2017.

Handschriftencensus: <http://www.handschriftencensus.de/4208>, accessed 18/5/2017.

Schweizerisches Idiotikon Digital: <www.idiotikon.ch>, accessed 20/6/2017.

CHAPTER 6

How To Be Remembered: Securing the *Memoria* of a Slain Person in Medieval Denmark

Helle Vogt[1]

After David Bowie's death of cancer in 2016 many people all over the world—including Bill Miller—were fascinated by how, via a music video, someone could create an image to shape the way people would remember the last stage of his life. Unlike Bowie, most people today are not particularly concerned about being remembered by posterity. Rather, what they are concerned about is how their friends, loved ones, and peers—their contemporaries and near-contemporaries—will remember them. This was surely not the case in the Middle Ages, however. As the Danish noblewoman Cecilie Pedersdotter in 1274 stated in her will, the reason for her donation to an abbey was so that 'my memory may be everlasting' (mei perpetua sit memoria).[2] What Bowie and the medieval donors have in common is that they had time to prepare for how they would be remembered after their death, and in the case of the medieval donors to make provisions for how to shorten their immortal soul's stay in Purgatory by both giving donations for masses for their soul and receiving the Last Rites on their deathbed.[3] But a person who was killed could not always receive absolution before dying, and had not necessarily made arrangements by wills or donations for his funeral and afterlife.[4] In these cases, the task of securing the dead person's memory and the health of his soul fell to his heirs and

1 I thank Kim Esmark and Hans Jacob Orning for their useful comments.

2 *Diplomatarium Danicum* (herafter cited as DD), various editors and publishers, Det danske Sprog- og Litteratur Selskab (1938–), vol. 2, ser. 2, 6 May 1274, no. 229.

3 Countless studies of *memoria* and donation cultures have been published. The standard works on *memoria* are Otto Gerhard Oexle, 'Memorialüberlieferung im früheren Mittelalter', *Frühmittelalterliche Studien* 10 (1976), 70–95; Otto Gerhard Oexle, 'De Gegenwaert der Toten', in *Death in the Middle Ages*, ed. Herman Braet and Werner Verbeke, Mediaevalia Lovaniensia series I studie (Leuven: 1983), 19–77; Arnoud-Jan A. Bijsterveld, Do ut des*: Gift Giving, Memoria, and Conflict Management in the Medieval Low Countries* (Hilversum: 2007).

4 On wills and donations in general in the Danish material see Kristian Sindballe, *Af Testamentarvens Historie i dansk Ret* (Copenhagen: 1915); Helle Vogt, 'Protecting the Individual, the Kin and the Soul—Donation Regulations in Danish and Norwegian Medieval Legislation', in *Inheritance and Property in the Nordic and Western World from Late Antiquity*

© KONINKLIJKE BRILL NV, LEIDEN, 2018 | DOI 10.1163/9789004366374_010

other relatives. The focus in this essay is upon how kinsmen of slain persons executed that obligation in medieval Denmark.

In his 2005 book *An Eye for an Eye* and elsewhere in his writings,[5] Bill Miller has considered the question of how kinsmen ought to react when one of their relatives is killed, concluding that 'To remember means to revenge'.[6] This conclusion is based primarily on an analysis of Shakespeare's *Hamlet*,[7] with additional references to some of the Icelandic sagas and the Old Testament story about the revenge of Abel. Miller views these narratives as expressions of cultures built on honour—and hence also upon shame, since a person's honour depended on his acting according to certain norms, such as the expectation that he avenge a wrong done to him. 'In honor cultures it matters not only how you die but also that you are avenged if you die in a way that demands revenge be taken'.[8] According to Miller, in honour societies remembering is intimately connected to reward and punishment. It is true that in the narrative universes that Miller works with, we find the notion that revenge is a way to honour a dead kinsman. However, if we step out of the world of fiction and start to look at revenge killings or bloodfeuds in medieval Iceland, Western Europe, or for that matter, Shakespeare's England around 1600, the bloodfeud is very difficult to find in the nonfiction sources. As the English historian Peter Sawyer summarised it in his article about bloodfeud in the Middle Ages, 'The bloodfeud flourished best, not in the real world, but in the fictions of poets, storytellers and lawyers'.[9] The Danish sources from the High Middle Ages confirm Sawyer's

until Today, ed. Ole-Albert Rønning, Helle Sigh, and Helle Vogt (London and New York: 2017), 130–45.

5 William Ian Miller, *An Eye for an Eye* (Cambridge: 2005); William Ian Miller, 'Choosing the Avenger: Some Aspects of the Bloodfeud in Medieval Iceland and England', *Law and History Review*, vol. 1, no. 2 (Autumn, 1983), 159–204.

6 Miller, *Eye for an Eye*, 99. Miller also recognises that compensation was an important factor in peace settlements, but he claims that compensation is closely linked to revenge. 'Compensation is a possibility only if revenge is a very likely probability. Who is going to pay you enough to assuage your honor if he does not fear your ability to reclaim your honor by killing him if he does not pay up?' *Eye for an Eye*, 105.

7 Unlike Miller, John Kerrigan claims that Hamlet never promised to avenge his father, but only to remember him, and hence he concludes that remembering and revenge are not necessarily connected. John Kerrigan, *Revenge Tragedy: Aeschylus to Armageddon* (Oxford: 1997), 182. Miller disagrees with this interpretation: Miller, *Eye for an Eye*, 227, n. 18.

8 Miller, *Eye for an Eye*, 100.

9 Peter Sawyer, 'The Bloodfeud in Fact and Fiction', in *Tradition og historieskrivning. Kilderne til Nordens ældste historie*, ed. Kirsten Hastrup and Preben Meulengracht Sørensen, Acta Jutlandica LXIII:2 Humanistisk Serie 61 (Aarhus: 1987), 27–38 at 36. I know that you cannot equate vengeance and feud in general; however, it is hardly controversial to identify

conclusion. Although feuds occurred, they were seldom the result of a killing, but rather due to enmity or rival economic interests among the elite. These feuds were often not fought as bloodfeuds, but more like proxy feuds, where one party plundered or sacked the other party's resources and occasionally attacked some of the opponent's men from a lower social stratum than the conflicting parties themselves.[10]

Since there is nothing in the Danish sources from the High Middle Ages to confirm Miller's statement that revenge was the normal way to remember and honour slain kinsmen, one has to ask how they might have been remembered and honoured instead. This essay will investigate if and how slain persons were honoured and remembered by the paying of man's compensation or other kinds of compensation. The focus of the investigation is medieval Danish practice, and as with all studies about medieval Scandinavia, the sources are problematic. Very few sources are preserved, and those that exist are almost exclusively from the absolute top of society, where transactions involving material goods and rituals were closely related and economic agreements so important that they needed to be recorded. The majority of the sources that mention killing compensation just inform us that a compromise was reached and the peace was restored. In some cases we are also told that compensation was given, but there are no details about the nature of the compromise or what the compensation covered.[11]

---

bloodfeud with vengeance. Bloodfeud necessarily involved revenge, though of course revenge could take many other forms besides bloodfeud. Countless pages have been written about how to characterise feud, bloodfeud and vengeance, and collective responsibility, and I do not want to stir up that hornets' nest of controversy, since it is not the purpose of this essay. I will just say that in general, the kinsmen of a slain person did not avenge or honour their deceased kinsmen by killing the killer or one of his kinsmen, which is characteristic of bloodfeud.

10 The feuds in the Danish sources have been studied in detail by Jeppe Büchert Netterstrøm. See for example *Fejde og magt i senmiddelalderen: Rosenkrantzernes fejder med biskop Jens Iversen og Lage Brok, 1454–1474* (Viborg: 2012); and 'Criminalization of Homicide in Early Modern Denmark (16th–17th centuries)', *Scandinavian Journal of History* 42 (2017), no. 4, 459–75. This kind of feud was not exclusively Danish; similar feud patterns are known from other parts of Europe. For an overview and references to further reading see Jeppe Büchert Netterstrøm, 'Introduction: Feud in Medieval and Early Modern Europe', in *Feud in Medieval and Early Modern Europe*, ed. Bjørn Poulsen and Jeppe Büchert Netterstrøm (Aarhus: 2007), 9–67.

11 These sources are mostly agreement letters, letters of *orfeydhe*, which documented that the parties had entered a formal settlement and had given a final promise of peace and reconciliation. For the second part of the fifteenth century, when the number of sources begins to increase, the number of these settlements increases as well. Jeppe Büchert

The payment of wergeld, or man's compensation, as I prefer to call it,[12] was the fundamental principle in Danish penal law. With respect to compensation for homicide, the kinsmen played a crucial role in paying and receiving it, because a killing was regarded as not only a matter between the killer and the heir of the slain person, but a matter for all blood-related men within the degree of consanguinity defined by the Church.[13] The compensation consisted of three instalments, of which the male members of the father's side of the family were to pay a third, the mother's side another third, and the killer the remaining third. In addition, a fine to the king was to be paid for the breaking of the peace, if the killing was committed intentionally. After the compensation was paid, oaths were exchanged between the killer and his relatives and the kinsmen of the deceased, and the peace restored.[14] According to law the value of the man's compensation was the same for both sexes and all social groups,

---

Netterstrøm, 'Bondefejder i Danmark 1450–1650', in *Feider og fred i nordisk middelalder*, ed. Erik Opsahl (Oslo: 2007), 35–72.

12 The word *wergeld* (or *wer*) does not exist in Old Danish. Instead the word *manbot* (man's compensation) is used. I disagree with the view expressed by Bill Miller in *An Eye for an Eye*, 104–13 that wergeld—the price for a man—was an expression of talion. As the German historian Stefan Esders has convincingly argued, it disregards the complexity of wergeld just to see it as a response to the threat of revenge. Stefan Esders, '"Eliten" und "Strafrecht" im frühen Mittelalter. Überlegungen zu den Bußen- und Wergeldkatalogen der Leges barbarorum', in *Théories et pratiques des élites au haut Moyen Âge*, ed. François Bougard, Hans-Werner Goetz, and Régine Le Jan, Collection Haut Moyen Âge 13 (Turnhout: 2011), 261–82 at 266.

13 Kinship was calculated using the canonical measurement, which before the Fourth Lateran Council in 1215 extended to the seventh degree removed and after the Council to the fourth degree. On 'canonical kinship' in the Danish laws see Helle Vogt, *The Function of Kinship in Medieval Nordic Legislation* (Leiden and Boston: 2010).

14 *Danmarks gamle Love med Kirkelovene*, 8 vols., ed. Johannes Brøndum-Nielsen et al. The chapters regulating the oath are found in: vol. 1: 1, Law of Scania, chs. 85, 92, 97, 113; vol. 5, Erik's Law of Zealand, book 3, chs. 26–32; vol. 2, Law of Jutland book 2, chs. 25, 27 and book 3, ch. 21. Det Danske Sprog- og Litteraturselskab (Copenhagen: 1933–1964). For an English translation see *The Danish Medieval Laws: The Laws of Scania, Zealand and Jutland*, ed. Ditlev Tamm and Helle Vogt (London and New York: 2016). The Danish laws were written down in the first half of the thirteenth century, and the system whereby kinsmen collectively paid man's compensation was upheld until 1537, when the principle of 'a life for a life', i.e. capital punishment, was introduced in the wake of the Lutheran Reformation that was imposed in 1536. See Helle Vogt, 'The Kin's Collective Responsibility for the Payment of Man's Compensation in Medieval Denmark', in *Wergild, Compensation and Penance: The Monetary Logic of Early Medieval Conflict Resolution*, ed. Lukas Bothe, Stefan Esders, and Han Nijdam (Leiden and Boston: forthcoming); and Netterstrøm, 'Criminalization'.

with the exception of slaves. However, in practice, as with so many other things in the medieval law, this was a starting point for negotiation: a rule that the parties could fall back on if they could not reach a compromise. In general the amount of the compensation and the form it would take were open to negotiation, and here status and honour could be important factors.

The Church often played an important role in negotiating settlements, and bishops and other ecclesiastical persons often took an active part in reaching an agreement and restoring the peace.[15] However, although forgiveness and reconciliation were Christian ideals, it was apparently not always easy to get the wronged party to agree to a settlement and forgive the killer, as is well illustrated in the following story from Arnold of Lübeck's *Chronicle of the Slavs*. The incident took place in Northern Germany and not Denmark, but it reveals so neatly the difficulties that had to be overcome in reaching a settlement that I cannot resist quoting it. The hero in the story, which takes place in the late twelfth century, is Bishop (later Saint) Evermod of Ratzeburg. Arnold describes the scene in the following way:

> And while the man of God was celebrating a public mass in the presence of the archbishop, it happened that a certain man of Thetmark had killed one of the best men of the region, with an effusion of blood. When this thing came to the attention of the bishop, he took pains to effect a reconciliation, as is the custom during the solemnities of masses; he strenuously pleaded with the man whose kinsman had been killed that he show forbearance toward his neighbour, repeating from the Sunday prayer, 'forgive us our trespasses', etc. And when he [the slain man's kinsman], hardened by his enraged mind, did not reflect upon these things, the bishop, descending from the pulpit, approached him and, with the relics of the saints, threw himself at his feet. And when he [the kinsman] began fettering himself with terrible oaths by God and his mother and the names of other saints, never to have released himself, instead of countering with a blessing the bishop gave him a great blow. And very promptly, with outstretched hands, he assented to what was being asked, and accepted his

15 On mediating and litigation in high medieval Denmark see Helle Vogt, 'The Power to Judge: Jurisdiction in Property Conflicts in Thirteenth-Century Denmark'; and Kim Esmark, 'Disputing Property in Zealand: The Records of the Sorø Donation Book', both in *Disputing Strategies in Medieval Scandinavia*, ed. Kim Esmark et al. (Leiden and Boston: 2013), 161–218.

> neighbour in peace. We believe that to have been done through divine intervention, that the demon was driven from the man by a blow.[16]

Being unwilling to forgive your enemy and reach a settlement is here explained as possession by an evil demon, which is used to illustrate the holiness of bishop Evermood, and also the theological ideal of forgiveness. However, the story also suggests that bishops saw it as their responsibility to get people to reach a settlement and restore the peace, and that it was not always an easy task. Because of the hatred and anger that kinsmen of a slain person were likely to feel toward the killer, they would not necessarily want a peaceful solution.

After this little intermezzo we return to man's compensation and remembrance when an agreement was entered into. There is no doubt that honour was an important factor when settlements were negotiated, and that rituals were needed to re-establish the honour of the wronged party, something that could not be bought with money. Thus the kinsmen of the killer, when they paid the man's compensation, were expected to swear not only an oath that they would not seek revenge but also a so-called levelling oath or oath of equality that they would do the same, i.e. accept compensation and renounce revenge, if the situation were reversed and it was their kinsman who was killed. The logic behind this levelling oath is laid out by the Archbishop of Lund, Anders Sunesen, in his convoluted early thirteenth-century Latin explanation of the Law of Scania: 'Moreover, the oath of equality is always enforced with such great diligence because when those who are harmed have been made equivalent to those who have harmed, the contempt for the perpetrators customarily stirred up by those who have suffered injury from their oppression is seen to be taken away.

16 Arnold of Lübeck, *Arnoldi Chronica Slavorum*, MGH SS rer. Germ. 14 (Hanover: 1868), 2; 7, 43. <http://www.dmgh.de/de/fs1/object/display/bsb00000766_00045.html>, accessed 14/6/2017. 'Cumque vir Dei missam publicam presente archiepiscopo celebraret, accidit ut effusione sanguinis facta quidam Thetmarsus quendam de melioribus terre occidisset. Quod cum innotuisset episcopo, ad reconciliationem laborare studebat, ut moris est inter missarum sollempnia, illum cuius cognatus ceciderat obnixe deprecabatur, ut proximo indulgeret, replicans de oratione dominica: "Dimitte nobis debita nostra" etc. Cumque ille, tumida mente induratus, hec non reputaret, episcopus de ambone descendens ad ipsum accessit, et cum sanctorum reliquiis ad pedes illius se optulit. Cumque ille iuramentis terribilibus per Deum et matrem eius et aliorum sanctorum nomina se ipsum constringeret, nunquam se dimissurum, episcopus pro benedictione contradicenti alapam maximam dedit. Et ille promptissime extensis manibus quod petebatur annuit et proximum in pace recepit. Quod divinitus factum credimus, per alapam demonem ab homine fugatum'. My thanks to Kate Gilbert for this and the other Latin translations in the present essay.

For prudent men always value the integrity of their reputation and the restoration of the honour due to them more than pecuniary compensation'.[17]

Anders Sunesen's focus here is on the honour of the living on both sides of the conflict and restoration of the peace through the acceptance of compensation. Not a word is said about the slain person and his honour. However, this is not surprising, since Anders Sunesen wrote about legal procedure and the logic behind the rules. If we want to figure out what role the remembering of the deceased played in the settlements, we must look at practice. There is no doubt that the honour aspect was linked to social standing. For those who were dependant on the labour of a slain person, financial compensation was very welcome. This group is seldom represented in the few surviving sources, but after man's compensation was replaced by capital punishment in 1537,[18] we find in the letter books of the Royal Chancery a large number of petitions from relatives of slain persons who ask permission to have 'a life for a life' changed to man's compensation in view of their poverty.[19]

In the following discussion, four examples will be used to illustrate the variation there could be in the strategies and settlements, depending on the circumstances of the killing and on who entered into the settlement. The first two cases involve two groups of relatives, whereas the two others are examples of persons who were killed under circumstances in which no single person could be held liable. In these latter cases, the inhabitants of a town were held responsible collectively.

The first example I have chosen is from the 1340s.[20] The full extent of the homicide settlement, as is almost always the case,[21] cannot be determined from the sources. What we know is that the maternal half-brother and other kinsmen of the deceased killer Niels Thygesen promised to establish an altar

17 'Equalitatis autem tanto diligencius semper exigitur juramentum, quod per ipsum, lesis ledentibus adequatis, auferri videatur contemptus, qui perpessis iniuriam ex oppressione solet inferencium suscitari; plur[e]s enim semper prvdentes faciunt integritatem fame et honoris debiti restitucionem quam pecuniariam satisfactionem'. *Danmarks gamle Love*, vol. 1, 2, ch. 46, 530.

18 'Kong Christian 3.s anden københavnske reces 24. august 1537', *Den danske Rigslovgivning 1523–1558*, ed. Aage Andersen, Det Danske Sprog- og Litteraturselskab og Selskabet for Udgivelse af Kilder til dansk Historie (Odense: 2015), 198–9.

19 *Kancelliets Brevbøger vedrørende Danmarks indre Forhold i Uddrag*, ed. C. F. Bricka et al. (Copenhagen: 1885–2005). Netterstrøm, 'Criminalization of Homicide'.

20 *DD*, vol. 3, ser. 2, 23 Nov. 1345, no. 193.

21 Often it is impossible to see how a settlement was made, because only the agreement letter is preserved in which the parties confirm that a settlement is established and that the peace is restored, but the specific terms are not mentioned.

in the cathedral town of Roskilde. The altar was to be finely equipped, and to be endowed with enough land to generate income for three weekly masses to be held for the soul of the slain man. In addition, for the sake of the slain man's sins Niels Thygesen's kinsmen were to pay for a pilgrim to be sent to Rome to pray at the saints' graves. The altar was established in 1348, and we know about the settlement via the donation letter from that year, wherein land and farms were transferred to the maintenance of the altar. The letter also reveals that the bishop of Roskilde had acted as mediator when the settlement was made.[22]

In this settlement the soul of the slain man was paramount. There are no traces of gifts or other kinds of financial compensation made to the slain man's kin, and man's compensation is not mentioned.[23] This is not the same as saying that other financial transactions did not take place, but they were clearly not so important that they have survived in writing. Nor is there evidence that the half-brother or the other kinsmen of the killer were expected to humiliate themselves while asking the slain man's relatives for forgiveness, but this is perhaps not surprising since the actual killer was dead, and his half-brother had 'inherited' the responsibility for settling the case. In addition, the slain man was from Jutland, and hence had been killed far away from his home, so the kinsmen of the slain man and the kinsmen of his killer would not meet regularly. Perhaps for that reason the restoration of honour might not have been so consequential. This was not always the case, however.

In the example above, the religious gifts and the soul of the slain man were in focus. Religious gifts also played a crucial role for the settlement in the next example, but they were only a part of the settlement agreement. Because the parties belonged to some of the richest and most influential families in the realm it is hardly surprising that in this case from 1405 the settlement was negotiated by their peers and entered into in the presence of Margrethe, first lady

---

22 *DD*, vol. 3, ser. 3, 26 Sept. 1348, no. 60. No letter of agreement is preserved from this case, but the agreement is known from the donation letter.

23 In 1348 a similar settlement was entered into, and here was it stated that when the killer had built and equipped an altar for the departed's soul and donated enough land to pay for a priest and masses in perpetuity, the killer would be completely free from obligations: *DD*, vol. 3, ser. 2, 9 Dec. 1346, no. 300. In this case the settlement was a family affair, since the killer and the slain man were brothers, and the common kinsmen had acted as mediators between uncle and nephew. Under the circumstances it would have been very strange if the kinsmen had contributed to payment of man's compensation, or had humiliated themselves in front of their own relative.

and lord of Denmark, the de facto ruling queen, and her stepson King Erik VII.[24] The settlement consisted of three parts: 1) gifts for the soul of the departed, 2) public humiliation of the killer, and 3) gifts to the closest relatives.[25] As in the first example, there was no mention of man's compensation.

The knight Jens Nielsen had killed Jens Jensen, son of the knight Jens Andersen. The gifts to be made for the soul of Jens Jensen alone were enormous. According to the settlement Jens Nielsen was to establish an altar in Aarhus cathedral, over which Jens Jensen's heirs would have the patronage. In addition, perpetual masses were to be endowed for the dead man's soul in two other churches. Gifts were to be given to the poor; and Jens Nielsen would also pay the costs for six pilgrims to travel to different holy places such as Jerusalem, Rome, and Santiago de Compostela, and for nine pilgrims to travel to various holy places in the Nordic kingdoms. What probably hurt more than the financial burden of the settlement was the act of humiliation. Witnessed by 200 knights and squires, Jens Nielsen had to beg forgiveness from Jens Jensen's father and sons while on his knees, and say these words: 'Even if I were the best and the mightiest knight in Denmark, and you had killed my son or my father in this manner, I would still enter this reconciliation and atonement with you'.[26] This was the same formula as the levelling oath used when man's compensation was paid, as mentioned above. Jens Nielsen was to give a sword or a knife to the slain man's father and to his sons while begging on his knees for their forgiveness, and to have the peace restored. Swords and knives were expensive in themselves, but they were first and foremost symbolic gifts. The same probably goes for the gifts given to the widow and daughters of the deceased, each of whom was to have a precious gift in the form of jewels. Again, Jens Nielsen had to kneel. In return for forgiveness, the gifts and payment for the religious services were promised by Jens Nielsen on behalf of all his kinsmen, on both his mother's and his father's side, born as well as unborn; and Jens Jensen's father and sons promised for themselves and their kin to forgive the killing and restore the peace. Both the settlement charter and the royal confirmation were witnessed by a large number of men from both the kin groups.

---

24 King Erik's confirmation, 24 Feb.1405: <http://diplomatarium.dk/dokument/14050224003>, accessed 14/6/2017. The *Diplomatarium Danicum* no longer publishes documents in print; those dating from 1401 onwards are published only online.

25 Compromise between Jens Nielsen and Jens Andersen 24 Feb. 1405, http://diplomatarium.dk/dokument/14050224001, accessed 19/6/2017.

26 'denn beste och mechtigste riddere y Danmarck, och hafde de slagidt min sønn eller min fader y saadan maade, da ville ieg hafve saadann en læghe och saadan en saane af dem der for'. <http://diplomatarium.dk/dokument/14050224001>, accessed 21/6/2017.

It was not only noblemen who could be forced to perform humiliating rituals as part of the settlements. Humiliation was also an important part of the two examples in which the inhabitants of towns were held collectively responsible for a killing. In 1301 the knight Josef Magnussen was killed in the town of Lund. The circumstances of the killing are unknown, but probably the city's mayors and town councillors were involved in some way, either by actively sanctioning the killing or by looking the other way.[27] Judging from the harsh terms of the settlement, it seems most unlikely that these officials did not bear some kind of responsibility, be it direct or indirect.

In 1310[28] King Erik V witnessed an agreement between the townsmen of Lund and the brothers and other relatives of Josef Magnussen. The settlement was reached with the archbishop of Lund and the bishop of Roskilde, among others, acting as mediators. The charter includes a long list of acts of penance and humiliation that the mayors and town councillors and the other inhabitants of Lund were supposed to undergo as part of the agreement. The penances comprised religious gifts for the soul of the departed, and symbolic humiliation of the townsmen. The townsmen promised to establish three new altars, two in Lund and one in Roskilde, where masses would be sung for the soul of the departed. The altars were to be finely equipped and endowed with enough land to provide income to support priests who could serve them in perpetuity. Yearly gifts were to be given to the poor. Additional money was allocated to vigils; donations were given to a long list of churches; and two pilgrims apiece received endowments to go to Rome and to Santiago de Compostela. As a sign of their penitence some of the mayors and town councillors were expected to carry a funeral litter around town in a procession from church to church, followed by all the barefooted townsmen, both male and female. The townsmen were also required to appear at the provincial assembly in Lund and, on their knees, ask the departed's brothers and other kinsmen for forgiveness and follow the procedure with security and levelling oaths and peace kisses as prescribed above. In the agreement there was no mention of man's compensation or additional gifts to the brothers or other kinsmen. The only mention of personal gain for the heirs was to the effect that one of the brothers, Juris, who was a canon at the cathedral in Lund, should have the profit from two of the altars

27 For further information on Josef Magnussen and the people of Lund's motives for killing him see Kurt Villads Jensen, 'A Knight in Town', in *Medieval Spirituality in Scandinavia and Europe: A Collection of Essays in Honour of Tore Nyberg*, ed. Lars Bisgaard et al. (Odense: 2001), 139–44. Like other towns in the region, Lund had more than one mayor.

28 *DD*, vol. 2, ser. 6, 20 Sept. 1310, no. 305.

during his lifetime, and after his death the benefit should go the other brothers as long as they lived.

Since Josef Magnussen was one of King Erik V's trusted men, and his brothers and kinsmen were powerful people, it was not an easy task to get the parties to enter a settlement. Thus, powerful mediators were needed. The bishop of Roskilde and the archbishop of Lund functioned as mediators and the settlement was witnessed by the king, so in that way the leaders of both the spiritual and secular powers in Denmark were represented. For the townsmen and town council the settlement was not entered into lightly: According to the agreement, if they not did not fulfil what was promised within a period of four years, at the demand of Josef Magnussen's brothers the archbishop would excommunicate all the mayors and town councillors and their wives and sons, and the entire town would be put under interdict. If the archbishop for some reason would not do it—after all, Lund was his residential town—the bishop of Roskilde would be entitled to place the town and all its inhabitants under interdict.

The last example, from the 1350s, concerned the town of Lübeck on one side and on the other, the kinsmen of the slain knight Markvard von Westensee, who were acting on behalf of his minor son and the minor son of his deceased brother. The boys were Markvard's closest kin, and thus were the ones who should raise a claim against those responsible for the killing.[29] Markvard belonged to a powerful Holstein noble family with close ties to the Danish king, and one of the relatives who acted on behalf of the minor boys was Benedikt von Ahlefeldt, a member of the king's council. Markvard himself belonged to a group of noblemen from Holstein who rebelled against the counts of Holstein after the counts rebelled against the Danish king in 1351. It is possible that Markvard was one of the king's men. His relationship to the king is unknown, but the large part King Valdemar played in the settlement makes it very likely that it was a close one.[30] The circumstances surrounding Markvard's death are unclear, but apparently he was killed not in Lübeck but in the countryside, and the body was afterwards brought to the town by those who had killed him. Nevertheless, the town was held liable for the killing by Markvard's relatives. Who the killers were is unknown, but it is likely that they were in the service of the mayors and town councillors. The fact that the killers brought the body to Lübeck suggests that they expected to be rewarded. Markvard and his relatives

29 I would like to give my thanks to Kim Esmark and Anders Leegaard Knudsen for valuable discussion and comments on the case.

30 On Markvard and the Westensee family see Wilhelm Mantels, *Beiträge zur Lübisch-Hansischen Geschichte. Ausgewählte historische Arbeiten* (Jena: 1881), 133–67.

had been in conflict with Lübeck, and for some periods even outlawed, meaning that they could be killed without reprisal when found, but each time a compromise was arranged and the peace restored. However in 1350 Lübeck and Markvard, together with some of Markvard's allies, had entered into a formal settlement. Markvard's killing thus broke the peace, and since it had taken place on Lübeck's territory, the town and not the killers was held liable. To resolve the conflict the parties agreed on arbitration, with the bishop of Lübeck; a Holstein knight, probably representing Lübeck; and the king's official all acting as arbitrators. The agreement letter specifically mentioned that the townsmen had handed over the case to arbitration 'for the sake of God, and subsequently in accordance with the wishes of the highborn lord King Valdemar'.[31]

The arbitrated settlement made by the litigants differed from the one in Lund in three ways. First, there was no act of humiliation; second, monetary compensation was paid to the kinsmen; and third, monuments for the memory of the deceased were to be raised. However, the largest part of the atonement consisted of a number of religious acts for the benefit of the soul of the departed. Markvard was to be remembered in all the town's parish churches 'as it is custom here' (alse hiree en seede is);[32] three altars were to be built and equipped and eternal masses for his soul instituted; and six pilgrims were to be sent to six different places, including Jerusalem, Santiago de Compostela, and Rome. Finally, Markvard was to be granted confraternity in three monasteries posthumously, thereby making him a beneficiary of the good deeds done in the monasteries.

Not only was Markvard's soul to benefit from the settlement; his memory was to be preserved for the Lübeckers by physical monuments. At the location outside the town walls where his corpse was deposited after the homicide, a cross was to be raised. At his grave the townsmen were to place a tombstone carved after their wishes. The raising of the cross is quite spectacular, because it would stand as an everlasting symbol of the consequences, not only of breaking the peace, but also of harming one of the king's men.

The last part of the agreement was the monetary compensation. The town agreed to pay 1000 marks to Markvard's son and 'those who have a right to it' (den, de dar recht to hebben), which must refer to his kinsmen, according to the law as mentioned above.[33] The compensation was to be paid by the

31 *DD* vol. 3, ser. 4, 22 May 1354, no. 120: 'dor godes willen vnde dar neghest dor ere willen des hochgheboren heren koning Woldemeres'.

32 Ibid. This was the only part of the agreement that was not fulfilled: Mantels, *Beiträge*, 163.

33 This was an enormous sum, even taking into account the fact that the coinage was devalued considerably from the mid-thirteenth to the mid-fourteenth century. The Law of

townsmen out of consideration for King Valdemar, another indication that the king played a large role in the settlement, and that the representation of the Lübeckers as agreeing to it voluntarily was more rhetorical than real. In addition the Lübeckers were to promise to defend Markvard's son in all his rights (*rechtes*) without specifying which rights. Presumably this was standard language, rather than a specific reference to the case.

What is most striking however, is not the elements of the settlement, but the fact that all the mayors and town councillors together with 100 townsmen had to free themselves 'according to the law' (entleghen mit rechte) and swear on the saints that they were innocent of the killing and had not participated in it either by oath or advice, and that they deplored it. The swearing of this oath seems incompatible with the fact that the town was collectively punished for the killing—for how could the people be innocent on the one hand, and on the other hand be punished? This apparent contradiction can only be resolved and the underlying logic of the oaths be understood if we take account of the fact that the king's peace was violated and assume that the killing was committed by persons in the service of the town, but not at the command of the town council. One could also argue that here we find the element of humiliation: given the fact that the Lübeckers were clearly seen as being responsible for the killing, some of them ran the risk of committing perjury, especially because they had to swear not only that they were innocent of the actual killing, but that they did not approve it. The huge cost of restoring the peace, financial and otherwise, probably made many of the townsmen wish Markvard had never been killed.

• • •

From these four very different examples of killing compromises, it can be concluded that religious gifts played a very big part in the settlements, and that they were arguably as good as monetary compensation given directly to the relatives. Often the closest family members were also expected to pay for perpetual masses for the soul of the departed, and the sum would most likely have to be larger than if they had died in bed of old age or illness. In the latter situations the death could be prepared for, but when someone was killed and (unless it was a lingering death) was thus robbed of the chance to receive the Last Rites, their stay in Purgatory would be very long and the prayers undertaken to shorten it correspondingly expensive. In the first three examples no

Jutland from 1241 prescribed three times 18 marks in man's compensation. In Lübeck the normal amount of man's compensation was 60–80 marks. Mantels, *Beiträge*, 164.

man's compensation was paid to the kinsmen, but the gifts for the slain man's soul could be seen as indirect man's compensation. In addition, the different humiliating rituals can be seen as a way for the kinsmen to regain the honour lost when one of their relatives was killed, and to show that they had accepted a settlement.

Finally we return to the question raised at the beginning of the essay: if the slain were not remembered and honoured by their kinsmen via revenge, were they remembered and honoured by agreements about compensation for killing? The answer to that is: yes. The departed person was remembered by perpetual prayers so that his name was kept alive, and the guilty party would often be reminded of the dead man not only by the financial costs of the settlement, but also by the humiliation he underwent in front of the slain person's relatives and friends. However, I would also argue that it was not just the slain person who was remembered and honoured by these concords. His kinsmen, too, gained tremendously, even if the economic gain was in some cases only indirect. Their symbolic capital of honour and prestige was increased by getting a powerful opponent to humiliate himself or themselves, or at least swear to protect the kinsmen's interests. In addition, in not settling a homicide case by taking man's compensation[34] the kinsmen could show both that they did not care about wretched mammon and that their honour could not be bought. In such cases not only was the departed remembered by the homicide settlement, but the relatives were as well, since they too were both honoured and remembered.

Works Cited

Printed Sources

Arnold of Lübeck. *Arnoldi Chronica Slavorum.* Edited by Johann Martin Lappenberg. MGH SS 14. http://www.dmgh.de/de/fs1/object/display/bsb00000766_00045.html>, accessed 14/6/2017. Hannover: 1868.

Bijsterveld, Arnoud-Jan A. Do ut des*: Gift Giving, Memoria, and Conflict Management in the Medieval Low Countries*. Hilversum: 2007.

Bricka, C. F. et al., eds. *Kancelliets Brevbøger vedrørende Danmarks indre Forhold i Uddrag*. Copenhagen: 1885–2005.

Brøndum-Nielsen, Johannes et al., eds. *Danmarks gamle Love med Kirkelovene*, 8 vols. Det Danske Sprog- og Litteraturselskab. Copenhagen: 1933–1964.

34 Unless the man's compensation was dictated by one's lord, and hence not demanded by the relatives.

Esders, Stefan. '"Eliten" und "Strafrecht" im frühen Mittelalter. Überlegungen zu den Bußen- und Wergeldkatalogen der Leges barbarorum'. In *Théories et pratiques des élites au haut Moyen Âge*, edited by François Bougard, Hans-Werner Goetz, and Régine Le Jan, 261–82. Collection Haut Moyen Âge 13. Turnhout: 2011.

Esmark, Kim. 'Disputing Property in Zealand: The Records of the Sorø Donation Book'. In *Disputing Strategies in Medieval Scandinavia*, edited by Kim Esmark et al., 181–218. Leiden and Boston: 2013.

Kerrigan, John. *Revenge Tragedy: Aeschylus to Armageddon*. Oxford: 1997.

Miller, William Ian. 'Choosing the Avenger: Some Aspects of the Bloodfeud in Medieval Iceland and England'. *Law and History Review*, vol. 1, no. 2 (Autumn, 1983): 159–204.

Miller, William Ian. *An Eye for an Eye*. Cambridge: 2005.

Netterstrøm, Jeppe Büchert. 'Bondefejder i Danmark 1450–1650'. In *Feider og fred i nordisk middelalder*, edited by Erik Opsahl, 35–72. Oslo: 2007.

Netterstrøm, Jeppe Büchert. 'Criminalization of Homicide in Early Modern Denmark (16th–17th centuries)'. *Scandinavian Journal of History* 42 (2017), no. 4, 459–75.

Netterstrøm, Jeppe Büchert. *Fejde og magt i senmiddelalderen: Rosenkrantzernes fejder med biskop Jens Iversen og Lage Brok, 1454–1474*. Viborg: 2012.

Netterstrøm, Jeppe Büchert. 'Introduction: Feud in Medieval and Early Modern Europe'. In *Feud in Medieval and Early Modern Europe*, edited by Bjørn Poulsen and Jeppe Büchert Netterstrøm, 9–67. Aarhus: 2007.

Oexle, Otto Gerhard. 'De Gegenwaert der Toten'. In *Death in the Middle Ages*, edited by Herman Braet and Werner Verbeke. Mediaevalia Lovaniensia series I studia IX. Leuven: 1983.

Oexle, Otto Gerhard. 'Memorialüberlieferung im früheren Mittelalter'. *Frühmittelalterliche Studien* 10 (1976): 70–95.

Sawyer, Peter. 'The Bloodfeud in Fact and Fiction'. In *Tradition og historieskrivning. Kilderne til Nordens ældste historie,* edited by Kirsten Hastrup and Preben Meulengracht Sørensen, 27–38. Acta Jutlandica LXIII: 2 Humanistisk Serie 61. Aarhus: 1987.

Sindballe, Kristian. *Af Testamentarvens Historie i dansk Ret*. Copenhagen: 1915.

Tamm, Ditlev and Helle Vogt. *The Danish Medieval Laws: The Laws of Scania, Zealand and Jutland*. London and New York: 2016.

Vogt, Helle. *The Function of Kinship in Medieval Nordic Legislation*. Leiden and Boston: 2010.

Vogt, Helle. 'The Kin's Collective Responsibility for the Payment of Man's Compensation in Medieval Denmark'. In *Wergild, Compensation and Penance: The Monetary Logic of Early Medieval Conflict Resolution*, ed. Lukas Bothe, Stefan Esders, and Han Nijdam. Leiden and Boston: forthcoming.

Vogt, Helle. 'The Power to Judge: Jurisdiction in Property Conflicts in Thirteenth-Century Denmark'. In *Disputing Strategies in Medieval Scandinavia*, edited by Kim Esmark et al., 161–80. Leiden and Boston: 2013.

Vogt, Helle. 'Protecting the Individual, the Kin and the Soul—Donation Regulations in Danish and Norwegian Medieval Legislation'. In *Inheritance and Property in the Nordic and Western World from Late Antiquity until Today,* edited by Ole-Albert Rønning, Helle Sigh, and Helle Vogt, 130–45. London and New York: 2017.

'Kong Christian 3.s anden københavnske reces 24. august 1537'. In *Den danske Rigslovgivning 1523*–1558, edited by Aage Andersen. Det Danske Sprog- og Litteraturselskab og Selskabet for Udgivelse af Kilder til dansk Historie, 198–9. Odense: 2015.

Online Sources

<http://diplomatarium.dk/dokument/14050224003>, accessed 14/6/2017. (King Erik's confirmation, 24 Feb.1405).

http://diplomatarium.dk/dokument/14050224001, accessed 19/6/2017. (Compromise between Jens Nielsen and Jens Andersen 24 Feb. 1405).

PART 2

Emotion, Violence, Vengeance, and Law in Medieval Literary Sources

CHAPTER 7

Telling Evidence in *Njáls saga*

Carol J. Clover

Readers of *Njáls saga* cannot but be struck by its trials—not only their number and intensity, but their lavish attention to procedure at the expense of substantive matters. The formalism of early Icelandic legal process may not be "of the sort that traditional legal history has attributed to prerational prebureaucratic law," writes Bill Miller of the collection of laws known as *Grágás*, but "procedure was still a good nine points of the law."[1] Make that more like 9.8 points in *Njáls saga*, for if other saga trials "show more colloquy and ad hoc argumentation than formal pleading," *Njála*'s show pleadings and more pleadings. The most dramatic moments in *Njála*'s trials turn on the performance and qualities of those pleadings (which audiences judge letter-perfect, flawed, eloquent, forceful, and so on) or on procedural trickery. Where, modern readers may wonder, are substantive matters—considerations of evidence, proof, facts? It's hard to believe that such an otherwise fiercely causal and ardently legal a narrative as *Njála* should go slack where these things are concerned. If ever a text were designed to pay heed to facts, we'd think it would be this one.[2]

And heed facts, I submit, it does—just not where or in the forms we might expect. In what follows, I want to extend the search for evidential reasoning in *Njála* beyond the trials proper, back into the running text, i.e., those parts of the saga that precede the trial (or other action). My point is that, especially where what I'll call "murky" matters are concerned ("murky" referring to things that are either unwitnessed or otherwise invisible), *Njála* can go to remarkable, if not always credible, lengths to adduce and vet evidence—and in configurations fully recognizable to modern readers.

Before I begin, two caveats and one confession. The first caveat is that my compass is narrow: I'll be considering just *Njála*, and within it, just four episodes. The other is that I proceed not as a legal scholar, but as a literary one with an abiding interest in saga narrative and its origins—though, as I'll suggest, the

1 William Ian Miller, *Bloodtaking and Peacemaking: Feud, Law, and Society in Saga Iceland* (Chicago and London: 1990), 248, 249.

2 I use the word "fact" advisedly in these pages to refer to a notion that seems to me implicit in *Njáls saga*, i.e., of evidence that has met some unstated standard of proof and is thus so robust that both parties accept it as beyond dispute. See also note 7, below.

© KONINKLIJKE BRILL NV, LEIDEN, 2018 | DOI 10.1163/9789004366374_011

legal and the literary-historical may on this point be linked. The confession has to do with my unease at venturing my thoughts on legal matters in *Njáls saga* to the world's expert on legal matters in *Njáls saga*. Miller, you've helped me before with questions I've had in this area, and I hope I got it right here.

• • •

Before I turn to murky events, let me take up an emphatically non-murky one: Flosi's killing of Helgi Njalsson in the beginning phase of the retaliatory burning of Njal and his family in their house at Bergthorshvall.[3] The burning attack is a massive and complex event, claiming eleven victims and involving more than a hundred attackers, of whom an untold number, but presumably more than a few, were also witnesses to Helgi's death.[4] It all happened two months before the beginning of winter, though it does not come to trial until the following summer at the Althing.

I'll begin with an excerpt from that trial. It's one of Mord Valgardsson's many pleadings (Mord being the lawyer asked to prosecute Flosi).

> Mord named witnesses—"to testify that I give notice of an action against Flosi Thordarson for unlawful assault, inasmuch as he assaulted Helgi Njalsson at the place where he assaulted Helgi and inflicted on him an internal wound, brain wound, or marrow wound, which did cause Helgi's death. I demand that Flosi be sentenced to full outlawry on this charge, not to be fed nor forwarded nor helped nor harbored. I claim that all his possessions be forfeit, half to me and half to those men in the Quarter who have a lawful right to receive his confiscated goods. I refer this manslaughter action to the proper Quarter Court. I give lawful notice of it, in public, at the Law Rock. I give notice of an action, to be heard at this session, for full outlawry against Flosi Thordarsson, as assigned to me by Thorgeir Thórisson." There was loud approval at the Law Rock for the eloquent and forceful way Mord had spoken. (141)

---

3 *Njáls saga*, written down in the late thirteenth century, is about events occurring around the year 1000. The Old Icelandic text is from *Brennu-Njáls Saga*, ed. Einar Ól. Sveinsson, Íslenzk fornrit 12 (Reykjavík: 1954). English translations are from *Njal's Saga*, trans. Magnus Magnusson and Hermann Pálsson (London: 1960), with some silent adjustments of my own. Numbers after quotations from both the original and the translation refer to chapters, not pages.

4 The account of the burning refers several times to men outside, some by name, thus making it clear that this was a public affair.

> Mǫrðr nefndi sér vátta; "nefndi ek í þat vætti," segir hann, "at ek lýsi lǫgmætu frumhlaupi á hǫnd Flosa Þórðarsyni, er hann hljóp til Helga Njálssonar á þeim vættvangi, er Flosi Þórðarson hljóp til Helga Njálssonar ok veitti honum holundar sár eða heilundar eða mergundar, þat er at ben gerðisk, en Helgi fekk bana af. Tel ek hann eiga at verða um sǫk þá sekjan skógarmann, óalanda, óferjanda, óráðanda ǫllum bjargráðum; tel ek sekt fé hans allt, hálft mér, en hálft fjórðungsmǫnnum þeim, er sektarfé eigu at taka eptir hann at lǫgum. Lýsi ek vígsǫk þessi til fjórðungsdóms þess, er sǫkin á í at koma at lǫgum; lýsi ek lǫglýsing; lýsi ek í heyranda hljóði at lǫgbergi; lýsi ek nú til sóknar í sumar ok til sektar fullrar á hǫnd Flosa Þórðarsyni. Lýsi ek handseldri sǫk Þorgeirs Þórissonar." At lǫgbergi var mikill rómr at því gǫrr, at Mǫrðr hefði mælt vel ok skǫruliga. (141)

And so on and on. But for the first line or two, this speech is repeated almost verbatim several times before and during the trial, which itself goes on for some twenty pages in modern edition.[5] The wording regarding the three types of wounds, one fatal, repeats almost exactly the wordings of *Grágás*.[6] When the defense takes its turn, there is no objection, or even reference, to this statement. Bill Miller suggests that such a declaration would be understood to "have attained the status of fact by formal procedures," namely, Mord's pleading and the absence of counterpleading by the other side, so it becomes a fact when no one objects.[7]

I'll come back to the trial of Flosi. First let's jump back seven chapters to the event itself—the account of Helgi's death, as it happens. Here, in the running text, we are told how, inside the burning house, he reluctantly puts on

5 This pleading pertains to the assault only, not the death wound, which requires a separate pleading with a different opening phrase (though it is largely identical otherwise). Bill Miller speculates on this and other repetitions, and also on why the act of killing Helgi looms so much larger in the trial than does the act of burning (in which so many more died), in his *"Why Is Your Axe Bloody?": A Reading of Njáls Saga* (Oxford: 2014), 266–7.

6 A man who, for example, publishes a wound or blow before witnesses is to state what the injuries are: "hvarz er heilvnd eða holund. eða merg und. eða þa er hann særðe hann þvi sáre er at ben gerðiz þa er hann fec bana" (whether it was a brain wound or internal wound or marrow wound; or that he wounded the other with a wound which proved mortal when he [got] his death): *Grágás. Islændernes Lovbog i Fristatens Tid, udgivet efter det Kongelige Bibliotheks Haandskrift*, 3 vols., ed. Vilhjálmur Finsen (Copenhagen: 1852, 1879, 1882; rpr. Odense, 1974), vol. Ia, p. 157. *Laws of Early Iceland: Grágás*, 2 vols. trans. Andrew Dennis, Peter Foote, and Richard Perkins (Winnipeg: 1980, 2000) vol. 1, p. 148.

7 William Ian Miller, private communication; see also *Bloodtaking*, 250 et passim.

a woman's scarf and cloak and files outdoors with the women, children, and servants who've been allowed egress. Then:

> When Helgi came outside, Flosi said, "That's a very tall and broad-shouldered woman; seize her!" When Helgi heard this, he threw off the cloak; he was carrying a sword under his arm, and now he struck out at one of the men, slicing off the bottom of the shield and severing his leg. Then Flosi came up and struck at Helgi's neck, cutting off his head with one blow. (129)
>
> En er Helgi kom út, þá mælti Flosi: "Sú er há kona ok mikil um herðar; takið þér hana ok haldið henni!" En er Helgi heyrði þetta, kastaði hann skikkjunni; hann hafði haft sverð undir hendi sér ok hjó til manns, ok kom í skjǫldinn, ok af sporðinn ok fótinn með. Þá kom Flosi at ok hjó á háls Helga, svá at þegar tók af hǫfuðit. (129)

That's it; the next sentence turns to something else.

This description of the killing is chillingly blunt. It also has a legal quality insofar as its wording fills in the blanks in advance, as it were, of the *Grágás* formula as to the assault and wound-type. It may be so that Flosi's killing of Helgi becomes a formal fact only at the Althing, when the other side fails to counterplead. But in a world in which bloodfeud and lawsuits were alternatives, can't it have been the case that something like facts—serviceable facts—came into being simply by virtue of their having been publicly witnessed when they happened? I can't help thinking that the killing of Helgi was such a fact—that its plain-view nature made it, for all practical purposes, subject to consensus on the spot, and thus rather like what our legal system calls "stipulated." In either case, nothing more is said about Flosi's killing of Helgi until the trial is at hand, when Mord simply declares it in his pleadings.

•••

But what about things that are unwitnessed, or indeed unwitnessable—what I'm calling murky matters? The sagas give us a number of cases of proof by admission, e.g., an unwitnessed killing that the perpetrator "publishes" to someone in the vicinity. Such an act is known as a *lýsing*—a telling term, implying, as it does, a "bringing to light." (Mord, in his above-quoted trial-pleading on Flosi's behalf, uses the verb *lýsa*, in that context usually translated as "give notice," no fewer than six times.)

And unwitnessed matters that are not admitted? For an example of how these may be processed, we need only follow *Njála*'s narration as it takes us, after Helgi's death, from outside to inside the blazing building. There—in private, as it were—we are told how, in the midst of smoke and flames, Njal charges the steward, who is about to leave, to take note of where and how he himself, Bergthora, and the child Thord are arranging themselves to die in bed. The narrator goes on to tell how the steward covers those three with an ox-hide and then leaves the house—whereupon Ketil, one of the attackers outdoors, "seized his arm and dragged him clear and questioned him closely about his father-in-law Njal" and the steward "told everything that had happened"(129).[8] So we have the steward's witness testimony as to how and where Njal will almost certainly die. And moments later, Skarphedin (back indoors) will determine when that happens, as he tells Kari, "Now my father must be dead, for not a groan or a cough has been heard from him" (129).[9]

That leaves Skarphedin, Grim, and Kari in the burning house. After a bit more fight-back, they set about trying to escape. With some heroic help from Skarphedin, Kari gets out through a back way ("Kari's clothes and hair were on fire by now, as he threw himself down off the wall and dodged away in the thick of the smoke.")[10] That brings us down to two still indoors: Grim and Skarphedin. Then:

> Skarphedin went over to his brother Grim. They joined hands and stamped on the fire. But when they reached the middle of the room, Grim fell dead. Skarphedin went to the gable-end of the house; then, with a great crash, the whole roof fell in. Skarphedin was pinned between roof and gable, and couldn't move from there at all. (130)
>
> Skarpheðinn gekk þá til Gríms, bróður síns; heldusk þeir þá í hendr ok tráðu eldinn. En er þeir kómu í miðjan skálann, þá fell Grímr dauðr niðr. Skarpheðinn gekk til enda hússins; þá varð brestr mikill; reið þá ofan ǫll þekjan. Varð hann þá í millum þess ok gaflaðsins; mátti hann þaðan hvergi hrœrask. (130)

---

8 Ketil "tók í mót honum ok kippti honum út ok spurði vandliga at Njáli, mági sínum; hann sagði allt it sanna." (129).

9 "'Nú mun faðir minn dauðr vera, ok hefir hvárki til hans styn né hósta'." (129).

10 "Þá loguðu klæðin ǫll á Kára ok svá hárit. Hann steypir sér út af þekkjunni ok stiklar þá með reykinum." (129).

But no one sees Skarphedin and Grim's last actions, and neither of them will live to tell the tale. Nor is there a handy steward or other such witness around to pass the information along. So how do we know these things?

Almost as if to preempt that question, the narration's very next sentence brings us back outdoors to this curious scene:

> Flosi and his men stayed by the blaze until broad daylight. Then a man came riding towards them. Flosi asked him his name, and he replied that he was Geirmund, a kinsman of the Sigfussons. "You have taken drastic action here," said Geirmund. "People will call it a drastic action [*stórvirki*], and a malicious one [*illvirki*], too," said Flosi, "but nothing can be done about it now." Geirmund asked, "How many people of note have perished there?" Flosi said: "Among the dead here are Njal and Bergthora, their sons Helgi, Grim, and Skarphedin; Kari Solmundarson and his son Thord; and Thord Freedman. We're not sure about those others who are less well known to us." "You've listed among the dead a man who to my certain knowledge has escaped," said Geirmund, "for I talked to him only this morning." "Who is that?" asked Flosi. "Kari Solmundarson," said Geirmund. "My neighbor Bard and I met him with his hair burnt off and his clothes badly charred, and Bard lent him a horse." "Had he any weapons with him?" asked Flosi. "He was carrying the sword Life-Taker," said Geirmund, "and one of its edges was blue and discoloured. We said that the metal must have softened, but Kari replied that he would soon harden it again in the blood of the Sigfussons and the other Burners." 'What did he tell you of Skarphedin and Grim?" asked Flosi. "He said that they were both alive when he left them," replied Geirmund, "but that they must be dead by now." (130)

> Þeir Flosi váru við eldana, þar til mjǫk var morgnat. Þá kom þar maðr ríðandi at þeim. Flosi spurði hann at nafni; hann nefndisk Geirmundr ok kvezk vera frændi Sigfússona ok mælti: "Þér hafið mikit stórvirki unnit." Flosi svarar: "Bæði munu menn þetta kalla stórvirki ok illvirki. Ok þó má nú ekki at hafa." Geirmundr mælti: "Hversu mart hefir hér fyrirmanna látizk?" Flosi svarar: "Hér hefir látizk Njáll ok Bergþóra, Helgi ok Grímr ok Skarpheðinn Njálssynir, Þórðr Kárason ok Kári Sǫlmundarson, Þórðr leysingi. En þá vita vér ógǫrla um fleiri menn, þá er oss ókunnari." Geirmundr mælti: "Dauðan segir þú þann mann, er vér vitum, at á braut hefir komizk ok ek hefi talat við í morgin." "Hverr er sá?" segir Flosi. "Kára Sǫlmundarson fundu vit Bárðr, búi minn," segir Geirmundr, "ok fekk Bárðr honum hest sinn, or var brunnit af honum hárit ok svá klæðin."

> "Hafði hann nǫkkut vápna?" segir Flosi. "Hafði hann sverðit Fjǫrsváfni," segir Geirmundr, "ok var blánaðr annar eggteinninn á, ok sǫgðu vit, at dignat mundi hafa, en hann svaraði því, at hann skyldi herða sverðit í blóði Sigfússona eða annarra brennumanna." Flosi mælti: "Hvat sagði hann til Skarpheðins eða Gríms?" "Á lífi sagði hann þá báða, þá er þeir skilðu," segir Geirmundr, "en þó kvað hann þá mundu nú báða dauða." (130)

To which Flosi responds that the attackers will soon pay with their own lives.

This dialogue sounds for all the world like an evidence-vetting process. First, Flosi grants that the burning is not only a *stórvirki*, but an *illvirki*—both *Grágás* categories. We then get four witness accounts: (1) Flosi's about the loss of life as nearly as he could see it from outdoors; (2) Geirmund's, which corrects Flosi's on several points, including the escape of Kari, badly burned and bent on revenge; (3) Kari's, as reported by Geirmund, regarding the condition of Grim and Skarphedin when he left them (speaking in the first person plural, Geirmund makes clear that his neighbor Bard, who was with him the whole time, could confirm these things); (4) and to these three I'll add a fourth, which comes just moments later, with the earwitness account of these men and others as to Skarphedin's own "testimony" as, down in the flames, he utters some garbled verse that may have been his dying words. I'm going to call this scene with Geirmund, in which so much crucial evidence is brought into the record, a "proof segment."

That proof segment will be supplemented by yet another as Kari and others excavate the burning site and both locate and identify the corpses. The discovery of the bodies of Njal, Bergthora, and the boy Thord in bed under the hide confirms the steward's testimony to that effect. The location of Grim's body at the "middle of the main room" confirms the narration's earlier claim that that's where he fell dead. Similarly the location of Skarphedin's body between gable and roof. And so on. The narrator uses the bodily remains as systematically as a modern crime-scene investigator might. Yes, the excavation sequence also reads like a brief for Njal's martyrdom; but that should not detract from its other, plainly secular purpose: to confirm who died and how, where, and when. The murkiness of the indoor burning thus produces not just one, but two, proof segments: the Geirmund one, which has to do with comparing partial witness accounts; and the excavation one, which has to do with the physical evidence of the bodies themselves. The excavation scene is the premier proof segment in *Njála* and perhaps in all the Íslendingasögur.[11]

11 *Njála* is remarkably preoccupied, here and elsewhere, with just where and when (including in what order) people die.

So plain-sight matters and murky ones would seem to entail very different narrative strategies. Helgi's public beheading can be told just once, when it happens, and that's it: no further evidence needed. But a murky death, like Grim's or Skarphedin's, needs more—sometimes a lot more, as these proof segments show. Only after the evidence is in and a deed proved can it be acted upon. In fact, at the risk of circularity, I would suggest that the elaboration of proof segments after murky events but not after plain-sight ones confirms that public witnessing itself does the job—on the spot, wordlessly. In which case it does indeed amount to something like stipulation in our trial, though apparently so self-evidently that it didn't need spelling out in either the laws or the saga.

•••

I'll come back to the Geirmund scene later. First I want to look at two other murky examples, both having to do at least indirectly with Gunnar of Hlidarend. The first is back in chapters 47–49, an elegant mini-saga that tells of a food-theft and the discovery thereof. It begins in the summer, when Gunnar and his neighbors over at Kirkby are at the Althing. Gunnar's wife Hallgerd, at home in Hlidarend and still angry at the Kirkby people for having refused to sell Gunnar food and hay in a time of shortage, sends a slave named Melkolf there to steal two horse-loads of butter and cheese and then burn down the storehouse so that the loss will seem accidental.[12] This the slave does, in the process forgetting his knife and belt near the scene of the crime. When the Althing is over and men return to their homes, the Kirkby people are taken aback at the fire damage but assume natural causes. In the meantime, over at Hlidarend, Hallgerd serves her husband and his friends, also just back from the Althing, a lavish dinner, including cheese and butter. Gunnar, knowing they had no such provisions in stock, asks Hallgerd where they came from. "From a source that should not spoil your appetite," she replies, adding that kitchen matters are in any case not a man's business. In anger, Gunnar says, "It will be an evil day when I become a thief's accomplice," and slaps her. Hallgerd says she will remember that slap and pay him back one day.[13]

---

12 For a brief but astute defense of Hallgerd's action, see Miller, *Bloodtaking*, 329, n. 30; and on the episode more generally, see his "Food and Feud" and "The Theft" sections in *Axe* (85–93; 110–6; and 304–5).

13 "'Þaðan, sem þú mátt eta,' segir hon, 'enda er þat ekki karla at annask um matreiðu.' Gunnar reiddisk ok mælti: 'Illa er þá, ef ek em þjófsnautr,'—ok lýstr hana kinnhest. Hon

Meanwhile, over at Kirkby, the knife and belt are found and identified as those of the slave Melkolf from Hlidarend. The finger of suspicion thus points to Gunnar and Hallgerd. The Kirkby people go to Mord Valgardsson, described as maliciously cunning and long hostile to Gunnar, and pay him to come up with a plan.[14] Mord advises them to send women round the district to trade small wares to housewives on the assumption that people "are inclined to rid themselves of any stolen goods that may be in their possession; and that's what will happen now if a crime is involved."[15] The women are to show Mord what they were given in each place, and then, if the evidence is established (ef uppvíst verðr), he says, he wants nothing more to do with the matter. The women leave and return after a fortnight with bulging packs.

> Mord asked them where they had been given the most; they replied that it had been at Hlidarend, and that Hallgerd had been particularly generous. Mord asked what they had been given there. "Cheese," they replied. Mord asked to see it, and they showed it to him; there were a number of slices. Mord took charge of the cheese, and a little later he went [over to Kirkby] to see Otkel. He asked Otkel to fetch his wife's cheese-mold and, when it was brought, he laid the slices into it. They fitted perfectly. They discovered that the women had been given a whole cheese. Mord said, "You can now see that Hallgerd must have stolen it." They assembled all the evidence [*dœmi*], and with that Mord said that he had fulfilled his part of the bargain, and took his leave. (49)
>
> Mǫrðr spurði, hvar þeim hefði mest gefit verit. Þær sǫgðu, at þeim hefði at Hlíðarendi mest gefit verit ok Hallgerðr yrði þeim mestr drengr. Hann spyrr, hvat þeim væri þar gefit; þær sǫgðu, at þeim væri ostr gefinn. Hann beiddisk at sjá; þær sýndu honum, ok váru þat sneiðir margar; tók hann þær ok varðveitti. Litlu síðar fór hann at finna Otkel; bað hann, at taka skyldi ostkistu Þorgerðar, ok var svá gǫrt; lagði hann þar í niðr sneiðirnar, ok stózk þat á endum ok ostkistan. Sá þeir þá, at þeim hafði heill hleifr gefinn verit. Þá mælti Mǫrðr: "Nú meguð ér sjá, at Hallgerðr

---

kvazk þann hest muna skyldu ok launa, ef hon mætti." (49) For a discussion of the social and sexual politics of the slap scene, see Miller, *Axe*, 57–9.

14 Mord was "illa til frænda sinna ok einna verst til Gunnars; hann var slœgr maðr í skapferðum ok illgjárn í ráðum." (25).

15 "'... því at allir hafa þat skap at gefa þat upp fyrst, er stolit er, ef þat hafa at varðveita, ok svá mun hér, ef af mannavǫldum er'." (49).

> mun stolit hafa ostinum." Drógu þeir ǫll dœmi saman; segir þá Mǫrðr, at hann þóttisk lauss þessa máls; skilðu þeir at því. (49)

Icelanders were hard on secret crimes exactly because they *were* secret (stealing food, regardless of its value, could earn full outlawry). But as the forensically-gifted Mord demonstrates, even the murkiest of deeds can be brought to light. Sending women off to trade under false pretenses is clever, if devious; the fitting of the cheese to the mold is pure Sherlock Holmes. One could hardly ask for a neater proof segment than this. It nails down an episode that has the important function of explaining at least some of the mounting enmity toward Gunnar in those districts—enmity that will eventually result in his death. And, for good measure, it occasions the slap that Hallgerd will indeed remember and repay in the last moments of her husband's life.[16]

But Gunnar is the object of hostilities long before he's actually slain. My last "murky" example comes in chapters 68–70, which tell of a thwarted conspiracy to kill him. The difference here is that the murkiness is not visual: it's mental. The question is whether some fully-armed men who set out one evening do so with the aim of killing Gunnar. At issue, then, is the state of mind known as intent, which, as in our own time and system, is proved by circumstances from which it may be inferred.

Here's the story. Thorgeir Starkadarson and his friend Thorgeir Otkelsson have a grudge against Gunnar. At the end of Chapter 68, they decide to do something about it.

> They agreed to make an attack on Gunnar. Thorgeir Starkadarson then said that Gunnar would be alone at home in a few days' time. "Meet me with eleven men," he said, "and I shall bring the same number." After that, Thorgeir rode home. (68)

> Ok semja þeir þat með sér at fara at Gunnari; segir þá Þorgeirr, at Gunnarr myndi á fara nátta fresti einn heima vera;—"skalt þú koma við inn tólfta mann til móts við mik, en ek mun hafa jafnmarga." Siðan reið Þorgeirr heim. (68)

16 Gunnar, defending himself with bow and arrow inside a house surrounded by enemies intent on taking his life, suddenly finds himself with a broken bowstring. When he asks Hallgerd for a strand of her long hair as a makeshift solution, she reminds him of the slap and refuses. To which Gunnar replies with a proverb: "To each his own way of earning fame" (Hefir hverr til síns ágætis nǫkkut). Now defenseless, he is killed just four sentences later. (77).

So: another unwitnessed one-on-one conversation that will soon be proved true—meaning that the Thorgeirs' intent will be revealed.

That's chapter 68. In chapter 70, at the Althing, Njal, on Gunnar's behalf, brings a charge of conspiracy to an arbitration hearing.

> People now rode to the Althing as usual, and both parties attended. Njal asked for a hearing, and then asked all good men present what claim, in their opinion, Gunnar had against the Thorgeirs for the conspiracy against his life [*fjǫrráð*]; they answered that in their opinion a man of Gunnar's standing had claims for heavy compensation. (70)

> Ríða menn nú til alþingis at vanða; eru nú hvárirtveggju á þingi. Njáll kvaddi sér hljóðs, spurði alla ina beztu menn, er þar váru komnir, hvert mál þeim þœtti Gunnarr eiga á þeim nǫfnum fyrir fjǫrráðin. Þeir svǫruðu, at þeim þótti slíkr maðr mikinn rétt á sér eiga. (70)

Between chapters 68 and 70, the plan to kill Gunnar evidently became an outed and actionable fact. What happened in the in-between chapter to cause that? We can almost smell a proof segment.

Chapter 69 begins at Thorolfsfell, where Njal is talking with his daughter-in-law Thorhild. It's late at night, and a shepherd has been out looking for some missing sheep. Then, the saga says, the shepherd returns. He rides up to the door, dismounts, and enters.

> Thorhild asked, "did you find the sheep?" "I found something much more important," he replied. "What was that?" asked Njal. "I found twenty-four men up there in the wood," he replied. "They had tethered their horses and were fast asleep, and had hung their shields in the branches." He had observed them so closely that he could describe the weapons and clothing of all of them, and Njal could tell exactly who each one was. (69)

> [Þórhildr] mælti: "Fanntu sauðina?" "Fann ek þat, er meira myndi varða," segir hann. "Hvat var þat?" segir Njáll. "Ek fann fjóra ok tuttugu menn," segir hann, "í skóginum uppi; þeir hǫfðu bundit hesta sína, en sváfu sjálfir; þeir hǫfðu fest skjǫldu sína í limar." En svá hafði hann gǫrla at hugat, at hann sagði frá allra þeira vápnabúnaði ok klæðum. Njáll vissi þá gǫrla, hverr hverrgi var … (69)

Njal thanks the shepherd, sends him to warn Gunnar, and then mounts a horse himself and rides to the woods where the men lie sleeping. Calling out, he rouses them:

> "You are careless, lying about like this," he said, "and what's the point of this expedition, anyway? Gunnar is not a man to be messed with, and this is a flagrant case of conspiracy to kill [*fjǫrráð*]. You had better know that Gunnar is gathering forces; he'll be here soon and will kill you, unless you flee back home." They jumped to their feet in panic, grabbed their weapons, mounted their horses, and fled back to Thrihyrning. (69)

> "Óvarliga liggið þér," segir hann, "eða til hvers skal fǫr sjá gǫr hafa verit? ok er Gunnarr engi klekktunaramaðr. En ef satt skal um tala, þá eru þetta in mestu fjǫrráð. Skuluð þér þat ok vita, at Gunnarr er í liðsafnaði; ok mun hann hér brátt koma ok drepa yðr, nema þér riðið undan ok heim." Þeir brugðusk við skjótt, ok varð þeim mjǫk við felmt, ok tóku vápn sín ok stigu á hesta sína ok hleyptu heim undir Þríhyrning. (69)

So the shepherd is the first witness. He has observed the men so carefully that he can identify them; and he also reasons, given their weapons and shields, that they must be up to no good. The second witness is Njal, who in addition to confirming the who, gets at just what the no-good is—that is, their intention to kill Gunnar. For intent, that murkiest of matters, we need at least circumstantial evidence, and that is exactly what Njal's accusation, joined to the Gunnar threat, produces: a panicky reaction that proves that they have indeed been caught redhanded. In much the way that Mord outed Hallgerd as a thief, then, Njal outs the Thorgeirs as conspirators.

With the players identified and their intent exposed, a triumphant Njal goes to Gunnar and suggests bargaining with the two Thorgeirs. The result is the Althing arbitration at which Njal wins a handsome settlement for Gunnar. Of course the matter doesn't end there; after some more back-and-forth conflict over the coming months, Gunnar will be killed after all. But the immediate outcome of Njal's midnight ride is proof enough to do the legal job for the moment.

Chapter 69 could hardly be more opportune. What the narrative needs at this point (and apparently presumes its audience needs) is evidence for *fjǫrráð*, and that's exactly what it gives us. So it's super convenient. But is it credible? Do we really believe that a shepherd memorizes the clothing and weapons of not just a few men, but twenty-four of them? And that from his descriptions Njal recognizes every one? And isn't there something almost comical about the idea of a sixty-year old Njal, never a man of action, jumping onto a horse in the middle of the night, charging solo into the woods, waking two dozen would-be killers, and calling them out so menacingly that they flee?

Now that we're on the subject of plausibility, let's go back to the Geirmund-Flosi conversation during the burning sequence. That proof segment too is awfully convenient. It's also a little strange. Who is this Geirmund? Flosi doesn't seem to recognize him, for he must ask his name. Nor does Geirmund offer a patronymic, which would have identified him more closely than the vague "kinsman of the Sigfussons." And he appears nowhere in *Njála* but here; after another quick mention a half-page later, he evaporates from the saga. A Fornrit footnote observes that this Geirmund is otherwise unknown, as is Bard, his claimed neighbor (the other half of the "we").[17] The whole scene is a little spectral. As to its origins, we can only speculate. In any case, its job in the burning episode is clear: to give the narration of actionable events the source footnote—the proof—it needs.

These two episodes—the Geirmund encounter and Njal's midnight ride—are equivalents, both functionally and compositionally. Both proceed from some murky matter: unseen events in one, state of mind in the other. Both serve to bring fresh evidence into the public record. Both strike a legalistic tone: Njal's precise accusation of *fjǫrráð*; the crafted questions and answers of the Geirmund-Flosi exchange. And finally, both scenes have the loud ring of inauthenticity.

What interests me, though, is not so much the authenticity or inauthenticity of such proof segments as the narration's systematic need to have them. It's as though, following every murky matter of consequence, there's a slot marked "proof segment" that needs filling with conclusive evidence, direct or circumstantial. Njal's midnight ride may or may not be a later invention, but the fact that tellers and/or writers along the way knew that the narrative needed evidence of intent to kill at this point speaks volumes about the legal paradigm that underlies the text. Likewise the Geirmund-Flosi conversation: it speaks to the same paradigm. Even if we doubt such scenes—even if we suspect them of being backformations from the lawsuits or revenge actions they look forward to—we are still looking at a protocol whereby the next move was expected to be based on facts as proved by evidence.

• • •

Where matters related to legal process are concerned, *Njáls saga* has long been recognized as a special case. To its other unusual features I would add

17 "Geirmundr er annars ókunnur og slíkt hið sama Bárður, búi hans ..." *Brennu-Njáls saga*, p. 334, n. 1.

the methodical lengths to which it goes, in long stretches of pre-trial text, to adduce evidence that will prove facts necessary to future actions. As we have seen, these evidence-pursuits can be quite substantial, especially in the case of murky matters. (Plain-sight matters do not seem to require the narrative attention that covert ones do.) Taken together, the Bergthorshvall burning passages discussed above—the sequence of witness accounts both during the burning itself and during the later excavation—yield an impressive range of specific evidence about who died (and who escaped) and when and where. And the elaborate pair of episodes having to do with Gunnar (his wife's cheese-theft; the Thorgeirs' conspiracy to kill him) are stories in their own right, each with its own plot-line; each with a smoking-gun moment (the fitting of the cheese to the mold, the panicky retreat of the plotters); and each with its master-investigator, Mord and Njal respectively. (Evidently exposing matters like theft and intent required the finest minds. Indeed, I can't help thinking that *Njála*'s heart lies less in trials proper than in the prior processes of on-site detection and proof.) Proving facts is not a minor matter in *Njáls saga*, in short. These four passages alone—and there are more—add up to some forty of the saga's 350 pages, and they contain some of its finest moments.

Works Cited

Brennu-Njáls saga. Edited by Einar Ól. Sveinsson. Íslenzk fornrit 12. Reykjavík: 1954.

Dennis, Andrew, Peter Foote, and Richard Perkins, trans. *Laws of Early Iceland: Grágás*, vol. 1. Winnipeg: 1980.

Grágás. Islændernes Lovbog i Fristatens Tid, udgivet efter det Kongelige Bibliotheks Haandskrift, vol. Ia, edited by Vilhjálmur Finsen. Copenhagen: 1852, rpr. Odense 1974.

Miller, William Ian. *Bloodtaking and Peacemaking: Feud, Law, and Society in Saga Iceland*. Chicago and London: 1990.

Miller, William Ian. "*Why Is Your Axe Bloody?*": *A Reading of Njáls Saga*. Oxford: 2014.

Njal's Saga. Translated by Magnus Magnusson and Hermann Pálsson. London: 1960.

CHAPTER 8

Widening Horizons in *Njáls saga*

Theodore M. Andersson

In his Icelandic studies Bill Miller has combined the analytical skills of jurisprudence and sociology with the esthetic sensibilities of a literary scholar. He has therefore focused on the best texts, *Njáls saga* among the long sagas and "Auðunar þáttr" among the shorter narratives.[1] For the most part saga scholars avoid discriminating between texts of the highest order and lesser creations, but Miller's choices betray him. His book about *Njáls saga* is an unabashed tribute to the quality of this masterpiece, though other scholars may prefer more neutral rankings.

An example of esthetic dispassion in saga study is the order of the texts in the Íslenzk fornrit series, on which we are all dependent. The order is not determined by narrative distinction but by geographical location. The series starts in the southwest corner of Iceland with *Egils saga*, moves up the west coast, across the north coast, and down the East Fjords until it comes to rest in the south with *Njáls saga*. Since this text is so frequently classed as the latest and greatest of the sagas, such an ordering is not without a, perhaps unintentional, sense of progression. But it surely suggests as well that the sagas are, generally speaking, regional. The argument in what follows is that *Njáls saga*, although it was caught up in an organizational scheme by region, is decidedly not regional. In fact it may be read to declare overtly an end to the regional principle.

The earlier sagas of similar weight and narrative ambition, *Egils saga* and *Laxdœla saga*, are quite self-consciously regional. They celebrate the colonization of their respective regions, Borgarfjord and Breidafjord, and their coverage hardly extends beyond their home regions except to describe how

1 The consensus that *Njáls saga* is the best of the sagas goes back as far as Peter Erasmus Müller, *Sagabibliothek med anmærkninger og indledende afhandlinger*, vol. 1 (Copenhagen: 1817), 51. Karl Lehmann and Hans Schnorr von Carolsfeld follow suit in *Die Njálssage insbesondere in ihren juristischen Bestandtheilen* (Berlin: 1883), 1, and introduce it as "[die] schönste aller isländischen Sagen" (the most beautiful of all the Icelandic sagas). Miller himself classifies it as "indisputably the greatest" in *"Why Is Your Axe Bloody?": A Reading of Njáls saga* (Oxford: 2014), 2. On "Auðunar þáttr" see his *Audun and the Polar Bear: Luck, Law, and Largesse in a Medieval Tale of Risky Business* (Leiden and Boston: 2008).

© KONINKLIJKE BRILL NV, LEIDEN, 2018 | DOI 10.1163/9789004366374_012

their leading personalities are exalted at the Norwegian court or other remote scenes of high adventure. They do not shed distinction on Iceland so much as they promote the greater glory of the leading local families.[2] In the final section of *Egils saga* Borgarfjord in fact becomes a kind of family preserve when Egil expels a neighbor on the implied grounds that the land he occupies was a gift from Egil's father.[3]

Laxdœla saga is even more extravagant in its promotion of family history. It is constructed in a way quite similar to what we find in *Egils saga*: family history, colonization, distribution of land, youthful adventures, interaction with royalty, a central love story, and an account of Gudrun Osvifrsdottir's old age parallel to Egil Skallagrimsson's last days. It is not unlikely that there is an element of imitation in these correspondences, but in addition the imitation seems pointedly competitive. The founding mother Unn is a grander figure than Skallagrim Ulfsson and is indeed the grandest colonist to be found anywhere in the sagas. Hoskuld, the son of her distinguished fellow-colonist Kol, cohabits with an Irish princess and begets the incomparable Olaf Peacock, who, though illegitimate, is deemed worthy of marrying the greatest lady in Borgarfjord, Thorgerd Egilsdottir. This rank-conscious promotion of a semi-certified grandee in Breidafjord could be read as a relativizing of the neighboring district in Borgarfjord.

The tacit comparison does not stop there. Whereas Egil and the two Thorolfs in *Egils saga* make their way in foreign lands with military prowess, no such requirement burdens the young gallants of *Laxdœla saga*. They merely appear before the Norwegian king and are acknowledged as persons of quality without further ado.[4] Romantic hyperbole follows suit. Egil's passion for his brother's widow Asgerd gets a memorable, though brief, mention, but is largely understated (ÍF 2:148–49). On the other hand, the tragic romance of Kjartan and Gudrun in *Laxdœla saga* is as arresting a story as can be found anywhere in the sagas, modeled as it is on the Eddic love story of Brunhild and Sigurd. Such examples of escalation in *Laxdœla saga* may suggest that it is in

2 Miller, *Axe*, 98, notes that the author of *Laxdœla saga* is "obsessed with birth and filiation to noble blood."

3 *Egils saga Skallagrímssonar*, ed. Sigurður Nordal, Íslenzk fornrit 2 (Reykjavik: 1933), 287. Hereafter the Íslenzk fornrit series, including *Laxdœla saga*, ed. Einar Ólafur Sveinsson, Íslenzk fornrit 5 (Reykjavik: 1934) and *Brennu-Njáls saga*, ed. Einar Ólafur Sveinsson, Íslenzk fornrit 12 (Reykjavik: 1954), will be abbreviated ÍF with the volume number and placed in parentheses in the text.

4 Thus grand receptions are conferred on Hoskuld Kollsson (ÍF 5.25) and Olaf Peacock (ÍF 5.52).

deliberate competition with *Egils saga* and aspires to exalt one district at the expense of another.

Accordingly we might expect *Njáls saga*, representing the southern quarter, to enter into this apparent regional competition, but it does not. The first departure to take note of is that the settlement narrative that looms so large in both *Egils saga* and *Laxdœla saga* is missing altogether in *Njáls saga*; there is only the faintest accounting of the ancestry of either Njal or Gunnar (ÍF 12.52, 55–56). The two earlier sagas cover a generous time span of some 200 years, but *Njáls saga* confines its action to not much more than fifty years.[5] There is no latitude for genealogical displays or ancestral inflation. Although both Njal and Gunnar live in the south and were born into southern families, there is no perceptible southern bias.

A particularly conspicuous anomaly is that *Njáls saga* does not even begin in the south, where most of the action will unfold.[6] Instead it borrows a character from *Laxdœla saga* and resurrects a relationship that we know very well from that saga, the relationship between the two half-brothers Hoskuld Dala-Kollsson and Hrut Herjolfsson. In the telling of *Laxdœla saga* the two of them share an inheritance and high status, Hoskuld at home in Breidafjord and Hrut abroad as a retainer of the Norwegian king Harald Graycloak (ÍF 5.44), where he becomes the favorite of the queen mother Gunnhild. King and queen mother vie with each other in admiration, and they grieve when Hrut returns to Iceland. Here he wins an inheritance dispute, marries several times, and fathers twenty-six children, sixteen sons and ten daughters. At the age of eighty he kills a local tough named Eldgrim, who tries to seize horses belonging to his half-brother Hoskuld. Even by the high standards of *Laxdœla saga* Hrut is a heroic specimen without a trace of detraction.

But what becomes of this paragon in *Njáls saga*? In a quite unexampled departure from common practice in the sagas Hrut, who turns out to be a minor character, appears immediately in the second paragraph with an exceptionally positive portrait (ÍF 12.6): "Hrut was a handsome man, big and strong, a good warrior but peaceable in disposition, a very wise man, tough toward his enemies but a good helper in important matters." Despite this glowing characterization he wastes no time in committing a breathtaking tactlessness. His half-brother Hoskuld is keen to show off his beautiful girl child, Hallgerd, and asks Hrut what he thinks of her. After some hesitation Hrut replies (ÍF 12.7):

---

5 Richard F. Allen, *Fire and Iron: Critical Approaches to Njáls saga* (Pittsburgh: 1971), 30, estimates the time span in *Egils saga* between 165 and 310 years and estimates *Njáls saga* at 65 years.

6 See Miller, *Axe*, 18.

"The girl is quite good-looking, and many men will pay the price, but I do not know how the thief's eyes got into our family." The prophecy, as almost always in the sagas, turns out to be accurate, but that may not excuse the heavy-handed candor.[7]

Hrut now arranges a betrothal to a woman in the South Quarter named Unn, but he delays the wedding for three years to allow for the collection of an inheritance in Norway. Here he is received by King Harald Graycloak and is promptly taken to bed by the queen mother Gunnhild, famed for her sorcery. She also offers to collect his inheritance, which has fallen into the hands of the villain Soti. She does so and is rewarded with half the proceeds. In the spring Hrut falls silent and yearns to return to Iceland. Gunnhild quickly sizes up the situation and asks if he has some woman out in Iceland. Sensing jealousy, he denies it, but Gunnhild, with her supernatural powers, easily sees through his disavowal. She therefore counters with a curse that will prevent him from consummating his marriage in Iceland, though he will continue to have access to other women.

He proceeds with the marriage, but it fails in due course and Unn, relying on the legal expertise of her father, contrives a divorce. This becomes a public humiliation when children playfully reenact the divorce (and the cause of it) in an assembly of grown-ups, some indignant and others gleeful. Hrut saves what face he can by refusing to return the dowry to Unn's father, unless he can prevail in a duel. Unn then appeals to her relative Gunnar of Hlidarendi to challenge Hrut in reprisal. Hrut is advised by his friends that he has no chance against a champion like Gunnar. He must therefore decline and suffer further humiliation.

In this story Hrut scarcely lives up to the praise initially accorded him. He does not become an object of unmitigated admiration on the part of Queen Gunnhild, as in *Laxdœla saga*, but instead he becomes a kept man. He performs sexual service in place of military service, which is the preferred mode for most Icelandic warriors at the Norwegian king's court. He does not collect his inheritance but leaves that task to his royal mistress, a woman to do a man's job. He is in fact so cowed by her that he does not dare to tell her the truth about his engagement in Iceland and must suffer a disabling curse. In addition, he becomes the victim of an elaborate divorce scheme. Not only that, but the divorce, as well as the cause, are reenacted by children in public so as to redouble the indignity. Hrut takes the children's comedy in stride, but he responds to the divorce proceedings by bullying his aging father-in-law and challenging

7 Ibid., 20.

him to an unequal duel. That hardly redounds to his credit.[8] Unn manages to keep the upper hand by recruiting Gunnar to trick Hrut and discountenance him one more time. Gunnar finally challenges Hrut to a duel, forcing him to back down and play the part of a coward.

There is little left of the imposing figure that was Hrut in *Laxdœla saga*. An awe-inspiring presence at the Norwegian court in the first saga has become the queen mother's sex slave in the second saga. The father of twenty-six children in one text has become partially impotent in the other. There cannot be much doubt that the author of *Njáls saga* knew *Laxdœla saga*, but how are we to account for such a narrative transformation? Should we simply assume that the two authors used two differing oral traditions?[9] The match seems a little too close for that, and we might rather suspect that one author is disparaging the account of another with malice aforethought. Hrut certainly suffers disparagement, but perhaps there is a larger issue at stake. Perhaps it was in more general terms the glossy surface, the historical glorification, and the past grandeur foregrounded in *Laxdœla saga* that goaded the author of *Njáls saga* into a response. This author seems to have had a more jaundiced vision of the past and a more sober view of past realities.

We will return to this possibility presently, but for the moment we must deal with the anomaly that the author begins a saga about southern Iceland with a long story about two westerners, Hrut Herjolfsson and Hallgerd Hoskuldsdottir. There is a dual focus on west and south from the outset, and that is a conspicuous departure from the single-region tradition in the earlier sagas. We should ask ourselves whether there are other indications of a supra-regional perspective in *Njáls saga*. Richard Allen noted this feature briefly, but as far as I can see, it has not become a matter for discussion.[10]

In the western prelude the coverage is extended to northern Iceland in a peculiar episode in which Gunnar is recruited to retrieve Unn's dowry from Hrut.[11] He seeks the counsel of Njal, who advises him to impersonate an itinerant peddler, visit Hrut, and claim to be from the north (Eyjafjord). Njal foresees that Hrut will ask about the people in Eyjafjord and instructs Gunnar to denounce them as scoundrels. He is also urged to report on the people of Reykjadal in the northeast in the same manner and dismiss them as thieves and villains. Finally, he is to devise some analogous defamation for the people in the East Fjords (ÍF 12.61). This slander is apparently calculated to put Hrut in a jolly and

8 On the problems inherent in this episode see ibid., 29.

9 See the discussion in Einar Ólafur Sveinsson, *Um Njálu* (Reykjavik: 1933), 106–20.

10 See Allen, *Fire and Iron*, 78, 140.

11 On the peculiarities see Miller, *Axe*, 62.

receptive mood and make him open to Gunnar's subsequent questions about the law. The ruse works, and Gunnar is able to learn from his host how to reopen the case. But why choose this particular form of levity that discredits the people of two more regions? Westerners, northerners, and easterners have all become the victims of deprecation.

This pattern continues in the famous sequence at the Allthing when Njal's party circulates to the booths of various chieftains in search of allies. Most of the chieftains are cautious or decline and are treated to degrading abuse by Skarphedin one after the other (ÍF 12.297–306). The sequence begins with Gizur the White at Mosfell, who is accommodating, then goes on to Skafti Thoroddsson. The appeal to Skafti goes awry when he declares neutrality and singles out the unprepossessing appearance of Skarphedin, who responds with a detailed account of Skafti's humiliating escape after a killing. The next stop is with a cautious Snorri the Chieftain, whom Skarphedin duly accuses of failing to avenge his father. From here the party proceeds to the booth of the men of Skagafjord in the northwest, where they attempt to enlist the help of Hafr the Wealthy. He too declines to become involved and again singles out Skarphedin in unflattering terms. Skarphedin responds by calling him a *mjólki* (milquetoast) and challenging him to recover his sister, who has been abducted from his house.

At this point the drama escalates as the party approaches the great chieftain in Eyjafjord, Gudmund the Powerful. Gudmund puts off any decision in the matter and comments on Skarphedin less disparagingly than the other chieftains. Skarphedin nonetheless retorts with an oblique reference to the charge of homosexuality brought against Gudmund by Thorkel Hake and Thorir Helgason and well known to saga readers familiar with *Ljósvetninga saga*. The final stop is at the booth of Thorkel Hake, who has distinguished himself among the men of Ljosavatn and is famous for heroic deeds abroad. Thorkel rejects the appeal for help sarcastically and heaps the customary abuse on Skarphedin. This time Skarphedin gives no quarter at all and responds with a particularly compromising personal attack. Thorkel leaps up in a fury and draws his sword, but Skarphedin reacts so forcefully that Thorkel is discountenanced and is obliged to sit down in disgrace.

These confrontations all take place on the grounds of the Allthing, but it will be apparent that they describe a topographical arc from the Ǫlfúsingar in the south to the Breiðfirðingar in the west to the Skagfirðingar in the northwest, the Eyfirðingar in the central north, and finally the Ljósvetningar in the northeast. The appeal is not confined to regional recruitment but approximates a national call to arms. A circling embrace of Iceland in fact becomes something of a motif in the saga. The East Fjords are omitted in the recruitment of allies for Njal, but they are included elsewhere, for example in Thangbrand's conversion mission (ÍF 12.256–69). This passage is usually discussed in connection with a perceived Christian orientation in the saga, but it is also characteristic of the widening historical lens. Ari Thorgilsson pinpointed the conversion moment at the Allthing, but the author of *Njáls saga* transforms it into a gradual progression across the country.

Thangbrand lands in the southern part of the East Quarter at Gautavík, proceeds to Svínafell on the western edge of Vatnajökull, and goes on to Dyrhólmar on the southernmost tip of Iceland. From there he turns inland to Fljótshlíð and Haukadalr before heading cross country to Barðaströnd in the West Fjords. He returns along a similar route and embarks again in Álptafjord not far from Gautavík. This is not the only mention of the East Fjords. When Flosi gathers forces after the burning of Njal and his family, the author focuses on the East Fjord region as far north as Vápnafjord. The itinerary is considerably more detailed and specific than in the case of Thangbrand's journey, with all the stopping places named and accounted for (ÍF 12.349–53).[12] We learn from Asgrim Ellida-Grimsson that Flosi also expects help from the people in Reykjadalr, around Ljósavatn, and in Øxafjord (ÍF 12.359). The recruitment in these areas is not narrated, but we learn that Flosi did indeed prevail on the Ljósvetningar (ÍF 12.365).

We have seen that Thangbrand's mission took him as far as Bardaströnd in the West Fjords, and even this somewhat remote and less populated region gets several mentions. At the very outset (ÍF 12.22) Hrut sells his merchandise there, and toward the end Eyjolf Bolverksson is characterized as being the great legal expert in the West Fjords (ÍF 12.364). He accordingly figures prominently in the final negotiations over the burning. The unsavory wizard and henchman of Thjostolf, Svan, is at home in Bjarnarfjord north of Steingrímsfjord in the West Fjords. It seems unlikely that the ubiquitous location of persons and narrative coverage in *Njáls saga* is happenstance and more likely that the author is making a deliberate effort to be broadly inclusive. Einar Ólafur Sveinsson indicated that *Njáls saga* has been characterized as "a history of the entire country," but he did not provide a footnote that would allow me to trace that idea.[13] Richard Allen also noted the national appeal for universal contributions to the fund for compensating the victims of the great burning: "The pile of money thus symbolizes the stake and interest the whole national assembly has in bringing

12 See Schnorr von Carolsfeld in *Die Njálssage*, 168–9, who found inaccuracies in the passage; and Einar Ólafur Sveinsson, *Um Njálu*, 349, who found no such inaccuracies.

13 Einar Ólafur Sveinsson, *Njáls saga: A Literary Masterpiece*, trans. Paul Schach (Lincoln, NE: 1971), 54.

about a peaceful settlement ..."[14] The finale of *Njáls saga* is thus a matter of national importance, not just a regional event.

I concluded the discussion of Hrut Herjolfsson with the surmise that *Njáls saga* is a conscious revision of the more naïve version of Saga-Age events that we find in *Laxdœla saga*. But the story of Hrut does not exhaust our author's apparent misgivings about "the west." As soon as the narrative of Hrut and Unn is complete, Hrut's niece Hallgerd is reintroduced, the girl with the thief's eyes. Without rehearsing the longstanding detractions and vindications surrounding this character, we may say that her entry onto the stage is not flattering (ÍF 12.29): "She was profligate and harsh-tempered."[15] Even worse is her companion and foster father, the Hebridean Thjostolf. The author devises a short sentence that convicts both with a single turn of phrase (ÍF 12.30): "It was said that in temperament he was no improvement on Hallgerd."

She is nonetheless given great narrative prominence, inasmuch as the next 160 pages tell the story of her three marriages down to the death of her third husband Gunnar. His death adds not a little to her notoriety, no matter how fantastical the idea that, had she been willing, a lock of her luxuriant hair could have restrung his bow and saved his life.[16] But that is only the beginning. She goes from bad to worse, devising a string of assassinations and authenticating her thief's eyes. Thus the good name of the Laxdœlir and the promotion of their regional distinction in their own saga are roundly dismissed.

Such disparagement is not restricted to western Iceland. We will recall how Gunnar, disguised as an itinerant peddler, slanders northerners and easterners alike to entertain and gull Hrut. This is a joke and a ruse, but it seems strained. There were surely other ways to humor Hrut, but our author seems to be preoccupied with regional self-promotion, and the slandering of northerners and easterners may be a variation on the same refrain. The author may be saying that regional disparagement is just as absurd as inflated regional pride. A variation on this theme is the deflation of the proudest chieftains when they are skewered by Skarphedin's barbs.

There is thus a coordinated assault on the inhabitants and personalities in other regions. We might be tempted to believe that a southern writer is promoting his own region by denigrating others, but the villainy of such characters as Mord Valgardsson or Hrapp at Grjótá or the deceitful pair Otkel and Skammkel

14 See Allen, *Fire and Iron*, 140.

15 On Hallgerd see Einar Ólafur Sveinsson, *Njáls saga*, 117, and his bibliography of discussions not easily available to readers outside of Iceland, Appendix B, 207–8.

16 On this curious motif see Kristján Jóhann Jónsson, *Lykillinn að Njálu* (Reykjavik: 1998), 131–4.

makes it clear that the author did not have it in mind to spare the southerners.[17] The negative valences extend even to the Atlantic interlude. The reception of Njal's sons at the court of Hakon jarl is not what youthful Icelandic adventurers were accustomed to in other sagas. Hakon jarl is not impressionable, and Njal's sons are lucky to escape with their lives. They return to Iceland not in a glow of admiration but with a serious grudge against Thrain Sigfusson, who is implicated in Hakon jarl's displeasure and therefore has a role in the narrow escape of Njal's sons.

The subsequent antagonism with Thrain is the spark that ignites the great feud leading up to the burning of Njal and his family. The voyage to the Norwegian court does not enhance the family reputation, as it does elsewhere in the sagas, but it serves as a prelude to the family's destruction. Despite Gunnar's heroics and Njal's imposing command of the law it is difficult to find faultless characters in *Njáls saga*, and it seems likely to this reader that the author had real reservations about the glorification of Saga-Age Icelanders in the earlier sagas. He read the history of Iceland less credulously.

It is also tempting to believe that *Njáls saga* promotes an almost self-consciously nationalizing perspective on Icelandic history. It embodies an inclusiveness that overrides the regional emphasis in previous sagas and focuses a unified political entity. This may not be unexpected after the incorporation of Iceland under the Norwegian crown in 1262–1264, and it may reflect a Norwegian view of Iceland as a single territory. On the other hand, the inclusiveness seems so emphatic that it may also represent a homegrown evolution in thinking and even an authorial argument. The legal negotiations toward the end of the saga focus on the East as much or more than the South and also assign prominent roles to the northerner Gudmund the Powerful and the westerner Snorri the Chieftain.

Njáls saga is famous, if not notorious, for the attention it gives to the niceties and quibbles in the law. This is also an area that is subject to a nationalizing perspective. Legal business is transacted almost exclusively at the Allthing, the national assembly, and, unless I have missed something, there is only one mention of business at a local assembly meeting (ÍF 12.118). The national perspective is reinforced by the institution of the *fimmtardómr* (fifth court), whether that speaks to Njal's credit or discredit. Njal begins by undermining the functioning of the Allthing to pave the way for a new court of appeals, which he favors as a means to procure a chieftainship for his foster son Hoskuld. Perhaps this reflects a long view of judicial reform, but it certainly

---

17 On Mord see ibid., 120; and on Hrapp, ibid., 141–2.

suggests an element of self-interest as well and may accord with the author's skeptical view of Icelandic history (ÍF 12.244–46).[18]

Interpretations of *Njáls saga* have laid considerable emphasis on the Christian coloring of certain episodes, but Sverre Bagge has recently argued compellingly that an overall interpretation must account for the text as a whole, not isolated episodes.[19] National inclusiveness and historical skepticism may be more widespread in *Njáls saga* than Christian sympathy, and we may bear in mind Miller's comment: "This is a saga about political and social competition, about tactic and strategy, almost Thucydidean in its intelligent social and political analysis …"[20] These narrative angles extend even to the aftermath of the saga, which may strike some readers as not quite relevant and stretching the normal boundaries of a saga text. Such appended stories carrying the reader beyond the confines of Iceland are not unexampled in the other sagas, but they are usually short (as in *Heiðarvíga saga, Fóstbræðra saga, Ljósvetninga saga*, and *Droplaugarsona saga*). The exception is *Grettis saga*, but the unusually full narrative in "Spesar þáttr" could have been inspired by the precedent in *Njáls saga.*

The Celtic epilogue in *Njáls saga* may have been added because it concludes the vengeance for Njal's burning with the death of fifteen more arsonists at the Battle of Clontarf, but Miller derides this explanation as a product of desperation or distraction.[21] The story as a whole is about perfidy and aggression, with eerie overtones foregrounded in the poem "Darraðarljóð."[22] These matters are prefaced by the voyage of Flosi and the last of the arsonists from Iceland. They are shipwrecked on Hrossey (Main Island) in Orkney and are obliged to take refuge with Jarl Sigurd Hlodvisson, who, as luck would have it, has been the

18 On the creation of the *fimmtardómr* see Lehmann and Schnorr von Carolsfeld, *Die Njálssage*, 124–36. On the evaluation of Njal's role see Einar Ólafur Sveinsson, *Njáls saga*, 165–6; Lars Lönnroth, *Njáls saga: A Critical Introduction* (Berkeley: 1976), 188–91; Miller, *Axe*, 168.

19 Sverre Bagge, "The Old Norse Kings' Sagas and European Latin Historiography," *JEGP* 115.1(2016), 1–38. On Christian coloring see Allen, *Fire and Iron*, 154, 157–8, 177, but cf. 43; Einar Ólafur Sveinsson, *Njáls saga*, 179; Lönnroth, *Njáls saga*, 106, 129, 161; Kristján Jóhann Jónsson, *Lykillinn að Njálu*, 143, 161, 165, 197; Daniel Sävborg, "Konsten att läsa sagor: Om tolkningen av trosskiftets betydelse i *Njáls saga*,' *Gripla* 22 (2011), 181–209; Lars Lönnroth, "Christianity, Revenge and Reconciliation in *Njáls saga*" in Lönnroth, *The Academy of Odin: Selected Papers on Old Norse Literature* ([Odense]: 2011), 179–87; Miller, *Axe*, 180, 191.

20 Miller, *Axe*, 17.

21 Ibid., 296.

22 Russell G. Poole, "Darraðarljóð: A Viking Victory over the Irish," in *Viking Poems on War and Peace: A Study in Skaldic Narrative* (Toronto: 1991), 116–56.

liege lord of one of Njal's fallen sons. Despite that special relationship Flosi and his men are spared.

One day one of the arsonists, Gunnar Lambason, is charged to provide entertainment by telling the story of the burning, but he delivers a seriously distorted version. At that very moment Kari Solmundarson arrives at the hall and overhears the distortion, one of those coincidences of which *Njáls saga* is not entirely free. Accordingly Kari rushes in and beheads Gunnar Lambason with a single stroke. Flosi speaks on the killer's behalf and saves his life, then delivers a more truthful version of events in Iceland. The story may have some figurative significance to the extent that it deals with the issue of reliable transmission, the question of when history is accurate and when it is falsified.[23]

Also present at the telling is King Sigtrygg Olafsson of Dublin, who now weaves a political thread into the narrative. He appeals to Jarl Sigurd to join him in a campaign to overthrow the model King Brjann in Ireland. He tries to make the conspiracy palatable by promising Sigurd the hand of his mother Kormlod and the throne in Dublin, or, as Einar Ólafur Sveinsson thought, the throne over all Ireland (ÍF 12.144n4). This appears to be a case of naked aggression because no charges are leveled against King Brjann. The malice is only heightened when the aggressors seek the alliance of two viking chieftains named Ospak and Brodir. Brodir is eager, but Ospak demurs on the ground of King Brjann's irreproachable character. He subsequently allies himself with Brjann, who falls in the ensuing battle, although his army emerges victorious. The battle itself is foreshadowed by drone-like weapons flying through the air and iron-clawed crows attacking Brodir's men. All of them perish, and Brodir himself is tortured to death.

This is a story of unmotivated warfare inspired by unprovoked malice and played out by a villainous cast of characters, including Sigtrygg's mother Kormlod. There is no reason for its being told in such detail; the death of fifteen arsonists could have been mentioned in a single sentence. But the dark shading of the Clontarf story may have fitted into the author's historical perceptions. Since the tale of Clontarf could have been available in written form, that text, with its lugubrious overtones, may very well have contributed to the author's critical view of history.[24]

---

23 Miller, *Axe*, 299.

24 Einar Ólafur Sveinsson argued for a lost written source, *Brjáns saga, in *Um Njálu*, 76–86 and 271–2. Lars Lönnroth rejected the written source in *Njáls saga*, 40, 231–6, but I find the verbal echoes between *Njáls saga* and *Þorsteins saga Síðu-Hallssonar* sufficient to suggest that there was a common written source. Also important is Einar Ólafur Sveinsson's observation in *Um Njálu*, 82–83, that the tone of "Brjáns þáttr" is quite distinct from what

Another possible explanation for the inclusion of the Clontarf episode is that the author, inspired by his view of Iceland as a unified state, wanted to place it in the context of the Celtic nations that were Iceland's nearest neighbors. The internal tensions among these nations may have been viewed as a historical deterrent, an unenviable contrast to what might be hoped for in Iceland and a disguised plea for unity, a reminder that unity was not always the guiding principle in Iceland and that it was a hard-earned new perspective.[25]

Njáls saga as a whole may be about a new Iceland arising from a feud-ridden past in the Saga Age and the Sturlung Age and headed toward an era of consolidation. It does not focus narrowly on the events in the South Quarter but embraces all parts of Iceland, as well as staging three expeditions to Norway and one to the Celtic lands. It appears to campaign against a regional focus and take deliberate aim at the local patriotism in *Laxdœla saga* (perhaps also in *Egils saga*) and the Saga-Age nostalgia that characterizes the earlier sagas generally. This author's history is not a glorification of ancient days but a sharp interrogation of the past to determine how people really behaved and what values really prevailed. The determination is not always positive and projects a full array of disreputable or compromised characters both at home and abroad.

One of the most persistent conventions in saga writing is to end on a conciliatory note. The author of *Njáls saga* does not depart from this convention but reconciles the residual heroes Kari and Flosi in the final scene, but the path leading to their reconciliation is the most fraught and difficult to be found anywhere in the sagas. The author reserves his enthusiasm not for the failed past but for the as-yet untested future.

Works Cited

Allen, Richard F. *Fire and Iron: Critical Approaches to Njáls saga*. Pittsburgh: 1971.

Bagge, Sverre. "The Old Norse Kings' Sagas and European Latin Historiography." JEGP 115.1 (2016): 1–38.

Brennu-Njáls saga. Edited by Einar Ólafur Sveinsson. Íslenzk fornrit 12. Reykjavik: 1954.

Egils saga Skallagrimssonar. Edited by Sigurður Nordal. Íslenzk fornrit 2. Reykjavik: 1933.

Einar Ólafur Sveinsson. *Um Njálu*. Reykjavik: 1933.

Kristján Jóhann Jónsson. *Lykillinn að Njálu*. Reykjavik: 1998.

---

we find in *Njáls saga*. I find Lönnroth's search for stylistic analogies in *Njáls saga*, 231, less convincing.

25 See especially Kristján Jóhann Jónsson, *Lykillinn að Njálu*, 223.

Laxdœla saga. Edited by Einar Ólafur Sveinsson. Íslenzk fornrit 5. Reykjavik: 1934.

Lehmann, Karl and Hans Schnorr von Carolsfeld. *Die Njálssage insbesondere in ihren juristischen Bestandtheilen*. Berlin: 1883.

Lönnroth, Lars. *Njáls saga: A Critical Introduction*. Berkeley: 1976.

Lönnroth, Lars. "Christianity, Revenge and Reconciliation in Njáls saga." In Lönnroth, *The Academy of Odin: Selected Papers on Old Norse Literature*, 179–87. [Odense]: 2011.

Miller, William Ian. *Audun and the Polar Bear: Luck, Law, and Largesse in a Medieval Tale of Risky Business*. Leiden and Boston: 2008.

Miller, William Ian. *"Why Is Your Axe Bloody?": A Reading of Njáls saga*. Oxford: 2014.

Müller, Peter Erasmus. *Sagabibliothek med anmærkninger og indledende afhandlinger*. Vol. 1. Copenhagen: 1817.

Poole, Russell G. "Darraðarljóð: A Viking Victory over the Irish." In *Viking Poems on War and Peace: A Study in Skaldic Narrative*, edited by Russell G. Poole, 116–56. Toronto: 1991.

Sävborg, Daniel. "Konsten att läsa sagor: Om tolkningen av trosskiftets betydelse i Njáls saga." *Gripla* 22 (2011): 181–209.

CHAPTER 9

Feud in the State: The Conflict between Haakon Haakonsson and Skule Baardsson

Hans Jacob Orning

Introduction

As a fresh M.A. student at the University of Oslo, in my first medieval seminar I had to present "Making Sense of the Sources," the introductory chapter of the (then) recently published *Bloodtaking and Peacemaking* by William Ian Miller. His argument that historians have shunned sagas because of guildish conventions that they are too much fun to be historical—"no pain, no gain"—was such a treat, showing that it is possible to write entertaining history and still be serious![1] More importantly, Miller participated in retrieving the sagas as sources that historians could use, in spite of their questionable historicity:

> Fictionalizing dialogue, fictionalizing events, inventing characters and their psychologies might unnerve the political historian, but they need not upset the social historian at all. Even these fictions are constrained by the ranges of the possible in the culture, and hence have useful social information to reveal.[2]

However, most importantly of all, Miller's book came to form my—and many others'—view of Old Norse history in a decisive way, launching a perspective on stateless societies which was neither Hobbesian nor Rousseauian, neither determinist nor centred on (ir)rational choice. Miller was of course no isolated actor in this movement, as there had been discussions in French history for quite a while, but he brought the train to Iceland for sure. And his book immediately attracted attention in Norway. My supervisor Kåre Lunden, who had introduced Karl Polanyi twenty years earlier, was very enthusiastic; and Sverre Bagge worked in much in the same vein in *Society and Politics in Snorri*

1 William Ian Miller, *Bloodtaking and Peacemaking: Feud, Law and Society in Saga Iceland* (Chicago: 1990), 45.

2 Ibid., 46.

© KONINKLIJKE BRILL NV, LEIDEN, 2018 | DOI 10.1163/9789004366374_013

Sturluson's Heimskringla.[3] But particularly a younger generation was inspired by Miller, using his results from stateless Iceland to discuss political cultures in kingdoms as well.[4]

In the following, I will analyse the last serious rebellion in Norway in the high Middle Ages, Duke Skule Baardsson's uprising against King Haakon Haakonsson in 1239–40, which marks the transition from civil war to a period of more stable conditions in Norway. I will first investigate it as what it has been called: a rebellion, and then I will use the anthropological lens to investigate it as a feud. The major source for this account is *Hákonar saga Hákonarsonar* (*The Saga of Haakon Haakonsson*). We are lucky to know quite a lot about this saga compared to other kings' sagas. It was commissioned by King Magnus Haakonsson shortly after the death of his father, King Haakon (r. 1217–63). Its author was Sturla Þórðarson, an Icelandic chieftain (nephew of the more famous Snorri Sturluson) who had opposed King Haakon in the final days of Iceland's independence, which came to an end in 1262/64.[5] Actually, Sturla came to Norway as a delinquent to receive the king's verdict for opposing him. Instead of being sentenced, he was given the honourable task of writing the recently deceased king's saga. Considering this dramatic backdrop of the saga, it is startling that it is so "dry and lifeless," to cite the Norwegian historian Knut Helle.[6] The reason for this is probably a combination of King Haakon's elevated position and Sturla's heavy indebtedness towards Haakon's son, who gave him the assignment. Since the rebellion of Skule Baardsson a quarter of a century earlier, Haakon had ruled without opposition as Norwegian king. He was by definition God's chosen one, and therefore raised above the political game of challenges and posturing which previous Norwegian kings had been

3 "Though we ... have to reject them as evidence of the individual events they describe, it is a little more likely that these stories, whether true or invented, contain some accurate information on society." Sverre Bagge, *Society and Politics in Snorri Sturluson's* Heimskringla (Berkeley: 1991), 239.

4 A legal anthropological perspective has inspired the anthologies *Gaver, ritualer, konflikter: Et rettsantropologisk perspektiv på nordisk middelalderhistorie*, ed. Hans Jacob Orning, Kim Esmark, and Lars Hermanson (Oslo: 2010); and *Disputing Strategies in Medieval Scandinavia*, ed. Kim Esmark, Lars Hermanson, Hans Jacob Orning, and Helle Vogt (Leiden and Boston: 2013). I was also much inspired by Miller in my doctoral thesis, published as *Unpredictability and Presence: Norwegian Kingship in the High Middle Ages* (Leiden and Boston: 2008).

5 Sturla Þórðarson's Festschrift comes later than Bill's, 803 years after his birth. See *Sturla Þórðarson: Skald, Chieftain and Lawman*, ed. Jón Viðar Sigurðsson and Sverrir Jakobsson (Leiden: 2017).

6 Knut Helle, *Innleiing, Soga om Håkon Håkonsson* (Oslo: 1963), p. 12.

constantly involved in.[7] Whereas these rivalries had been openly expressed in previous kings' sagas, here they were tamped down. King Haakon Haakonsson was not a king to be challenged anymore.

Yet *Hákonar saga Hákonarsonar* should not be underestimated as a reliable historical source. First, the mere quantity of details recounted in the saga makes it likely that Sturla had archival material at his disposal. For instance, in describing a public meeting in 1223, more than forty years before Sturla was writing, he names sixty participants: earls, royal officials and clerics from four different regions.[8] Second, the saga recounted recent incidents, making it improbable that Sturla could "invent" events that had not taken place, simply because there would have been too many witnesses if he had cheated. Third, Haakon's opponent Skule was firmly entrenched in the royal dynasty as the father-in-law of Haakon and the grandfather of King Magnus. He could not therefore be ridiculed or belittled without restraint. Thus, when embarking upon an analysis of the relationship between Haakon and Skule in *Hákonar saga Hákonarsonar*, the dual character of the saga should be kept in mind: It is a saga permeated by ideology, but also filled with petty, trivial stuff which cannot possibly have been purely invented.

Skule Baardsson's Rebellion

I will first analyse the conflict between Haakon and Skule as a rebellion, which is how Sturla explicitly described it. First some basic facts: Haakon Haakonsson was made king of Norway in 1217, at the age of thirteen. The circumstances

7 The *rex iustus*-ideology, whereby the king was viewed as the God's elected, a supporter of the Church, and as an upholder of law with a particular responsibility for the poor, had a breakthrough in Norway with the coronation of Magnus Erlingsson in 1163/64. See Torfinn Tobiassen, "Tronfølgelov og privilegiebrev," *(Norsk) Historisk tidsskrift* 43 (1964), 181–273; Erik Gunnes, *Kongens ære. Kongemakt og kirke i "En tale mot biskopene"* (Oslo: 1971); Sverre Bagge, *The Political Thought of The King's Mirror* (Odense: 1987). A different conception of kingship emerges from Snorre Sturluson's *Heimskringla*, written around 1230, where the king was regarded as *"primus inter pares"*: a chieftain principally on a par with other mighty magnates, who had to succeed in the political power struggle in order to maintain his authority. See Bagge, *Society and Politics*; Bagge, *From Gang Leader to the Lord's Anointed* (Odense: 1996).

8 Narve Bjørgo, "Om skriftlege kjelder for Hákonar saga," *(Norsk) Historisk Tidsskrift* 46 (1967), 185–229. Moreover, Sturla was probably not very versed in Norwegian conditions, so that he was dependent upon informants. See Randi Bjørshol Wærdahl, "Gautr Jónsson of Mel: Craftsman of Battle and Chief Oral Source of *Hákonar saga*," in Jón Viðar Sigurðsson and Sverrir Jakobsson, *Sturla Þórðarson*, 107–19.

surrounding the choice of Haakon are unclear, as there were several candidates for the throne. One of them was Skule Baardsson, half-brother of the recently deceased king Inge Baardsson. When Haakon was acclaimed king, Skule was made earl, but during the first years of King Haakon's reign, Skule was probably close to being the real governor of the country. He became more firmly rooted in the royal dynasty through his daughter's marriage to the king in 1225. However, Skule gradually lost ground, probably as a result of King Haakon's coming of age. During the late 1220s there were no major disagreements between them, but in the 1230s tensions arose, and in 1239 Skule openly defied King Haakon. After approximately six months of open enmity, Skule's party was decisively defeated and shortly thereafter he was killed.[9]

When Sturla wrote the saga in 1264–65, a quarter of a century had passed since Skule's rebellion, and since then no one had challenged King Haakon openly. In the meantime, the king's position had solidified correspondingly. In 1247 he was crowned king by a papal legate, as the second king in Norwegian history. Towards the end of his life, a new law of succession was issued (1260), strengthening royal dynastic control over succession, and in the following years Greenland and Iceland were brought under Norwegian supremacy (1261–64). Moreover, in this period (between 1240 and 1263) the ideological work *Konungs skuggsiá* (*The King's Mirror*) was written, probably by a person close to royal circles.[10] Many of its examples from the Old Testament echo aspects of the conflict between Haakon and Skule, and it might even have been intended as commentary upon this conflict. So how was Skule's rebellion depicted in *Hákonar saga Hákonarsonar* from an ideological point of view?

•••

Skule was bound to to King Haakon both formally by oath and informally through obligations of loyalty, serving as his earl from 1217 to 1237 and as his duke from 1237 to 1239. We do not know the exact wording of the earl's oath from 1217, but according to *The Law of the Retinue* from 1274–77, an earl should swear to be "loyal ... both openly and secretly" (hollær oc trur ... bæðe løynilega oc opinbærlega) to the king, to show him obedience (*lýðni*), and to be loyal in

9 These facts and basic interpretations are of course based on *Hákonar saga Hákonarsonar*, in *Det Arnamagnæanske Haandskrift 81a Fol.*, ed. A. Kjær (Oslo: 1985–87, orig. 1919), hereafter cited as Hs; and on Knut Helle, *Norge blir en stat 1130–1319* (Bergen: 1974, orig. 1965); Kåre Lunden, *Norge under Sverreætten 1177–1319* (Oslo: 1976); Orning, *Unpredictability and Presence*; Sverre Bagge, *From Viking Stronghold to Christian Kingdom* (Copenhagen: 2010).

10 Bagge, *Political Thought*, 209–22.

holding land from the king and in keeping the oaths to the common people.[11] The specific wording of Skule's oath was definitely of crucial importance, because the saga states that "the earl had in advance formulated the oath as he wished" (jarl hafdi skipad eidinum adr, sem han likadi), making the earl's loyalty contingent on the king's compliance with all agreements made between the two of them.[12] Sturla hints that this initiative of Skule was illegitimate, but he nevertheless had his way.

Late in 1239 Skule decided to rebel against Haakon, sending out men in all directions to try to kill as many of the king's men as possible and even trying to ambush the king himself.[13] King Haakon's first reaction upon receiving news of Skule's actions was that "what has now been disclosed has been planned for a long time" (þetta var fyrir longu ætlat, sem nu er fram komit).[14] When he later made a speech to his men, the king emphasised that Skule had "proclaimed himself king without having terminated the peace" (let gefa sier kongsnafn at osogdum gridum [sic] milli vor).[15] This was unprecedented in Norwegian history and implied that Skule had killed men who were as equally obligated to him as they were to the king and "expected nothing but good" (ser visv einskis von nema gods).[16]

Konungs skuggsiá pays a great deal of attention to rebellions against divinely sanctioned kings. King Saul in the Old Testament had been installed as king by God, but he ran into trouble after he refused to comply with God's commands, and in particular when his prosperous general David threatened to outshine him. Saul was suffused with envy, and he sought to eliminate David, even though the latter had done nothing to deserve such a fate, serving him faithfully and without suspicion. David, on his side, refused to lay his hands on Saul, even after he was informed that God had deserted Saul and instead chosen himself as king, and in spite of Saul's attempts on his life.[17] For contemporaries, the parallels between this story and the rivalry between Haakon and

---

11 *Hirdloven til Norges konge og hans håndgangne menn* [*The Law of the Retinue*], ed. and trans. into modern Norwegian by S. Imsen (Oslo: 2000), 7. Hereafter cited as H.

12 Hs 24.

13 Hs 202–5.

14 Hs 207.

15 Hs 229.

16 Ibid. However, this was not a precise statement, as retainers had since 1233 sworn oaths of loyalty only to the king, and Haakon was much on the alert in 1239, evidently not at all ignorant about what could come about (Hs 181, 197, 205).

17 *Konungs skuggsiá*, ed. L. Holm-Olsen (Oslo: 1983, orig. 1945), 107–15. Hereafter cited as KS. The work has been quite imprecisely translated into English: see Laurence Marcellus Larson, *The King's Mirror* (London and Oxford: 1917).

Skule must have been fairly evident. Skule was next in line to the king, as was David, but instead of obeying the king as David did, Skule schemed to kill him, even though Haakon had never sought to kill him, and God had given Skule no confirmation that the present king was out of favour with God.

King Haakon's statement that Skule's rebellion had been planned for a long time is in keeping with the depiction of Skule elsewhere in *Hákonar saga Hákonarsonar*. Skule is typically described as a schemer who plots secretly against the king. Nowhere is this more evident than during the first years of Haakon's reign. First, Skule tries to obstruct the election of Haakon as king, using his influence among the clergy to postpone the kingmaking ceremony.[18] The illegitimacy of this course of action is revealed by the secrecy surrounding Skule's actions, as he consults with his friends "all day and night.... But people were told nothing about their decision."[19] When the people signal that they want Haakon as their king, Skule changes strategy and demands that Haakon's mother Inga undergo the ordeal of hot iron to prove that her son is of royal blood. However, when Inga is to perform the ordeal, the hot iron is nowhere to be found, and the saga insinuates that Skule's men have thrown it away.[20] It is unclear how powerful Skule was at this stage, but according to Sturla, he used whatever powers he had in an inappropriate manner.[21]

How did Haakon survive these first years, barely a teenager himself and dominated by a mighty and experienced earl intent on having things his own way? Sturla makes no secret of the fact that Haakon was inept as a governor at this stage: "The king was young, and because he was childish, he preferred playing to governance" (Kongrinn var ungur, ok [fyrir] bern[s]ku sakir sinnar gadi hann meir leiks sins enn landrada).[22] When Skule, without informing the king, sends letters to other kings and magnates who had previously been enemies in order to ask for friendship, Haakon has no objection: "I hold it as harmless that he gets numerous friends, since he will certainly keep our settlement, and I do not intend to break it" (ætla ek mer þat meinlaust, þo at hann eige ser marga uine, þuiat hann man uel hallda uor einkamal af sinne hende; ætla ek ok eigi

18 Hs 12, 15–17.

19 Ibid. On secrecy, see Miller, *Bloodtaking*, p. 89.

20 Hs 13–14. On the use of ordeals as a vehicle to squeeze or threaten opponents, see Stephen D. White, "Proposing the Ordeal and Avoiding It," in White, *Feuding and Peace-Making in Eleventh-Century France* (Aldershot: 2004), ch. 7, 89–123.

21 Lunden, *Norge under Sverreætten*, 181–98 holds Skule to be the more powerful; Bagge, *Gang Leader*, 107–19 disagrees.

22 Hs 19.

fyrri at bregda).[23] For an author like Snorri Sturluson, such qualities were not kinglike. In his *Heimskringla* the child king Inge Hunchback sends letters to his brothers at the age of three, complaining about their recklessness in protecting the realm from enemies.[24] For Sturla, on the contrary, Haakon's childish innocence does not attest to political foolishness, but rather to a combination of faith in other people's motives and in his own vocation. The king's goodwill is proof of his special connection to God, and emanates from his trust that God will provide for him.[25] What *could* have emerged as a conclusion from *Hákonar saga Hákonarsonar*—that Haakon is a naïve or even stupid politician who is almost outmanoeuvred by Skule's clever scheming—appears instead as an illegitimate plot whereby a treacherous subject seeks to ambush an innocent king.

Skule's suspect behaviour in *Hákonar saga Hákonarsonar* continues after the royal election is decided in Haakon's favour in 1217–18. It is insinuated that he is trying to exploit the conflict to his own advantage during the strife with rebel groups in the eastern part of the country, which goes on more or less continuously until 1227. It is not until 1233 that open rivalry surfaces again in the saga, however, as a result of Skule's being outnumbered when he meets with the king in Bergen.[26] Sturla links Skule's frustrations at this meeting to the impending rebellion: "People who knew them said that there was never again full confidence between them" (þat hafa men sagt, er vita þottuz huoratueggiu skaplynde, ath alldri hafi sidan ordit fullr trunadr mille þeirra).[27] The story in *Konungs skuggsiá* about Lucifer's rebellion can be read as a commentary aimed at demonstrating why Skule's actions leading up to his rebellion are not legitimate. In return for their being "obedient to their Creator and loving him humbly without deceit" (lyðni oc ast sæmð viðr skapara sinn mæðr litillæti ón alla flærð), God grants his angels "all beauty and honour" (allri fægrd oc allri annarri sæmd).[28] However, the angels are endowed with free will, so that they can decide whether to comply or not. Lucifer is the foremost among God's angels, and he attracts many angels "with service and full friendship" (mæð þionosto oc allri vinatto).[29] For a long time things go well, but eventually

23 Ibid.

24 *Ingi*. In *Heimskringla*, edited by Bjarni Aðalbjarnarson. Vol. 3, Íslenzk fornrit 28 (Reykjavík: 1979), 303–346 at 8. See Ian Grohse, "Fra småbarns munn—Myte og propaganda under kongene Inge og Sigurd Haraldsson c. 1136–1139," (*Norsk*) *Historisk tidsskrift* 4 (2016), 473–91.

25 Hs 6.

26 Hs 174–77.

27 Hs 177.

28 KS 79.

29 Ibid.

Lucifer grows discontented with the obedience that God requires, because he considers God's demands as a threat, and his own power as sufficient to equal God's. He therefore sets up his own high seat at the other side of the world, and refuses to obey God—yet without proclaiming open enmity.[30] Skule likewise has accepted the king's supremacy for a long time, and like Lucifer he has been forced to show obedience to the detriment of his own honour (in 1233). Moreover, he is made to sound much like Lucifer in complaining about "how much shame and dishonour he had received from King Haakon in return for his goodwill towards him" (huerssu mickla skomm ok suiuirdu hann hafdi haft fyrir sinn goduilia a Hakoni kongi).[31] Through the example of Lucifer, the author makes it perfectly clear that this course of action is unacceptable and that it qualifies for exclusion from society. In this way, *Hákonar saga Hákonarsonar*, backed by *Konungs skuggsiá*, could draw a distinction between Skule's (legitimate) frustrations and his (illegitimate) rebellion.

Finally, *Konungs skuggsiá* helped Sturla legitimise a delicate matter, namely how the historical Skule was killed: he died when a monastery where he was seeking refuge was set on fire, an act that violated the principle of church asylum.[32] Disrespecting church asylum was a major crime which was heavily condemned, both in the laws[33] and when perpetrated by Skule's men in the initial phase of the rebellion in *Hákonar saga Hákonarsonar*.[34] How then was it possible to get away with a royal violation of the same law? Sturla adopted a multi-fold strategy in order to justify the royal action. For one thing, he put the king at arm's length from the whole incident. Haakon is not present when the burning takes place, and nowhere does the king approve of the killing outright.[35] For another, the violation is legitimised by referring to the country's necessity (*nauðsyn*). Haakon's men thought "there were such men inside the monastery that it was necessary to break the peace, whether one thought it was good or bad" (naudsynn var til at giora þar ofrid, huort sem þætti vel ædr jlla).[36] *Nauðsyn*, Latin *necessitas*, was a key term in Roman law, referring to the king's authority to break laws in case of urgent concerns.[37] Such extraordinary

30 KS 79–80.

31 Hs 199.

32 Hs 241–42.

33 Jfr. Arne Bøe, "Kirkegård, Norge," in *Kulturhistorisk leksikon for nordisk middelalder VIII* (Copenhagen: 1981), 399.

34 Hs 202.

35 Hs 242–43.

36 Hs 241.

37 Bagge, *Political Thought*, 32 and 189–94.

pre-emptions had been introduced in Norwegian laws in the mid-twelfth century in the formula that the king had the right to sidestep established norms: "to punish [so as] to cleanse the country and create peace" (refsa til landreínsanar oc friðar).[38] Yet a paragraph in the saga allowing the king to override normal procedures was a novel measure that must have needed further bolstering if it was to emerge as convincing. *Konungs skuggsiá* could help with that. King Salomo experiences a similar situation after his chief commander Joab disobeys him and seeks shelter in a church. Then the king orders that he be dragged out of church and executed. The Son in *Konungs skuggsiá* is surprised that the right of church asylum can be infringed in this way, but the Father justifies Salomo's behaviour by saying that "his [Joab's] behaviour and the verdicts of the holy laws kill him, not us" (uverk hans ok domur heilagra laga drepr hann enn huargi ockar).[39] Executing an opponent was not usual during the "civil wars," when most opponents were pardoned; and when it also entailed the breach of church asylum, it must have been quite unheard-of. Sturla needed all the support he could get for explaining this mode of action, and *Konungs skuggsiá* gave him what he needed.

The Feud between Haakon and Skule

How far did Sturla Þorðarson's description from 1264–65 of the conflict between Skule and Haakon as a rebellion reflect the views of people who experienced this conflict in the 1220s–30s? There is of course no way of finding this out directly, since most of the events recorded in *Hákonar saga Hákonarsonar* have left no traces in other sources. Nevertheless, since the major events in the struggle were probably depicted in a reliable manner, given the short amount of time since they had happened, a careful analysis of behaviour during the conflict can throw light on how the agents may have perceived it at the time. It is of course difficult to distinguish between descriptions of events in the saga which seem reliable on the one hand, and interpretations which are more likely to have been added later (often to enhance the king's role) on the other. Working our way back from Sturla's "official" version in 1264–65 to the contemporary reality of Skule's struggle, we must take into consideration that these actions formed part of the last phase of the "civil wars" in a society which had not yet seen *Konungs skuggsiá* nor the quarter of a century of royal

---

38 *Den eldre Gulatingalova* [*The Older Gulathing Law*], ed. B. Eithun, M. Rindal and T. Ulset (Oslo: 1994), 32.

39 KS 121.

consolidation of power. Thus, Sturla's outlook when writing the saga must have been substantially different from that of the participants in the 1220s–30s.

If we analyse the conflict between Haakon and Skule, taking their actions as the point of departure, it does not look like an unjustifiable struggle between a legitimate king and a (soon-to-be) rebel, but rather like a rivalry between two major players contending for power in accordance with established social norms. The concept of feud can provide a key to understanding this conflict, even if, contrary to conflicts in typical "feuding societies," it occurred in a society with a central power (as did many if not most medieval European feuds). In *Bloodtaking and Peacemaking*, Bill Miller saw feuding as one of the "key structures" in which the struggle for political dominance is carried out, identifying nine features of feud in Freestate Iceland. In my opinion these nine features can be consolidated into three key elements:

- A hostile relationship between groups, in which there is collective liability
- Norms of honour controlling and limiting violence
- Keeping of scores according to a rough principle of balance, including settlement[40]

One could add an additional element, based on the fact that kinship was bilateral and hence overlapping, and groups therefore were fairly variable in composition in Old Norse society:

- Groups are variable and frequently change in size and composition.

The conflict between Haakon and Skule before 1239 comprised a more or less permanent state of rivalry rather than violent clashes with a beginning and an end. In line with this, Paul Hyams in *Rancor and Reconciliation* writes about a "feud culture" or "vengeance culture."[41] Jón Viðar Sigurðsson similarly opts for

40 Miller, *Bloodtaking*, 180–81.

41 Paul R. Hyams, *Rancor and Reconciliation in Medieval England* (Ithaca: 2003), xvii, xix, 8–9. In *Vengeance in the Middle Ages*, Throop and Hyams, drawing on Pierre Bourdieu, argue that a definition should be avoided, and limit themselves to providing a "rough account of the practice of medieval English men and women." See *Vengeance in the Middle Ages*, ed. Susanna A. Throop and Paul Hyams (Aldershot: 2010), 160. Basically, this approach is in line with that of Miller, who prefers discussing "distinctive features" of feud: Miller, *Bloodtaking*, 180. Similarly, Jeppe Buchert Netterstrøm and Helgi Þorláksson are careful to "despecify" their definitions in their introductory and methodological articles in the above-mentioned Nordic anthologies. See Jeppe Buchert Netterstrøm, "The Study of Feud in Medieval and Early Modern Europe," in *Feuds in Medieval and Early Modern*

a wider definition of feud that incorporates rivalries that persist beyond individual settlements, which often functioned only to interrupt tension for a short while.[42] In the following, the rivalry between Haakon and Skule, which lasted for twenty-three years, will be analysed as *one* feud, with two phases.

The First Phase of the Feud

In the early days of King Haakon's reign, we can see remnants of a "feud culture," in spite of Sturla's attempt to conceal the power play by making Skule the illegitimate schemer and Haakon the innocent, God-chosen king. However, in the saga the naïve youngster-king is surrounded by a group of councillors who definitely know better. When King Haakon applauds Skule for sending letters in secret to their former enemies, the experienced men around him see the danger and take measures to prevent Skule from doing so by trying to intercept the envoys.[43] And when the bishops refuse to show the king proper honour, the chief advisor Dagfinn *bóndi* is quick to act, arguing that "in that case, the honour that belongs to the royal office will soon evaporate" (þa man bratt af þuozt oll su sæmd, er konginum heyrir til).[44] In other words, the king will rapidly lose his power if he does not react against such encroachments. The saga makes no secret of the fact that Skule had a strong position in this phase, which he used to further his own interests. However, whereas Sturla depicts this as reprehensible, contemporary men probably saw it as the most natural of things. The issue was not to have Skule think or behave otherwise, but to counter his challenges with similar measures.

In the saga, the rivalry between Haakon and Skule is vividly exposed when conflicts arise among their men. In 1218, a relative of Haakon's cuts off the hand of a friend of Skule's at a feast with their combined retinues. This creates havoc, particularly because the king's relative is a rash man who is not popular. Skule gathers his men and utters his wish for revenge. He first goes towards the perpetrator, but seeing that he is protected by his fellows, he lends his ear to a follower who is urging him to kill the king:

Europe, ed. J. B. Netterstrøm (Århus: 2007), 9–68; Helgi Þorláksson, "Feud and Feuding in the Early and High Middle Ages: Working Descriptions and Continuity," in Netterstrøm, *Feuds in Medieval and Early Modern Europe*, 69–94.

42 Jón Viðar Sigurðsson, *Chieftains and Power in the Icelandic Commonwealth* (Odense: 1999), 155–70.

43 Hs 20–21.

44 Hs 18. See also Hs 39, 42.

> More of us will end up the same way, and then you yourself, lord, and it is my advice that we forestall this by pulling the ships and killing the king and all those who stand in front of him.[45]

However, other men object to this proposal, and instead Skule ends up wounding one of Haakon's men who had nothing to do with the misdeed. Still angry, Skule does not back down until a majority within the retinue declare that they will support the king if Skule wants to decide matters using violence.[46] In this situation, Skule does his best to appear as a staunch leader willing to protect his men and avenge them if necessary. Haakon by contrast is described as more peace-minded and elevated above the conflict. This might be true, but only to the extent that his role as a leader is performed by others, such as his councillors, who warn Skule about going too far. In this situation the pressure is on Skule, whose man has been injured, but Haakon has to live up to exactly the same expectations. In cases in which his men are insulted or wronged, he is no less eager than Skule to stand up for them and comply with the demands of honour.[47]

•••

The real-life conflict between Haakon and Skule took place in a society with formal institutions and offices which we would consider to be part of a state.[48] However, it is interesting to note that these formal institutions left considerable room for rivalry. We have seen that the formal arrangement between Haakon and Skule, as king and earl respectively, was regulated in law. Yet the laws admitted that earls could not only provide valuable assistance to the king through their authority; they could also be a threat to the monarchy, through disloyalty and demands for heritability of their office. *The Law of the Retinue*

---

45 "Ver munum sua fara fleire, ok þui næst þier, herra, ok er þat rad, at uier uerdum fyrri at bragdi ok drogum upp skip undir þeim ok drepum kongin ok alla þa, er fyrir honum standa" (Hs 50).

46 Hs 51.

47 King Haakon had no objection in principle against taking vengeance, as when he allowed Skule to do so in 1221 (Hs 70). Moreover, the king probably took revenge himself where the saga author has camouflaged his participation (Hs 193). Finally, abroad King Haakon's motive of taking revenge was openly admitted (Hs 107, 108, 111, 317). This is contrary to Theodore M. Andersson, who views Skule as the more vindictive person of the two. See Andersson, "Sturla Þórðarson's Narrative Personalities," in Jón Viðar Sigurðsson and Sverrir Jakobsson, *Sturla Þórðarson*, 156–67.

48 See Helle, *Norge blir en stat*.

therefore stated that the best option was not to make any earls or dukes, and the offices were abolished in 1309.[49] Earls could act in two roles in medieval Norway: as guardians of minor kings or as governors for parts of the realm.[50] In both roles they could be a challenge to royal authority, particularly in the first case, where in effect they acted as the highest leader. Skule probably acted as guardian until 1220–21, when he was given a part of the country to govern.[51]

The potential for "institutionalized" rivalry also applied to legal decisions, such as Haakon's claim to kingship. Haakon (or rather his councillors) had first to struggle to obtain kingship in 1217, and then in the subsequent year to prove that he was a king's son. The following year Haakon was engaged to Skule's daughter Margrete.[52] However, the rivalry did not end there. In 1223 the case came up again at a large public meeting, where the archbishop declared that there was uncertainty as to who was closest to the royal office, Haakon or Skule.[53] Considering the elaborate formal procedures undertaken in 1217–18 to establish Haakon as king, including the ordeal by hot iron, the persistent haggling about this demonstrates how little right could do without might. The reason for bringing this issue up again must have been that Skule calculated his position to be so strong that he could challenge Haakon.

As Sturla frames the scene, after the two protagonists have come up with their arguments the other magnates are encouraged to voice their opinion. This is no easy endeavour, as explained by the first law man who is asked to give his opinion: "most people are afraid of the power" (flestir eru hræddir fyrir valldinu).[54] No one wants to be the first to take a stand in an unsettled case, because the effects of choosing the wrong side could potentially be devastating. However, once the balance tips in one direction, there is a veritable rush of declarations in favour of the dominant party. As soon as Haakon receives a series of support declarations, the minority is quick to abandon Skule's case and rally to Haakon, even accusing one another of disloyalty.[55] In the end, Haakon is acclaimed king with no dissident votes. One would perhaps expect this unanimous assembly decision to mark the end of the rivalry in the favour of

49 H 14.

50 Grethe Authén Blom, *Samkongedømme, enekongedømme, Håkon Magnussons hertugdømme* (Trondheim: 1972), 21–27.

51 Hs 22; Helle, *Norge blir en stat*, 110.

52 Hs 54.

53 Hs 88.

54 Hs 91.

55 Hs 89–93.

King Haakon. However, there is nothing to suggest that this verdict produced such a decisive outcome.

The Second Phase of the Feud

According to *Hákonar saga Hákonarsonar*, the rivalry between Haakon and Skule resurfaced in 1233 after a lengthy pause. This is probably historically incorrect, as the rivalry did not stop in the decade after 1223.[56] However, from 1233 onward their rivalry was more expressly spelled out at annual meetings in Bergen. The pretext for this escalation was the demand made of Skule by a royal supporter at the first meeting in 1233: "We think that you show the king obedience only by taking off your outer garments and falling at the king's feet" (Oss þikir þu skylldugur til hlydni vid konginn, ok leggir af þier yfirklædin ok fallir til fota kongi).[57] *Lýðni*, obedience, was a key concept in the royal ideology, providing a basis for monarchy to transcend the personal and reciprocal elements of the friendship terminology.[58] Appearing without outer vestments before the king was also a crucial ritual for establishing monarchical authority, and *Konungs skuggsiá* highlighted its significance as a mark of deference.[59]

However, Skule refuses to do as he is told. The saga describes this as an act of defiance, but in reality the demands being put on him are unusually strict. When *Konungs skuggsiá* devoted so much space to explain the importance of taking off outer vestments in front of the king, this is a sure sign that it was considered a controversial issue. Moreover, even if earls were required to show obedience towards the king in *The Law of the Retinue*, such a claim is atypical in *Konungs skuggsiá* and the kings' sagas. Here the term *lýðni* was normally reserved for the ordinary people's relationship to the king, whereas retainers were asked for their service (*þjónusta*), a requirement that Skule was prepared to fulfil.[60] Thus the situation in 1233 must have been intolerable to Skule, and it is indeed possible that the ritual was planned as a deliberate provocation. This

---

56 According to the saga, the end of the rivalry was a result of Haakon's strengthened position vis-à-vis Skule, partly because of the termination of the Ribbung rebellion in 1227, partly due to Haakon's coming of age meanwhile. Yet we should not overestimate the changes in the relationship between the two leaders at this time, because Skule was hardly as humble as the saga indicates, and the later rivalry suggests that this was a latent condition (Hs 157, 160, 172).

57 Hs 177.

58 Orning, *Unpredictability and Presence*, 69–85.

59 KS 47.

60 Orning, *Unpredictability and Presence*, 69–85. Skule's response is: "I knew how to serve [*þjóna*] kings when you did otherwise" (Hs 177). A story in the kings' sága *Morkinskinna* from c. 1220 contains a request for both obedience and taking off one's cloak, where

interpretation is strengthened by the fact that no chair was prepared for Skule at his arrival in Bergen.[61] Hence, what reignited or reinforced the conflict was an attempt to humiliate or offend Skule.

In *Hákonar saga Hákonarsonar* King Haakon states in 1240 that Skule's rebellion had been planned long beforehand. However, this is not a likely conclusion if we follow Skule's actions. The tension between Haakon and Skule in the 1230s does not concern whether Skule should be subordinate to the king or not—as the king's earl, he definitely is—but how their relationship should be framed. This is a straightforward business, as strength determines negotiating position. Every time they meet after 1233, Skule tries to match the king's fleet and manpower, on the grounds that "he would not be dominated by others in deciding things" (eiga eigi allt vndir odrum, huat sem j yrdi).[62] However, on every occasion he fails, always being outnumbered, with the result that Haakon can set the agenda and terms for their cooperation.

This pattern forms the immediate backdrop for the rebellion in 1239. Before their annual meeting in Bergen that summer, Skule agrees on how many ships to bring along. Then he comes up with the idea of mustering a larger fleet than he had agreed to come with, so that he can outmanoeuvre Haakon.[63] It is only upon hearing that his scheming has been revealed to King Haakon that Skule begins to consider a rebellion, because it arouses his anxiety that Haakon's response to his manoeuvre with the ships will be to strip him of all his powers.[64] Skule probably has broad backing for his frustrations and for using the "shame and dishonour" (skomm ok suiuirdu) he has been subjected to by Haakon as a justification of his rebellion.[65] Skule is acting from the view that his relationship to the king is a reciprocal one even though he owes the king subordination, and that it entails a large element of rivalry, albeit within the confines of society. Between obedience and rebellion there was considerable scope of action for a man like Skule. Only the prospect of losing everything could trigger an escalation of the conflict, from feud to war.

King Haakon acts from much the same presuppositions as Skule does. He engages in the rivalry with the aim of coming out on top, and from the

---

the latter ritual was considered the more degrading. See *Morkinskinna I*, ed. Ármann Jakobsson and Þórður Ingi Guðjónsson, Íslenzk fornrit 23 (Reykjavík: 2011), 51.

61 Hs 177.

62 Hs 195. See also Hs 181: "I am more disinclined than previously to come into their power" (ek em ofusari at vera j valldi en fyr).

63 Hs 197.

64 Hs 195, 198.

65 Hs 199.

1230s onwards probably because he thinks he has the power to squeeze Skule. However, his intention is not to eliminate his earl / duke and father-in-law. First, even if he tries to outmanoeuvre Skule at their joint meetings, he makes no effort to humiliate him, apart from the one incident in 1233, when he is clearly goaded by some of his men.[66] To the contrary, norms for avoiding conflict escalation and bloodshed come into play as soon as one party threatens to withdraw from a mutual understanding of the conflict. When Skule does not turn up for their meeting in 1235, Haakon and the archbishop take the initiative of setting up a provisional division of the realm to avoid trouble, and two years later Haakon tries to please Skule by giving him the title of duke.[67]

Even after Skule has rebelled, the prospect of settlement as a way of solving their conflict does not vanish. In the winter of 1240, after Skule has taken his men to the eastern part of the country, the archbishop proposes to mediate a settlement.[68] Such a suggestion was of course almost mandatory coming from a cleric. Yet Haakon refuses it not on principle, but because he reckons that a meeting will diminish hostilities, at a time when he thinks he has a good chance of winning if hostilities continue.[69]

After Skule defeats Haakon's men in eastern Norway in a battle in March 1240, however, the situation changes dramatically, making Skule's party the more prosperous one: "People thought that nothing could withstand him" (þotti mönnum þa, sem eingi hlutur mundi vid honum standa).[70] Now people switch to Skule's side in large numbers, especially in the east. In Trondheim, Skule's men are so convinced they will win that they openly scorn Haakon's men.[71] Even among King Haakon's closest supporters defection is now a pressing issue. They nickname him "Haakon Sleep" (*suefn*) and want to disband their forces, a clear sign that they are reluctant to commit themselves.[72] Exactly the same had happened five years earlier when Skule backed out of a meeting with King Haakon. At that time the following poem was made: "The oaths to Inge's brother were broken; no one wanted to follow anymore" (eidar rufuz vid Jnga brodr, eingi villdi fylgia leingra).[73]

---

66 Hs 175–77.

67 Hs 184, 190, 187. In 1237, the division of the realm had been rearranged, so that his third was scattered throughout the country, probably to his disadvantage as compared to previously; see Lunden, *Norge under Sverreætten*, 200–3 on the rearrangement.

68 Hs 222.

69 Hs 222.

70 Hs 226.

71 Hs 221.

72 Hs 211, 223–5.

73 Hs 182.

•••

Such unstable situations are the most revealing when it comes to laying bare the fragility in the relationship between leaders and their men. What seemed like solid groups with clear-cut dividing lines could evaporate all of a sudden, based on the evaluations that people made of their leaders. It reminds us that even in a society with kings and formal institutions, power in the last instance was based on the very same thing as in state-less societies, on what Bill Miller formulates as "having others think one had the ability to muster forces."[74] It also implies that kings constantly had to cope with two challenges in relation to their men: to make them fight, and to make them fight for the right cause. Goading speeches before battles are of course a genre heavily loaded with clichés in the kings' sagas, but they can nevertheless provide information on these problems. King Sverre was the first military leader in Norwegian history to abandon the organization of the army into a *svinfylking*, a unit where farmers were placed in the centre and flanked (and closed off) by retainers. The prime concern of this mode of fighting was to prevent the farmers from fleeing by locking them in, and as the Norwegian historian Kåre Lunden formulated it, clashes resembled natural disasters where two blocks rolled against one another.[75] King Sverre instead made his warriors run free, stinging like bees where the possibility offered itself. One precondition for this change was the professionalization of warriors; another was that they had sufficient interest in fighting for the king, something that years of guerilla warfare had secured.[76] Still, this change can easily be exaggerated, and it surely only applies to a minor proportion of the army. When goading men to fight in the sagas, both King Sverre and King Haakon refer to the benefit of the realm and to their obligations towards the king, but they are always quick to move on to their men's personal motives for fighting. "Remember that you have lost men and goods," King Haakon urges his men in Oslo in 1240, "and show in both advice and behaviour what you have to avenge on them ..." (Birtid nu huortueggia j ydrum rædum ok atferdum, huers þer eigit at hefna).[77]

This personal aspect is most visible in the aftermath of battles, when the issue of who should be given mercy (*grið*) arose. According to *Sverris saga*, before the battle against the Croziers in the Strindsea in 1199 King Sverre had

74 Miller, *Bloodtaking*, 245.

75 Lunden, *Norge under Sverreætten*, 109–14.

76 Ibid., 101–15; Helle, *Norge blir en stat*, 190–2.

77 Hs 229.

instructed his men, the Birchlegs, not to give mercy to anyone who did not ask it from the king himself. However, after the battle, the army leaders gave quarter to their friends and relatives among the enemy. When other warriors killed them in accordance with the king's orders, the leaders complained about their mercy being violated. Sverre then advised them to kill those who had killed their relatives: "After this, groups of Birchlegs went all over town and killed one another's relatives until all of them were killed" (Eptir þat gengu sveitirnar um bøin oc hendu þa hvarir annara frendr þar til er allir varo drepnir).[78] Such criss-crossing bonds were probably also a crucial factor in determining the course of battles, even if sagas are far more eager to describe heroic battles than more prosaic mechanisms of this kind. Men went for targets against whom they had personal grudges, and conversely they protected and gave mercy to opponents with whom they were related or acquainted.[79]

This undercurrent of personal motives in the kings' sagas was probably much stronger in reality, since the sagas were primarily concerned with enhancing the king's role in society. Kings tried to take advantage of such motives by juxtaposing their own enmity with their men's, but the latter aspect often worked in the opposite direction. Whereas the kings wanted their men to fight relentlessly or else keep peace, their men were less intent on risking their lives for the king. Therefore outright victories were rare, and the fruits of victories often tended to be counterbalanced by warriors conducting their own private feuds under the auspices of royal authority. Feuds were not only fought in the highest echelons of society.

However, at certain points the style of feuding could change. At the top level, 1240 marks a watershed in this respect. King Haakon's bad luck in the winter of 1240 spurred him into swift action in order to prevent large-scale defection. And his strategy succeeded better than he could have dreamt of, when a surprise attack on Skule and his men in Oslo in April 1240 ended in total victory.[80] This is as close to war as we can get: two large armies meeting in a pitched battle with many killed and wounded, with one party emerging victorious. After this Skule's side was simply too weak to enter into negotiations about a settlement.

78 *Sverris saga etter AM 327,4°*, ed. G. Storm (Oslo: 1981, orig. 1920), 159.

79 See also this mechanism in the battle of Oslo in 1240, Hs 236–7.

80 Hs 238.

The End of Feud?

Skule Baardsson's total defeat in 1240 marks the close of the "civil wars" in Norway, which had been going on for approximately a century. Now the "period of greatness" lay ahead, eighty years of internal peace, external expansion and royal dominance: a success story of which *Hákonar saga Hákonarsonar* forms an integral part. However, it is easy to forget the role played by coincidence when dealing with such epochal changes. Had not King Haakon profited from such good winds in sailing from Bergen to Oslo, and if Skule had not been so overconfident that he was careless in scouting—this is actually the only instance when a surprise attack on Oslo succeeds in the sagas—there would probably have been a more dragged-out struggle, maybe resulting in a more balanced settlement between the parties. What is sure is that the last feud-like conflict in Norwegian history ended in a highly atypical, spectacular manner. Moreover, as we have seen, even if Skule's opposition ended up as a rebellion, this is not how his conflict with King Haakon was perceived in its contemporaneity. Then it looks more like a feud between two leaders who had ample space for manoeuver in a society where rivalry was part of the political culture.[81]

Furthermore, there is no reason to assume that feud had played out its role after 1240. In Norway it was mostly sheer luck that prevented strife from breaking out at subsequent royal successions, as both King Haakon Haakonsson's and his son King Magnus's oldest sons died just in time to pave the way for their younger and more able brothers (Magnus and Haakon respectively). If this had not happened, fraternal strife could have erupted, as in the neighbouring kingdoms. In Denmark, the brothers Abel and Kristoffer fought one another; in Sweden, Birger, Erik and Valdemar.[82] These conflicts have normally been classified as rebellions or dynastic struggles, not as feuds, since they were based on rivalry for the throne, and soon resulted in divisions between a dominant group and a rebel group. However, rebel groups found support in other Scandinavian countries, where the power play between kingdoms encouraged dissidents to seek shelter and support from rival kings. In the Swedish case,

81 On feuding in Norway prior to this period, see Hans Jacob Orning, "Conflict and Social (Dis)order in Norway, c. 1030–1160," in *Disputing Strategies in Medieval Scandinavia*, ed. Kim Esmark et al. (Leiden and Boston: 2013), 45–82.

82 On the struggles in Denmark, see Aksel E. Christensen, *Kongemagt og Aristokrati. Epoker i middelalderlig dansk statsopfattelse indtil unionstiden* (Copenhagen: 1976); Kai Hørby, *Velstands krise og tusind baghold. 1250–1400*, Gyldendal og Politikens Danmarkshistorie 5 (Copenhagen: 1989). On the Swedish case, see Tor Einar Fagerland, *Krigføring og politisk kultur i nordisk middelalder. De mellomnordiske konfliktene 1286–1319 i et europeisk perspektiv* (Trondheim: 2006).

the rivalry went on for decades, with the result that that the ablest brother, Duke Erik, established a large realm (often called the "Middle Nordic realm") in what was then the borderland between Norway, Sweden and Denmark. Here again it was only coincidence that prevented this realm from becoming permanent, when the oldest brother Birger captured Erik and his younger brother and let them starve to death. This act aroused so much anger and opposition that it swept Birger from the throne and paved the way for a joint Norwegian-Swedish kingdom under Erik's infant son.[83] These rivalries between pretenders retained many characteristics of feud. The conflicts were fought between fairly small groups who normally avoided large-scale bloodshed and aimed for settlements—even though they sometimes included glaring misdeeds that broke with the feud paradigm. And they often went on for decades, in a state of permanent rivalry with occasional outbursts of violence.

Even in the "period of greatness" feuds were fought in the midst of the royal entourage in Norway: we just do not have the sources to tell us about this anymore. However, we can get scattered glimpses into this from Icelandic sources such as *Þorgils saga skarða*, which recounts a major skirmish in King Haakon's retinue in 1250–51.[84] Moreover, feuds went on below this top level, even after King Haakon formulated a prohibition against taking kin vengeance in 1260.[85] As sources from the fourteenth century onward make abundantly clear, local feuding cultures persisted for centuries to come. The state did not suppress the feud; it only pushed it one step down the ladder and made it accommodate to a society where some sorts of violence became banned, but other forms lived on.[86]

---

83 Sverre Bagge, *Cross and Scepter: The Rise of the Scandinavian Kingdoms from the Vikings to the Reformation* (Princeton: 2014); Fagerland, *Krigføring og politisk kultur*.

84 *Þorgils saga skarða*, in *Sturlunga saga*, ed. Jón Jóhannesson, Magnús Finnbogason, and Kristján Eldjárn (Reykjavik: 1946), 9.

85 *Frostatingslova* [Frostathing Law], in *Norges gamle Love indtil 1387*, vol. 1, ed. R. Keyser and P. A. Munch (Oslo [Christiania]: 1846), Intro, 8. In Magnus Lawmender's National Law from 1274 fines paid to a victim's kin (*wergeld*) were abolished. See *Norges gamle Love indtil 1387*, vol. 2, ed. R. Keyser and P. A. Munch (Oslo [Christiania]: 1848), IV 12, 16. The prohibition is mentioned as one of King Haakon's major contributions at the end of his saga (Hs 332).

86 See i.a. Steinar Imsen, "Den gammelnorske drapsprosessen," (*Norsk*) *Historisk tidsskrift* 2 (2009), 185–229; Helgi Þórláksson, "Vald og ofurvald. Um innlent vald, erlent konungsvald og líkamlegt ofbeldi á 15. Öld," in *Leiðarminni. Greinar gefnar út í tilefni 70 ára afmælis Helga Þorlákssonar 8. Ágúst 2015* (Reykjavík: 2015), 279–95; Hans Jacob Orning, *The Reality of the Fantastic: The Magical, Political and Social Universe of Late Medieval Saga Manuscripts* (Århus: 2017).

Works Cited

Andersson, Theodore M. "Sturla Þórðarson's Narrative Personalities." In *Sturla Þórðarson: Skald, Chieftain and Lawman*, edited by Jón Viðar Sigurðsson and Sverrir Jakobsson, 156–67. Leiden and Boston: 2017.

Bagge, Sverre. *Cross and Scepter: The Rise of the Scandinavian Kingdoms from the Vikings to the Reformation*. Princeton: 2014.

Bagge, Sverre. *From Gang Leader to the Lord's Anointed*. Odense: 1996.

Bagge, Sverre. *From Viking Stronghold to Christian Kingdom*. Copenhagen: 2010.

Bagge, Sverre. *The Political Thought of The King's Mirror*. Odense: 1987.

Bagge, Sverre. *Society and Politics in Snorri Sturluson's Heimskringla*. Berkeley: 1991.

Bjørgo, Narve. "Om skriftlege kjelder for Hákonar saga." (*Norsk*) *Historisk Tidsskrift* 46 (1967): 185–229.

Blom, Grethe Authén. *Samkongedømme, enekongedømme, Håkon Magnussons hertugdømme*. Oslo: 1972.

Bøe, Arne. "Kirkegård, Norge." In *Kulturhistorisk leksikon for nordisk middelalder VIII*. Copenhagen: 1981.

Christensen, Aksel E. *Kongemagt og Aristokrati. Epoker i middelalderlig dansk statsopfattelse indtil unionstiden*. Copenhagen: 1976.

Den eldre Gulatingalova. Edited by B. Eithun, M. Rindal and T. Ulset. Oslo: 1994.

Esmark, Kim et al., eds. *Disputing Strategies in Medieval Scandinavia*. Leiden and Boston: 2013.

Fagerland, Tor Einar. *Krigføring og politisk kultur i nordisk middelalder. De mellomnordiske konfliktene 1286–1319 i et europeisk perspektiv*. Trondheim: 2006.

Grohse, Ian. "Fra småbarns munn—Myte og propaganda under kongene Inge og Sigurd Haraldsson c. 1136–1139." (*Norsk*) *Historisk tidsskrift* 4 (2016): 473–91.

Gunnes, Erik. *Kongens ære. Kongemakt og kirke i "En tale mot biskopene."* Oslo: 1971.

Hákonar saga Hákonarsonar [*The Saga of Haakon Haakonsson*]. In *Det Arnamagnæanske Haandskrift 81a Fol.*, edited by A. Kjær. Oslo: 1985–87, orig. 1919.

Heimskringla. Edited by Bjarni Aðalbjarnarson. Vol. 3. Íslenzk fornrit 28. Reykjavík: 1979.

Helgi Þorláksson. "Feud and Feuding in the Early and High Middle Ages: Working Descriptions and Continuity." In *Feuds in Medieval and Early Modern Europe*, edited by J. B. Netterstrøm, 69–94. Århus: 2007.

Helgi Þorláksson. "Vald og ofurvald. Um innlent vald, erlent konungsvald og líkamlegt ofbeldi á 15. Öld." *Leiðarminni. Greinar gefnar út í tilefni 70 ára afmælis Helga Þorlákssonar 8. Ágúst 2015*, 279–295. Reykjavík: 2015.

Helle, Knut. *Innleiing, Soga om Håkon Håkonsson*. Oslo: 1963.

Helle, Knut. *Norge blir en stat 1130–1319*. Bergen: 1974, orig. 1965.

Hirdloven til Norges konge og hans håndgangne menn [*The Law of the Retinue*]. Edited and translated into modern Norwegian by S. Imsen. Oslo: 2000.

Hørby, Kai. *Velstands krise og tusind baghold. 1250–1400*. Gyldendal og Politikens Danmarkshistorie 5. Copenhagen: 1989.

Hyams, Paul R. *Rancor and Reconciliation in Medieval England*. Ithaca: 2003.

Imsen, Steinar. "Den gammelnorske drapsprosessen." (*Norsk*) *Historisk tidsskrift* 2 (2009): 185–229.

Jón Viðar Sigurðsson. *Chieftains and Power in the Icelandic Commonwealth*. Odense: 1999.

Jón Viðar Sigurðsson and Sverrir Jakobsson, eds. *Sturla Þórðarson: Skald, Chieftain and Lawman*. Leiden and Boston: 2017.

Keyser, R. and P. A. Munch, eds. *Norges gamle Love indtil 1387*, vols. 1 and 2. Oslo (Christiania): 1846 and 1848.

The King's Mirror. Edited and translated into English by L. M. Larson. London and Oxford: 1917.

Konungs skuggsiá. Edited by L. Holm-Olsen. Oslo: 1983, orig. 1945.

Lunden, Kåre. *Norge under Sverreætten 1177–1319*. Oslo: 1976.

Miller, William Ian. *Bloodtaking and Peacemaking: Feud, Law and Society in Saga Iceland*. Chicago: 1990.

Morkinskinna. Edited by Ármann Jakobsson and Þórður Ingi Guðjónsson. 2 vols. Íslenzk fornrit 23–24. Reykjavík: 2011.

Netterstrøm, Jeppe Buchert. "The Study of Feud in Medieval and Early Modern Europe." In *Feuds in Medieval and Early Modern Europe*, edited by Jeppe Buchert Netterstrøm, 9–68. Århus: 2007.

Orning, Hans Jacob. "Conflict and Social (Dis)order in Norway, c. 1030–1160." In *Disputing Strategies in Medieval Scandinavia*, edited by Kim Esmark et al., 45–82. Leiden and Boston: 2013.

Orning, Hans Jacob. *The Reality of the Fantastic: The Magical, Political and Social Universe of Late Medieval Saga Manuscripts*. Århus: 2017.

Orning, Hans Jacob. *Unpredictability and Presence: Norwegian Kingship in the High Middle Ages*. Leiden and Boston: 2008.

Orning, Hans Jacob, Kim Esmark, and Lars Hermanson, eds. *Gaver, ritualer, konflikter:Et rettsantropologisk perspektiv på nordisk middelalderhistorie*. Oslo: 2010.

Sverris saga etter AM 327,4°. Edited by G. Storm. Oslo: 1981, orig. 1920.

Þorgils saga skarða. In *Sturlunga saga*, edited by Jón Jóhannesson, Magnús Finnbogason, and Kristján Eldjárn. Reykjavik: 1946.

Throop, Susanna A. and Paul Hyams, eds. *Vengeance in the Middle Ages*. Aldershot: 2010.

Tobiassen, Torfinn. "Tronfølgelov og privilegiebrev." (*Norsk*) *Historisk tidsskrift* 43 (1964): 181–273.

Wærdahl, Randi Bjørshol. "Gautr Jónsson of Mel: Craftsman of Battle and Chief Oral Source of *Hákonar saga*." In *Sturla Þórðarson: Skald, Chieftain and Lawman*, edited by Jón Viðar Sigurðsson and Sverrir Jakobsson, 107–19. Leiden and Boston: 2017.

White, Stephen D. "Proposing the Ordeal and Avoiding It." In Stephen D. White, *Feuding and Peace-Making in Eleventh-Century France*, ch. 7, 89–123. Aldershot: 2004.

CHAPTER 10

'Waltharius': Treasure, Revenge and Kingship in the Ottonian Wild West

Simon MacLean

Those of us who make a living researching the post-Roman world of the Franks do not, give or take a Gregory of Tours, spend our days reading texts quite as complex or interesting as Bill Miller's Icelandic sagas. As fascinating as they are as historical sources, few would claim that the dry pages of the *Royal Frankish Annals* or even Einhard's *Life of Charlemagne* should be considered classics of world literature. The Latin epic poem *Waltharius* is, however, something different from the Frankish norm. It is a psychologically complicated story about greed, revenge, and the etiquette of violence. Set in the age of Attila the Hun, its story is built around the conflicting loyalties of three protagonists, none of whom emerges unharmed either morally or physically. The poet's black humour, his sharp appreciation of secular aristocratic culture, and his refusal to offer up a clean resolution call to mind the world of Njal and Egil as much as the straight-faced Christian chronicles of the ninth and tenth centuries. The text was popular in its own time, finding numerous known readers and copyists from the late tenth century until the thirteenth. Related stories of Walter's exploits spread widely, turning up in epics and poems including the *Nibelungenlied*, the Old English *Waldere*, and the *Song of Roland*. Eventually, Walter even made it into the Old Norse tradition via the stories collected by the author of *Thidrekssaga*.[1] The text and manuscripts of *Waltharius* have proved no less fascinating to modern historians and philologists, inspiring hundreds of scholarly studies since the poem was first edited by Jacob Grimm in 1838, and especially since the appearance of the standard edition by Karl Strecker in 1951.[2] Many of these studies deal with the vexed question of authorship.

1 P. Dronke, 'Waltharius–Gaiferos', in Dronke, *Latin and Vernacular Poets of the Middle Ages* (Aldershot: 1996), 29–79. For reasons of space I will not be able to cite more than a small sample of *Waltharius* scholarship.

2 *Waltharius*, ed. K. Strecker, in *Der Lateinischen Dichter des deutschen Mittelalters* (Weimar: 1951), 1–85. A more recent edition and English translation is provided by D. M. Kratz (ed. and trans.), *Waltharius and Ruodlieb* (New York: 1984). I will cite the poem by line numbers only, which are the same in both editions. Translations are based on Kratz.

© KONINKLIJKE BRILL NV, LEIDEN, 2018 | DOI 10.1163/9789004366374_014

In this article I will approach authorship via a question about readership: what might the poem have meant to its first known reader, the tenth-century bishop of Strasbourg to whom the earliest version of the poem is dedicated? I will emphasise two key themes, inspired by a reading of Miller's work on the sagas: the poet's depiction of the Vosges, where most of the action is set, and the role played in the text by treasure and gifts. First, however, we need an outline of the poem and theories on its authorship.

Poem and Poet

The poem, which comes in at just under 1500 lines, is set in a pseudo-historical version of fifth-century Europe. It has three main sections. In the first, Attila the Hun leads his armies across the Rhine and extorts tribute and hostages from the kings of the Franks, Burgundians, and Aquitanians. The hostages, Hagen, Hildegund, and Walter respectively, gradually rise to high positions at the Hunnic court, and Walter becomes the leader of the army and its most feared warrior. When news arrives that the Frankish king Gibicho has died, and that his son Gunther has broken his father's peace treaty with Attila, Hagen flees. Walter and Hildegund, now betrothed, follow him some time later after getting the Huns drunk at a banquet. They bring with them two coffers of treasure, about which Attila is not best pleased. The poem's second section follows Walter and Hildegund as they travel through the Frankish kingdom. Gunther catches wind of them as they pass through the royal city of Worms, and works out that they are carrying treasure from Attila's court. The king is greedy for the gold and, despite the protestations of Hagen, takes twelve warriors to track down the fugitives in the forested hills of the Vosges. When they find Walter, he is barricaded into a gorge or cleft in the hills, which means the warriors have to take him on one at a time. Walter lives up to his reputation as a saga-style killing machine and takes out each of the champions in a series of gory encounters enlivened by threats and accusations. Each of these is described with some relish. In the third act, Gunther (maliciously) and Hagen (reluctantly) lure Walter into the open and engage in the final battle, after which all three are left graphically mutilated but alive. Gunther is too badly injured to speak, but the other two share some wine and joke about their wounds (Hagen has lost an eye, Walter a hand) before departing for home. Hagen carries the very ill Gunther back to Worms, while Walter and Hildegund go back to Aquitaine to reign for thirty years.

The poet may not have been inventing the story as a pure act of imagination: to judge by diverse references to him in a variety of later sources, Walter had an independent life in numerous oral traditions. Nonetheless, the Latin *Waltharius* (which is our earliest witness to the Walter tradition) was not simply a repository of orally transmitted tales but a carefully composed work in its own right, deeply influenced by patristic writings and classical epics such as Virgil's *Aeneid.* It was also treated as a complete work by medieval readers and copyists. For example, the eleventh-century Italian monk who incorporated *Waltharius* into his eccentric history of the monastery of Novalesa bent the poem to his own purposes by careful epitomisation, but in a way that nonetheless respected the original structure and content of the work.[3]

Scholarship on the poem has long been dominated by questions about its genre: how should we understand such a superficially profane work as the product of a profoundly Christian literary culture? Could a clerical audience really appreciate a story about the deeds of a hero who kills eleven men in a variety of inventive ways (including four by decapitation)? How did the author balance Classical, Christian, and 'Germanic' elements? Debates over such questions have generated many valuable insights about the way the poet used, interacted with, and perhaps even parodied the pagan epics by which he was inspired or repelled.[4] But the problem with this line of analysis is that the categories it deals in were inextricably linked elements of early medieval culture, to the point of being indistinguishable. The notion of the 'Germanic' as a cultural category is highly contestable, as is the notion of a sharp distinction between the tastes and perspectives of religious and lay aristocrats. Apart from anything else, we know that stories from mythical heroic pasts were widely enjoyed in early medieval monasteries—otherwise they would not have survived to the present day.[5] And, as Rachel Stone has shown, the violent excesses of *Waltharius* cannot be interpreted as a parody of lay conduct because they are wholly consistent with the much more laconic descriptions of aristocratic atrocity and violence found in Carolingian annals (which were also written by churchmen).[6] As with the Icelandic sagas, then, we are entitled to read

3 *Chronicon Novaliciense*, ed. L. Bethmann, MGH SS 7 (Hanover: 1846), 2.7–12, 85–94; A. Bisanti, 'La leggenda di Walthario e i distici "Vualtarius fortis" nel "Chronicon Novaliciense"', *Bollettino di Studi Latini* 40 (2010), 76–85.

4 D. M. Kratz, *Mocking Epic: Waltharius, Alexandreis and the Problem of Christian Heroism* (Madrid: 1980); C. Ratkowitsch, '*O vortex mundi, fames, insatiatus, habendi, gurges avaritiae.* Das *Waltharius*-Epos zwischenaltgermanischem Sagenstoff, Vergils Aeneis und christlicher Moral', *Mittellateinisches Jahrbuch* 51 (2016), 1–38.

5 P. Wormald, 'Bede, Beowulf and the Conversion of the Anglo-Saxon Aristocracy', in *Bede and Anglo-Saxon England*, ed. R. T. Farrell (Oxford: 1978), 32–95.

6 R. Stone, 'Waltharius and Carolingian Morality: Satire and Lay Values', *Early Medieval Europe* 21 (2013), 50–70. Stone's argument would be equally applicable to the post-Carolingian period:

Waltharius as an artefact of its era—a source for the tastes and social assumptions of the time in which it was written rather than a staging point on the road from antiquity to some 'fully Christianised' future.[7]

But to which era did it belong? Dating the poem is, like dating Einhard's *Life of Charlemagne*, one of the great parlour games of early medieval historiography. The old consensus, that it was written by a monk of St-Gall in the 920s and revised a century later, was tenuously based on an enigmatic passage in Ekkehard IV's eleventh-century *Casus Sancti Galli* and is now generally rejected as incompatible with the manuscript evidence.[8] Most recent opinion has preferred to locate the work in the rich textual environment of the Carolingian Renaissance. Via claims that poem shares a 'similar poetic energy' to other works of the earlier ninth century, and emphasising the poet's evident familiarity with the work of the Carolingian writer Walahfrid Strabo, much effort has been expended to make the poem fit the court circles of Charlemagne (d. 814) or Louis the Pious (d. 840).[9] More recently still, *Waltharius* has been read as a kind of allegory of late Carolingian politics, an admonition about the chaos that could result from conflicts between friends and allies which was especially pertinent in the years after the civil wars among the sons of Louis the Pious in the early 840s.[10] These arguments are worthy of much more serious consideration than is possible here, but the reason that all (including those made in this article) are unprovable on textual grounds is that the direction of influence between the poem and the ninth- and early tenth-century works it seems to cite is impossible to determine with certainty.[11]

---

see e.g. the straight-faced account of prisoners being beheaded and mutilated in Widukind, *Rerum Gestarum Saxonicarum Libri Tres*, ed. P. Hirsch (Hanover: 1935), 3.55, 134–35. This text is translated in B. Bachrach and D. Bachrach, *Deeds of the Saxons* (Washington, DC: 2014).

7 W. I. Miller, *Bloodtaking and Peacemaking: Feud, Law, and Society in Saga Iceland* (Chicago and London: 1990), 44–51.

8 A. M. Turcan-Verkerk, 'Langue et littérature latines du Moyen Âge', *Annuaire de l'École pratique des hautes études, section des sciences historiques et philologiques* 146 (2015), 122–33 summarises and evaluates the various theories.

9 R. Schieffer, 'Zu neuen Thesen über den Waltharius', *Deutsches Archiv für Erforschung des Mittelalters* 36 (1980), 193–201 critiques the early Carolingian argument. 'Similar poetic energy': Dronke, 'Waltharius', 77.

10 A. Rio, 'Waltharius at Fontenoy? Epic Heroism and Carolingian Political Thought', *Viator* 46 (2015), 41–64; A. M. Turcan-Verkerk, 'La diffusion du *Waltharius* et son anonymat: Essai d'interprétation', *Filologia Mediolatina* 23 (2016), 59–122.

11 B. Vollmann, 'Gesta Berengarii und Waltharius-Epos', *Deutsches Archiv für Erforschung des Mittelalters* 61 (2005), 161–4.

One major obstacle for a Carolingian dating is the fact that some of the manuscripts—including the earliest—carry a preface by a certain Gerald, who dedicates the poem to a bishop called Erchanbald. Walter Berschin has convincingly identified this bishop, via comparisons to other poems and dedications written in his circle, as Erchanbald of Strasbourg (965–91).[12] Because this presents a problem to both of the most common theories about the poem's context (tenth-century St-Gall and the Carolingian Renaissance), the preface is commonly explained away as the work of a copyist, especially as the Latin does not match the main body of the poem. The preface was, however, a kind of acrostic encoding a hidden message in praise of God and should not therefore be expected to resemble the Virgilian hexameters that follow.[13] Gerald also seems to claim the work as his, describing it as 'my *libellus*' and the product of his own 'long effort'—a peculiar thing for a mere copyist to say.[14] The connection with Erchanbald is in any case circumstantially strong. In the preface, Gerald asks his reader to remember him as his 'dear Adelphus'. This is apparently a pun on 'dear *amicus* [friend]' and seems to be a knowing reference to St Adelphus, whose cult at nearby Neuweiler was actively promoted by the bishops of Strasbourg in the tenth century.[15] Erchanbald was originally from Swabia, which would explain why someone in his entourage was so familiar with the work of the Reichenau poet Walahfrid. He also had close links to the Swabian monastery of St-Gall, from where he recruited scholars to Strasbourg, and it may or may not be a coincidence that the leader of the St-Gall school until about 970 was a man called Gerald.[16] The poem itself is largely set in Alsace, whose main ecclesiastical centre was Strasbourg. Moreover, the manuscript transmission seems to begin in the later tenth century and is attached to centres along the Rhine upstream from Strasbourg.[17] Occam's razor would therefore suggest that the possibility that Gerald was the author and Erchanbald the original dedicatee should not be dismissed so easily.

12 W. Berschin, 'Erkanbald von Straßburg (965–991)', *Zeitschrift für die Geschichte des Oberrheins* 134 (1986), 1–20; accepted by e.g. Turcan-Verkerk, 'Langue et littérature'.

13 H. Haefele, 'Geraldus-Lektüre', *Deutsches Archiv für Erforschung des Mittelalters* 54 (1998), 1–21 (together with the additional note by G. Silagi at 119–20).

14 *Waltharius*, preface, v. 9–16.

15 M. Tischler, 'Die Gorzer Reform in Neuweiler bei Zabern an der Schwelle zum XI. Jahrhundert. Beobachtungen zu einigen Handschriftenfunden', *Archives de l'Eglise d'Alsace* 51 (1993/94), 69–90, at 73.

16 K. Langosch, *Waltharius: Die Dichtung und die Forschung* (Darmstadt: 1973), 92–93.

17 Berschin, 'Erkanbald', 13–16; Turcan-Verkerk, 'La diffusion', 64–104 (who speculates that the earliest manuscript, a fragment, might not have contained the preface).

But setting aside the question of authorship, what we can say with near certainty is that Erchanbald was the earliest reader of the poem whose name we know, and that he received it at or near the beginning of his pontificate.[18] Why did Gerald think the poem would amuse his bishop? How might Erchanbald have related to its narrative? Whether or not it was written for him, we are entitled to ask what he might have got from it. And even if he did not compose the text, Gerald's rewriting of it was an act of authorship which we are entitled to interpret in some way as a reflection of his own time. In addressing these overlooked questions, I will focus in particular on the poem's striking depiction of King Gunther as a villain: as the personification of greed, as a man who was out of his mind, and indeed as the antithesis of good kingship.[19] Why might a bishop of Strasbourg have been entertained by a tale of greed, revenge, and bad kingship, delivered to him at a moment when his own king, Otto I (936–73), had just reached the zenith of his power with an imperial coronation at Rome? The answer, I think, lies in consideration of two core themes: the poet's depictions of geography and treasure. I will address these in turn before returning to the question of Bishop Erchanbald and King Otto.

Place and Perspective

The comprehensibility of *Waltharius*'s setting to an audience in mid-tenth century Strasbourg has not been fully explored. Strasbourg was the main city and chief bishopric of Alsace, part of the kingdom of the Ottonians, the Saxon dynasty which ruled the former Carolingian East Frankish kingdom from 919 until 1024. One of the main challenges faced by the Ottonians as they established their power was extensive raiding by Hungarians, nomadic warriors from Pannonia who had been brought into the Frankish world by one of the last Carolingian kings around 891. The ethnography of the Hungarians was a source of fascination for contemporary observers, and they were frequently identified as successors to earlier peoples from the same region: specifically, the Avars and the Huns. This is explicit in the main history of Otto I's reign, *Deeds of the Saxons* by Widukind of Corvey, which was finished at about the same time that Erchanbald became bishop. The Hungarians, according to Widukind, 'are also called Avars', and he adds that 'some believe [the Avars] are the remainder

18 It was definitely in use as a schoolbook in Speyer by 981: Turcan-Verkerk, 'Langue et littérature', 132–3.

19 J. Peeters, 'Guntharius—Die Fehler eines Königs', *Amsterdamer Beiträge zur älteren Germanistik* 34 (1991), 33–48.

of the Huns'.[20] A similar set of associations is implied by the terminology of *Waltharius*, which uses 'Avar' and 'Hun' interchangeably. The threat posed by the Hungarians has generally been used as an argument against a tenth-century date for the poem, since it is hard to square with the poet's relatively benign (even comical) depiction of Attila.[21] But this objection dissolves if the text were written—or at least read—after 955, when Otto I definitively crushed the Hungarians and killed their leaders at the Battle of the Lech.[22] There may even be a knowing reference to this longer history in the poem itself, which refers to the Huns enjoying more than a thousand years of rule, and in which Walter speaks of the '*for now* [*nunc*] unconquered people of the Pannonians'.[23] There were other resonances that a contemporary audience might have noticed. In 935 the Hungarians, like the Huns in the poem, had attacked Burgundy. In 926 they had passed through Alsace, and as recently as 954 they had even been seen on the edges of the Vosges, about fifty miles north-west of Strasbourg, as confederates of Otto I's rebellious son-in-law Conrad the Red.[24]

If the Huns must have called to the bishop's mind the Hungarians, the poet's description of their Frankish opponents also echoed contemporary conditions. The Ottonians were from Saxony, but the empire they controlled was figuratively Frankish in the eyes of contemporaries.[25] Erchanbald was himself addressed as 'bishop of the Franks' in another poem written during his lifetime.[26] The *Waltharius* poet's characterisation of Gunther as a 'king of the Franks' was thus relevant to contemporary definitions of political geography, and to the bishop of Strasbourg's sense of the political sphere in which he himself operated. It was also specific to the Latin poem: in other versions of the Walter story, Gibicho and Gunther are identified as Burgundian kings (which was, in historical terms, probably correct).[27] It is also interesting that the poem places Gunther's 'royal seat' (*sedes regiae*) at Worms.[28] Worms was a Roman city and

20 Widukind, *Rerum Gestarum Saxonicarum*, 1.17–18, 27–28; trans. Bachrach and Bachrach, *Deeds*, 28–29.

21 Kratz, *Waltharius*, xix on the depiction of Attila.

22 C. Bowlus, *The Battle of the Lechfeld and its Aftermath* (Aldershot: 2006).

23 *Waltharius*, v. 10, 166 (my italics).

24 Adalbert, *Continuatio*, ed. F. Kurze. In *Reginonis abbatis prumiensis Chronicon, cum continuatione treverensi*, 154–79. Hanover: 1890; Flodoard, *Annales*, ed. P. Lauer (Paris: 1906), s.a. 954, 137–8.

25 C. Brühl, *Deutschland-Frankreich: Die Geburt zweier Völker* (Cologne: 1995).

26 *Clavis Scriptorum Medii Aevi Auctores Galliae 735–987, Tomus I*, ed. M. H. Jullien and F. Perelman (Turnhout: 1994), 361.

27 Dronke, 'Waltharius', 39.

28 *Waltharius*, v. 433.

had been an important royal centre under the Carolingians, particularly under Charlemagne before 800. But this was not the case in the first half of the tenth century, when it was barely visited by kings: only two royal appearances (925 and 926) are known from the period 900–950. In the 960s, however, Otto I took residence there four times, despite spending all but two years of the decade in Italy. These visits were not routine transits on the royal itinerary, for Worms was in the 960s an important venue for the staging of Ottonian majesty: the ruler's son Otto II was crowned king in the city in 961 and held his first autonomous royal assembly there in 967.[29] Our best contemporary source for these assemblies is Adalbert, the continuator of Regino of Prüm's *Chronicle*, who also reports that when the Carolingian king Charles the Simple wanted to take control of Alsace in 923, he first came to Worms; and that Otto I had passed through Alsace from Worms ('in Francia') en route to Italy in 966.[30] Adalbert's perception of Worms as the chief seat of a Frankish king, and as a springboard for royal campaigns into Alsace, was a perspective from Alsace itself: when he wrote his chronicle in the mid-late 960s Adalbert was abbot of Wissembourg, about forty miles north of Strasbourg.

A Frankish king from Worms facing Hunnic antagonists, both threatening to intervene in Alsace: these were features not just of the fictional landscape depicted in *Waltharius*, but also of tenth-century political geography as viewed from the area around Strasbourg at the time Erchanbald became bishop. This coincidence should encourage us to pay more attention to the fact that much of the action in *Waltharius* is set in the Vosges mountains near Strasbourg. Geographical description was a narrative element that writers of this period inherited from the historians of Late Antiquity, but *Waltharius*'s setting is more than simply the backdrop to the poem. The topography of Walter's hideout is described in some detail, its inaccessibility essential to the structure of the narrative as a series of single combats. The Vosges region, characterised as a harsh wilderness, is itself personified in the poem.[31] The poet introduces the region as 'a massive woodland, having many lairs of beasts, accustomed to echo with the sound of hounds and horns'.[32] It was not, though, a benign environment: Walter's hideout was 'a place well suited to bloodthirsty bandits'.[33] Elsewhere, one of Walter's opponents is described in death as 'giving his body to the wild

29 C. Brühl, *Palatium und Civitas. Studien zur Profantopographie spätantiker Civitates vom 3. bis 13. Jahrhundert* (Cologne: 1975), vol. 2, 115–7.

30 Adalbert, *Continuatio*, s.a. 923, 965, 966, 157, 175, 177.

31 For example, *Waltharius*, v. 823.

32 *Waltharius*, v. 491–92.

33 *Waltharius*, v. 496.

woodland beasts'; and even the heroic Walter himself, after despatching most of his enemies, is said to have 'feared the woodland with its unknown winding paths, which might lead him into impenetrable thorns or even wild beasts'.[34]

This emphasis on the character of the region as wilderness was not neutral, and drew its force from a deep cultural opposition between untamed and domesticated/civilised space.[35] Mastering wilderness, and the beasts it contained, was one of the ideological attributes of powerful kingship in the Frankish world.[36] Gunther's failure to control this environment, indeed the fact that he was bested by Walter with its assistance, adds to the poet's unambiguous picture of him as a bad king. It also meshes with Walter's complaints in the poem that the king should have guaranteed him safe passage through his realms, and that as a traveller he should have been protected, rather than assaulted, by royal authority—another important marker of appropriate kingship in this period.[37] That this use of the setting was an authorial choice, and not simply descriptive, is indicated by comparison with another famous description of the Vosges, written in the 820s by Ermold the Black in a letter to the Carolingian king Pippin of Aquitaine.[38] This is framed as a mocking dialogue between personifications of the Vosges and the Rhine, vying to claim pre-eminence as supporters of royal power. In response to the accusation that it was battered by rain and good only for firewood, the Vosges states that its wood was used to build palaces and churches, and that kings hunted in its forests. In Ermold's eyes, the Vosges was a region that did not rebuff kingship but nourished it. This was hardly surprising in that the Carolingian Emperor Louis the Pious, whom Ermold was ultimately trying to impress, was a regular visitor to the hunting grounds in the Vosges and used such occasions to perform his royal status.[39] But where Louis the Pious had hunted regally for animals, the 'mad' and 'arrogant' King Gunther hunted for humans and treasure, stalking Walter and Hildegund through the hills by following their footprints

34 *Waltharius*, v. 913, 1147–49.

35 F. Guizard-Duchamp, 'Les espaces du sauvage dans le monde franc: Réalités et représentations', *Actes des congrès de la Société des historiens médiévistes de l'enseignement supérieur public* 37 (2006), 117–29.

36 P. Dutton, 'Charlemagne, King of Beasts', in Dutton, *Charlemagne's Mustache and Other Cultural Clusters of a Dark Age* (New York: 2004), 43–68.

37 *Waltharius*, v. 594–95; T. Reuter, 'The Insecurity of Travel in the Early and High Middle Ages: Criminals, Victims and their Medieval and Modern Observers', in Reuter, *Medieval Polities and Modern Mentalities*, ed. J. L. Nelson (Cambridge: 2006), 38–71.

38 Ermold, *Ad Pippinum Regem*, in *Poème sur Louis le Pieux et Épîtres au roi Pépin*, ed. E. Faral (Paris: 1932), 202–17.

39 E. Goldberg, 'Louis the Pious and the Hunt', *Speculum* 88 (2013), 613–43.

in the dust.[40] For Ermold, the Vosges was a place where royal power was enhanced; for the *Waltharius* poet, where it failed.

This point is sharpened by the poet in his descriptions of the individual encounters between Walter and the eleven champions (plus Hagen) sent by Gunther to kill him. The poet gives names to all of these men, and brief biographical details to most.[41] Almost all of them come from towns which were central places of royal power in the west of the Ottonian kingdom. The first to be named, Gamalo, is described as a 'prefect of Metz', which brings to mind the position of the Metz-based aristocrat Frederick who had been made 'duke of the Lotharingians' in 959. Two others are from Speyer and, interestingly, Strasbourg. One is said to be a Frank, two are from Worms (the Frankish 'royal seat'), and one is from Saxony (the Ottonian homeland). Walter makes a bleak joke to the Saxon, Ekivrid, before killing him. Ekivrid asks him if he is a 'woodland demon' (*faunus*) and Walter fires back a threat, saying that if he comes any closer 'you will be really able to tell the Saxons that you saw a demon in the Vosges'.[42] Later, when his men begin to be dismayed at the body count and ask to end the expedition, King Gunther responds: 'If thus shamed I leave the Vosges, then what becomes of me? ... I would rather die than enter Worms after such a thing'.[43]

This 'here' vs 'there' contrasting of Worms and other royal centres with the peripheral wilderness of the Vosges makes it clear that Gunther and his men are strangers in a strange land, and reminds us that violence can have a geography. Epics and sagas often depict violence (as opposed to legitimate force) as characteristic of in-between places and outlying regions.[44] In Ottonian texts, the western parts of the realm—the so-called 'middle kingdom', including Alsace—were often depicted as a wild frontier.[45] According to Thietmar of Merseburg, 'the people of the West' were 'always fickle' and displayed a 'tendency towards arousal'—they were cowards who resisted the rule of God and king and 'serve[d] only their bodily desires'.[46] Already in the poem by Ermold (an exile who was anxious to win a recall to the royal court) we find

40 *Waltharius*, v. 512–13.

41 *Waltharius*, v. 582–1063.

42 *Waltharius*, v. 768–69.

43 *Waltharius*, v. 946–48.

44 Miller, *Bloodtaking*, 188.

45 T. Riches, 'Bishop Gerard I of Cambrai (1012–1051) and the Representation of Authority in the *Gesta Episcoporum Cameracensium*', University of London PhD thesis (2006), 188–245.

46 Thietmar, *Chronicon*, ed. R. Holtzmann, *Die Chronik des Bischofs Thietmar von Merseburg und ihre Korveier Überarbeitung* (Berlin: 1935), 6.48, 334; trans. D. Warner, *Ottonian Germany* (Manchester: 2001), 270–1.

the Alsatians described as 'an exceedingly ferocious people', drunk on wealth, barbarous of tongue, and ignorant of proper religion.[47] The views of Thietmar and Ermold represent the rhetorical disdain of the outsider, the sneering of the metropolitan at the provincial. Erchanbald would not have shared their perspective unquestioningly, for in tenth-century terms he was himself a provincial. If the bishop was able to appreciate the version of this discourse found in *Waltharius*, this implies a slightly different sensibility: a kind of reverse 'othering' in which the discourse of wilderness could be appropriated by members of the Alsatian ruling class to fashion their own sense of how they fitted into the Wild West of the Ottonian kingdom.

Treasure and Revenge

Although the poem deals overtly with themes such as heroism, fidelity, and the legitimacy of violence, it is not always fully appreciated that these are secondary to the core motif of the whole poem: the status of the treasure stolen by Walter from Attila, and his attempts to carry it home to Aquitaine through Gunther's kingdom. The poet repeatedly mentions that the treasure was what the king really desired, and he is explicitly described as greedy, arrogant, and 'insane' in terms which echo the personifications of avarice and pride in one of the poet's main sources, Prudentius's fifth-century *Psychomachia*.[48] At the heart of the poem is a speech by Hagen, seemingly acting here as the poet's interlocutor, on the evils prompted by greed for gold.[49] The emphasis on this theme in *Waltharius* means it is often read as a parable on greed, and even as a satire on aristocratic acquisitiveness. Students of the poem have even argued that Walter himself is not immune from the text's critique, given his taking of the treasure from the Huns and his anxiety to hold on to it.[50] But this underrates the realism and subtlety with which Frankish churchmen understood aristocratic society (to which, after all, they belonged)—as long as it was not deemed excessive, they did not necessarily regard the pursuit of wealth as a matter for condemnation.[51] In keeping with the latter observation, I suggest that the wealth issue in *Waltharius* is not an ecclesiastical suspicion that

47 Ermold, *Ad Pippinum Regem*, 214–5.

48 Kratz, *Mocking Epic*, 33–36; Rio, 'Waltharius at Fontenoy', 47–52.

49 *Waltharius*, v. 857–75.

50 Kratz, *Mocking Epic*, 47–48.

51 Stone, 'Waltharius and Carolingian Morality', 61–65.

treasure was corrupting per se, but rather an expression of anxiety about deciding *whose* gold it was.

The starting point here is the observation that the poet treats the treasure as the same body of gold throughout the poem: the gold given by Gibicho to the Huns in tribute is the same gold that Walter steals from Attila, and which Gunther then tries to extort from the hero. Gunther states this explicitly when he realises that the stranger passing through his lands is Walter: 'Rejoice ... the tribute treasure [*gaza*] sent by Gibicho to the eastern king is now sent by the Almighty back to me here in my kingdom!'[52] Gunther then urges his men to pursue Walter and get his 'stolen money' (*furata talenta*), which Walter should be made to 'return' (*reddere*) to him.[53] Walter, in response, sarcastically asks the first man sent against him how he expects him to 'return' something to Gunther that was not his in the first place, and wonders aloud how he could be said to have stolen anything from the king.[54] The wealth is his, and Gunther is in fact the thief.[55] The dramatic tension in the poem therefore derives not from a generalised suspicion of lay desire for treasure, but from the fact that Gunther and Walter are driven by conflicting narratives of the history of this *particular* treasure. The king claims that the story began with his father's possession of the gold, and that it was therefore a gift which he is now reclaiming. The hero, on the other hand, follows a different script. Ignoring the fact that the wealth had previously been given as tribute by the Franks, he implicitly claims that the beginning of its story was his own seizing of the treasure from Attila—which was, by dint of the same argument, a legitimate act.[56]

All of the above examples are given in direct speech: they are represented as the views of the protagonists, not of the poet. The poet's sympathy with Walter's position is nonetheless made very clear in that he refers to Gunther as '*superbus*' (arrogant), '*infelix*' (misguided) and '*demens*' (mad) in precisely these passages. Why, though, does the poet take this point of view? His anxieties appear to relate not to the inherently corrupting influence of wealth, but to the etiquette of its distribution between members of the elite. One aspect of this is the fact that *Waltharius* begins with tribute paid by the Frankish king to

52 *Waltharius*, v. 470–72.

53 *Waltharius*, v. 517, 641, 724.

54 *Waltharius*, v. 654–57.

55 *Waltharius*, v. 659, 1218.

56 On the competing classifications of gifts and similar transactions see Miller, *Bloodtaking*, 77–110; W. I. Miller, *Humiliation* (Ithaca: 1993), 15–52; W. I. Miller, *Audun and the Polar Bear: Luck, Law, and Largesse in a Medieval Tale of Risky Business* (Leiden and Boston: 2008), 99–113.

the Huns in return for peace. The word used is *censum*—a payment or fee—and the poet emphasises that the decision was legitimised by the consent of all at a council.[57] One of the champions sent by Gunther against Walter is compared to the Trojan warrior Pandarus, 'who was once ordered to break a treaty'; and another is said to have rendered his soul at death to Orcus, in classical literature not only a personification of death but also a punisher of broken oaths.[58] Orcus is also said to await Gunther when he dies.[59] The oath broken by Gunther and his men can only be the original Frankish peace deal with Attila: in attempting to regain the Frankish treasure after having broken the treaty with the Huns, the king was trying to have his cake and eat it. The poet's insinuation seems to be that the breaking of the oaths meant that the Franks had in effect relinquished their claim to the gold before Walter had asserted his own.

A second argument embedded in *Waltharius* is that Gunther does not observe proper etiquette in the distribution of booty—in fact he is shown up in this respect by the other main characters. He explicitly states that the treasure is destined to be his, personally.[60] In a long passage at the heart of the poem, just before the first champion is sent against him, Walter offers some of the gold to Gunther in return for peace, even though he thinks he is entitled to expect safe passage by default. Gunther is intent on taking all the treasure for himself, and despite Hagen's attempts to persuade him otherwise, he refuses the offer.[61] Later, Walter renews the offer, this time explaining to Hagen what should have happened if the king were behaving appropriately. In this alternative scenario, Walter would have been recognised and received with hospitality, and would have surrendered gifts to his hosts voluntarily.[62] Hagen himself observes the etiquette of warfare by saying that he will not fight his former friend, but in so doing will not claim his share of any spoils.[63] In seeking all the treasure for himself, Gunther manifests not only greed, but also a refusal to observe the rules for royal comportment in dealing with the distribution of such wealth. Those rules, or expectations, are articulated in the poem by Hagen and Walter, whose magnanimous attempts to show good faith by giving up their claims to gold mark them as more kingly than the king. Gunther's actions are depicted as tasteless and excessive, and disproportionate to his position and to

57 *Waltharius*, v. 20–24.

58 *Waltharius*, v. 728, 913.

59 *Waltharius*, v. 1327.

60 *Waltharius*, v. 471–72, 641.

61 *Waltharius*, v. 566–665.

62 *Waltharius*, v. 1239–63.

63 *Waltharius*, v. 637.

the situation.[64] The violence that unfurls in consequence of Gunther's refusal is therefore on his hands. Walter's killing of the first champion is portrayed as legitimate because he first offered gold to avoid the fight. Some of the other warriors then claim that they are fighting Walter not for gold, but in vengeance for his killing of their colleagues.[65] Not least among them is Hagen, who is distraught at the death of his nephew Batavrid, the sixth champion. Hagen laments that Batavrid died as a result of (Gunther's) greed, and explains to Walter that he cannot walk away because his need to avenge the young man overrides their friendship.[66] The king responds by trying to manipulate his faltering men into fighting Walter for revenge rather than treasure.[67] When it comes to the crunch, though, he himself will not avenge his own men.[68] For him, it's all about the money. The actions of Gunther's men, motivated by loyalty to the king and the desire for vengeance after their fellows had been killed, are described (even validated) by the poet as comprehensible in themselves. The actions of the king himself are not. Everything that happens follows from Gunther's belief—mistaken, in the poet's opinion—that the treasure was his and not Walter's. This is the original sin of *Waltharius*, from which stems the ensuing cycle of revenge, death, and mutilation.[69]

The distribution of treasure in the form of tribute and booty was a sensitive, rule-bound issue in many medieval societies, and one whose categories and vocabulary were open to misunderstanding and dispute.[70] It needed to be handled with great care. This is why, when Hrut takes booty from a pirate in *Njal's saga*, he is careful to agree to the terms of its redistribution with the Norwegian king before taking a cut for himself.[71] A cluster of analogous codes and expectations surrounded the distribution of plunder among the elites of the Carolingian Empire (though its systems for gathering and paying tribute to outside aggressors were extremely controversial).[72] Indeed, the poem's extended rumination on Hunnic treasure is sometimes linked by modern commentators to Charlemagne's crushing of the Avars in 796: contemporaries

64 I borrow the language here from W. I. Miller, *Eye for an Eye* (Cambridge: 2006), 18–25; Miller, *Audun*, 117–8.

65 *Waltharius*, v. 699–701, 914.

66 *Waltharius*, v. 846–85, 1266–79.

67 *Waltharius*, v. 950–53.

68 *Waltharius*, v. 1060–65.

69 Cf. Miller, *Humiliation*, 59–60.

70 Miller, *Audun*, 81–82, 124.

71 *Njal's Saga*, trans. M. Magnusson and H. Palsson (Harmondsworth: 1960), ch. 5, 47–48.

72 T. Reuter, 'Plunder and Tribute in the Carolingian Empire', in Reuter, *Medieval Polities*, 231–50.

commented on the vast amount of wealth this yielded for the king, who then distributed it to his important followers and lesser kings around Europe.[73] But the story in *Waltharius* is about a king paying tribute to the Huns in return for peace, and the subsequent revocation of that treaty. This resembles the events of the 790s much less than those of the 920s, when the first Ottonian king Henry I bought peace from the Hungarians and then, nearly a decade later, broke it. A tenth-century source even tells us that Henry did this deal because his soldiers were not up to the job, which is the same reason the poem gives us for Gibicho's equivalent decision.[74] Henry's deal should be seen as part of a broader post-Carolingian landscape whose politics in the first half of the tenth century were dominated by the negotiation of treaties and alliances, not just with invaders, but also between kings and their aristocratic elites.[75] The battle in the Vosges, and Gunther's refusal to deal with Walter, reads like the result of just such an agreement going wrong. To an audience in the middle of the tenth century, this failure of dialogue could readily have been interpreted as a comment on the fragility of contemporary political dynamics, transposed into a mythical historical register.

As part of their depiction of a world glued together by deals and agreements, narrative sources make it clear that the etiquette of plunder, tribute, and treaty-making was a subject of anxiety and discussion in Ottonian political culture. Widukind of Corvey makes numerous references to the distribution of spoils and booty among one's followers as a vital component of good lordship.[76] In a passage about margrave Gero, leader of the Saxon forces on the eastern frontier, he describes the declining loyalty of soldiers who were inadequately compensated with an appropriate share of booty.[77] In Widukind's telling, even the very origins of the Saxons were tied up in a story about the distribution of treasure. The story revolves around an exchange of gifts sealing a treaty between the Saxons and the Thuringians. Coming to the lands of the latter, a Saxon youth trades gold arm-rings (the same type of treasure carried by Walter in the poem) for dust, which he scatters on the ground, allowing the Saxons to claim that this land is now theirs—inevitably provoking a battle with

73 Einhard, *Vita Karoli Magni*, ed. O. Holder-Egger (Leipzig and Hanover: 1911), ch. 13, 15–16.

74 Widukind, *Rerum Gestarum Saxonicarum*, 1.38, 55–57.

75 G. Althoff, *Amicitiae und Pacta: Bündnis, Einung, Politik und Gebetsgedenken im beginnenden 10. Jahrhundert* (Hanover: 1992).

76 Widukind, *Rerum Gestarum Saxonicarum*, 1.35, 1.36, 2.11, 2.15, 2.17, 3.66, 3.68, 48–54, 74–78, 79–83, 141–3; Thietmar, *Chronicon*, 8.32, 530–1.

77 Widukind, *Rerum Gestarum Saxonicarum*, 2.30, 91–92.

the Thuringians, who take a rather different view of the transaction.[78] This is obviously a legend, but it shows that contemporaries were very well aware that an exchange of gifts in the making of an agreement could be open to opposing interpretations. The legalistic one used by the Saxons in their use of the dust, and approved of by Widukind, was pretty implausible—but not much more far-fetched than the *Waltharius* poet's interpretation of Gunther's obligation to relinquish his claim to the Frankish treasure because of the expiry of his father's deal with the Huns.

Widukind's discussion of the peace deal done between Henry I and the Hungarians in 924 is also suspiciously defensive. Seeking to narrate it as a staging point on the road to Otto I's routing of the same enemy in 955, the historian claims that Henry extorted peace from the enemy and in return only gave up a prisoner and 'some gifts'.[79] But elsewhere in his text he makes clear that gifts given in such a situation constituted an acknowledgement of tributary status, and indeed lets slip that Henry I thought so too—as shown by his apology to his people for 'plundering' their churches and families to pay the Hungarians their 'customary gifts'.[80] Given that Widukind had not baulked at describing two major rebellions faced by his own king Otto I, it may seem surprising that he felt the need to neutralise Henry's tribute to the Hungarians by recategorising it as mere giving of 'gifts'. The reason for Widukind's caution is indicated by the *Waltharius* poet's characterisation of Gibicho's tribute to the Huns as an act of cowardice: it was very easy for such transactions to be become, in the eyes of hostile observers, evidence of weakness, corruption, or avarice.

Henry I's dealings with the Hungarians obviously still mattered to the narratives of Ottonian history told in Erchanbald's time, but to the ruling elites of Alsace the events of the 950s would have been much fresher in the memory. The Hungarian army which appeared on the fringes of the Vosges in 954 was in the employ of two rebellious dukes: Liudolf of Swabia (the king's son) and Conrad the Red of Lotharingia (the king's son-in-law).[81] Lotharingia to the north and Swabia to the east were the two duchies with the closest links to Alsace, and the powerful of the region intermittently traded their loyalties

78 Widukind, *Rerum Gestarum Saxonicarum*, 1.4–6, 5–7.

79 Widukind, *Rerum Gestarum Saxonicarum*, 1.32, 45.

80 Widukind, *Rerum Gestarum Saxonicarum*, 1.10, 1.35, 1.38–39, 17–18, 48–51, 55–59.

81 Ruotger, *Vita Brunonis*, ed. I. Ott, *Ruotgers Lebensbeschreibung des Erzbischofs Bruno von Köln* (Weimar: 1951), ch. 19, 17–19.

between them.[82] Just before Easter 954 the Hungarians had been 'received publicly', at Worms no less, and given 'abundant gifts of gold and silver' by the rebels.[83] Later in the year, after the rebellion had been subdued, Otto lamented not only that Liudolf had worked alongside 'the enemies of God', but also that the Hungarians were returning home 'loaded down with my gold and silver with which I enriched my son and son-in-law'.[84] Liudolf threw himself on his father's mercy, claiming he had acted under pressure: he had only 'gathered' money for the Hungarians out of fear.[85] Here is another situation that echoes the dynamics found in *Waltharius*: a tribute paid to 'Avars' and a king claiming that the money was his—even though it had been 'gathered' from the coffers of the kingdom's churches and paid over without the ruler's knowledge.

With his triumph over the Hungarians at the Lech a few months later, Otto had the opportunity to actualise his claim to this treasure. One source says that the king had promised to reward all those who joined him in the battle; another, that in the aftermath of the battle 'trophies' were sent round the realm to advertise the king's great victory.[86] But it is not at all likely that the money 'gathered' by Liudolf in the previous year found its way back to its previous owners. Widukind usually refers to a distribution of booty in the wake of Ottonian victories, but the Lech is an exception.[87] In fact, the king's triumph was principally celebrated in Saxony, and it was the distant Saxon church of Magdeburg which received much of the wealth that Otto had acquired.[88] This was despite the fact that very few Saxons fought at the Lech, where the army was primarily made up of fighters from the west and south of the kingdom: Lotharingia, Swabia, Alsace, Franconia, and Bavaria—the same areas which had been at the heart of the rebellion of 953–4 and whose churches and landowners had been prevailed upon (willingly or not) to pay for Liudolf's and

82 T. Zotz, 'Das Elsaß—ein Teil des Zwischenreichs?', in *Lotharingia: Eine europäische Kernlandschaft um das Jahr 1000*, ed. H. Herrmann and R. Schneider (Saarbrücken: 1995), 49–70.

83 Widukind, *Rerum Gestarum Saxonicarum*, 3.30, 11–18; trans. Bachrach and Bachrach, *Deeds*, 116; Adalbert, *Continuatio*, s.a. 954, 168; Flodoard, *Annales*, s.a. 954, 137–38.

84 Widukind, *Rerum Gestarum Saxonicarum*, 3.32, 118–9; trans. Bachrach and Bachrach, *Deeds*, 117.

85 Widukind, *Rerum Gestarum Saxonicarum*, 3.32, 118–9; trans. Bachrach and Bachrach, *Deeds*, 118.

86 Thietmar, *Chronicon*, 2.9, 49; Ruotger, *Vita Brunonis*, ch. 35, 36.

87 E.g. Widukind, *Rerum Gestarum Saxonicarum*, 2.17, 81–83 on the Battle of Birten during the great rebellion of the late 930s.

88 Thietmar, *Chronicon*, 2.11, 50.

Conrad's Hungarian mercenaries.[89] These regions were thus forgiven for their uprising, and reintegrated into the expanding Ottonian kingdom. But they were almost certainly not compensated for the treasure they had lost—which ended up, via the Hungarians, in the hands of the triumphant king.

Erchanbald and Otto

The above analysis of two prominent but under-appreciated themes in *Waltharius* shows that the poem would have had strong resonances for a mid-tenth-century Alsatian audience. Its depiction of the Vosges as a place where kingship was tested and failed, and its expressions of anxiety around the etiquette of plunder and tribute, were not only relevant but integral to the political discourse of the 960s. But the poet hitched these two themes to a pretty savage critique of a king. Why would Gerald have thought his bishop would be receptive to such a commentary? This seems a hard circle to square because, as has been long noted, Erchanbald was a conspicuous supporter of Ottonian authority during his long tenure, receiving in return a number of generous privileges connected to jurisdiction and coinage which made him in theory at least one of the most powerful bishops in the whole kingdom.[90] In a document of 981 describing the military forces to be sent to the king from each of the realm's major churches, Strasbourg was the first named bishopric.[91] It is noticeable, however, that almost all the evidence for the close relationship between the bishop of Strasbourg and the king comes from after 973: in other words, from the reign of Otto II, not that of Otto I. Although the relationship between Otto I and Erchanbald before 973 is not clear from the sources, we should not simply assume that it was unambiguously positive.

This is especially so because the king's attempts to govern Alsace in the second half of his reign were anything but smooth. In the first half of the tenth century, kings had occasionally fought for control of Alsace: there was a violent three-way competition for the Upper Rhine region—including the sacking and burning of Strasbourg—between the rulers of Burgundy, East Francia, and West Francia in the early 910s, and a similar conflict at the end of

89 Widukind, *Rerum Gestarum Saxonicarum*, 3.44, 123–5.

90 *Die Urkunden Otto des II.*, ed. T. Sickel (Hanover: 1888), nos. 72, 73, 129, 267. Commentary: H. Büttner, *Geschichte des Elsaß I*, ed. T. Endemann (Sigmaringen: 1991), 176–7; Berschin, 'Erkanbald', 3–4.

91 *Indiculus Loricatorum*, ed. L. Weiland, MGH Constitutiones 1 (Hanover: 1893), no. 436.

the 930s during the first major rebellion against Otto I. On the latter occasion the region nearly became the graveyard of Ottonian rule when, during a siege of Breisach in Alsace 'many of the king's supporters abandoned him because they no longer had hope that the Saxons would continue to rule'.[92] One of the most high-profile deserters was Bishop Rothard of Strasbourg, Erchanbald's predecessor-but-one.[93] Such flare-ups of hot conflict aside, the more regular exercise of kingship and royal authority was virtually absent from the region for several decades after the end of the Carolingian Empire. This doesn't mean that Alsace was lawless, but it was more or less free from direct royal intervention for the best part of half a century.[94] All this changed markedly in the early 950s, when Otto I began to pay close attention to the southern parts of his kingdom, driven by his increasing interest in Italy, which he conquered by means of three invasions in 951–52, 961–65, and 966–72.

Otto's approach to controlling Alsace in the 950s and 960s was highly intrusive in comparison to the laissez-faire approach which had prevailed hitherto, involving the sudden dispossession of local bigwigs and the attempted dismantling of their families' positions. The dominant aristocratic family in the region is known as the Etichonids, and by some accounts their position went back to the seventh century.[95] Even taking a less optimistic view of the continuity of family consciousness, a branch of the Etichonids characterised by the names Guntram, Eberhard, and Hugh had been the leading noble kin group in Alsace for well over a century by the time Otto I took a hostile interest in their affairs in the 950s. The first manifestation of this interest was the king's deposition of a count called Guntram at a large assembly in 952. This was the assembly at which Otto attempted (not altogether successfully) to cement his recent invasion of Italy, and it was attended by bishops and aristocrats from south of the Alps as well as East Francia.[96] The charge was treason or infidelity, though we don't have the details because the trial is only known to us through passing references in a number of charters via which the count's confiscated lands were

92 Widukind, *Rerum Gestarum Saxonicarum*, 2.24, 87; trans. Bachrach and Bachrach, *Deeds*, 84.

93 Widukind, *Rerum Gestarum Saxonicarum*, 2.25, 87–88.

94 M. Borgolte, 'Geschichte der Grafengewalt im Elsaß von Dagobert I. bis Otto dem Großen', *Zeitschrift für die Geschichte des Oberrheins* 131 (1983), 3–54 at 46–49.

95 F. Vollmer, 'Die Etichonen: Ein Beitrag zur Frage der Kontinuität früher Adelsfamilien', in *Studien und Vorarbeiten zur Geschichte des grossfränkischen und frühdeutschen Adels*, ed. G. Tellenbach (Freiburg: 1957), 137–84.

96 Adalbert, *Continuatio*, s.a. 952, 166.

subsequently redistributed.[97] The accusation may have been deeply cynical if, as has been persuasively argued, the charges were revenge-served-cold from Guntram's participation in the mass rebellion against Otto more than a decade earlier, in 938–9.[98] A second manoeuvre against the same family was prosecuted in 959, with the king putting the monastery at Lure, controlled by Guntram's brothers, under direct royal control in the guise of monastic reform.[99]

However sincerely he believed in his rhetoric of treason and reform, Otto's moves against Guntram and his brothers were highly opportunistic, because the lands at stake were strategically important. Guntram's estates were essential for controlling key routes through the Upper Rhine region, especially access to the Bündner Pass across the Alps, while Lure controlled access to the Burgundian Gate, a pass connecting Alsace and Burgundy to the west via the Vosges.[100] The main beneficiaries of these dispossessions, moreover, were the family of Otto's second wife Adelheid, whom he had married in Italy in 951. Adelheid was a figure with important connections in all the regions surrounding Alsace: descended on her mother's side from the dukes of Swabia, she was daughter and sister of kings of Burgundy and widow of a king of Italy. In the 950s and 960s Otto placed key Alsatian lands in the hands of her brother Conrad III of Burgundy, her mother Bertha, and Adelheid herself. Her other brother Rudolf was 'duke' of the Alsatians by 962.[101] The purpose of Otto's strategy was not only to link together the power-bases of his new in-laws in the south-west of his kingdom, but also to transform Alsace from a frontier zone into a centre of royal activity on the Upper Rhine, binding it more closely with its neighbours and facilitating access to Italy. The marginalisation of Liudolf of Swabia and Conrad the Red which led to the rebellion of 953–4 was a direct consequence of Otto's marriage to Adelheid and the promotion of her family. In fact, the trigger for the rising was the granting of the palace-monastery of Erstein, in Alsace, to Bertha.[102] This was much more than a bit of regional

---

97 *Die Urkunden Konrad I., Heinrich I. und Otto I.*, ed. T. Sickel (Hanover: 1879–84), nos. 155, 166, 189, 201, 236; *Die Urkunden Heinrichs II. und Arduins*, ed. H. Bresslau et al. (Hanover: 1900–3), no. 77.

98 T. Zotz, 'König Otto I., Graf Guntram und Breisach', *Zeitschrift für die Geschichte des Oberrheins* 137 (1989), 66–77.

99 *Die Urkunden Ottos I.*, no. 199; Büttner, *Geschichte des Elsaß*, 164; H. Hummer, *Politics and Power in Early Medieval Europe: Alsace and the Frankish World 600–1000* (Cambridge: 2006), 229–31, 240–46.

100 Borgolte, 'Geschichte der Grafengewalt', 50; Büttner, *Geschichte des Elsaß*, 165–6.

101 Büttner, *Geschichte des Elsaß*, 164–72; T. Zotz, 'Die Ottonen und das Elsaß', in *Kaiserin Adelheid*, ed. F. Staab and T. Unger (Speyer: 2005), 51–68 at 53–60.

102 Adalbert, *Continuatio*, s.a. 953, 166.

housekeeping: members of the old guard in the south and west certainly understood which way the wind was blowing.

What Erchanbald of Strasbourg thought about any of this in the years after his accession can be no more than a matter of speculation. He must, though, have been aware of the controversy surrounding Otto's intervention in Alsace. He had been a member of his own predecessor's entourage during the earlier 960s, when the king was still issuing charters reminding people of Guntram's infidelity. In fact, the redistribution of strategic Alsatian lands and monasteries to members of Otto's family and other Saxon allies continued into the second half of the 960s.[103] After the loss of Lure, Guntram's brothers refocused their family network on new residences high in the Vosges and also established a new monastery at Altdorf near Strasbourg, with a large endowment including property in the city itself. The new house was consecrated by Erchanbald in 974.[104] The royal intervention at Lure had itself been a blow to the Strasbourg bishops, who (according to a tenth-century source) had had ambitions of their own at the house, and who were now expressly excluded by the terms of Otto's reform.[105]

The idea that a bishop might have entertained a negative attitude to the southern expansion of royal authority is not so far-fetched (especially since we don't know that Erchanbald—unlike his predecessor Udo—was a royal appointment). A text written at a royal nunnery in the Ottonians' Saxon heartland in the early 970s was openly critical of Otto I's Italian adventures.[106] In 972 Archbishop Adalbert of Magdeburg—the same Adalbert who had written the unambiguously pro-Otto chronicle at Wissembourg in the mid-960s—made the same point by publicly treating a Saxon duke in the manner of a king while Otto was south of the Alps.[107] Prior to its foundation in 968, Otto's long-gestated plan to establish an archbishopric at his favourite church of Magdeburg was itself a matter of great controversy among the East Frankish bishops, with the main opponent being Otto's own son, Archbishop William of Mainz.[108] Strasbourg was a subordinate diocese of Mainz. When in 966 Otto marched

103 E.g. *Die Urkunden Ottos I.*, nos. 284, 365, 368–69.

104 Büttner, *Geschichte des Elsaß*, 173–4; Hummer, *Politics and Power*, 247–9.

105 Hummer, *Politics and Power*, 238.

106 *Vita Mathildis Reginae Antiquior*, ed. B. Schütte, in *Die Lebensbeschreibungen der Königin Mathilde*, MGH SRG 66 (Hanover: 1994), 109–42 at ch. 15, 139–40.

107 Thietmar, *Chronicon*, 2.28, 73–74; G. Althoff, 'Das Bett des Königs in Magdeburg: Zu Thietmar II, 28', in *Festschrift für Berent Schwineköper zu seinem 70. Geburtstag*, ed. H. Maurer and H. Patze (Sigmaringen: 1982), 141–53.

108 M. Becher, *Rex, Dux und Gens: Untersuchungen zur Entstehung des sächsischen Herzogtums im 9. und 10. Jahrhundert* (Husum: 1996), 289–90, 296.

from Worms en route to Italy through Alsace (his last visit to the region, and the first time we can be sure he met Erchanbald) he paused at Strasbourg only long enough to reallocate more confiscated lands to support his hoped-for archbishopric in Magdeburg.[109] This was a supremely confident king in action, not only brushing aside opposition and dismantling the power of those who got in his way, but rubbing it in their faces and shouting it from the rooftops.

We can't know what the bishop of Strasbourg thought about these matters, but we do know that he read *Waltharius*. Did its stories of Hunnic invaders, Burgundian queens, and Frankish kings remind him of his own day? Would Gunther's fixation on 'his' treasure have made him think wryly of Otto I's appropriation of the gold given by the western churches to the Hungarians, via Liudolf of Swabia and Conrad the Red? Might he have relished the poem's haughty king coming a cropper in the Vosges when considering Otto's rapid dismantling of time-immemorial political arrangements among the ruling class of Alsace? And when he considered Walter's heroic stand in the forests and gorges west of Strasbourg did the bishop think about what had happened at Lure, itself situated in a gap in the mountains, or of Guntram's brothers building their new hilltop residences high in the Vosges? *Waltharius* is not a *roman à clef*. It does not map neatly onto the contours of contemporary politics. But, knowing what he knew about Otto and the Vosges, how could the bishop not be reminded of his own times? This, surely, is one reason why Gerald thought the poem would amuse Erchanbald ('it is for playing rather than praying') and hoped that it would make his long days pass more quickly.[110]

Conclusion

The recent consensus that *Waltharius* is best contextualised in the Carolingian period undersells the poem's compatibility with the Ottonian world in which we know it found an audience. The arguments made in this article reinforce Berschin's case for Gerald as the author of the text and Erchanbald as its original recipient. The fact that the earliest manuscripts were made in the later tenth century at centres along the Rhine valley was an important part of Berschin's case. To this we might now add that the monastery which produced what seems to be the earliest copy of all was directly connected to the events we have been describing: Lorsch was one of the institutions which benefited from the dismantling of Guntram's estate, receiving rights in his major estate

109 *Die Urkunden Ottos I.*, nos. 331–33.

110 *Waltharius*, v. 18–20.

of Brumath.[111] Control of Brumath, in fact, may have been the issue at the heart of Guntram's alleged treachery.[112] But even if we don't insist on a mid-tenth century origin for the text, we can still gain some insights into that period by thinking about how Erchanbald might have read the poem. We need not doubt that he would have appreciated the arguments of numerous modern scholars that he had in front of him a Christianised version of epic poetry which took much of its moral meaning from a sophisticated dialogue with classical and patristic sources. The poem's puzzling ending, with the main protagonists maimed and joking with each other about their injuries should be read in this light: Hagen's loss of an eye and some of his teeth, adumbrated earlier in the poem, can be read as a Christian parable on the futility of revenge—literally, an eye for an eye.[113] 'Thus was the treasure of the Avars shared!' adds the poet, archly.[114]

But the contemporary resonances of the poem mean that it can't have been interpreted only as an intellectual exercise predicated entirely on a deep appreciation of its profound intertextuality, nor as a single-minded clerical condemnation of lay greed. It was also an ironic commentary on the complex world in which the protagonists lived, and in which the poet and his readers could recognise their own. The poet was not only a neo-Prudentius, but also a proto-Miller. The drama and tension in the narrative resides not in simple moral lessons but in the poet's wry acknowledgement of the competing demands that operated on Walter and Hagen. Their loyalty to each other was ultimately incompatible with Hagen's loyalty to Gunther and Walter's to Attila. Their friendship was compromised by Walter's killing of Hagen's nephew, which in turn was perfectly justified as a response to Gunther's arrogance and greed. Revenge, killing and the desire for wealth were not satirised per se—the poet's much more subtle point was that such things could in themselves be justified, but that the irreconcilable perspectives of the protagonists turned them into chapters of a tragi-comic story in which nobody could truly win. This is all made explicit in Hagen's agonised exchanges with Gunther and Walter in which he laments his impossibly compromised position.[115] Hagen, caught between the other two characters, understood precisely the etiquettes of loyalty by which he was inexorably crushed. Walter was driven by the knowledge that

111 *Die Urkunden Ottos I.*, no. 201; Büttner, *Geschichte des Elsaß*, 166.

112 Zotz, 'Guntram', 70–71, 75–76.

113 Kratz, *Waltharius*, xxii. On body-parts as value-bearing see Miller, *Eye for an Eye*, 46–48, and Eva Miller's article in the present volume.

114 *Waltharius*, v. 1404.

115 *Waltharius*, v. 1067–1125, 1239–79.

he was in the right. Gunther, on the other hand, was driven by an inflexible belief in the authority of the king's will which led him to reject all attempts at compromise. Individually, each might have had a case, but in combination their motivations led only to conflict. In such circumstances, the regular rhythms of a politics based on deals and truces could not work. The fragile cultural balance on which perched the smooth operation of politics was placed in jeopardy when presided over by a king who could not be trusted to follow the rules—or to adhere to the spirit as well as the letter of the deals which he himself had made.[116]

Works Cited

Adalbert, *Continuatio*. In *Reginonis abbatis prumiensis Chronicon, cum continuatione treverensi*, edited by F. Kurze. MGH SRG 50, 154–79. Hanover: 1890.

Althoff, G. *Amicitiae und Pacta: Bündnis, Einung, Politik und Gebetsgedenken im beginnenden 10. Jahrhundert*. Hanover: 1992.

Althoff, G. 'Das Bett des Königs in Magdeburg: Zu Thietmar II, 28'. In *Festschrift für Berent Schwineköper zu seinem 70. Geburtstag*, edited by H. Maurer and H. Patze, 141–53. Sigmaringen: 1982.

Bachrach, B. and D. Bachrach. *Deeds of the Saxons*. Washington, D.C.: 2014.

Becher, M. *Rex, Dux und Gens. Untersuchungen zur Entstehung des sächsischen Herzogtums im 9. und 10. Jahrhundert*. Husum: 1996.

Berschin, W. 'Erkanbald von Straßburg (965–991)'. *Zeitschrift für die Geschichte des Oberrheins* 134 (1986): 1–20.

Bisanti, A. 'La leggenda di Walthario e i distici "Vualtarius fortis" nel "Chronicon Novaliciense"'. *Bollettino di Studi Latini* 40 (2010): 76–85.

Borgolte, M. 'Geschichte der Grafengewalt im Elsaß von Dagobert I. bis Otto dem Großen', *Zeitschrift für die Geschichte des Oberrheins* 131 (1983): 3–54.

Bowlus, C. *The Battle of the Lechfeld and its Aftermath* (Aldershot: 2006).

Brühl, C. *Deutschland-Frankreich: Die Geburt zweier Völker* (Cologne: 1995).

Brühl, C. *Palatium und Civitas. Studien zur Profantopographie spätantiker Civitates vom 3. bis 13. Jahrhundert*, vol. 2. Cologne: 1975.

116 For comments on a draft of this article I am grateful to Rob Bartlett, Eric Goldberg, and Matthias Tischler; and to Chris Callow for discussing the sagas with me. This article forms part of the HERA JRP III project 'After Empire: Using and Not Using the Past in the Crisis of the Carolingian Empire'.

Büttner, H. *Geschichte des Elsaß I*. Edited by T. Endemann. Sigmaringen: 1991.

Chronicon Novaliciense. Edited by L. Bethmann. MGH SS 7, 73–128. Hanover: 1846.

Die Urkunden Heinrichs II. und Arduins. Edited by H. Bresslau et al. Hanover: 1900–3.

Dronke, P. 'Waltharius—Gaiferos'. In Dronke, *Latin and Vernacular Poets of the Middle Ages*, 29–79. Aldershot: 1996.

Dutton, P. 'Charlemagne, King of Beasts'. In Dutton, *Charlemagne's Mustache and Other Cultural Clusters of a Dark Age*, 43–68. New York: 2004.

Einhard. *Vita Karoli Magni*. Edited by O. Holder-Egger. MGH SRG 25. Leipzig and Hanover: 1911.

Ermold, *Ad Pippinum Regem*. In *Poème sur Louis le Pieux et Épîtres au roi Pépin*, edited by E. Faral, 202–17. Paris: 1932.

Flodoard. *Annales*. Edited by P. Lauer. Paris: 1906.

Goldberg, E. 'Louis the Pious and the Hunt'. *Speculum* 88 (2013): 613–43.

Guizard-Duchamp, F. 'Les espaces du sauvage dans le monde franc: Réalités et représentations'. *Actes des congrès de la Société des historiens médiévistes de l'enseignement supérieur public* 37 (2006), 117–29.

Haefele, H. 'Geraldus-Lektüre', *Deutsches Archiv für Erforschung des Mittelalters* 54 (1998): 1–21, together with the additional note by G. Silagi at 119–20.

Hummer, H. *Politics and Power in Early Medieval Europe: Alsace and the Frankish World 600–1000*. Cambridge: 2006.

Indiculus Loricatorum. Edited by L. Weiland. MGH Constitutiones 1, no. 436. Hanover: 1893.

Jullien, M. H. and F. Perelman. *Clavis Scriptorum Medii Aevi Auctores Galliae 735–987*, vol 1. Turnhout: 1994.

Kratz, D. M. *Mocking Epic: Waltharius, Alexandreis and the Problem of Christian Heroism*. Madrid: 1980.

Langosch, K. *Waltharius: Die Dichtung und die Forschung*. Darmstadt: 1973.

Miller, W. I. *Audun and the Polar Bear: Luck, Law, and Largesse in a Medieval Tale of Risky Business*. Leiden and Boston: 2008.

Miller, W. I. *Bloodtaking and Peacemaking: Feud, Law, and Society in Saga Iceland*. Chicago and London: 1990.

Miller, W. I. *Eye for an Eye*. Cambridge: 2006.

Miller, W. I. *Humiliation*. Ithaca: 1993.

Njal's Saga. Translated by M. Magnusson and H. Palsson. Harmondsworth: 1960.

Peeters, J. 'Guntharius—Die Fehler eines Königs'. *Amsterdamer Beiträge zur älteren Germanistik* 34 (1991): 33–48.

Ratkowitsch, C. '*O vortex mundi, fames, insatiatus, habendi, gurges avaritiae*. Das *Waltharius*-Epos zwischenaltgermanischem Sagenstoff, Vergils Aeneis und christlicher Moral'. *Mittellateinisches Jahrbuch* 51 (2016): 1–38.

Reuter, T. 'The Insecurity of Travel in the Early and High Middle Ages: Criminals, Victims and their Medieval and Modern Observers'. In Reuter, *Medieval Polities and Modern Mentalities*, edited by J. L. Nelson, 38–71. Cambridge: 2006.

Reuter, T. 'Plunder and Tribute in the Carolingian Empire'. In Reuter, *Medieval Polities and Modern Mentalities*, edited by J. L. Nelson, 231–50. Cambridge: 2006.

Riches, T. 'Bishop Gerard I of Cambrai (1012–1051) and the Representation of Authority in the Gesta Episcoporum Cameracensium'. University of London PhD thesis (2006).

Rio, A. 'Waltharius at Fontenoy? Epic Heroism and Carolingian Political Thought'. *Viator* 46 (2015): 41–64.

Ruotger. *Vita Brunonis*. In *Ruotgers Lebensbeschreibung des Erzbischofs Bruno von Köln*, edited by I. Ott. MGH SRG NS 10. Weimar: 1951.

Schieffer, R. 'Zu neuen Thesen über den Waltharius'. *Deutsches Archiv für Erforschung des Mittelalters* 36 (1980): 193–201.

Sickel, T., ed. *Die Urkunden Konrad I., Heinrich I. und Otto I.* Hanover: 1879–84.

Sickel, T., ed. *Die Urkunden Otto des II.* Hanover: 1888.

Stone, R. 'Waltharius and Carolingian Morality: Satire and Lay Values'. *Early Medieval Europe* 21 (2013): 50–70.

Thietmar. *Chronicon*. In *Die Chronik des Bischofs Thietmar von Merseburg und ihre Korveier Überarbeitung*, edited by R. Holtzmann. MGH SRG NS 9. Berlin: 1935.

Tischler, M. 'Die Gorzer Reform in Neuweiler bei Zabern an der Schwelle zum XI. Jahrhundert. Beobachtungen zu einigen Handschriftenfunden'. Archives de l'Eglise d'Alsace 51 (1993/94): 69–90.

Turcan-Verkerk, A. M. 'La diffusion du *Waltharius* et son anonymat: Essai d'interprétation'. *Filologia Mediolatina* 23 (2016): 59–122.

Turcan-Verkerk, A. M. 'Langue et littérature latines du Moyen Âge'. *Annuaire de l'École pratique des hautes études, section des sciences historiques et philologiques* 146 (2015): 122–33.

Vita Mathildis Reginae Antiquior. In *Die Lebensbeschreibungen der Königin Mathilde*, edited by B. Schütte, 109–42. MGH SS SRG 66. Hanover: 1994.

Vollmann, B. 'Gesta Berengarii und Waltharius-Epos'. *Deutsches Archiv für Erforschung des Mittelalters* 61 (2005): 161–4.

Vollmer, F. 'Die Etichonen: Ein Beitrag zur Frage der Kontinuität früher Adelsfamilien'. In *Studien und Vorarbeiten zur Geschichte des grossfränkischen und frühdeutschen Adels*, edited by G. Tellenbach, 137–84. Freiburg: 1957.

Waltharius. In *Der Lateinischen Dichter des deutschen Mittelalters*, edited by K. Strecker. MGH Poetae 6, 1–85. Weimar: 1951.

Waltharius and Ruodlieb. Edited and translated by D. M. Kratz. New York: 1984.

Warner, D. *Ottonian Germany*. Manchester: 2001.

Widukind. *Rerum Gestarum Saxonicarum Libri Tres*. Edited by P. Hirsch. MGH SRG 60. Hanover: 1935.

Wormald, P. 'Bede, Beowulf and the Conversion of the Anglo-Saxon Aristocracy'. In *Bede and Anglo-Saxon England*, edited by R. T. Farrell, 32–95. Oxford: 1978.

Zotz, T. 'Das Elsaß—ein Teil des Zwischenreichs?' In *Lotharingia: Eine europäische Kernlandschaft um das Jahr 1000*, edited by H. Herrmann and R. Schneider, 49–70. Saarbrücken: 1995.

Zotz, T. 'König Otto I., Graf Guntram und Breisach'. *Zeitschrift für die Geschichte des Oberrheins* 137 (1989): 66–77.

Zotz, T. 'Die Ottonen und das Elsaβ'. In *Kaiserin Adelheid*, edited by F. Staab and T. Unger, 51–68. Speyer: 2005.

PART 3

Comparative Perspectives

CHAPTER 11

Braveheart and Sexual Revenge

Robert Bartlett

Bill Miller is, of course, fascinated by revenge, and one of my many happy times with him was an afternoon at home in St Andrews with a few beers watching the highlights of the best revenge films of all time. *Once Upon a Time in the West*, naturally. *Witchfinder General* (aka *The Conqueror Worm*), indispensable. But perhaps the most gratifying part of the afternoon was introducing Bill to a film he did not know, *The Princess Bride*,[1] which has one of the most satisfactory revenge climaxes of any film. The obsessional Spanish swordsman Inigo Montoya has been pursuing the evil six-fingered man for decades, determined to avenge himself on his father's murderer. He finally tracks him down and has him at his mercy. "Offer me money!" he says to the villain. "Yes!" "Power, too, promise me that," demands Inigo. "All that I have and more. Please …," begs the six-fingered man. "Offer me anything I ask for," says Inigo. "Anything you want …," he is promised. "I want my father back, you son of a bitch!" Inigo says, and runs him through with his sword. At that time the 1995 Mel Gibson film *Braveheart*[2] had not yet been released, and it is interesting to contemplate whether it would have merited an inclusion in the afternoon's viewing. In this essay I argue the case that it is a revenge film, and, more specifically, a sexual revenge film.

The hero of the film is the Scottish patriot William Wallace, and it may be worth summarizing briefly what is known of the actual historical events through which William Wallace acquired his heroic reputation. Edward I of England (the "Longshanks" of the film) seized the opportunity offered by a succession crisis in the kingdom of Scotland to secure the crown for John Balliol, sometimes rather harshly described as a puppet king, but certainly one whom Edward regarded as his inferior. When Balliol attempted to assert his independence, Edward invaded Scotland, deposed him, and annexed the country to his realm. This happened in 1296 and is the situation presented at the beginning of the film. Although the chronology in the film is hopelessly inaccurate, the basic sequence of events is not: Wallace leading resistance to the English,

1 *The Princess Bride*, dir. Rob Reiner. (1987).

2 *Braveheart*, dir. Mel Gibson. (1995).

© KONINKLIJKE BRILL NV, LEIDEN, 2018 | DOI 10.1163/9789004366374_015

winning a battle at Stirling but then losing one at Falkirk, finally being captured and brutally executed in London.

In the film, it is the attempted rape and the execution of William Wallace's wife that leads the Scottish patriot from quietist and family man to English-slaughtering killing machine. The root of this idea can be found, not in historical sources from Wallace's time, but in later legendary elaborations. The earliest sources say nothing about any woman in Wallace's life, but by the fifteenth century the themes of sexuality and revenge had entered his story. Andrew Wyntoun, who composed a Scots verse chronicle in the period 1390–1420, devotes a chapter to Wallace's rising in 1297, beginning with the description of an exchange of insults between Wallace and the English occupiers at Lanark.[3] Wallace enters the town with his "sword both sharp and long," such as befits "manly men," and resists when one of the English tries to grab it. "Thou should not bear so fair a knife," says the Englishman, provoking Wallace's derisive reply, "So said the priest who fucked your wife. So long he called that woman fair, until his babe was made your heir." "Methinks you subject me to scorn," replies the perceptive Englishman. "Your mother was fucked before you were born," answers Wallace, perhaps seeking to make things quite clear. These verbal insults culminate in a fierce brawl in the market square, with Wallace fighting off a crowd of English.

Wallace's insults here are drawn from a traditional, and deeply unoriginal, well: the taunts of men who cast doubts on the masculinity of other men by questioning the sexual behaviour of their wives and mothers. The Englishman is being cuckolded by a priest, who is the real father of his son, and his mother is a slut. Even today, "*et ta mère*" is a recognized insult in France. The manly Wallace thus first appears in Wyntoun's work deriding the masculinity of his English enemies.

Wyntoun next introduces a character not previously recorded: Wallace's lover (*lemman*), who lives in Lanark, and is presumably the reason Wallace has come to the town. Seeing him pursued by a crowd of English, she opens her door to him and brings him into her house. By the time the English have broken down the door, Wallace has escaped through another exit, and his lover keeps his pursuers talking until he has time to make it to the woods. But she is to suffer for the help she has given him. The sheriff comes to Lanark and has her seized and executed. Wallace witnesses this from a nearby hiding place. He summons thirty friends and, that same night, enters Lanark stealthily and

3 *The Original Chronicle of Andrew of Wyntoun*, ed. F. J. Amours, 6 vols., Scottish Text Society 50, 53–4, 56–7, 63 (Edinburgh: 1903–14) vol. 5, pp. 300–5. All quotations from medieval Scots have been modernized.

bursts in on the sheriff. He explains his purpose—"That woman dead of yesterday, I shall be quit now, if I may"—and kills the sheriff. And so Wallace is launched on his career.

There is no doubt that the historical William Wallace killed the sheriff of Lanark, a man named William Hesilrig, for this was the first charge against him in the indictment at his trial in 1305.[4] Moreover, one of the sheriff's entourage at that time, who was left for dead at Lanark but was found the next morning and made a recovery, was Thomas Gray, father of the chronicler of the same name, who tells the story in his *Scalacronica*.[5] But these accounts lack the love interest that Wynton brings to the tale. Here he was probably drawing on oral traditions about Wallace. Wyntoun himself is a witness to the fact that "Of his good deeds and his manhood, Great tales and songs are made," and this invisible world of story-telling must lie behind the legendary figure who emerges into writing in the fifteenth century.[6]

But Wyntoun's story presents problems if an audience wanted a Wallace who was unreservedly heroic. He makes his escape through his (unnamed) lover's house, leaving her to the mercy of the English. He watches her execution "from a hiding place (*in hiddillis*)" without intervening.[7] Robin Hood would surely not just watch at such a moment—the arrow would already have gone through the sheriff's heart. The next Scots writer to describe this incident obviously did feel the plot could be improved, for, while he certainly knew Wyntoun's account, and cited the sexual insult exchange and other lines, he made some important changes. This author was Blind Harry (or Hary), who composed his rabidly anti-English poem about Wallace in the 1470s, partly in order to stiffen the resolve of the war party at the Scots court.[8] His *Wallace*, almost 12,000 lines in length, formed the basis of all later literary and popular tradition, and Randall Wallace, the screenwriter of the film *Braveheart*, acknowledges him as his inspiration and source.

Blind Harry had a wide canvas on which to paint, and he expanded Wyntoun's account in many ways. He gives Wallace's sweetheart a background story: she

---

4 *Documents Illustrative of Sir William Wallace, His Life and Times*, ed. Joseph Stevenson (Maitland Club, Edinburgh: 1841), no. 28, p. 191; and *Annales Londonienses*, ed. William Stubbs, in *Chronicles of the Reigns of Edward I and Edward II*. 2 vols., RS 76 (Edinburgh: 1882–3), vol. 1, p. 140, both from BL Add. MS 5444, fol. 138, an eighteenth-century transcript from Cotton Otho B iii, a manuscript destroyed in the fire of 1731.

5 Thomas Gray, *Scalacronica*, ed. Joseph Stevenson (Maitland Club, Edinburgh: 1836), 123–4.

6 *Wyntoun*, 5, p. 318.

7 *Wyntoun*, 5, p. 304.

8 *Hary's Wallace*, ed. Matthew P. McDiarmid. 2 vols. Scottish Text Society, 4th ser. vols. 4–5 (Edinburgh: 1968–9); Blind Harry, *The Wallace*, ed. Anne McKim (Edinburgh: 2003).

has a named father, Hugh Braidfute, although he and his wife are dead, and she had had an older brother, who has been killed by Hesilrig; she lives respectably on her inheritance; she has purchased protection from the English king. Harry eulogizes her virtues: "courteous and sweet, filled with nobleness."[9] One day Wallace catches sight of her as she goes to Lanark church (that great opportunity for seeing the other sex) and he is pierced by love for her. She agrees to meet him, and he is moved by her account of her family's troubles and her own struggle to preserve her virginity against the advances of the English. On one point she is quite clear: "With my good will I will no *lemman* be, To no man born."[10] It is marriage or nothing. At this point Wallace feels that the demands of the war of liberation must take priority, although he pictures future possibilities: "if it might be, Through God's will that our kingdom were free, I would you wed with all heartfelt pleasure."[11] He then departs to continue slaughtering Englishmen.

After 440 lines, Harry returns to the topic of Wallace's love for the young maiden of Lanark. Despite continuing tensions in his mind between the claims of love and war, Wallace does marry her, and they are happy and have a child, a pretty young girl, who, we are told, grew up to marry a man called Shaw. We do not learn the girl's first name, any more than we know that of her mother, Wallace's wife. It is at this point that Harry begins to borrow heavily from Wyntoun's account, with the insults and the fighting, although in his version Wallace is at the head of a band of followers, not alone. Again, Wallace's wife (not his lover, as in Wyntoun), lets the Scots through her house and delays the English, who kill her. But there is no mention of Wallace witnessing this in hiding. Instead, a serving girl takes news to him of his wife's killing. Wallace and his men descend on Lanark, kill Hesilrig and "twelve score Englishmen," and burn their houses (the burning is attested in Thomas Gray's account). Scots flock to him when they hear the "fine tidings."[12]

The film deals with this rather entangled sequence of events as follows. William Wallace and his beloved, called Murron in the film, have married, but secretly. A hideous English soldier attempts to rape her but she resists fiercely. At this point Wallace turns up, throws the soldier off, and helps Murron to a horse, which he sends galloping off with a smack to its rump. Meanwhile the English soldiers have gathered and are intent on seizing or killing the unarmed

9 *Hary's Wallace*, 5, lines 579–604, ed. McDiarmid, 1, p. 91; ed. McKim, pp. 90–1.

10 *Hary's Wallace*, 5, lines 693–4, ed. McDiarmid, 1, p. 94; ed. McKim, p. 94.

11 *Hary's Wallace*, 5, lines 705–7, ed. McDiarmid, 1, p. 94; ed. McKim, pp. 94–5.

12 *Hary's Wallace*, 6, lines 17–267, ed. McDiarmid, 1, pp. 108–16; ed. McKim, pp. 110–19.

Wallace. What the viewer then sees, but Wallace does not, is that Murron has been intercepted, knocked off the horse, and captured. So when Wallace finally makes his escape, by a subterfuge, he expects he will be meeting Murron at the spot they have agreed. We see him waiting there in vain, and then cut to the execution of Murron by the English magistrate. The very next scene, one of great power, shows a dead-eyed Wallace riding to take his revenge. The slow motion, the music, the pace, create tension which then explodes into one of the film's many frenetic combat scenes. Wallace and his friends seize the English fort, Wallace knocks the magistrate down the steps (just as happens in Wyntoun and Blind Harry), and then kills him at the very spot where he had killed Murron.

The film script has taken some elements from the medieval legendary version of events: the execution of Wallace's beloved, his swift revenge. Others have been omitted: there is no prior brawl, no help offered to Wallace by his lover/wife. There is no Wallace observing the execution from a hiding place, as in Wyntoun. The poems show Wallace escaping with the help of his beloved; the film has Wallace helping her to escape (even though ultimately unsuccessfully). The fifteenth-century picture is that the sheriff executes Wallace's lover/wife because of the help she gives to the Scottish patriots. In the film, resistance to rape is the catalyst. It is true that in Blind Harry's poem, Wallace's beloved mentions the threat of rape from English soldiery, but this is in passing. All versions concern an occupied land and resistance to the occupiers, but the film puts sexual violence at the heart of the story.

This sexual element in the occupiers' behaviour has already been introduced as a main theme very early in the film. After the opening sequences, in which Wallace's father and brother are killed by the English, there is a jump in time, indicated by a voice-over ("many years later"), and we are introduced to the English court, and its curious sexual dynamics. The threateningly masculine Edward I ("Longshanks") has arranged for his patently homosexual son to marry a beautiful French princess, but the prince can hardly bear to touch her and has eyes only for his presumed male lover. After these relationships have been quickly and crudely established, events at the English court take a shocking turn. King Edward holds a council to decide how to deal with Scotland. While his eyes explore the gorgeous French princess, his mind concocts a plan for the sexual humiliation of the Scots, and he proceeds to authorize the "old custom" of permitting a noble to sleep with a common woman on her wedding night. "We'll breed them out!" he exclaims. This imposition of the right of an English lord to take a Scottish bride to his bed on her wedding night then provides the narrative thread of the next part of the film (it explains, for example, why Wallace and Murron wed secretly).

Longshanks calls this "old custom" *prima nocte* (although not all the actors in the film are quite clear about the pronunciation). This is the imaginary *ius primae noctis*, meaning literally "the right to the first night," also known by the French term *droit du seigneur* (lord's right). It has a long literary and ideological tradition, although no basis in reality. Alain Boureau, who studied the subject in depth in a book which appeared in English translation as *The Lord's First Night*, concluded that "this 'right' is certainly mythical."[13] But it is not mythical in the sense of being invented by Hollywood, like the idea of armoured knights having to be mounted on their horses by cranes. The curious thing about the *ius primae noctis* is that some people in the late Middle Ages and early modern period believed that *it had once existed*, although it was no longer current. One of those people was the Scottish scholar Hector Boece, friend of Erasmus, first principal (head) of the university of Aberdeen, and author of a history of the Scots from earliest times to the fifteenth century, which was published in 1526. Boece explains that the sex-mad Scottish king Evenus III, a contemporary of the emperor Augustus, had ordained that "the local lord should be the first to take the chastity of a newly wedded maiden." According to Boece, the young nobles liked this idea so much that the law was only abrogated a millennium later, under King Malcolm III Canmore (d. 1093).[14] So when the screenwriter of *Braveheart* made the sexual rights of the lord a central plot device in the film, he was not just exercising his own inventiveness (great though that clearly is) but was drawing on widespread traditions of what once had been, the harsh inequalities of the imagined past.

Braveheart was not the first Hollywood film to see the potential of this devil's brew of feudal tyranny and cuckoldism. Thirty years before *Braveheart*, Charlton Heston had also claimed the right in his film *The War Lord*.[15] In this case, though, the custom was presented differently: it was not an oppressive imposition of alien conquerors, but an ancient rite acknowledged by the village headman. Trouble blew up in *The War Lord*, not because the lord demanded the right to the first night, but because he refused to release the girl on the following morning. In this film true love blossomed between Charlton Heston's virile knight and the peasant girl he had demanded. Not so in *Braveheart*. Here, the odious English lord turns up in the midst of an idyllic Scottish wedding

---

13 Alain Boureau, *The Lord's First Night: The Myth of the* Droit de Cuissage, trans. L. G. Cochrane (Chicago: 1998), 6. The French original was published as Boureau, *Le droit de cuissage: La fabrication d'un mythe (XIIIe–XXe siècle)* (Paris: 1995).

14 Hector Boece, *Scotorum historiae a prima gentis origine* (Paris: 1526), Book 3, fol. 36.

15 *The War Lord*, dir. Franklin Schaffner (1965). The film is based on a play: Leslie Stevens, *The Lovers* (1956).

scene, with its rustic music, jugglers, and country dancing, to demand "the right of *prima nocta*," as he calls it. He is backed by a large body of armed men, and it looks as if the Scots who resist, including the husband, will clearly come off worst, but the young bride herself, crowned with a chaplet of leaves, intervenes. She must be thinking that only by going with the lord can she save the lives of her groom and the other Scots. She whispers to him and kisses him before she is taken off, while the wedding party disperses in gloom and silence. We then move on to Wallace's wooing of Murron.

Just like Wallace himself, this wronged husband avenges himself by killing the man who has deprived him of his wife. The second English fort captured by Wallace and his men is commanded by the lord who had earlier taken the Scottish bride to his bed. Among the followers who seize the fort is the husband. "I never did her any harm," says the lord. "It was my right." "Your right," says the husband contemptuously. "Well, I'm here to claim the right of a husband." He then smashes the lord's head in. What has been infringed by "*prima nocte*" is not a woman's right but "the right of a husband." The arrogant English noble and the furious Scottish husband seem to agree that they are talking about rights *over* women, not rights *of* women.

Alain Boureau has shown how the myth of the *ius primae noctis* could be used politically in France. Sometimes it was the king's lawyers and officials who denounced it as a wicked abuse of the seigneurs whose power they were seeking to undermine in the interests of royal centralization. Boureau cites a sixteenth-century French jurist:

> It is execrable that in some places of the kingdom ... we can find the custom observed and tolerated that the lord of the place had the right to lie the first night with the bride ... These are barbaric and brutal acts, unworthy not only of Christians but of men.[16]

During the Age of Enlightenment and the French Revolution, the custom could be invoked in attacks on "feudalism," which the French National Assembly famously abolished in 1789.

In these cases the right is being used to criticise the harsh power of feudal lords; in the film, these feudal lords are also representatives of an occupying power. Hence the right of the first night, which Edward I supposedly "declares" in Scotland, is used to show how low and unprincipled the occupying enemy is. Just as the attempted rape of Murron introduces sexual violence into the story, so the theme of the lord's first night is used to stress the harshness of this

16 Boureau, *The Lord's First Night*, 203.

foreign domination by sexualizing it. It is a common enough piece of propaganda: "they are taking our women."

Personal and national motives thus mix. Sometimes the film shows them in conflict, as in the dream sequence, when the dead Murron appears to the sleeping Wallace and urges him to wake even as he says he wishes to stay in that dream-world with her. The conflation of Wallace's love for his country and his love for his murdered wife is clear enough to be commented upon by one of the characters in the film, Hamish, Wallace's childhood friend: "Your dream isn't about freedom. It's about Murron. You're doing this to be a hero because you think she sees you." One can see the same link in the medieval literary sources that the script borrows from. In Blind Harry's poem Wallace describes the death of his wife, then says at once, "Then I ranged forth in cruel war and pain, Until we redeemed part of our land again."[17] The connection is implicit but unmistakable: revenge for his wife's death involves the recovery, the redemption, of the land. It is a common patriotic step to identify the beloved country with a woman's body. If it is woman's body, it can be raped, and hence invasion and conquest can be personified. "The Rape of Belgium" in 1914 is only the most famous use of the metaphor. The Latin for one's country is *patria*, literally "fatherland," but the noun is itself feminine. Male patriots love their female *patria*.

But what country are they fighting for? Historians have noted not only the huge historical inaccuracies and impossibilities in the film, especially the absence of the bridge at the Battle of Stirling Bridge and the sexual relationship between Princess Isabella and Wallace, but also the way that the Scottishness depicted in the film is almost exclusively a Highland Scottishness. Scots wear tartan and live surrounded by mountains. Wallace urges Bruce to "unite the clans." And some elements have drifted in from the eighteenth-century Jacobite risings, which had considerable support in the Highlands. The most notable example occurs after Wallace's father and brother have been killed. They are buried with a Latin funeral service conducted by a priest, but that night there is a separate and clandestine ritual, with the playing of bagpipes. Young Wallace asks what is happening and his uncle replies, "saying goodbye in their own way, playing outlawed tunes on outlawed pipes." This is a clear reference to the supposed (but mythical) suppression of the bagpipes by the British government after the 1745 Jacobite rising. Later in the film Hamish, Wallace's friend from childhood, refers to the English ban on the Scots bearing arms (this is why the

17 *Hary's Wallace*, 8, lines 1359–60, ed. McDiarmid, 1, p. 219; ed. McKim, p. 227; and see also Wallace's reflections on the competing claims of war and love, *Hary's Wallace* 5, lines 611–50, 6, lines 29–40, ed. McDiarmid, 1, pp. 91–3, 109; ed. McKim, pp. 91–3, 110–11.

initial attacks undertaken by Wallace and his followers use improvised weapons). Unlike the ban on the bagpipes, this really was a government policy after the suppression of the 1745 rising, enshrined in the Act of Proscription.

Braveheart opens with a voice-over explaining that "the king of Scotland had died without a son" but then proceeds to forget this. The general portrayal of the situation is that Scotland has been subject to rape and murder by the English for a hundred years; that Wallace's grandfather as well as his father had died in the struggle; and that if Bruce gives firm leadership then the Scots will have, in Wallace's words, "what none of us have ever had—a country of our own." What then had the king of Scotland ruled? It is hard to avoid the conclusion that someone has confused Scotland and Ireland. Scotland was a separate kingdom in the Middle Ages and early modern times, at times at war with England, at times at peace—in the 200 years before Edward I's invasion of 1296 there had been only nine years of war between the two kingdoms. Eventually, in 1707, both Scotland and England gave up their status as separate kingdoms to form the United Kingdom. Ireland, on the other hand, had been invaded and mostly subjected by the English in the twelfth and thirteenth centuries, but had maintained resistance to English rule, even if sometimes desperately, until achieving independence, for most of its territory, in the twentieth century.

Hollywood has a long tradition of not being able to distinguish, or not being interested in distinguishing, Ireland from Scotland. Both are "Celtic," dreamy and not English. The star and director of *Braveheart*, Mel Columcille Gerard Gibson, is of Irish descent and most of the film was shot in Ireland with Irish soldiers as extras. The film highlights a fey Irishman who joins up with Wallace because he wants to kill Englishmen. He is actually based on a character in Blind Harry's poem and not pure invention, but more purely fictional is an incident of fraternization at the Battle of Falkirk between the Scots and the Irish serving in the English army. It has been claimed that this fraternization was introduced into the film after the Irish soldiers who were playing the parts were "unhappy at the idea of the Irish fighting the Scots."[18]

Some features of *Braveheart* recur in other films directed by or starring Mel Gibson. The vivid depiction of atrocities and the anti-Englishness appears in his film *The Patriot* of 2000, which is often regarded as simply *Braveheart* set in the America of 1776. His interest in torture recurs in *The Passion of the Christ* and *Apocalypto*. These themes have purposes. "Our" atrocities are justified by "their" prior atrocities: the treacherous hanging of the Scottish nobles justifies the burning alive of English soldiers. The prolonged torture of Wallace at the end of the film, which corresponds to the slow and painful death he

18 Lin Anderson, *Braveheart: From Hollywood to Holyrood* (Edinburgh: 2005), 82 (cf. also 115).

actually experienced, underlines his heroism while stressing the inhumanity and sadism of the English. The end result of all this is to create a picture which suggests colonial freedom fighters struggling against an entrenched imperial power. By borrowing from the history of the Highlands, the Jacobite risings and their suppression, and by shaping a history of Scotland that is more like Ireland, *Braveheart* thus heightens the victimhood and long suffering of the Scots. In fact, Scots had had an independent kingdom until the year before Wallace's rising.

Braveheart is not only about fighting for the freedom of your country. It is also about manhood. When Wallace encounters his old friend Hamish again after many years away, Hamish challenges him by dropping a large rock at his feet. He explains what this means: "Test of manhood." So, manhood is something that needs to be tested, and is measured by physical aggression. It is a striking feature of *Braveheart* that, although the plot hinges on romantic, heterosexual unions, a great deal of emotional weight is also placed on relationships between men, often between fathers and sons. This is not a point that is put into words in the film, but it is remarkable that all of the chief male protagonists are motherless. Our first view of the young William Wallace shows him running after his father and older brother, who are setting off on a journey. No mother is seen or mentioned. Later, after the death of his father and brother, the young William is all alone until his somewhat alarming uncle turns up to adopt him. This uncle is clearly his mother's brother, for he comments, with an initially unexpected softness, that William has the look of his mother. That is all we hear of her. There is a brief mention of the mother of William's childhood friend Hamish, but only in a bawdy aside. The effeminate Prince Edward and Robert the Bruce have powerfully depicted fathers, but no mothers. These father-son relationships, of very different kinds, weave through the film.

The relationship between Longshanks and his son hinges on "manhood." The film's depiction of Prince Edward as a raving queen understandably annoyed gay activists. This mincing misogynist who spends his time looking in the mirror, soaking up the flattery of his gorgeously dressed young companions and avoiding physical contact with his wife, is both distasteful as a stereotype and historically inaccurate. Edward in fact fathered four children with his wife Isabella and seems to have been brave in battle. But this portrayal of Edward follows necessarily from the film's hard and simple template of masculinity. Masculinity means physical courage, involving the infliction of suffering as well as the bearing of it, sexual virility, and rough male camaraderie.

Longshanks himself is virile in the old-fashioned way. The voice-over tells us, "It was widely whispered that for the princess to conceive, Longshanks would have to do the honors himself. That may have been what he had in mind all along." This picture of heterosexual vigour corresponds to the historical Edward I. He was a famous warrior king, and about his virility in the narrow sense there can be no doubt. Edward married a French princess, as his second wife, when he was sixty and his bride twenty, and she gave birth to three children. But to challenge English rule is also to challenge Edward's masculinity. When the princess returns from her embassy to Wallace, she reports to King Edward: "He waits for you at York. He says he will attack no more towns or cities, if you are man enough to come and face him."

It would probably be an over-statement to say that, in the film, Wallace is a father figure to Robert Bruce. Perhaps he is an ideal elder brother. Bruce's own father is mired in cynicism and physically decaying through leprosy (a disease that actually did strike the historical Robert Bruce in later age). The father is amused at the way his son admires Wallace. Bruce is, until the end, a waverer, conscious of English power and of his own noble status, impressed by Wallace's complete and selfless commitment to the cause but not sharing it: "I want to believe as he does," he says. The dynamic is a recurrent theme in the film, with Bruce, despite regarding Wallace as a hero, being hesitant, even fighting for Longshanks at Falkirk before eventually leading the Scots to victory against the English in the final scene of the film. All that is known of the historical figure of Robert Bruce in the years before 1306, when he claimed the Scottish throne, a point of no return, makes this a plausible picture. Whether he actually fought against Wallace at the battle of Falkirk is uncertain, but it was undoubtedly believed to be the case by the middle of the fourteenth century, when the story is recorded in the historical compilation of John of Fordun.[19] Fordun in fact writes that "it is commonly said" that King Edward's victory was due to Bruce, who launched a surprise attack on the Scots from the rear.

The idea that Bruce fought on the English side at the battle also occurs in Wyntoun, in Blind Harry and in the Latin chronicle of Walter Bower, which was compiled in the 1440s. Blind Harry and Bower report a conversation between Bruce and Wallace that took place in the aftermath of the battle. In Bower, when Bruce's pursuit of Wallace is halted by a deep gorge, he calls out to him, asking him why he fought against the king of England and the more powerful people of Scotland. Wallace replies: "O Robert, Robert, it is your inactivity and effeminate cowardice that are stirring me to the liberation of the rights of your homeland." It is because Bruce is a "half-man" (*semivir*) that Wallace has been driven to champion the cause himself. This is a turning point for Bruce, planting a seed in his mind: "because of this, Robert was like a man waking from a

19 John of Fordun, *Chronica gentis Scotorum*, ed. W. F. Skene (Historians of Scotland 1 and 4, 2 vols., Edinburgh: 1871–2), 1, p. 330 (*Gesta annalia* 101).

deep sleep."[20] Blind Harry, with his cinematic instincts, describes a brief single combat between Bruce and Wallace at Falkirk, and he also has an exchange between them after the fighting.[21]

Blind Harry's account of the conversation begins with a blunt assertion of masculinity. Bruce, on one side of a river, sees Wallace on the other and calls out, "Who are you there?" "A man," replies Wallace. Bruce recognizes him: "That have you proved today." Wallace has clearly moved on from proving his manhood by having rocks thrown at him. Bruce and Wallace engage in private conversation, in which Wallace derisively rejects the suggestion that he could live in peace in Scotland as a loyal lord of Edward's, and spurns Bruce as "a renegade devourer of thy blood." After this, Bruce returns to King Edward's camp, still all bloody from the fighting. As he sits down to eat, the English lords mock him: "Behold, yon Scot eats his own blood." Bruce reflects regretfully on Wallace's words. Harry then reports, "From that day on he did not fight against Scots."[22] He is on the way from being a "half-man" to being a man, like Wallace.

An important part in the plot of *Braveheart* is played by the French princess, wife of Longshanks' son. In Blind Harry's poem there is no such figure, but some of the components of the role are found in the way Harry presents the English queen. She too is French, is intrigued by Wallace and heads an embassy to negotiate with him. As King Edward musters his forces for his expedition into Scotland, she begs on her knees that he should change his plans: "They are Christians, that is their heritage. To rob that crown, that is a great outrage."[23] The king ignores his wife's high-minded objections, of course, but later, after Wallace has made incursions deep into England, and the English have decided to seek peace, she volunteers to be the envoy to him. The queen is fairly frank about one of her motives: "As I desire that chieftain for to see. For he is known both hardy, wise and true."[24] Likewise, the princess in *Braveheart* is fascinated by the accounts that have reached her of Wallace and his deeds.

After the queen has been given permission to negotiate with the Scottish leader, the poet reflects on the fascination with Wallace that some women show:

---

20 Walter Bower, *Scotichronicon*, 11. 34, ed. Donald Watt et al. (9 vols., Aberdeen and Edinburgh: 1987–98), 6, pp. 94–6.

21 *Hary's Wallace*, 11, lines 363–72 (single combat), 442–526 (conversation), ed. McDiarmid, 2, pp. 52, 54–7; ed. McKim, pp. 315, 317–20.

22 *Hary's Wallace*, 11, lines 527–46, ed. McDiarmid, 2, p. 57; ed. McKim, pp. 320–1.

23 *Hary's Wallace*, 6, lines 293–4, ed. McDiarmid, 1, p. 117; ed. McKim, p. 120.

24 *Hary's Wallace*, 8, lines 1126–7, ed. McDiarmid, 1, p. 212; ed. McKim, p. 220.

> Some of them said the queen loved Wallace on account of his great reputation for high nobility. One sees in many places that a hardy man who is also handsome will happen to win great favour in the opinion of women. So it happened in his time with Wallace.[25]

So the queen sets off to meet Wallace, accompanied only by a unthreateningly pacific entourage of widows, nuns and aged priests. When she finally encounters him, he prevents her from kneeling before him by taking her in his arms and kissing her: "Straightaway he caught this crowned queen in his arms, and kissed her without another word. So he had never done to a Sotheron before." A Sotheron is someone from the south, usually meaning English, although a French lady who was queen of England might well qualify too. Negotiations between Wallace and the queen lead to no definite outcome. He refuses her offer of money, and gives a brief account of the origins of the war and of his involvement in it, an account that emphasizes the death of his beloved. Finding him intransigent, the queen tries another tactic: "'Wallace,' she says, 'you were called my love, and so the more boldly did I put you to the test, trusting to slake your anger. I think you should do something for my sake.'" But Wallace is not to be allured by ladies any more than he can be bribed by gold. Nevertheless, they part on good terms.[26]

Much of this goes straight into the film: the embassy itself; the offer of gold, which both the queen in the poem and the princess in the film distribute generously when Wallace refuses it, rather than bringing it back to the English king; the fascination with Wallace, both with his manliness and with the romantic story of his lost love. What is not in the medieval tradition is the love-making, the actual sexual encounter of Wallace and the princess. Just as in the case of the attempted rape of Murron and authorization of the *ius primae noctis*, the film gives the political and national conflict a sexual twist. And this sex forms part of the theme of revenge.

Both in the literary traditions of the later Middle Ages and in the film, Wallace is motivated by a desire for revenge. As already mentioned at the beginning of this essay, Wyntoun gives Wallace's words as he confronts the sheriff William Hesilrig after the execution of his love: "That woman dead of yesterday, I shall be quit (*quyte*) now, if I may."[27] The word *quyte* has a modern equivalent in "quits," as in "now we are quits," a word the Oxford English Dictionary defines crisply as "Even or equal with, especially by means of repayment or retaliation."

25 *Hary's Wallace*, 8, lines 1137–42, ed. McDiarmid, 1, p. 212; ed. McKim, p. 220.

26 *Hary's Wallace*, 8, lines 1215–1468, ed. McDiarmid, 1, pp. 215–2, ed. McKim, pp. 223–31.

27 *Wyntoun*, 5, p. 304.

It is linked to the word "quiet," since you achieve quiet only when you get even. In Blind Harry's poem, on hearing of the death of his beloved, Wallace vows revenge: he will not rest "until this deed be avenged (*wrokyn*)"; he swears to God that he will spare no English man: "for her sake there shall ten thousand die." And he suppresses his tears: "Where men may weep, their courage is the less, it slakes the ire for wrong they should redress (*radres*)."[28] These words *wrokyn* and *radres* are central components of the vocabulary of vengeance and compensation. Even in modern English people still wreak vengeance.

The film certainly shows Wallace wreaking revenge, and it would be reasonable to classify Wallace's revenge as "sexual revenge" since he kills those who have killed his wife after they have attempted to rape her. But there is a deeper sense in which he takes sexual revenge. A standard form of revenge is to do to your enemy what they did to you (or to do to their cousin what they did to your cousin). But the revenge that Wallace takes is not to capture his enemy's women and rape them, which would undermine his heroic status, but to captivate them and impregnate them. This is the role of the French princess, who falls for Wallace and becomes pregnant by him, thus not only cuckolding her husband, the effeminate Prince Edward, but also uprooting the family line of his demonic father Edward I. In this world of dynasties, the blood line was the most important thing, and that blood line was established sexually, through the dissemination of semen, which was, according to medieval theory, the same thing as blood. This equation of blood and semen in medieval (and later) thinking was not just a learned theory but part of general knowledge and found its way into popular song. In Child Ballad 67, "Glasgerion," for example, the well-born lady who has been tricked into having sex with a servant boy, and then decides to kill herself when she realizes the deception, says, "There shall never no churl's blood/Spring within my body."

In the early part of the film we have seen the romantic masculinity of Wallace's wooing of Murron, who becomes his wife, although secretly, to avoid "*prima nocte*," and the princess is also susceptible to his charms. The English, as we learn from the princess' pert lady-in-waiting, are sexual oafs—"they do not know what tongues are for"—but Wallace is both virile and sensitive. And he not only manages a night of consensual sex with the princess, but impregnates her. However, this is complex. Wallace has indeed impregnated his enemy's woman, but has managed to do so without mingling his blood with English blood, for he impregnates a *French* not an *English* princess. This way he can keep his racial purity while also despoiling the hated English line. Likewise, what Wallace is avenging, the death of his wife, had not involved any previous

28 *Hary's Wallace*, 6, lines 209–24, ed. McDiarmid, 1, p. 115; ed. McKim, p. 117.

mixing of Scottish and English bodily fluids, for Murron had resisted the attempted rape. She has neither consented nor been penetrated. She is executed but she has not been defiled. Wallace's wife has kept her purity; and he is set on revenge for a murdered, not a raped, wife.

The princess has her own revenge on her monstrous father-in-law. As Longshanks lies dying, his breath rasping, she whispers into his ear: "You see, death comes to us all. But before it comes to you, know this. Your blood dies with you. A child who is not of your line grows in my belly. Your son will not sit long on the throne, I swear it." Longshanks is unable to speak but conveys his distress. In this fiercely dynastic world, the perpetuation of one's line was a fundamental goal. The princess has denied it to the dying king, when he can do nothing about it. And when she predicts that her husband will not reign for long, she is wrong literally (Edward II was king for twenty years) but right in a deeper sense: the historical Isabella was responsible for her husband's deposition and murder, after she seized power in 1326 alongside her lover Roger Mortimer.

Longshanks had threatened to "breed out" the Scots when introducing the *ius primae noctis*. His daughter-in-law has turned the tables by breeding him out. His son's successor will not be of his own blood, but of the blood of William Wallace. This audacious fiction on the part of the screenwriter would, if believed, imply that Edward III of England was Wallace's son. It might then seem awkward that the real Edward III spent years in warfare in Scotland, backed a rival claimant to the Bruce dynasty and held David II, the son of Robert Bruce, as his prisoner for more than a decade. Being the biological son of a famous Scottish patriot hardly seems a counterweight to this hammering of the Scots. But the point is paternity. The film shows the English taking and trying to take the wives of the Scots (seen as such rather more than as Scots women), but, in the person of William Wallace, the Scots men have their revenge, cuckolding the English prince, and bringing their blood/semen into the royal line of England. The message is clear: You take our women, we'll take yours.

Works Cited

Printed Sources

Anderson, Lin. *Braveheart: From Hollywood to Holyrood*. Edinburgh: 2005.

Annales Londonienses. In *Chronicles of the Reigns of Edward I and Edward II*, edited by W. Stubbs. RS 76. 2 vols. London: 1882–3.

Blind Harry. *The Wallace*. Edited by Anne McKim. Edinburgh: 2003.

Boece, Hector. *Scotorum historiae a prima gentis origine*. Paris: 1526.

Boureau, Alain. *The Lord's First Night: The Myth of the Droit de Cuissage*. Translated by L. G. Cochrane. Chicago: 1998. Originally published in French as Boureau, *Le droit de cuissage: La fabrication d'un mythe* (*XIII*e*–XX*e *siècle*). Paris: 1995.

Bower, Walter. *Scotichronicon*. Edited by Donald Watt et al. 9 vols. Aberdeen and Edinburgh: 1987–98.

Gray, Thomas. *Scalacronica*. Edited by Joseph Stevenson. Maitland Club. Edinburgh: 1836.

John of Fordun. *Chronica gentis Scotorum*. Edited by W. F. Skene. 2 vols. Historians of Scotland 1 and 4. Edinburgh: 1871–2.

McDiarmid, Matthew P., ed. *Hary's Wallace*. 2 vols. Scottish Text Society, 4th ser., 4–5. Edinburgh: 1968–9.

Stevenson, Joseph, ed. *Documents Illustrative of Sir William Wallace, His Life and Times*. Maitland Club. Edinburgh: 1841.

Wyntoun, Andrew. *The Original Chronicle of Andrew of Wyntoun*. Edited by F. J. Amours. 6 vols., Scottish Text Society 50, 53–4, 56–7, 63. Edinburgh: 1903–14.

Films Cited

The War Lord (1965). Directed by Franklin Schaffner.

Braveheart (1995). Directed by Mel Gibson.

The Princess Bride (1987). Directed by Rob Reiner.

CHAPTER 12

Stringer's Saga: Njal and *The Wire*

John Hudson and Mark D. West

An immediately recognisable feature of Bill Miller's work is its combination of extraordinarily diverse reading and its repeated resort to the semi-standard Western literary canon.[1] The Hebrew Bible, Shakespeare's tragedies, Montaigne's *Essays*, the nineteenth-century Russian novelists (especially Dostoevsky) all recur in his writings, as they do in his conversation. Beyond such traditional classics, there are further works less universally familiar but of nearly as high standing, such as Robert Burton's *The Anatomy of Melancholy* and Adam Smith's *The Theory of Moral Sentiments*. Most prominent amongst such works are the Icelandic sagas, above all *Njal's Saga*.

However, it is with literature that the Miller canon largely stops: there are practically no references in his work to music, only the very occasional reference to film. Just one television series penetrates the literary citadel, sneaking into a coda and footnote in his 2011 book, *Losing It*. That series is *The Wire*, the creation of former journalist David Simon in association with former police detective Ed Burns, shown on HBO over five seasons between 2002 and 2008. Trying to summarise *The Wire* is like participating in the Monty Python game-show 'Summarise Proust', but suffice it to say that it is a study of the decline of an American city (Baltimore), of the failure of institutions, and of the impact of these on individual and collective lives. Both the viewer's subjective assessment of the quality of the work,[2] and the makers' aspirations for it,[3] justify

1 For the diversity of reading, note e.g. the soldiers' diaries and memoirs that underpin Miller's *The Mystery of Courage* (Cambridge, MA: 2002). The flow of e-mailed recommendations continues unabated, for example a Japanese probation officer's diary from 1943: <https://www.scribd.com/document/51752924/Diary-of-Probational-Officer-Kan-Nakamura-Sept-1942-Jan-1943>, accessed 16/5/2017. In this essay, we follow Miller in quoting from the translation of *Njáľs Saga* by Magnus Magnusson and Hermann Pálsson (Harmondsworth: 1960). Episodes of *The Wire* are cited by series number and episode number, in the form 1.1, etc.

2 On the aspirations of *The Wire* to differ from other television entertainment, see e.g. R. Alvarez, *The Wire*, rev. ed. (New York: 2010), 3; one may consider whether the author of *Njála* had similar aspirations. On the Greek tragedy fatalism of *The Wire*, see e.g. Alvarez, *Wire*, 384–5; saga-fatalism might be an even more appropriate parallel.

3 Note e.g. Alvarez, *Wire*, 298; audio-commentary on 3.3. Note also e.g. the care with which characters are introduced; in 1.1 Wee-Bey and D'Angelo talk, the former in front of a burger

© KONINKLIJKE BRILL NV, LEIDEN, 2018 | DOI 10.1163/9789004366374_016

its subjection to the type of close reading that will form part of this essay. Attentive viewers also know how carefully constructed the whole work is. We will do violence to it by concentrating on one strand pulled from its seamless web.[4] Nevertheless, this one strand is certainly central, particularly for the first three seasons: the triangular conflict between the police, a drug gang headed by Avon Barksdale and his adviser and lieutenant Stringer Bell, and other players in the drug market, including rising competitor Marlo Stanfield and individualist raider Omar Little.[5]

We have no doubt that *The Wire* is an appropriate subject of scholarly study, especially for comparison with the sagas. But we chose it for this essay for an additional reason: we know that Miller also believes it worthy, not only because he chose to cite it and only it as the television representative in his canon, but also because he is so clearly a fan. Both of us have enjoyed extensive discussions with him about the series, and one of us had the distinct pleasure of receiving Miller's episode-by-episode real-time reactions one summer, as he attempted to bridge the self-described 'I'm-out-of-ideas' gap between books. Most reactions began with an open mouth and ended with head in hands.

In this essay, we attempt to follow a few of Miller's rules of writing—although we won't even try to emulate his deep mining of the Western canon and indeed will rely simply on the two works themselves together with a very limited number of associated studies, primarily those by Miller himself. We have, though, been able to follow his rule of relentlessly informative titles: that is, we titled the essay precisely after our subject matter, a rule Miller preached to one of us (who ignored it) and followed precisely throughout his career (*Humiliation, The Anatomy of Disgust, The Mystery of Courage, Faking It*, and so on), until he parodied it in 2011 with a 38-word title (*Losing It: In which an aging professor laments his shrinking brain, which he flatters himself formerly did him noble service: A plaint, tragic-comical, historical, vengeful, sometimes satirical*

---

sign, the latter in front of a chicken sign. They are speaking of D'Angelo having talked in a car about matters that should not be discussed there; immediately it is clear that D'Angelo may not have in him the capacity to follow the basic rules required of those participating in The Game. Cf. e.g. W. I. Miller, *'Why Is Your Axe Bloody?': A Reading of Njáls saga* (Oxford: 2014), 18–19, on the self-conscious skill of the *Njála* author.

4 The web metaphor is used in a quotation mentioned in relation to *The Wire* by Alvarez, *Wire*, 197; the 'seamless web' metaphor goes back to Sir Frederick Pollock and F. W. Maitland, *The History of English Law before the Time of Edward I* (2nd ed., Cambridge: 1898; reissued with a new Introduction by S. F. C. Milsom, Cambridge: 1968), vol. 1, 1.

5 An alternative view would be that it is a quadrilateral conflict, the fourth dimension being conflict between, on the one hand, the police trying to do their job on the street, on the other, the authorities above them.

and thankful in six parts, if his memory does yet serve) and thereafter seems to have thrown out the window in 2014 in favour of cleverness (*'Why Is Your Axe Bloody?'*). Like Miller, we offer no roadmap here as to where the essay is headed, as we believe readers can follow along, just as they can follow *Njála* or *The Wire*. And like Miller, we attempt to present sufficient evidence to ensure that readers will agree with our point of view, whilst providing sufficient caveats to make clear when we're not so sure of ourselves. And with that we begin.

Njál's saga and The Wire

The purpose of this essay is not to seek strict parallels between *Njál's saga* and *The Wire*. Rather, just as one might look to anthropology for inspiration, or Miller might look to Shakespeare or the Bible, we attempt simply to think about *Njála* in light of *The Wire* and its various themes and elements, whilst also hoping to say something of interest to admirers of *The Wire* through the comparison with *Njála*. To be clear: The sandbox in which we play in this essay is far simpler than Miller's more sophisticated pit. We note the ways in which the series might suggest elements that would otherwise escape notice of all but the most attentive, informed, and imaginative saga reader.[6]

That there are similarities, indeed parallels, in both subject matter and characters, is obvious to any reader and viewer.[7] Take perhaps the most memorable pair of characters in the two works: Skarphedin, Njal's warrior son, and Omar, the drug raider. Omar's thin face, obtrusively marked by extensive scar, is at its most chilling when he grins, a grin that renders still more believable his utterances such as 'Omar don't scare'.[8] Except for skin tone, the impression is nearly identical to that produced by descriptions of Skarphedin: 'His face was very pale and his features sharp. He had a crooked nose and prominent teeth, which made him ugly round the mouth. He looked every inch a warrior'.[9] Skarphedin's grin and words, like Omar's, are mutually reinforcing:

6 We should, meanwhile, admit that our essay has profited from surreptitiously obtaining and incorporating answers from Miller on points of Icelandic law.

7 Note also: how neither work has a single heroic figure who dominates; the lack of interior monologue; and the comment of Miller, *Axe*, 47: 'We may not like to think that thugs can have high IQs, but why should an intelligent person not like his violence as well as the next man or woman?'.

8 1.6. For Omar's grin, see also e.g. 2.3; his laugh seems less sinister. Other characters grin too, notably Cheese, but his grin—whilst perhaps slightly deranged—seems to lack the quiet menace of Omar's or indeed Skarphedin's; see esp. 3.2, 5.10.

9 Ch. 25.

close to the climax of the story, and faced with his opponents, 'Skarphedin stood there grinning, with his axe raised and said, "This is the axe I carried when I leapt twelve ells over Markar river and killed Thrain Sigfusson while eight men stood by and could not lay a hand on me. And I have never raised weapon against anyone and missed my mark."'[10] Equally clear are the parallels between the two characters who most obviously seek a route to success other than the warrior's: Njal, who plans, advises, and litigates to achieve his and others' aims; and Stringer Bell, devoted to study, analysis, and negotiation as a path to dominance.[11]

There are also parallels in the pairings of characters, most obviously in the pairing of adviser and advisee, the latter often the man of action.[12] Essential to the first three seasons of *The Wire* is the pairing of Stringer and Avon Barksdale, described by show creator David Simon as 'mind' and 'heart'.[13] In the saga there is the pairing of Njal and Gunnar, although the latter seems to lack the type of instinctive astuteness that characterises Avon.[14] Such relationships continually raise the issue of the balance between adviser and advisee, between planner and man of action. Disruption of the balance can be a sign of impending trouble, especially when the apparently subordinate figure of the adviser may be seen as becoming dominant. When a character named Proposition Joe

---

10 Ch. 120. For Skarphedin's grin, see further esp. ch. 123; also e.g. chs 36, 37; Miller, *Axe*, 86, 91, 208–9, 212, 216, 235–7, 243–4. The only other person in the saga who grins is the dangerous Thjostolf; ch. 16, and see Miller, *Axe*, 244. Just as Omar's laugh is less effective than his grin, so too does Skarphedin's grin work best when accompanied by appropriate cool; cf. ch. 44: Skarpheddin 'grinned: but the sweat broke out on his forehead and two red spots flared on his cheeks, which had seldom happened before'. On this and Skarphedin's normal self-control, see Miller, *Axe*, 106.

11 For Stringer studying, and his position as outsider, see 1.8; note also 2.4, his desire to study for a mid-term showing him to be above lesser matters. Note e.g. 2.3 for Stringer and shares and market saturation.

12 Note also Miller, *Axe*, 43, on pairings of advisers and advisees. Other types of pairing are also deployed with skill, for example that between characters such as Njal and Mord, who are presented as having comparable characteristics but are treated in very different fashions by the author/narrator, as respectively planner and schemer; note Miller, *Axe*, 269–70. There are also pairings between opponents, for example Stringer Bell and Detective McNulty.

13 Audio-commentary on 3.12. For Avon acting by instinct, note also e.g. 3.9, where he uses the phrase 'I can smell it' to show his sense of a situation.

14 Miller, *Axe*, 71. Note e.g. ch. 21 where Gunnar says that he knows hardly anything about law and then is persuaded to go to see Njal.

refers to Avon as Stringer's 'dog', whom Stringer is to call off, it may paradoxically signify that Stringer's apparently ever-rising career is in peril.[15]

At the same time, there are many major differences between *Njála* and *The Wire*. For instance, marriage is of quite small significance in this strand of *The Wire*, but very prominent in *Njála*, particularly the three marriages of the beautiful *femme fatale* Hallgerd, by-named 'Long-Legs'.[16] Powerful women are few in *The Wire*, particularly among the drug gangs, although there are exceptions, most notably Avon's sister Brianna (mother of D'Angelo Barksdale) and also De'Londa, mother of the imprisoned 'soldier' Wee-Bey's son, Namond.[17] Both women seek to shame their men into acting in what they consider the proper fashion, according to the 'rules of The Game'. In *Njála* women are much more prominent, above all Njal's formidable wife, Bergthora. She is assertive in her powers—'I'm Njal's wife, and I have no less authority in hiring than he does'[18]—and in her goading:

> 'You men amaze me. You kill when killing is scarcely called for, but when something like this happens you chew it over and brood about it until nothing comes of it. Hoskulf Hvitaness-Priest will be here as soon as he hears about it; he will ask you to settle the matter peacefully, and you will grant his request. So if you really want to do anything, you must do it now'.
>
> 'Our mother is trying to spur us on', said Skarphedin, 'and not without good reason'.[19]

Furthermore, institutions and the state loom much larger in *The Wire* than in *Njála*.[20] Some parallels do exist; for example, in both tales parties pursue private vendettas through institutions.[21] However, arguably the local courts, or 'Things', and the central 'Althing' are the only institutions in *Njála*; particularly the latter comes to fail in the later stages of the saga. Institutions are present

15 3.10.

16 Ch. 9; for her creating disputes, note esp. chs 1, 9–17, 34–48.

17 For Brianna, see e.g. 1.12 (her first appearance), 1.13; in 4.6 she is in charge. She is treated more sympathetically in the drama than is De'Londa, for whom see e.g 4.6.

18 Ch. 36.

19 Ch. 98.

20 Note, though, the importance of doing favours in *The Wire*, within both institutional and non-institutional frameworks; e.g. 1.3, 1.4, 2.7. An attempt is made to institutionalize mutual favour-rendering through the drug sellers' co-op (see e.g. 4.9), but this proves unsustainable; see esp 5.6.

21 See esp. 2.6 for Omar testifying against Bird because Avon Barksdale's men have tortured and killed his lover.

throughout *The Wire*, their failings one of its major themes. If part of *The Wire*'s purpose is to show the limits of the difference between the state and other forms of exercise of power,[22] it also suggests that the growth of institutions is in some sense natural: the state of nature of the free zone for drug selling, known as 'Hamsterdam', is shown to be failing, and participants seek routinisation, taxation, and other state-like methods to make it work.[23] So there are marked differences, but such differences too make *The Wire* an aid in thinking about *Njála*.

Feud and 'The Game'

Much of Njála is concerned with feud, especially that between Njal and his sons on one side and the family sometimes known as the Sigfussons on the other. Likewise much of *The Wire* is concerned with 'The Game', a term used to encompass not only the drug ecology of buyers, sellers, and in particular the use of violence to control sales, but also the institutional system in which the players function.[24] The Game has explicit parallels to an actual game, as D'Angelo Barksdale demonstrates while teaching chess to two younger players (while simultaneously explaining The Game to the audience):

> D'ANGELO: You see this? This the queen. She smart, she fierce. She move any way she want, as far as she want. And she is the go-get-shit-done piece.
> WALLACE: Remind me of Stringer.
> ...
> D'ANGELO: These right here, these are the pawns. They like the soldiers. They move like this, one space forward only. Except when they fight, then it's like ... like this. And they like the front lines, they be out in the field.

22 This is done not just literally but also metaphorically, for example in Series 1 and 2 through the police cloning of pagers and computers of those under surveillance.

23 E.g. 3.7, 3.8.

24 For The Game, note e.g.: 1.7; 1.12; 2.11 ('The Game is The Game'). In 4.13 Wee-Bey tells Colvin 'That's The Game', but both sides of the discussion are revealing of the problem of the individual's struggle with the impersonal power of The Game. Cf. 4.6 for the phrase 'all in the game' being used concerning electoral politics; for 'The Game' being used in further contexts, see also e.g. 2.6, 2.7. The quotation at the end of the title sequence for 1.13, the last episode of Series 1, is ' "all in the game ..." ', attributed to 'Traditional West Baltimore'; this is a very rare instance of the opening quotation not being attributed to a specific character who makes the quoted statement in the episode that follows.

WALLACE: So how you get to be the king?
D'ANGELO: It ain't like that. See, the king stay the king, a'ight? Everything stay who he is. Except for the pawns. Now, if the pawn make it all the way down to the other dude's side, he get to be queen. And like I said, the queen ain't no bitch. She got all the moves.[25]

Furthermore, the Game can be expressed as a set of personal values, personal characteristics, personal motivations: 'The Game ain't in me no more' admits Cutty, long ago a most reliable soldier.[26]

A characteristic of the violence within both feud and Game is its reciprocity.[27] One of the nine 'features and impressionistic observations' that Miller says 'seem ... to characterise feud' is that 'A notion of exchange governs the process, a kind of my-turn/your-turn rhythm, with offensive and defensive positions alternating after each confrontation'.[28] But as Miller argues, feuding practice was not bound by such a model, and as we will see, *Njála* can be regarded as providing a critique of the model.[29]

Both *Njála* and *The Wire* prompt a further thought about the reciprocal nature of feud. If the violence of feud is a reciprocal process, how does one explain not just the first violence that sets in motion individual feuds, but the very first violence that created the overall pattern of the feuding society? In both *Njála* and *The Wire*, individual feuds can have identifiable starting and end points, although these may depend on who is telling the story of the feud, and may have a degree of imprecision. Much of the feuding in *Njála* can be seen as starting with a woman, Hallgerd, and her actions. Such might seem a predictable starting point for ill-fated events in a medieval tale. Yet there is then the mysterious and insoluble question of the origin of her disruptiveness: in the saga's very first chapter her uncle says of her, 'I cannot imagine how

25 1.3. This famous scene can feel rather forced in its exposition of symbolism; cf. Miller, *Axe*, 32 on the subtlety of symbolism in *Njála*. Bodie returns to the metaphor of the pawn and chess in 4.13.

26 3.6. The shared values of The Game can momentarily unite the most deeply opposed characters; see below, p. 278, on Avon and Marlo. Note further that feud and Game are the matter depicted, but also external to individual events, acting as drivers of the narrative.

27 Not all violence within *Njála* or *The Wire* had this characteristic: Omar's raids are not intended to be part of a pattern of reciprocal violence, and nor are the encounters with Vikings in *Njála*, e.g. chs 5, 30.

28 W. I. Miller, *Bloodtaking and Peacemaking: Feud, Law, and Society in Saga Iceland* (Chicago: 1990), 180–1. For the my-turn, your-turn rhythm of violence in *The Wire*, note esp. 5.6.

29 See below, pp. 286–92.

thief's eyes have come into our kin'.[30] Likewise, although feuds might seem to have clear ends, they were often in danger of continuation, perhaps indeed perpetuation. Bergthora quite rightly warns: 'even though a settlement has been made, you must be on your guard; for Hallgerd honours no settlement'.[31]

As for the culture of feud and The Game, *The Wire* makes explicit what seems implicit in *Njála*. *The Wire* suggests that The Game is in a certain sense eternal: '"The Game's the Game", "Always"', as is said in the single conversation between Avon and Marlo.[32] Characters in *Njála* likewise take feud as a natural part of their society and culture. The conversion to Christianity does not change this, and indeed violence continues to escalate after the conversion. The lack of a conceivable end to conflict is pithily summarised by one of *The Wire*'s detectives with reference to the so-called War on Drugs: 'You can't even call this shit a war.... Wars end'.[33]

Limiting and Escaping the Feud or 'The Game'

What means, then, might exist to limit or escape the apparently all-embracing feud or Game? We will focus particularly on two—planning and law—but there were of course others. One was to look beyond the specific truces negotiated within a dispute to general truces covering places or times, a method very familiar to medieval historians with the phenomena of the Peace and Truce of God as means of countering social and political disorder.[34] In *Njála* we have no signs of specific times of peace. Rather, there were in Iceland notions of a kind of peace (*thinghelgi*) covering the meetings of the courts (*things*) and above all of the Althing; such a peace breaks down completely in the later part of the saga.[35] In *The Wire* we have the Sunday Morning Truce, when violence is to be in abeyance, an institution that has been around 'as long as The Game itself'.[36] In a dramatic incident, this Truce is broken, as members of the Barksdale gang spot an opportunity to kill their number-one target, Omar. The power of the

30 Ch. 1. Theft, with its stealth as well as the threat to livelihood in an economy of narrow margins, was considered a more serious offence than many forms of homicide.

31 Ch. 37.

32 5.2.

33 1.1.

34 See e.g. *The Peace of God: Social Violence and Religious Response in France around the Year 1000*, ed. T. Head and R. A. Landes (Ithaca: 1992).

35 See below, p. 287.

36 3.9.

Truce is such that they have to seek higher authorization to break it, which they duly receive from Stringer Bell. The shooting, however, does not result in Omar's death; instead the target has to bundle his aged grandmother unceremoniously into a car, losing her hat in the process. Had Omar been killed with no one else involved, it may well be that justificatory explanations could have been found for the breach of the Truce—for example, that his prior actions had broken so many rules that he was effectively outlawed from the benefits of the Truce. But the involvement of an aged, female, behatted citizen, clearly on her way to church, places the action beyond justification.

It is also interesting that it is Stringer Bell who provides authority for the attempted hit—Stringer, who is usually keen to avoid problematic violence. In contrast, a leading soldier, Slim Charles, criticizes breach of the Truce.[37] Why does Stringer act in this way? Is it because he is focused on another issue, not concentrating on this request? Because he is acting on limited information? Because he is operating according to a different set of norms, seeing this opportunity in terms of business-advantage rather than the customary rules of The Game? Or because he has in fact not sufficiently internalised his own rules of Business to follow them if emotion or lack of concentration get in the way? As we go on, we will see repeatedly in both *The Wire* and *Njála* the problems of characters trying to act according to a set of norms different from the dominant ones.

An alternative method of limiting, even of escaping feud or Game was to have a preference, a default-setting, for settling rather than fighting.[38] Although he is a great warrior, Gunnar states his worry that others will regard him as less of a man for his unwillingness to kill.[39] Yet this preference is not enough to stop him becoming a perpetrator of major violence and finally a victim of it. Likewise one of the growing tensions between Avon Barksdale and Stringer Bell is Stringer's preference for settling, even if only temporarily, in order to gain a greater long-term advantage whilst risking short-term loss of respect or honour. Avon holds the maintenance of respect or honour paramount,[40] and indeed does establish his reputation to good effect: Proposition Joe points out that Avon never backs down on anything.[41] Yet *The Wire* deliberately avoids

---

37 3.9.

38 Note also e.g. Miller, *Axe*, 173, for discussion of problems arising from Njal's preference for settling.

39 Ch. 54. On this, see Miller, *Axe*, 119–22.

40 For quarrels between Avon and Stringer, see esp. 2.12 (the 'street' against the 'business class'), 3.6. Note also 2.9 for Stringer talking to Bodie about the need for flexibility.

41 3.9.

indicating that one approach is right, the other wrong; rather, it suggests that neither approach can fully succeed. Avon, a 'soldier',[42] does survive, but in a diminished position; Stringer ascends to considerable heights, but then plummets and meets his death.

If Stringer sees 'Business' as a continuation of The Game by other means, some may instead seek simply to opt out of participation either from individual disputes or more fully.[43] In *Njála* we are told of people going 'out of the saga'.[44] This takes them away from at least the feuds recorded within this saga, although there was of course plenty of opportunity for dispute even 'out of the saga'. Rare is the individual such as Ingjald Hoskuldsson, who seems to enjoy at least some success in limiting his participation in feud on behalf of one party or the other.[45] Geir the Godi is an unusual instance of a character who succeeds in getting out of the saga because a settlement works.[46] Few too are the characters in *The Wire* who escape The Game successfully. One is Cutty, recently released from long imprisonment. Lured back into involvement in The Game, he finds he no longer has it in him and manages to pursue life running a boxing gym. Perhaps escape is easier for him not only because of the high value attached to his past reputation but also because he is not a family member and perhaps had always been a paid soldier rather than a close associate.[47] Other attempts to escape The Game end in tragedy—indeed in some of the most tragic events of the whole story—as in the case of Avon's nephew D'Angelo and of the young Wallace, executed by his friends as a potential liability.[48]

Related to these courses of action, and also to each other, are the two main methods alternative to violence suggested by *Njal's saga* and *The Wire*: Planning and Law.[49] Both Stringer and Njal plan intently. And if Stringer is not a lawyer, his first appearance makes clear that he might have been one in another world, for example in the world of Njal. He is seated in court. His suit signifies his prosperity. He is handsome, clean-cut if not completely clean-shaven. He has

42 2.9.

43 Note also the discussion of the laws of King Edmund of England in J. G. H. Hudson, *The Oxford History of the Laws of England: Volume II 871–1216* (Oxford: 2012), 173.

44 Note also Miller, *Axe*, 301. Cf. D'Angelo's use of the phrase 'out of The Game' with reference to Wallace; 1.12 (and note also the discussion between D'Angelo and Wallace in 1.9).

45 See esp. chs 116, 124, 130–2.

46 Ch. 80. Note the case of Hogni, who is said to be out of the saga at ch. 80 but reappears at ch. 93. Gunnar's brother Kolskegg manages to leave the saga by leaving Iceland and getting as far as Byzantium; ch. 81. For more on the term *godi*, see n. 70 below.

47 See esp. 3.6.

48 1.12, 2.6.

49 Note also that another planner, Proposition Joe, is killed in the end: 5.4.

glasses and a yellow legal pad. And his planning has worked, as acknowledged by Detective McNulty's passing comment of 'nicely done'.[50] All of this can be compared to the first presentation of Njal:

> Njal was wealthy and handsome, he had one peculiarity: he could not grow a beard. He was so skilled in law that no one was considered his equal. He was a wise and prescient man. His advice was sound and benevolent, and always turned out well for those who followed it.[51]

Yet both Stringer and Njal end up being killed. Stringer does make specific mistakes, but most importantly his personal skills—of which he seems proud—let him down.[52] He fails fully to understand the soldiers who have contributed to the building up of his and Avon's power, and cannot bring them along with him.[53] Increasingly he patronises them, his attempts at consultation turning into formalised condescension. The absurdity of the meetings with their rules and procedures leads to Stringer himself appearing absurd,[54] and at the same time his bullying comes to resemble that of the tyrannical policeman Major (subsequently Colonel) Rawls.[55] Meanwhile his attempt to shift to the values, practices and discourse of business is flawed too. His behaviour retains aspects of the values of his old world; he has not fully internalised his desired new values.[56] When he makes mention of 'my world', that of the drug gang, in a business context, it may be a tactical move but it may indicate that he has not fully escaped that world: whichever is the case, the move does not bring major success.[57] And when he faces death, he initially talks money in the hope of being spared.[58] He has failed to recognise that an alternative set of values of honour and vengeance are at play, values that he had grown up within. If Njal dies surrounded by his family because of their loyalty and their desire for heroic demise, Stringer becomes isolated in values as in power and it is in such isolation that he dies.

---

50 1.1. On Stringer, note also esp. 1.8, 3.6.

51 Ch. 20.

52 2.9. For his mistakes, see e.g. 1.11.

53 2.12.

54 3.1.

55 3.3.

56 See esp. his outburst during a meeting in 3.1; he ends with the memorable phrase that we have of course both longed to use in our meeting-chairing duties, 'adjourn your asses'.

57 3.8.

58 3.11.

Like Stringer, Njal thinks that affairs are better dealt with in business-like fashion, through planning and without unnecessary violence. Yet just as Avon's tactics of survival preserve him whereas Stringer's strategic thinking ends with his death, so too one may ask whether Njal's elaborate plans are really more effective in the long-term than, say, Hallgerd's brief provocations.[59] As with Stringer, there appears to be change over time.[60] Sometimes Njal's cleverness and perceptiveness can come back to bite him.[61] He finds it hard to deal with the problem of people acting without consulting him.[62] And as he grows older and as the world around him becomes still more violent, with ever more situations requiring a martial response, his particular skills do not allow him the same control that he had previously exercised: 'Njal is still trying to write scripts, but people no longer are saying the lines he wants them to say'.[63]

Just as with Stringer, not all Njal's counsel and planning is for peaceful strategies. The advice on the conduct of feud he gives can be complex[64] or simple (one might say blindingly obvious): he warns Gunnar 'never to travel without company and always to carry his weapons'.[65] Yet in the end Njal makes a military misjudgement that is also a psychological misjudgement—and he is supposed to be very good on psychology if not necessarily on warfare:

> Njal said to his men, 'How many do you think they are?' 'They are a tight-knit force', said Skarphedin, 'and strong in numbers too; but they suspect that they will have a hard task to overcome us, and that is why they have halted'. 'I do not think so', said Njal. 'I want everyone to go inside, for they found it hard to overcome Gunnar of Hlidarend, even though he was only one against many. This house is just as strongly built as his was, and they will never be able to overcome us'. 'That is the wrong way to look at it', said Skarphedin. 'The men who attacked Gunnar were chieftains of such character that they would have preferred to turn back rather than burn him in his house. But these people will not hesitate to use fire if they

---

59 E.g. ch. 41. Note discussions of limits of Njal's prescience in Miller, *Axe*, 22, 62–72. Great patience and considerable tactical planning also occur, e.g., in Omar's activities; what makes Stringer different is that he plans at both tactical and strategic levels.

60 Miller, *Axe*, 96, finds as early as ch. 38 'the first indication that Njal's prescience is not seamless and his strategic success-rate, though very good, is hardly perfect'.

61 Note ch. 67.

62 Ch. 91, on which see Miller, *Axe*, 158–9.

63 Miller, *Axe*, 216, on ch. 121. Note also Miller, *Axe*, 72.

64 See e.g. chs 55, 91.

65 Ch. 60.

> cannot overcome us in any other way, for they will resort to any means to destroy us'.

Njal prevails, but Skarphedin is right in his military and his psychological assessments.[66]

So the Planning route fails both for Njal and for Stringer. Is this because it was impossible, or because there were failings in execution? Njal and Stringer suffer from becoming too distanced from dominant values of their world while necessarily having to operate within that world. Success would have required a full repertoire of different skills and values upon which to draw at appropriate times, but the authors do not allow the characters this omnicompetence. The thematic interplay of feud and law, of Game and Business, is worked out most fully by interplay between characters. Stringer's distancing from Avon is integrated in and epitomised by Slim Charles gradually displacing him, the all-round counsellor being displaced by the wartime consiglieri.[67] The differences between Njal and Skarphedin are made most clear as death approaches. Other genres might allow such dichotomies to be played out through individuals' internal debate; in the vast majority of instances *Njála* and *The Wire* encapsulate particular if complex values in particular if complex individuals.[68]

What then of Law? Its failings in *The Wire* are obvious. Its crucial agents, the detectives on the ground, are under-resourced. It is bureaucratised and politicised. And it is corrupt at every level, including that of legal practitioners. This corruption is most obvious in the case of the Barksdale gang's lawyer, Maurice Levy, yet opportunism tugs even at prosecutor Rhonda Pearlman, acting on behalf of and in concert with the police. In the very final episode of *The Wire* she is pulled into a process of deal-making with Levy in which what might be seen as 'common sense justice' becomes lost. Instead, a series of legal technicalities sets up a series of negotiations and shifts of power reminiscent of the trial of the Burners in *Njála*.

Law initially proves rather more successful in *Njála*.[69] In one sense law is far from under-resourced: in fact a huge amount of time is invested in it. On the other hand, it is a characteristic of Icelandic saga society that the state is absent, and this creates at the very least potential problems of enforcement in legal matters. Late in the saga Gudmund the Powerful asks, '"Is there any wish

66 Ch. 128. See also Miller, *Axe*, 225–31.

67 The shift starts at 3.6 and 3.7; note esp 3.11.

68 See Miller, *Axe*, 220, 289–92, on Flosi as a possible exception.

69 See also Miller, *Axe*, 260–5.

to impose either district outlawry or full exile?"' To which Snorri the Godi[70] replies, '"No, neither, for such sentences have often been disobeyed, and thus given rise only to further killings and further enmities."' At this point, as the saga draws towards the burning of Njal, law is ceasing to provide solutions. Njal says,

> 'I have long had the feeling that this case would go badly for us, and so it has turned out'. 'Not at all', said Skarphedin. 'They will never have any legal grounds for prosecuting us'. 'Then', said Njal, 'it will end in disaster for everyone'.[71]

Law might become corrupted when lawyers worked for pay. The Burner's lawyer Eyjolf does so, and his death goes uncompensated 'because of his unfairness and dishonesty'.[72] Njal himself is involved in the clearly political manipulation of legal matters, most notably in the creation of the Fifth Court. If there were good reasons for that Court to be set up, its creation is nevertheless an act of gerrymandering by Njal, intent on elevating his foster-son for a desired marriage. Moreover, in order to create demand for the new Court, Njal has to block existing litigation, regardless of the effect on participants:

> There was heavy litigation that year, and as usual many people came to consult Njal; but Njal, against all likelihood, gave them advice which each time led to deadlock between plaintiff and defendant. Bitter quarrels arose when legal agreement could not be reached, and people rode home from the Althing with their differences unsettled. The months passed until the next Althing was due.... It was uneventful at first, until Njal said it was high time that people gave notice of their lawsuits. But there were many who said there was little point in doing that, since no one could make any progress with actions that were brought before the court—'and we prefer to settle our claims with weapons now', they said. 'That must never happen', said Njal. 'It would be quite wrong to have no law in the

70 The term *goði* (anglicized as *godi*) is sometimes translated as 'priest' and sometimes as 'chieftain'.

71 Ch. 123.

72 Ch. 145. Accepting payment or gift to act as lawyer was not prohibited by the laws, but the author presents this as an improper payment for support, a prohibition of which he had inserted in his account of the setting up of the Fifth Court in ch. 97; see further Miller, *Axe*, 267.

> land. But your complaints are more than justified, and it imposes a responsibility on those of us who know the law and are the lawmakers'.[73]

As mentioned in the context of *The Wire*, law has become detached from 'common sense justice', and therefore from social expectation—and hence it has begun to lose its social purpose. The litigation involving Flosi and the Burners of Njal on one side, and on the other the party of Mord Valgardsson, who took up the case of the supporters of Njal and his sons, becomes a battle of technicalities.[74] These include technicalities arising from manipulation of jurisdiction, reminiscent of Njal's gerrymandering, and we also see the Burners and their lawyer seeking to employ the Fifth Court to further their case. Such use of the law was not popular: 'There was loud agreement that Mord was giving a good account of himself in the case, and that Flosi and his men were resorting to mere lawyers' quibbles and cheating'.[75] Eventually a procedural error gives a decisive advantage to Flosi and his party, whose lawyer announces, 'we shall now bring our own Fifth Court actions against them and have them all sentenced to outlawry'.[76] A messenger explains the situation to Thorhall Asgrimsson, the brilliant lawyer of Mord's party. His actions mark symbolically and literally the festering failure of law, the turn to war:

> When Thorhall heard this he was so shocked that he could not speak a word. He sprang out of bed, snatched with both hands the spear that Skarphedin had given him, and drove it deep into his own leg. The flesh and the core of the boil clung to the blade as he gouged it out of his leg, and a torrent of blood and matter gushed across the floor like a stream. Then he strode from the booth without a limp, walking so fast that the messenger could not keep pace with him, and hurried to the Fifth Court. There he encountered Grim the Red, one of Flosi's kinsmen. As soon as they met, Thorhall lunged at him with the spear. It struck Grim's shield, split it in two, and went right through Grim himself, so that the blade protruded from between his shoulders. Thorhall flung him off the spear, dead.[77]

---

73 Ch. 97.
74 Chs 141–4.
75 Ch. 142.
76 Ch. 144.
77 Ch. 145.

Law could overcome many difficulties, but the nature of some problems put them beyond legal solution. Just as Stringer's planning brought many successes but could not provide a complete way out from the values and practices of The Game, so too did law not provide a universal alternative to the values and practices of feud.[78]

Njal, The Wire, and 'The Peace in the Feud'

How do these conclusions fit with other interpretations of feud? Much work, first in anthropology, then in history, has been devoted to revealing the limits of the destructive effect of feud, examining the restraints upon feud, demonstrating the self-regulatory aspects of feud, and on occasion suggesting the cohesive effects of feud. Such studies of course accept that violence occurred, but in reaction against the tradition that feud was anarchic their emphasis is often upon 'The Peace in the Feud'.[79] The phrase is ambiguous. It may mean that simply there are periods of peace during individual feuds or within societies where feud is common; such peace may indeed be interpreted as the result of feud or the threat of feud. The more specific meaning—associated with Max Gluckman's famous 1955 article 'The Peace in the Feud'—is that feud has internal limits, and that these limits are intimately linked to settlement, i.e. feud is to a degree self-regulating. Such self-regulation works through various mechanisms, notably the conflicts of loyalty faced by some participants—the so-called cross-cutting ties; the fear of retaliation;[80] and the possibility of settlement through compensation. In *The Wire* there are periods of relative peace between rival drug gangs; these can occur through co-operation or when one group is dominant, enjoying a monopoly of the use of illegitimate force. There are also extended periods of peace within the feuds in *Njála*. These often are partially concealed by the brevity of their coverage, the close of chapters using terse phrases such as 'everything was quiet for a while' or 'there was peace for

78 See also Miller, *Axe*, 264. Even the possibility of such routes was, of course, restricted to a few individuals of sufficient intelligence and resources. Many others, most obviously in *The Wire*, were simply cannon-fodder, or 'pawns in the game'.

79 See esp. M. Gluckman, 'The Peace in the Feud', *Past and Present* 8 (1955), 1–14.

80 In *The Wire* 1.6, this is pithily summed up by Omar and McNulty in conversation: '"You do the thing on your name." "Anyone gonna come after Omar, they gonna know Omar's coming after him?" "Oh, indeed"'.

a long time'.[81] The growing-up of Hoskuld Thrainsson between the time when Njal took him in and the subsequent re-emergence of violence is largely covered by the words 'And so time passed', but this hiatus must have lasted about a decade.[82]

Yet despite the fact that it ends with a reconciliation, it is hard to read *Njála* in its entirety, or indeed to watch *The Wire*, as a story of a society that functions partly through self-regulating feud. Rather, lasting peace appears impossible in either setting. An upward spiral of violence, taking several of the main characters with it, occurs in *The Wire*. Slim Charles gives his pithy interpretation: 'The Game the same ... just got more fierce'.[83] In *Njála*, as Miller has written, the author presents a model of the self-regulating feud—'the balanced exchange model'—but 'then subjects the model to a substantial critique, showing that in many ways the model is incoherent'.[84] No self-regulating aspect of feud saves Njal from being consumed by it. Rather than balanced exchange, the saga recounts the escalation of feud, from the killing of slaves to the deaths of leading characters to the death of Njal by dishonorable means.[85] Even after Njal's death the upward spiral continues, to violence in the Althing and then clashes that resemble civil war.[86] Earlier actions produce later violence: deeds have reasons, men do what they have to do.[87] There is reconciliation at the end between Flosi, who was responsible for Njal's death by burning, and Kari, Njal's son-in-law who escaped the burning house in which Njal died.[88] However, the reader must wonder whether this can occur only because almost everyone has been wiped out, and anyone who believes that the settlement will be

81 Chs 51, 106; see also e.g. chs 37, 93. Note also e.g how in the Northumbrian feud recorded in the *De obsessione Dunelmi*, decades are shrunk into the phrase 'some time later'; C. J. Morris, *Marriage and Murder in Eleventh-Century Northumbria: A Study of* 'De Obsessione Dunelmi', University of York Borthwick Paper 82 (York: 1992), 3.

82 Ch. 94. On this period covered in chs 94–8, see Miller, *Axe*, 167.

83 3.4. Bodie and others' reaction to Marlo's actions confirms that there was a belief that violence was spiralling upwards. Note Wee-Bey's comments on how, 'back in the day', a newcomer like Marlo would not have got away with breaking the rules; 4.5. See further, e.g., the conversations between Wee-Bey and Colvin in 4.13.

84 Miller, *Axe*, 73. For problems with the 'balanced-exchanged model' beyond those discussed here, see Miller, *Axe*, 86–87; also *Bloodtaking*, 179–89.

85 See Miller, *Axe*, esp. 76, 200. A somewhat similar spiral may be identified elsewhere, for example in the Northumbrian feud recorded in the *De obsessione Dunelmi*: Morris, *Marriage and Murder*, 2–5.

86 Ch. 145; Miller, *Axe*, 255, and the qualifications at 278.

87 See Flosi on Kari in ch. 155.

88 Ch. 159.

permanently successful cannot have read the saga with care. It may be the end of this particular saga; it certainly need not be the end of the feuds.

In part the failure to find lasting peace results from the apparently inevitable emergence of new troubles and new troublemakers. Just as once Avon and Stringer had fought to obtain control of a territory, so a new challenger appears in the form of Marlo, and so, one feels, a new challenger will inevitably emerge to take on Marlo. The rhythm of these challenges would be well worth study, in the sagas as elsewhere.

However, the failure to find lasting peace also stems from the failure of the key mechanisms for feud's self-regulation to work consistently, just as alternative routes away from feud did not work consistently. Indeed, the difficulties with metaphors sometimes used of self-regulation are revealing: these are not mechanisms, acting as if they are operating within a machine. Nor does the metaphor of the rules of the game work with ease, even though the metaphor is employed by the very participants.[89] The metaphor endangers appreciation of individual choices, be it refusal to play according to the rules—for example refusing ever to pay compensation[90]—or playing within spaces allowed by or not covered by rules. The complexity of real life may prevent rules having the precision of those of games, even when rules are an attempt to give life stylised form.[91] There are also the questions of who sets the rules, and of who enforces them.[92] Indeed, enforcement may involve a possible paradox: the methods of enforcing norms limiting feud or Game may themselves be those of the feud or of The Game.[93]

What of specific aspects of the limitation of feud? We find that fear of retaliation sometimes restrains violent action, sometimes does not. Even threat of Skarphedin's vengeance does not prevent Thord being killed by Sigmund.[94] Cross-cutting ties, which may be created by marriage, are largely absent from

89 See Omar in 4.6; see also above, pp. 276–7, on chess; note references to The Game being rigged (i.e. not being played according to fair rules on a level playing field), e.g. 4.13, and also McNulty using the phrase in 5.2 with reference to legal process hindering the police gaining what they regard as just results.

90 See below, p. 290, on Thjostolf. For not playing according to the rules, see also e.g. Skammkel in ch. 50.

91 Note also Miller, *Axe*, 87: 'A turn is pretty clear in games like chess and tennis, but not in life or in a lot of other games'.

92 See also above, pp. 283–4.

93 Cf. the laws of Alfred the Great, c. 42, discussed in Hudson, *Oxford History*, 172–3.

94 Ch. 42.

The Wire[95] and feature less prominently in *Njála* than one might have expected from arguments such as Gluckman's.[96] On occasion they do work as a pressure for settlement, as happens after the killing of Thrain:

> Ketil of Mork was Thrain's brother; but he was married to Njal's daughter, Thorgerd, and he found himself in a difficult situation. He rode to see Njal and asked him if he intended to offer compensation for Thrain's killing. Njal said, 'I shall make such reparation as is required that all may be well; and I want you to persuade your brothers to accept a settlement, for they are parties to the claim'.[97]

Such conflicting ties do not keep Ketil out of participating in feud, but still provide him with some protection. Kari lets him flee, saying 'The man riding last is someone I have no wish to kill—Ketil of Mork. Our wives are sisters, and he has always been the most honourable of our enemies'.[98] Yet overall, connections through marriage do not weave much peace. A supernatural experience of a man from Caithness presents women as far from peace-weavers: he

> went outside and saw twelve riders approach a woman's bower and disappear inside. He walked over to the bower and peered through a window; inside, he could see women with a loom set up before them. Men's heads were used in place of weights, and men's intestines for the weft and warp; a sword served as the beater, and the shuttle was an arrow.[99]

The long poem that follows, chanted by the women, celebrates violence, not peace.

Njála certainly shows the close relationship between the violence of feud on the one hand, and, on the other, compensation and settlement. Settlements

95 There may be various reasons for the lack of cross-cutting ties between different competing groups in *The Wire*. The societies of East and West Baltimore may be too distinct to have such ties, a possibility covered by Gluckman in his discussion. Note also how the group headed by Marlo Stanfield seems to have very little or no familial background at all.

96 Cf. Gluckman, 'Peace in the Feud', esp. 7, 10.

97 Ch. 93.

98 Ch. 146, and also ch. 151. Note also chs 98 on Hoskuld Thrainsson; 116, 124, 126, 130–2 on Ingjald; 134 on Sorli Brodd-Helgason; 140 on Skapti, Thorstein Hollow-Mouth, and Jodis; 153 on Thorstein, Flosi, and Steinvor.

99 Ch. 157.

can work,[100] and even if they do not bring permanent peace, temporary 'time outs' could have their advantages.[101] Yet some choose to opt out of the system, temporarily or permanently, being known in some cases not to pay compensation, in others not to honour settlements. One of the first trouble-makers in *Njála* is Hallgerd's foster-father, Thjostolf, 'a Hebridean by descent. He was strong and skilled in arms; he had killed many men and paid compensation for none of them'.[102] Even for those who did not opt out, the values and processes of settlement and compensation raised problems. Opposing parties might differ irreconcilably about the appropriate payment (or revenge) to make things even, or their perceptions might change over time.[103]

Furthermore, the author 'shows that compensation, unless the specie is blood or exile, is at its core self-contradicting'.[104] The possibility of compensation creates incentives, and earlier compensation can finance settlements for later violence. The classic case in *Njála* is the purse containing the compensation that Gunnar pays to Njal for the killing of his servant Svart. Rather than entering general circulation, the money remains in the purse, no doubt a reminder of the earlier killing. Then, at the Althing, Njal takes out the purse and uses it to pay compensation to Gunnar for Atli's slaying of Kol, Svart's killer. Skarphedin is right when sight of the purse prompts him to say, with a grin, 'That will come in handy'.[105]

Moreover, even if the main parties come to a settlement, there is a multiplicity of interests that may not all be satisfied, any one of which may cause violence to erupt again.[106] There were not, and indeed could not be, hard rules, let alone enforced hard rules, to cover every situation. Njal promises Atli that his death will bring 'a freeman's compensation, Bergthora will promise—and no doubt provide—blood-revenge for you as well'. As we have seen, Atli is killed, and compensation is paid. On Njal's arrival home from the Althing,

> when Bergthora saw the money she said to Njal, 'you will be thinking that you have kept your promise to Atli; but my promise has still to be fulfilled'.

100 See e.g. ch. 80: 'At the Althing there was much discussion about the dispute between Hogni and Geir the Godi; in the end, a settlement was made, which proved lasting'.

101 See also Miller, *Axe*, 132–3.

102 Ch. 9. See above, p. 278, for Hallgerd being accused of not honouring settlements.

103 See Miller, *Axe*, 79.

104 Miller, *Axe*, 79.

105 Chs 36–37; on this, see Miller, *Axe*, 80–86.

106 Miller, *Axe*, 86–87: 'the model simply ignores the crucial issue of who has to be paid; how many people have an interest in the corpse who need to be bought out'.

> 'There is no necessity for you to keep it', said Njal. 'But you have already guessed otherwise', said Bergthora, 'and so it shall be'.[107]

Here the person excluded from the settlement has earlier made an explicit promise. In other cases, interest could arise simply from kinship. Thus Lyting says: 'Everyone knows that I received no compensation for the death of my brother-in-law Thrain. I shall never be content until he is avenged'.[108] Lyting himself has paid compensation for the killing of Hoskuld Njalsson,[109] but here again not everyone feels they have received compensation:

> 'I want to know what compensation you will pay me for my father [Hoskuld Njalsson]', replied Amundi. 'I am his illegitimate son, and I have received no compensation yet.' 'I have already paid in full for killing your father', said Lyting, 'and your grandfather and uncles received the money, while nothing was paid for my own brothers. Certainly, I committed a grave crime, but I had to pay dearly for it'. 'I'm not asking if you paid them any compensation', said Amundi. 'I know that you came to terms with them. I am asking what compensation you are prepared to pay me'. 'None whatever', replied Lyting. 'I cannot understand how that can be right and just before God', said Amundi, 'for you have struck me close to my heart. And I can tell you this, that if my eyes were blest with sight, I would get full compensation for my father or else take blood revenge. May God judge between us'. He walked out of the booth. At the door he turned once more, and at that moment his eyes opened. 'Praise be to the Lord my God', he said. 'His will is revealed'. He ran back into the booth right up to Lyting, and sank his axe up to the hammer into Lyting's head; then he wrenched the axe out, and Lyting fell forward, dead.[110]

The limits to the self-regulation of feud, the incapacity of feud to bring lasting peace, contributes to the sense of the feud, or The Game, as Grim Reaper. Skarphedin accepts that he must go into the house to meet his fate, even though he does not accept that Njal's decision is right: 'for he is a doomed man now. But still I do not mind pleasing my father by dying in the house with him,

107 Ch. 38.
108 Ch. 98.
109 Ch. 99.
110 Ch. 106.

for I am not afraid of dying'.[111] Or as Snoop, a cold killer unaware that death is approaching, puts it in *The Wire*, 'deserve got nothing to do with it ... it's just time'.[112]

The Problem of Ending

We have followed Miller in treating *Njála* as a representation of an imaginable society. However, it is, of course, literature, as one may well claim *The Wire* is too, so let us end with a partly literary issue: the problem of ending. Very happy to condemn the fifth and final series of *The Wire* as a fall from earlier standards, Miller long attempted to claim that the ending of *Njála* did not represent such a fall. Difficulties, however, did trouble him,[113] and eventually, between the draft and published version of *'Why Is Your Axe Bloody?'*, he arrived at 'the one true theory: sometimes some of the greatest writers are not good at writing endings'.[114]

Let us concentrate on two difficulties in the ending of the saga, 'difficulties' at least to our tastes. The first is the problem of the apocalyptic aspects of the ending, at least as executed. Just before the final reconciliation, the tone of the saga changes. There is the long poem of the death-weaving women, mentioned earlier.[115] There are descriptions of a rain of boiling blood. 'Swords leapt from the sheaths, and axes and spears flew up in the air and fought of their own accord. The weapons attacked the men so fiercely that they were forced to protect themselves, but several of them were wounded and one man on each ship was killed.... Ravens came flying at them with beaks and talons that seemed made of iron'.[116] Now, apocalyptic or near-apocalyptic endings can work—in Wagner, in the Bible—but not really in conjunction either with the type of reconciliation, perhaps hollow reconciliation, with which *Njála* closes, or with the economical realism that is such a distinguishing feature of the saga. So too in *The Wire*'s final series, some of the economical realism of the earlier series

111 Ch. 128. Note also how Gunnar comes to find that he cannot win endlessly through his martial success in feud, but nor can he win by not participating; rather, he is consumed by the feuding culture.

112 5.9.

113 Miller, *Axe*, 17, 294–300.

114 Miller, *Axe*, 300.

115 Ch. 157, above, p. 289. After the man had departed, 'the women mounted their horses and rode away, six to the south and six to the north'.

116 Ch. 156; note also the increasing importance of the Christian year in chs 156–7, as well as a miraculous healing and a series of portents.

is abandoned in the move, even a parodic one, towards a plot form that can lapse towards melodrama, the serial killer hunt—in this case concentrated on the homeless living in a near subterranean, twilit yet fiery world redolent of approaching apocalypse.

Secondly, and more closely tied to the rest of this essay, is the problem arising from the loss of crucial characters. Just as Stringer Bell dies some two-thirds of the way through the whole run of *The Wire* so does Njal die just over 70 percent of the way through his saga.[117] In Stringer's case, death feels as if the natural end point of the multiple stories has been reached; in Njal's, that just some final working out remains to be done. Both deaths can be seen as having martyr-like elements, fitting for the end of a work; this is much more so with Njal, but Stringer does seem to lie in crucifix position as the scene of his murder is examined.[118] The loss of Stringer and Njal weakens the thematic dialectic between planning and fighting, a dialectic played out between friends even more than between enemies. The high point of the dialectic between Stringer and Avon is reached as they look out over Baltimore from a balcony, the world apparently at their feet. They reminisce, but in ways that indicate long-standing incompatibility rather than the complementarity that until recently had apparently characterised their relationship. They recall Stringer having stolen a badminton set, a humorous recollection, yet the object stolen is as symbolically suggestive of Stringer's distinct character as the inability to grow a beard was of Njal's. In *Njála* the death of Gunnar removes one element of the dialectic between fighting and planning, but in the saga as in *The Wire* this thematic debate has a high point just before death, as Skarphedin and Njal debate how to take on the Burners.

The replacements for these leading characters, with the exception of Flosi,[119] somehow lack the depth of Njal and Stringer. It may be a matter of taste—and the makers are full of praise for 'restraint' in acting—but the very coldness and impersonality of Marlo Stanfield may remove something from the intensity of *The Wire*.[120] Readers of *Njála* may feel similarly detached from Kari,[121] and certainly he and Flosi do not provide the same sort of dialectic as that between

117 Ch. 129. Note that there was a gap of almost two years between Series 3 and 4 of *The Wire*, and some possible doubt that further series would be made; see e.g. Alvarez, *Wire*, 263.

118 Chs 129, 132; 3.11, 3.12.

119 See above, n. 68.

120 Audio-commentary on 4.1. The closing stages of *The Wire* deliberately, and skilfully, offer the possibility of Marlo following the Stringer Bell business route, but then have him refuse it; 5.10.

121 See Miller, *Axe*, 276–93.

Njal and Gunnar or Njal and Skarphedin. Nor do the new lawyer characters replace Njal as a suitable focus for law as an alternative to feud.[122] Eyjolf's corruption and his operating for pay exclude him from respect and themselves make him a subject of contention.[123] Thorhall, as we have seen, abandons law for violence. The thematic dynamic that has driven the saga is lost as the feud reaches its melodramatic climax and then its final, rather anticlimactic and potentially uncertain settlement.

Miller-like, we may worry about these suggestions: are these concerns with the ending simply a product of our tastes, the product of socio-cultural circumstance? Did Icelandic readers or listeners lap up the procedural detail (and repetition) which to us slows the narrative during the trial of the Burners, rather as viewers of a modern medical drama might lap up long flows of incomprehensible quick-fire requests from emergency room doctors?[124] Is our objection to an excess of new characters and new settings a result of deeply embedded assumptions about certain unities within the greatest literature?[125] Rather, we think we should just agree with Miller's assessment that the ending does not quite work, and explore, as we have, the possible reasons why this is so. Not every medieval epic ends in an unsatisfactory way for the modern reader. We suspect that Miller would wish the *Njála* author had come up with an ending like that of the Oxford version of *The Song of Roland*: '"God", said the king, "how wearisome is my life". His eyes flow with tears, he tugs his white beard'.[126]

Works Cited

Alvarez, Rafael. *The Wire*, rev. ed. New York: 2010.

Brault, Gerard J., ed. and trans. *The Song of Roland: An Analytical Edition*. Vol. 2, *Oxford Text and English Translation*. University Park, PA: 1978.

Gluckman, Max. 'The Peace in the Feud'. *Past and Present* 8 (1955): 1–14.

Head, Thomas and Richard Landis, eds. *The Peace of God: Social Violence and Religious Response in France around the Year 1000*. Ithaca: 1992.

122 Note also Miller, *Axe*, 269–72, on Mord.

123 Ch. 138; see above, p. 284.

124 Chs 141–4.

125 See esp. ch. 154; also Miller, *Axe*, 16–17.

126 *The Song of Roland: An Analytical Edition*, ed. and trans. G. J. Brault, vol. 2, *Oxford Text and English Translation* (University Park, PA: 1978) ll. 4000–1.

Hudson, John. *The Oxford History of the Laws of England: Volume II, 871–1216*. Oxford: 2012.

Miller, William Ian. *Bloodtaking and Peacemaking: Feud, Law, and Society in Saga Iceland*. Chicago: 1990.

Miller, William Ian. *The Mystery of Courage*. Cambridge, MA: 2002.

Miller, William Ian. *'Why Is Your Axe Bloody?': A Reading of Njáls saga*. Oxford: 2014.

Morris, Christopher J. *Marriage and Murder in Eleventh-Century Northumbria: A Study of 'De Obsessione Dunelmi'*. University of York Borthwick Paper 82. York: 1992.

Njál's Saga. Translated by Magnus Magnusson and Hermann Pálsson. Harmondsworth: 1960.

Pollock, Sir Frederic and F. W. Maitland. *The History of English Law before the Time of Edward* I. Second edition, 1898; reissued with a new Introduction by S. F. C. Milsom. Cambridge: 1968.

The Wire. Creator, producer, and head writer, David Simon. First broadcast on HBO in 2002–2004, 2006, 2008.

CHAPTER 13

'An Overdeveloped Sense of Vengeance'? The Middle Ages, Vengeance and Movies

Stuart Airlie

In AD 68 the noisy night-time streets of Rome became even more disturbed than usual. Cries of vengeance resounded in the city as householders threatened clumsy slaves with chastisement. 'An avenger (*vindex*) is coming to get you!' they bellowed. The real target of such cries, however, was not the cowering slaves but the emperor Nero himself. A general in Gaul had come out in rebellion against the tyrant; the general's name was Vindex. These warning cries of punishment to come were not isolated but were like a chant from the oppressed, savouring the pleasure of anticipated vengeance for their wrongs. But when is the avenger's work ever really finished? While Vindex's rebellion failed, Nero was eventually forced off the stage into oblivion in 68, though he was to come back to haunt western culture in such various media as fevered Christian imaginings of Antichrist in the apocalypse and the equally fevered form of scenery-chewing performances by the likes of Peter Ustinov in a variety of films.[1]

Bill Miller has spent a long time listening to cries for vengeance, acutely sensitive to the emotional power behind them, as well as to the workings of systems and discourses of law and honour within which vengeance operates. Miller's work here covers an impressively wide field and is of correspondingly wide appeal and interest. But it has a special resonance for medievalists, partly because of his own illuminating readings of these treasures of medieval literature, the Icelandic sagas, but also because of medievalists' concerns with 'stateless' societies in which feud, vengeance and honour seem to be

1 Suetonius, *The Twelve Caesars*, Book 6 (Nero), ch.45 2, in *Suetonius*, trans. J. C. Rolfe, 2 vols, vol. 2 (Cambridge, MA, 1970), 168–70; Thomas E. Kitchen, 'Apocalyptic Perceptions of the Roman Empire in the Fifth Century A.D.', in *Abendländische Apokalyptik. Kompendium zur Genealogie der Endzeit*, ed. Veronika Wieser, Christian Zolles, Catherine Felk et al. (Berlin: 2013), 644, 648; Maria Wyke, *Projecting the Past: Ancient Rome, Cinema and History* (New York and London: 1997), 110–46.

© KONINKLIJKE BRILL NV, LEIDEN, 2018 | DOI 10.1163/9789004366374_017

an integral part of the culture.[2] Despite his consuming interest in medieval Iceland, Miller's work ranges widely beyond the Middle Ages, not least in its focus on, for example, the films of Clint Eastwood as representations of the avenger in society.[3] As a medievalist who is also a movie enthusiast, I intend this essay as a tribute to the breadth of Miller's interests. I take inspiration from his work to offer a fellow medievalist's perspective on some themes of vengeance to be found in three films that can be illuminated by his work even as they themselves cast light on it. The films are *The Virgin Spring* (1960), a tale of a father's vengeance for the rape and murder of his daughter in medieval Sweden, directed by Ingmar Bergman; *Harakiri* (1962), also known as *Seppuku*, a story of an avenging samurai warrior set in seventeenth-century Japan, directed by Masaki Kobayashi; and *Unforgiven* (1992), probably the best known of the three, featuring Clint Eastwood as director and star in a bleak story of outrage and vengeance in the American West. The three films are very different in period, setting and style but are linked in a common concern with the nature of vengeance. And medieval films, i.e., films set in the western Middle Ages, may have much in common with films of other genres, periods and cultures; to juxtapose *The Virgin Spring* and *Harakiri* is to gesture towards that comparing of western feudal medieval society and samurai-era Japan that goes back to the work of Marc Bloch. Samurai films have in their turn caught the interest of western medievalists as well as of western film-makers.[4] Not only has

---

2 See, for example, Patrick J. Geary, 'Living with Conflicts in Stateless France', originally published in 1986, in his *Living with the Dead in the Middle Ages* (New York: 1994), 125–160; Guy Halsall, 'Reflections on Early Medieval Violence: The Example of the "Blood Feud"', *Memoria y Civilización* 2 (1999), 7–29; Paul R. Hyams, *Rancor and Reconciliation in Medieval England* (New York: 2003), e.g., in chapter 1; Stephen D. White, 'The Feelings in the Feud: The Emotional Turn in the Study of Vengeance', in *Disputing Strategies in Medieval Scandinavia*, ed. Kim Esmark et al. (Leiden and Boston: 2013), 281–311. The common citation and deployment of Miller's work by such scholars does not imply consensus among them.

3 William Ian Miller, 'Clint Eastwood and Equity: The Virtues of Revenge and the Shortcomings of Law in Popular Culture', in *Law in the Domains of Culture*, ed. Austin Sarat and Thomas Kearns (Ann Arbor: 1998), 161–202; William Ian Miller, *Eye for an Eye* (New York: 2006) 147–51. The bibliography to that book and the index to William Ian Miller, *Faking It* (Cambridge: 2003) give some sense of the range of Miller's interests and registers; his content, of course, also testifies to this. The quotation in my title comes from a line in the enchanting 1987 fantasy movie *The Princess Bride*, whose avenger character Inigo Montoya pops up in *Eye for an Eye*, 143–4.

4 Bettina Bildhauer and Anke Bernau, 'Introduction: The A-chronology of Medieval Film', in *Medieval Film*, ed. Bildhauer and Bernau (Manchester and New York: 2009), 1–19; and see also John M. Ganim, 'Medieval *Noir*: Anatomy of a Metaphor', ibid., 182–202. Japan: Marc Bloch, *Feudal Society* 2 vols, trans. L. A. Manyon (London: 1962), vol. 2, 446–7; on samurai films as

Miller written an extended analysis of Clint Eastwood's portrayal of avengers, but it was he himself who urged me, some years ago now, to watch the astonishing *Harakiri*, and I owe him a particular debt for that wise counsel.

Medievalists may be particularly aware of the fragility of institutions. The complexity of people's behaviour and the fallibility of human institutions, processes and judgement can be a haunting presence in medieval thinking on law precisely because they are haloed with the divine justice that casts them in such an unflattering light. Written after the Goths' sack of Rome in 410, Augustine's *City of God* has a chapter in Book 19 titled 'The mistakes of human judgement, when the truth is hidden'. Here Augustine takes a bleak view of the work of judges whose task is indispensable in society but which is also made impossibly complex by flaws in earthly procedures as well as by the deception and weakness of human beings:

> In view of this darkness that attends the life of human society, will our wise man take his seat on the judge's bench, or will he not have the heart to do so? Obviously, he will sit, for the claims of human society constrain him and draw him to his duty; ... the wise judge does not act in this way [using torture, being deceived by false evidence, etc.] through a will to do harm, but because ignorance is unavoidable—and yet the exigences of human society make judgement also unavoidable.[5]

Augustine sums up the grim bargain of our necessary subjection to flawed institutions and processes; the often extravagant rhetoric of our early medieval legal sources should not disguise the fact that the period's rulers and judges, plaintiffs and victims knew this too, even if Augustine's radical pessimism remained exceptional. Our own culture is one of law where feud and the actions of a lone avenger taking law into their own hands are not visible. Nonetheless, we too worry about our institutions' fragility (fallibility of witnesses, corruption of officials), and at times we are bound to feel some of that tension between

medieval films, see Randy P. Schiff, 'Samurai on Shifting Ground: Negotiating the Medieval and the Modern in *Seven Samurai* and *Yojimbo*', in *Race, Class and Gender in "Medieval" Cinema*, ed. Lynn T. Ramey and Tison Pugh (New York and Basingstoke: 2007), 59–72. Schiff focuses on Japanese culture and history; samurai films, however, are not simply to be equated with western medieval ones, or indeed with Westerns (Clint Eastwood appeared in *A Fistful of Dollars* (1964), based on *Yojimbo* (1961) directed by Akira Kurosawa), a point emphasised by Joan Mellen, *Seven Samurai* (London: 2002), 68–72.

5 Augustine, *City of God*, XIX, c. 6, trans. Henry Bettenson (London: 2003), 860; Robert Markus, *Saeculum: History and Society in the Theology of Saint Augustine* (Cambridge: 2nd ed., 1988), 99.

the mismatch of colourless law up against the heat of demands for revenge. Augustine's tough-mindedness always threatens to enlighten us. Why should we desire to be deceived? This is the tension between retribution (impersonal) and revenge (personal) that Bill Miller has explored in discussing equity. If the processes of law can leave us dissatisfied and hungry, no wonder the lone no-nonsense avenger of fiction is attractive. But as Miller also shows, such avengers are often more complex figures than we might think, and we should pay closer attention to their representation.[6]

Of course it is quite a step for medievalists from primary sources such as capitularies, law codes, chronicles and sagas to movies. But our stories, in medieval narratives, are precisely that: stories, representations. Just because a medieval text appears in its modern edition in the Monumenta Germaniae Historica does not mean that it is straightforwardly historical. The historical figure Adela of Melten's involvement in violent aristocratic rivalries and vengeance c. 1000 so impressed Karl Leyser that he labelled her a 'Lady Macbeth of the Lower Rhine'. But medieval authors did not tell her story straight; they manipulated that figure for their own narrative purposes, notably in the *Life* of her son Bishop Meinwerk of Paderborn. This *Life*, written in the mid-twelfth century, incorporated genuine past charters, but the author drastically transformed the pattern of Adela's story to serve the interests of her son's church.[7] Modern historians have of course turned to more manifestly literary sources such as the *chansons de geste* in order to produce acute analyses of violence and vengeance in high medieval aristocratic culture. But in reviewing such work, Steve White has warned against seeing such sources as transparent gateways to real and universal emotions such as anger and the desire for vengeance.[8] They too are representations.

I do not intend to say here that all representations are of equal historical value and that historians are not concerned with historical realities. Of course we are. But taking a holiday from our specialised *Quellenkritik* can refresh our view of the societies we study, and of how we study them and their representations of themselves. Human cultures and human natures vary and that variety deserves our attention, but we need not see these cultures as walled off from each other. In the present context it is worth recalling that Erich Auerbach's

6 Miller, 'Clint Eastwood', especially 174–8.

7 Karl Leyser, *Communications and Power in Medieval Europe: The Carolingian and Ottonian Centuries* (London and Rio Grande, OH: 1994), 40; Régine Le Jan, 'La vengeance d'Adèle ou la construction d'une légende noire', in *La Vengeance, 400–1200*, ed. Dominique Barthélemy, François Bougard and Régine Le Jan (Rome: 2006), 325–40 at 338–9.

8 White, 'Feelings', 285–9.

Mimesis includes a discussion of the classic Frankish feud narrative of Gregory of Tours as well as of more aesthetic literary texts by Stendahl and Woolf.[9] The films discussed here, like medieval texts, evoke and represent cultural and historical worlds remote from us (including the times of their making), but like Augustine's sombre reflections, they also proclaim *de nobis fabula narratur*.

Historical films are one way of representing history; the same is true of academic monographs with footnotes. Films are worth historians' time.[10] We are the audience who react with horror, anger, shame as well as enjoyment, like characters who witness or participate in acts of vengeance in these films and in medieval sagas, chronicles and *chansons de geste*. At least one historian has yearned for the fullness of movie narrative in lamenting that episodes of violence in some medieval legal sources are 'a snapshot that the historian needs to fit into an action movie that he does not possess'.[11] Movies are not academic texts and our enjoyment of them feels like a less complicated experience than our enjoyment of academic arguments and analysis. As Miller says, relatively straightforward revenge films such as some Clint Eastwood movies offer narratives that 'take us from indignation and outrage to satisfaction'.[12] The three films we will look at here do indeed follow that arc, but how deep is the 'satisfaction'? The films themselves explicitly ask this, and thus demand that we answer; the films' answer may not be final; we are not passive watchers but as 'third-party observers' are 'arbiters'.[13] Like characters in the films, we are observers, though we are privileged ones, and our view here is thus one of the three that Miller argues are necessary for understanding and weighing acts of

9 Erich Auerbach, *Mimesis: The Representation of Reality in Western Literature*, trans. Willard R. Trask (Princeton: 1968), chapter 4.

10 Robert A. Rosenstone, *History on Film/Film on History* (Harlow: 2006); Marnie Hughes-Warrington, *History Goes to the Movies* (Abingdon and New York: 2007); *A Companion to the Historical Film*, ed. Robert A. Rosenstone and Constantin Parvulescu (Malden, MA: 2013). On historians' approaches to medieval films, see, in addition to the works in n. 4 above, Stuart Airlie, 'Strange Eventful Histories: The Middle Ages in the Cinema', in *The Medieval World*, ed. Peter Linehan and Janet L. Nelson (London and New York: 2001), 163–83 (new edition forthcoming); and Bettina Bildhauer, *Filming the Middle Ages* (London: 2011).

11 Paul Hyams, 'Was There Really Such a Thing as Feud in the High Middle Ages?', in *Vengeance in the Middle Ages: Emotion, Religion and Feud*, ed. Susanna A. Throop and Paul Hyams (Farnham and Burlington VT: 2010), 151–76 at 154. See also Miller, 'Clint Eastwood', 171; and see White, 'Feelings', 290–1, 301 on participants as advisers in the dramas.

12 Miller, 'Clint Eastwood', 169–70; Miller, *Eye for an Eye*, 140–5.

13 Miller, 'Clint Eastwood', 171, 172.

violence (with the perspective of perpetrator and victim as the other two).[14] All three films make us work, make us think about vengeance and justice, not least because the avenger character in each of them ponders and questions the nature and meaning and rightfulness of the violence that they commit. In order to focus our gaze and guide our looking, I refer here to John Hudson's set of categories for comparative analysis of a range of disputes: 1) motivation and emotion (e.g., honour and vengeance), 2) the nature and scale of the violence involved, 3) widening of the circle of those affected beyond initial perpetrator and victim and 4) time, duration; that is, ripples or chains of acts subsequent to the original incident.[15] It is such institutions and processes that our chosen films anatomise; they don't just celebrate vengeance.

A couple of preliminary points before we turn to the films themselves. All three are prestigious, award-winning films, with famous directors at the helm. This does not mean that they, in particular *The Virgin Spring* and *Unforgiven*, are completely distinct from revenge or rape and revenge movies at the rowdier end of the movie spectrum, a point understood by Miller and by scholars such as Carol Clover, whose work *Men, Women and Chainsaws* repays reading here, not least because Bergman's film inspired the later Hollywood 'video nasty' *Last House on the Left* (1972).[16] That is not, however, a dimension that I explore here. And referring to these films' directors is a shorthand way of referring to the films' creators, who were many. I do not wish to suggest that films are the exclusive creation of their directors; they have many authors and creators.

All three films show the audience the initial act, the outrage that triggers the vengeance, but none of the avengers themselves witness these scenes directly. They are thus at a remove from the original violence, even if they are deeply affected by it, and we can judge their reactions because we have been witnesses of the outrage. In two of the films, *The Virgin Spring* and *Unforgiven*, a woman is the victim of the initial violence and women are also witnesses of it; the solitary woman in *Harakiri* is a removed victim and witness of the original

14 William Ian Miller, 'Getting a Fix on Violence', in Miller, *Humiliation, and Other Essays on Honor, Social Discomfort and Violence* (Ithaca: 1993), cited and discussed in Warren C. Brown, *Violence in Medieval Europe* (Harlow: 2011), 7–8.

15 John G. H. Hudson, 'Feud, Vengeance and Violence in England from the Tenth to the Twelfth Centuries', in *Feud, Violence and Practice: Essays in Medieval Studies in Honor of Stephen D. White*, ed. Belle S. Tuten and Tracey L. Billado (Farnham and Burlington, VT: 2010), 29–53 at 33–34.

16 Carol J. Clover, *Men, Women, and Chainsaws: Gender in the Modern Horror Film* (London: 1992); Miller, 'Clint Eastwood', 174–5.

act. In the societies depicted in these films, those women who survive cannot take vengeance. In *The Virgin Spring* a serving-woman can only watch as her stepsister is raped and murdered by a trio of herdsmen. She thus parallels the audience's situation, trapped in watching the young woman's ordeal, and it is a hard scene to watch. Later, consumed with horror and guilty self-loathing, she can only confess this to the dead woman's father, and then help him prepare ritually for vengeance. This woman's role in the story, however, is essentially passive, and it says much for the skill of the actress Gunnel Lindblom that she can invest the role with so much life.

In *Unforgiven*, it is again a woman (Delilah, played by Anna Thomson) who is the victim of the initial assault, a prostitute whose face is slashed by a cowboy infuriated by her mocking of his manhood. She survives his attack and remains in the film as witness to, and evidence of, the assault, a reminder to the audience of the crime and the call for vengeance/justice. When Clint Eastwood's character gets news of the assault, the woman's injuries are magnified in the telling, partly to suggest to us that there might be some honour as well as mercenary motives in his decision to claim the money that the prostitutes have offered for vengeance on the cowboys who assaulted Delilah. It is after this that the film shows us the cowboys returning to town to hand over horses to the saloon owner as compensation for the assault. The younger cowboy, less active in the assault, has brought an extra pony for Delilah, over and above the price agreed. The audience knows that he is not quite as guilty as his partner (the same is true of the youngest herdsman in *The Virgin Spring*), and also knows that false news of Delilah's injuries is spreading. It may well be tempting to hope that his offer will be accepted. The other women angrily reject it and chase him and his pony away. The film is careful not to give Delilah a chance to offer her testimony; she stands apart, behind the other jeering women, silent and watchful; a medium close-up of her head and shoulders shows the scars on her face and her straight gaze; music creeps in on the soundtrack, simultaneously elegiac and portentous, but it is up to us how we read her face. She bears the scars that are the sign of the vengeance-provoking assault, but she does not seem to be looking at the pony and cowboy with the hostility of the other women. The film makes us look at her: is there resignation or hope in her eyes, any sign that she dreads what might be coming, or that she wants the pony, or that she couldn't care less about this well-meant non-compensation? This makes the audience work: what do we think of her reaction, of the cowboy's offer? The film sets out the dilemma but does not force a choice upon us; the problem is ours. Of course as an audience we want Clint Eastwood to arrive and the story of vengeance to unfold. The rest of the film shows us what this means.

The initial act of violence in all three films drives the plot, but with varying degrees of complexity and sophistication. In some ways, the Bergman film is the most straightforward; it is also the shortest, a mere 89 minutes compared to *Harakiri*'s 133 minutes and *Unforgiven*'s seemingly slower 131 minutes. Based on a ballad and with a script, unusually, not by Bergman himself but by Ulla Isaaskson, it tells how a young woman, spoiled darling daughter of a minor lord (played by Bergman regular Max von Sydow) and lady in medieval Sweden, leaves her house on a beautiful spring day to take candles to the church in a nearby village. In sunny countryside, she encounters three herdsmen, shares her food with them and is then raped and murdered in an unflinchingly brutal scene. The herdsmen seek shelter for the night in what they do not realise is the girl's house and offer her mother the daughter's fine robes for sale. The mother says she must consult her husband and in the morning, in a long sequence of preparation for vengeance and its harsh execution, the father kills all three herdsmen. There is no public institution of justice in the film, no reference to law, or to the Church as mediator, no discussion of compensation.

Apart from some distracting nonsense about a cult of the pagan god Odin, the film is essentially a stark juxtaposition of these two acts of violence, and they remain spectacular nearly sixty years after the film was made; throughout, the film is beautiful to look at, though often hard to watch. The rape and murder appear as cause and justification for the father's violence. He has not witnessed the crime; his wife's showing him the bloodstained clothes of their daughter is all the information and justification that he needs. Vengeance is automatic in that he immediately plans to act. He doesn't need his stepdaughter's testimony to inform or motivate him. Her speech is followed by action, not by dialogue or by the father's reflection upon what he has heard from his wife and stepdaughter. We thus get no explanation or comment by the father or any other character about the justification of vengeance, or indeed any doubts about it. The audience's watching of the rape and murder scene is thus central to judgement. Do we think that the father's actions are justified, are they what we want to happen, morally and/or as spectators with a desire for 'satisfaction'?[17] This is one of the problems with the film. As it goes on, 'the narrative is more concerned with [the father] Töre's redemption than it is with [the daughter] Karin's trauma', as Alexandra Heller-Nicholas observes in a thoughtful account of the film.[18] But she also notes that the rape scene is one

17 See Miller, *Eye for an Eye*, 151–4 on audience expectations.

18 Alexandra Heller-Nicholas, 'Silence and Fury: Rape and *The Virgin Spring*', *Screening the Past* (2010): online article at <http://www.screeningthepast.com/2015/01/silence-and-fury-rape-and%C2%A0the-virgin-spring/>, accessed 20/6/2017.

of 'affective intensity (and undeniable beauty)'. This too is part of a problem with the film; the image of Karin's face before her death with some artfully placed shadows over her brow is distracting, and not in a Brechtian manner, in its calling attention to the fine camerawork. Bergman himself later unfairly dismissed the film as 'a lousy imitation of Kurosawa'.[19]

Overall, however, the rape and murder scene is stark: no dialogue or music, just the natural sounds of the river, with the sobs of Karin, the grunting of the men, the noise of their scuffling and struggling on the earth, the thump of the club on Karin's head, all this with the camera at some distance giving us the viewpoint of helpless observers of the crime unfolding in beautiful natural surroundings.[20] In the aftermath, the film's tone seems to soften; snow falls on the upturned face of the youngest herdsman, temporarily left behind by his seniors, and a plaintive flute plays on the soundtrack, the first non-diegetic sound in the film for a while. But the film manages to avoid dissolving into lyricism. Karin's body remains, but there is no close up of her peaceful in her beauty; the camera remains at a distance showing a body that is dead, inert, a ghastly object in the landscape; the boy scatters some earth on it, but not enough to cover it, and his throwing of the earth only underlines the corpse's unreacting passivity.

The crime scene is now to be balanced by a (longer) scene of vengeance.[21] This is a strange and powerful sequence. After seeing his daughter's clothes and hearing from the serving-woman the details of how she died, Töre (the father played by Max von Sydow) instructs the woman to heat the sauna. This abrupt and isolated line—there is very little dialogue indeed in the vengeance scenes—is followed by a cut to the open country outside the homestead and we see the father, a lone figure in the landscape, grasp a birch tree, grappling with it to uproot it and bring it to the ground; this unexpected scene shows the father as man of action and strength but also surely represents his emotional turmoil. It turns out to be practical preparation for the sauna scene, dominated by the striking image of the naked father beating himself with birch twigs passed to him in silence by the fully clothed serving-woman. No dialogue explains this, and we are left to enjoy the imposing physical presence of both actors, the play of light on the father's muscular body, the steam rising in the dark of the sauna and the relentless swish of the birching. This is a rite of purification, of preparation and, while it is very distinctive and actually quite puzzling

19 Stig Björkmann, Torsten Manns and Jonas Sima, *Bergman on Bergman: Interviews with Ingmar Bergman*, trans. Paul Britten Austin (London: 1973), 120.

20 Clover, *Men, Women and Chainsaws*, 124, 137.

21 Heller-Nicholas, 'Silence and Fury'.

and disconcerting on a first viewing, it parallels scenes in other films where the hero prepares for action, often in a montage that displays increasing physical strength and moral confidence. There is a witty example of this in the 'I'll Make A Man Out Of You' number in Disney's *Mulan*. *Unforgiven* also has a similar sequence, but it parodies the norm as Clint Eastwood (Clint Eastwood!), preparing to return to the world of gunslinging violence, practices shooting but fails spectacularly to hit the target. This parody itself has a grim echo towards the end of the film where Eastwood has to resort to alcohol to prepare himself for the final killing spree.

But Bergman films his scene straight and goes on to preface the killings with a grim and disturbing solemnity. Again, dialogue is very sparse. The father has been carrying his sword but now turns to the serving-woman and commands her to bring him the slaughter knife; he is going to kill the herdsmen like animals. He quietly enters the room where they sleep, followed by his wife, who will witness the killings as the women do at the end of *Unforgiven*. In silence he empties out the bag containing his daughter's clothes; the camera remains at a distance, there is no close-up of his face, no dialogue. He seats himself in his chair and we see him in a frontal shot, enthroned as a judge. He waits. And we wait with him, hearing the breathing of the doomed men, including the young boy who has been picked out in previous scenes as less vicious than his brothers, as brutalised by them. All this takes quite a bit of time and the film gives us no obvious signposts: no music, no dialogue to point us in a moral or narrative direction; just the waiting and looking at the dead woman's clothes, the sleeping killers, the impassive statuesque parents. We know that the storm will break and as spectators we surely want that, but the long austere sequence gives us an uncomfortably long time to think; what can the vengeance achieve? When the herdsmen finally awaken, the spell is broken and we get to see a virtuoso scene of scrabbling figures rushing to kill or escape in confined space. We do not get any speech of accusation or justification from the father, nor do the killers say anything in acknowledgement of their guilt. They probably see the daughter's clothing on the table and they probably know why they are being attacked, but the scene does not make this explicit. This denies the audience a level of satisfaction and pleasure in the vengeance narrative, and marks out *The Virgin Spring* as different from our other two films. All we get is killing; the grotesque death agony of the rapist who is slaughtered on the father's chair of justice is visually echoed in scenes of pain and collapse in later Bergman films.[22] Bergman remains the artist; the film is representation, not a

22 Miller, *Eye for an Eye*, 140–51. Jacques Aumont, *Ingmar Bergman. Mes films sont l'explication de mes images* (Paris: 2003), 174–5.

window. The father also kills the young boy; his lesser degree of guilt does not save him any more than it saves the younger cowboy in *Unforgiven*: avengers are not lawyers.[23]

The film does let the father articulate thoughts about vengeance and justice, but only *after* the killings, and this does not lead to satisfaction for the viewer. Max von Sydow does the best he can with lines expressing the father's anger, guilt and bafflement at his own killings and God's inaction while his daughter was dying, but this anguished eloquence is at odds with the stark silence of the film's key scenes where the viewer was not being told what to think. The father delivers these lines at the very site of his daughter's killing, where he and his household have journeyed to find the body. That, however, is not all they find; a spring of fresh water now bubbles up out of the ground after the father's speech, and he and the family form a stately tableau of ye olde medieval piety which the camera views from above while a choir chants on the soundtrack. But this is merely a formal ending. The camera also sees the girl's body, as dead as it was before, and it is the camera and us, not heaven, that look down on the mournful group, victims and perpetrators of violence in a world of indifferent nature. This is merely a close to the film; there is no balancing of accounts.

Our second film does explicitly confront the question of vengeance, retribution and satisfaction but there is not much for our comfort here either. This is the hypnotic *Harakiri*, a devastating attack on the 'honour' of the samurai warriors of a great house in seventeenth-century Japan. In its critical view of the warrior elite, *Harakiri* is not unique in Japanese samurai films.[24] Nevertheless, its presentation of warrior cultural values is quite different from what is probably the most famous samurai film in the West, Akira Kurosawa's *The Seven Samurai* (1954), and it does not match the fluid dynamism of Kurosawa's film. Much of *Harakiri* is slow and stately, as its cast (nearly all men) move calmly through space, above all the horizontal space of the rooms of the warrior house, or sit to deliver and hear narratives that gradually unfold the film's story through flashbacks.[25] All this, however, is the ticking of a time-bomb and the film culminates in an astonishing sequence of duels and combats.

---

23 Or are they? See Miller, 'Clint Eastwood', 176 and 187.

24 Lisa Spalding, 'Period Films in the Prewar Era', in *Reframing Japanese Cinema: Authorship, Genre and History*, ed. Arthur Nolletti, Jr and David Desser (Bloomington and Indianapolis: 1992), 131–44 ; David Desser, 'Toward a Structural Analysis of the Postwar Samurai Film', ibid., 145–64; Thomas Keirstead, 'The Anti-Samurai Film', in Rosenstone and Parvalescu, *Companion*, 425–42.

25 There is, however, much tension within the style; see Alain Silver, *The Samurai Film* (Cranbury NJ and London: 1977), 70–72; Desser, 'Toward a Structural Analysis', 151–3;

The story, set in the seventeenth century, seems simple. Tsugumo Hanshiro, a *ronin* (a masterless samurai whose lord's power has been broken up) seeks permission from the Iyi house to commit ritual suicide in the courtyard of their palace. A counsellor tells him the story of a previous visit, when a young *ronin* made the same request. The leaders of the Iyi house, wearied by a series of such importunate beggars seeking only shelter and food, not an honourable death, had called his bluff and pressured him to go through with the suicide immediately, even though his poverty meant that he possessed only a bamboo sword. We see this excruciating scene in the flashback but Tsugumo only hears about it from the counsellor; we are the witnesses. Nonetheless, he insists that he is no bluffer and the clan accept his request and assemble in the courtyard to witness his fate. All this takes place within the calm horizontal places of the palace and the courtyard. Tsugumo sits in the middle of the courtyard; he seems to be in the centre of the picture. But the clan is raised above him and the camera looks down on him; he is central, but he appears to be a humble petitioner, diminished.

Tsugumo then tells his story, revealing that he is the father-in-law of the young *ronin* with the bamboo sword. Flashbacks take us to a world outside the warrior castle, a world of falling blossom, the painting of parasols and fans, a world of daughter, wife, child, a world very different from that of the warriors, though Tsugumo is one himself. These flashbacks take the viewer away from the warrior world and mean that the castle, rigidly masculine, with movement formally controlled in its horizontal spaces, is gradually invaded by Tsugumo's memories. His world is also one of poverty and illness and it is this that had driven his son-in-law to the house of Iyi. As the lyrical but sad flashbacks catch up with the present (the film actually lasts only a little longer than the two hours of Tsugumo's visit to the palace), we see shadows lengthen across the courtyard and sense something of the coiled force of the solitary *ronin* amidst the haughty clan Iyi.

Tsugumo reveals that he saw the chief retainers of the clan bring his son-in-law's body home to his hovel; formally correct, they recited his honourable death and revealed the bamboo blade. That is why Tsugumo has sought entry to the palace of the Iyi. He rises to denounce the obduracy and cruelty of the warriors and their inhuman code of honour. Here the avenger, unlike in *The Virgin Spring*, does pronounce an indictment to his victims, and they respond to it, sticking to their code. But the avenger himself admits that nothing can bring back his family, though he had hoped to take the clan's expression of

---

Philip Kemp, 'Kobayashi's Anti-Samurai Movie' (booklet essay for the 'Masters of Cinema' DVD release of *Harakiri* (2011)), 13.

regret and understanding to his family in the next world. There is no real pay-back possible.[26] The film, however, will show the nature of the satisfaction that Tsugumo's actions provide.

What is to be destroyed is the whole notion of the warrior house's code of honour, a code whose deathly rigidity is symbolised by the ancestral armour shown at the very start of the film as a sort of mystical fetish preserved in the castle. The courtyard scene turns out to have been a scene of trial, of presentation of indictment, evidence and judgment. A medievalist cannot help but be reminded of the denunciations of the violence of the knights in the 'feudal revolution' in, for example, cases in the eleventh-century *Book of Sainte Foy*. The film, however, is more radical and systematic in its onslaught. As Steve White has observed, the monks of Sainte-Foy do not denounce feud, they take part in it via legal disputes and celebrate 'retaliatory vengeance' unleashed by God and the saints; we should not make a 'crude distinction between helpless, peaceable monks and violent lay nobles'.[27] But Tsugumo's attack on the house of Iyi is an attack on a whole system, in which one of his weapons is his extraordinary mocking laughter at the pretensions of the warriors (his varying laughter is only one of the elements in Tatsuya Nakadai's mesmerising performance, and is itself an echo and distortion of the laughter of the warriors). His clothes, his speech, his gestures rebuke and condemn the warriors. In a severely exciting duel between Tsugumo and one of the warrior champions outside the courtyard, a wind sweeps through a graveyard and an empty landscape, as if to blow all before it.[28]

But it is Tsugumo who sweeps all before him. In a masterly scene near the start of the final conflict, we see the clan counsellor sitting within the palace, still and dignified but anxiously attending to the sounds of chaos and fighting offscreen. These sounds and the actual fighting then burst into the house and now we see these calm horizontal spaces broken up, smashed, full of vertical figures in combat, with blood smeared across the elegant walls. Tsugumo invades the inner sanctum, knocking the ancestral armour off its shrine. The only way that he can be stopped seems to be by gunfire and in contrast to the honourable warriors in *Seven Samurai* the Iyi warriors do not hesitate to deploy

26 Cf. Miller, *Eye for an Eye*, 140–59.

27 Stephen D. White, 'Garsinde v. Sainte Foy: Argument, Threat and Vengeance in Eleventh-Century Monastic Litigation', in *Religious and Laity in Western Europe 1000–1400: Interaction, Negotiation, and Power*, ed. Emilia Jamroziak and Janet Burton (Turnhout: 2006), 169–81 at 180; Kathleen Ashley and Pamela Sheingorn, *Writing Faith: Text, Sign and History in the Miracles of Sainte Foy* (Chicago: 1999), at, e.g., 59–64 and 121–46.

28 See Mellen, *Seven Samurai*, 52, 65, 74 on the wind in that film.

guns to defend themselves.[29] But Tsugumo stabs himself before they can fire. The film ends with a voice-over that is the official house chronicle giving a misleading account of Tsugumo's suicide with no reference to the conflict; the armour is restored to its shrine and the film ends with a close-up of it, echoing the start. But we the audience have seen the conflict, the rigidity and hypocrisy of the warriors. The institution has been broken and its weaknesses and corruption exposed for us. Tsugumo failed to obtain the satisfaction of apology or repentance from the warriors, but the film offers its audience something else: the bleak satisfaction of analytical justice, not simple vengeance.

Unforgiven (1992), directed by and starring Clint Eastwood, is a sort of 'encyclopedia' of the Western movie and draws on Eastwood's persona as fashioned by him in a long series of films where he plays a lone avenger.[30] A rich, sombre movie, it traces an arc of vengeance and violence from the opening incident of an attack on a whore (the women are referred as such throughout the film), as discussed above. In this town, Big Whiskey in Wyoming (the film was shot in Canada), there is law in the person of the sheriff, Little Bill (wonderfully played by Gene Hackman). The barkeeper duly calls him in to punish the cowboys and to ensure settlement for the damage done to his property, the cut woman. The madam wants a hanging, the sheriff calls for his bullwhip and the barkeeper insists on recompense. Little Bill imposes the fine of the horses as compensation. The madam is outraged, furious that the cowboys won't even get a whipping. In a tone of weariness, the sheriff asks if there hasn't already been enough blood. The weary, reasonable tone of Hackman's voice pulls the audience to his side: perhaps the compensation is insufficient, but the imposing of a settlement is the imposing of an ending, a capping of violence. Still, as an audience, we want a story, and Hackman's mercurial performance goes on immediately to suggest to us that he is not simply the reasonable enforcer of impersonal law in this town.

As the film goes on, the sheriff is revealed as a monster, a sadist who keeps the peace through ferocious wilfulness. We also see the nature of the violence unleashed by Clint Eastwood and his partners in their taking vengeance on the men who assaulted the whores. On one level, it is hard to take satisfaction in all this, and the film warns us against this, as the characters react in horror to the actions that they themselves perpetrate or suffer. But the ever-tightening narrative spiral of explosive action surely enthrals us; we want more, we want

29 Mellen, *Seven Samurai*, 54, 57.

30 Mario Sesti, '*Unforgiven*', in *The Hidden God: Film and Faith*, ed. Mary Lea Bandy and Antonio Monda (New York: 2003), 201–5 at 201; on the making of the film and its place in Eastwood's career, see Richard Schickel, *Clint Eastwood: A Biography* (London: 1996).

to be satisfied.[31] What triggers the final explosion of vengeful violence is a second outrage: the torture and killing of Ned (played by Morgan Freeman), the partner of Eastwood's character, by a gloatingly sadistic Hackman, whose quiet whispered promises of more violence disturb us as much as the image of a white man whipping a black man. Again, the avenger does not see this. It is the women who hear the sounds of the torture whipping. They appear in the film as an increasingly silent and passive chorus of witnesses. This seems like an example of the typical marginalising of women in such films (though Frances Fisher as the madam is a fierce presence in every scene in which she appears, and there is a nicely played scene of an awkward encounter between the avenger and the scarred woman). But here the women's silence, their grave attentive faces force the audience to wonder what they think, and thus what they themselves, the audience, think. What do we want? Surely we want vengeance for Ned, we want to let Clint become Clint. It is one of the whores who tells Eastwood the story of Ned's death as she delivers the bounty money to him for killing the cowboys. She utters a distraught account of Eastwood's violent past as recounted by Ned; the women now know what they have conjured up and they know that Ned's death will lead to more killing. Even as we hear this speech and realise that no balance can be struck, that killing leads to killing, we watch Eastwood harden into cold killer mode and we want him to confront the sheriff. Demands of narrative, of genre, and our own desires, are irresistible; the two stars must have a final shoot-out. The film cannot treat us unjustly, it must show us this.

The final scenes are very impressive. Amidst rain and thunder, Eastwood rides alone into the town; he and we see Ned's body, degraded in public display, a display that is meant to help us see Eastwood's vengeance as legitimate. In the saloon a jovial Gene Hackman buys drinks for his followers and plans to hunt down Eastwood. The women look on. Into this crowd steps the lone avenger, and the sound of his gun being cocked brings deathly silence to the scene. Bill Miller's examination of this scene focuses on the sheriff's lack of guilt for his killing of Ned, his lack of moral acknowledgement, and Miller concludes that the solitary avenger of 'honor-based feuding cultures, model payback cultures', and his audience, do not need the perpetrator of the original outrage to acknowledge or feel guilt for the vengeance to be satisfying.[32]

But I think that Miller does miss one dimension of these last scenes of the movie, and that is their movie-ness. Miller writes that the Eastwood character is 'not a glorier or a gloater. The movie kills all who gloat and glory'.[33] This is

31 See Miller, *Eye for an Eye*, 140–6 on satisfaction.

32 Miller, *Eye for an Eye*, 150; and see 146–51.

33 Ibid., 149.

true but in the final scenes, the movie surely glorifies the Eastwood character. It becomes too much in love with itself and with the persona of Clint Eastwood. Not that this is a bad thing; it is glorious to watch and we want Eastwood to deal out death with snappy one-liners that cap any backchat from Hackman or bit-part players; the star has to have the last word. Everyone else in this scene is part of a group, but the camera picks out Eastwood as a lone figure, a superhuman figure in his erect posture and deadly action, and in the aura that he casts round himself as he acknowledges in that distinctive voice that he has brought death to every kind of creature ('I've killed women and children, I've killed everything that walks or crawls at one time or another'). After he mentions women and children, the camera cuts to the women looking down on the scene from the upper storey of the bar, but quickly returns to Eastwood, while thunder rolls in the background. If we are meant to register horror at Eastwood's admission (and he is not gloating when he says it) the film makes us look at him as something elemental, beyond good and evil. But this is not impersonality, this is star charisma and hugely enjoyable. This kind of enjoyment does tend, however, to suspend critical thought. After killing the sheriff, and several extras, Eastwood steps out into the darkness and rain where he 'hollers out threats into the stormy night to cow any would-be continuers of the feud and the movie'.[34] This is well put, but misses the overwhelming sense of an ending here. The music now adds sombre majesty. Mounted on his horse, Eastwood is hard to see and hear amidst the rain and thunder because he is part of the storm, he is the storm itself. And the movie begins with thunder over the town; the storm has now burst. The movie's beginning yearns for its ending in storm and darkness. Eastwood's cry 'You better not cut up no whores' offers only the prospect of the angry justice of an absent god to replace the lost monster of the sheriff. This is not social, this is an end of law, despite the glimpse of an American flag in the background—or is that flag meant to suggest some civic shelter for the women who now come out of the shadows to gaze upon Eastwood? The movie tries too hard to satisfy us here.

All three films show us the satisfaction of vengeance stories, and the limits of that satisfaction. *Harakiri* is perhaps the most unblinking and unflinching in its telling of all this, but each deserves careful viewing. All offer visual pleasure and provoke troubling thoughts. And that means that they send us, or some of us, back to reading Bill Miller and that is some satisfaction.[35]

---

34 Miller, *Eye for an Eye*, 158.

35 I gave a preliminary version of this paper at a gathering to honour Bill Miller at the University of St Andrews in Spring 2016. I am grateful to participants for comment, and I owe a particular debt to the late Nora Bartlett for some stimulating remarks. I am also

Works Cited

Printed Sources

Airlie, Stuart. 'Strange Eventful Histories: The Middle Ages in the Cinema'. In *The Medieval World*, edited by Peter Linehan and Janet L. Nelson, 163–83. London and New York: 2001; new edition forthcoming.

Ashley, Kathleen and Pamela Sheingorn. *Writing Faith: Text, Sign and History in the Miracles of Sainte Foy*. Chicago: 1999.

Augustine. *City of God*. Translated by Henry Bettenson. London: 2003.

Aumont, Jacques. *Ingmar Bergman. Mes films sont l'explication de mes images*. Paris: 2003.

Bildhauer, Bettina. *Filming the Middle Ages*. London: 2011.

Bildhauer, Bettina and Anke Bernau. 'Introduction: The A-chronology of Medieval Film'. In *Medieval Film*, edited by Bettina Bildhauer and Anke Bernau, 1–19. Manchester and New York: 2009.

Björkmann, Stig, Torsten Manns and Jonas Sima. *Bergman on Bergman: Interviews with Ingmar Bergman*. Translated by Paul Britten Austin. London: 1973.

Bloch, Marc. *Feudal Society*. Translated by L. A. Manyon. 2 vols. London: 1962.

Brown, Warren C. *Violence in Medieval Europe*. Harlow: 2011.

Clover, Carol J. *Men, Women, and Chainsaws: Gender in the Modern Horror Film*. London: 1992.

Desser, David. 'Toward a Structural Analysis of the Postwar Samurai Film'. In *Reframing Japanese Cinema: Authorship, Genre and History*, edited by Arthur Nolletti, Jr and David Desser, 131–44. Bloomington and Indianapolis: 1992.

Ganim, John M. 'Medieval Noir: Anatomy of a Metaphor'. In *Medieval Film*, edited by Bettina Bildauer and Anke Bernau, 182–202. Manchester and New York: 2009.

Geary, Patrick J. 'Living with Conflicts in Stateless France'. In Patrick Geary, *Living with the Dead in the Middle Ages* (New York: 1994), 125–60.

Halsall, Guy. 'Reflections on Early Medieval Violence: The Example of the "Blood Feud"', *Memoria y Civilización* 2 (1999): 7–29.

Heller-Nicholas, Alexandra. 'Silence and Fury: Rape and The Virgin Spring', Screening the Past (2010). Online article at <http://www.screeningthepast.com/2015/01/silence-and-fury-rape-and%C2%A0the-virgin-spring/>, accessed 20/6/2017.

Hudson, John G. H. 'Feud, Vengeance and Violence in England from the Tenth to the Twelfth Centuries'. In *Feud, Violence and Practice: Essays in Medieval Studies in Honor of Stephen D. White*, edited by Belle S. Tuten and Tracey L. Billado, 29–53. Farnham and Burlington, VT: 2010.

grateful to Jinty Nelson for encouragement, and to my daughter Madeleine, for her critical viewing of some films not always to her taste.

Hughes-Warrington, Marnie. *History Goes to the Movies.* Abingdon and New York: 2007.

Hyams, Paul R. *Rancor and Reconciliation in Medieval England.* New York: 2003.

Hyams, Paul R. 'Was There Really Such a Thing as Feud in the High Middle Ages?'. In *Vengeance in the Middle Ages: Emotion, Religion and Feud,* edited by Susanna A. Throop and Paul Hyams, 151–76. Farnham and Burlington VT: 2010.

Keirstead, Thomas. 'The Anti-Samurai Film'. In *A Companion to the Historical Film,* edited by Robert A. Rosenstone and Constantin Parvulescu, 425–42. Malden, MA: 2013.

Kemp, Philip. 'Kobayashi's Anti-Samurai Movie'. Booklet essay for the 'Masters of Cinema' DVD release of *Harakiri* (2011).

Kitchen, Thomas E. 'Apocalyptic Perceptions of the Roman Empire in the Fifth Century A.D.'. In *Abendländische Apokalyptik. Kompendium zur Genealogie der Endzeit,* edited by Veronika Wieser et al. Berlin: 2013.

Le Jan, Régine. 'La vengeance d'Adèle ou la construction d'une légende noire'. In *La Vengeance, 400–1200,* edited by Dominique Barthélemy, François Bougard and Régine Le Jan, 325–40. Rome: 2006.

Leyser, Karl. *Communications and Power in Medieval Europe: The Carolingian and Ottonian Centuries.* London and Rio Grande, OH: 1994.

Markus, Robert. *Saeculum: History and Society in the Theology of Saint Augustine.* 2nd ed. Cambridge: 1988.

Mellen, Joan. *Seven Samurai.* London: 2002.

Miller, William Ian. 'Clint Eastwood and Equity: The Virtues of Revenge and the Shortcomings of Law in Popular Culture'. In *Law in the Domains of Culture,* edited by Austin Sarat and Thomas Kearns, 161–202. Ann Arbor: 1998.

Miller, William Ian. *Eye for an Eye.* New York: 2006.

Miller, William Ian. 'Getting a Fix on Violence'. In Miller, *Humiliation: and Other Essays on Honor, Social Discomfort and Violence.* Ithaca: 1993.

Miller, William Ian. *Faking It.* Cambridge: 2003.

Rosenstone, Robert A. *History on Film/Film on History.* Harlow: 2006.

Rosenstone, Robert A. and Constantin Parvulescu, eds. *A Companion to the Historical Film.* Malden, MA: 2013.

Schickel, Richard. *Clint Eastwood: A Biography.* London: 1996.

Schiff, Randy P. 'Samurai on Shifting Ground: Negotiating the Medieval and the Modern in *Seven Samurai* and *Yojimbo*'. In *Race, Class and Gender in "Medieval" Cinema,* edited by Lynn T. Ramey and Tison Pugh, 59–72. New York and Basingstoke: 2007.

Sesti, Mario. 'Unforgiven', in *The Hidden God: Film and Faith,* ed. Mary Lea Bandy and Antonio Monda, 201–5. New York: 2003.

Silver, Alain. *The Samurai Film.* Cranbury, NJ and London: 1977.

Spalding, Lisa. 'Period Films in the Prewar Era'. In *Reframing Japanese Cinema: Authorship, Genre and History,* edited by Arthur Nolletti, Jr and David Desser, 131–44. Bloomington and Indianapolis: 1992.

Suetonius. *The Twelve Caesars*, Book 6 (Nero). In *Suetonius*, translated by J. C. Rolfe, vol. 2. Cambridge, MA, 1970.

White, Stephen D. 'The Feelings in the Feud: The Emotional Turn in the Study of Vengeance'. In *Disputing Strategies in Medieval Scandinavia*, edited by Kim Esmark et al., 281–311. Leiden and Boston: 2013.

White, Stephen D. 'Garsinde v. Sainte Foy: Argument, Threat and Vengeance in Eleventh-Century Monastic Litigation'. In *Religious and Laity in Western Europe 1000–1400: Interaction, Negotiation, and Power*, edited by Emilia Jamroziak and Janet Burton, 169–81. Turnhout: 2006.

Wyke, Maria. *Projecting the Past: Ancient Rome, Cinema and History*. New York and London: 1997.

Films Cited

A Fistful of Dollars (1964). Directed by Sergio Leone.

Harakiri (1962). Directed by Masaki Kobayashi (also known as *Seppuku*).

Unforgiven (1992). Directed by Clint Eastwood.

The Princess Bride (1987). Directed by Rob Reiner.

The Virgin Spring (1960). Directed by Ingmar Bergman.

CHAPTER 14

Getting a Head in the Neo-Assyrian Empire: Narratives of Enemy Decapitation in Ashurbanipal's Sources

Eva Miller

Although I work in a field geographically more than three thousand miles away and more than a millennium and a half earlier than the events of the Icelandic sagas, my connection to the work of William Ian Miller is foundational: Miller is my father and therefore my earliest academic mentor. His influence might explain how I have ended up, despite my temporal and geographical distance from his own field, with a shared interest in the bloodier side of history. This article will deal with topics that Miller has touched on in his own work, including the meaning and value of severed body parts, the ambiguity of messengers and their messages, and the intentions and worldview behind pre-modern texts.

In this article I look at the royal narratives of the last great king of the Neo-Assyrian empire (c. 911–605 BCE), Ashurbanipal (668–c. 627 BCE). With a heartland in what is now northern Iraq, the Neo-Assyrian empire under Ashurbanipal reached from the Persian Gulf to the Mediterranean, the Zagros Mountains through the Levant down into Egypt. Starting in the 1840s, successive Neo-Assyrian capitals began to be uncovered by French, British, and German excavators, revealing a material past for a civilisation that had previously been known mostly through garbled (and unfavourable) Biblical and Greek sources. Royal inscriptions of Assyrian kings in stone or on clay formed the basis of the decipherment of cuneiform, the world's first writing system, and the language Akkadian, an East Semitic language related to West Semitic Ugaritic, Hebrew, Aramaic, and Arabic.[1] The earliest excavations also uncovered Assyrian palace reliefs, limestone slabs with shallow carvings that adorned the walls of Assyrian palaces. These were highly coveted by European powers, although they were generally considered to be of little artistic merit.[2]

---

1 Cuneiform texts written in Sumerian, a linguistic isolate which was long dead as a spoken tongue by the Neo-Assyrian period, would not be deciphered until much later and are still much more poorly understood than Akkadian texts.

2 Mogens Trolle Larsen, *The Conquest of Assyria: Excavations in an Antique Land, 1840–1860* (London: 1996), 102–3.

© KONINKLIJKE BRILL NV, LEIDEN, 2018 | DOI 10.1163/9789004366374_018

This initial assessment saw the texts and art of Assyrian palaces as simplistic and highly stereotyped propaganda. However, a century and a half of scholarship has shown that reliefs, annals, and epigraphs were in fact dynamic forms of communication which evolved in style, content, and purpose over the period of the empire. Innovation is particularly apparent in the works of Ashurbanipal's reign. His reliefs exhibit previously undeveloped narrative techniques and subject matter, while his royal inscriptions show notable literary influences and a strong interest in Assyria's ancient past.[3] The culmination of Ashurbanipal's artistic and narrative innovation is generally agreed within the discipline to be represented by the palace wall reliefs and accompanying texts that deal with the Battle of Til-Tuba (c. 653) and the beheading on the field of Teumman, king of Elam (a traditionally hostile nation based east of the Zagros Mountains in modern-day Iran) as well as subsequent campaigns against Elamite allies in southeast Babylonia, the region to the south of the Assyrian heartland and part of its sphere of imperial control. This narrative, particularly in its visual form, is structured around Teumman's severed head, the image of which appears repeatedly across the reliefs of two palaces, sometimes attached to his body, more often not. Although Teumman's head is notable for its prominence in these visuals and in written narratives that discuss its treatment, it is not the only severed head to play a role in the account of the campaigns against Elam and its allies. Across a handful of royal sources about these events composed during Ashurbanipal's reign, severed heads appear in a variety of contexts and evidently serve a variety of purposes, although there are certain common features of how they are presumed to function.

The sources which feature the story of Teumman's and other enemies' heads are of several types, with different editions within these types. As outlined in Table 1, there are both visual and textual narratives of several forms. These include the shallow reliefs carved on palace walls (in this case, the Southwest Palace at Nineveh, built by Ashurbanipal's grandfather Sennacherib, r. 705–681, but renovated during his reign and, to a lesser extent, the North Palace of Ashurbanipal at Nineveh). Some of these wall reliefs contain so-called

3 On Ashurbanipal's role in his court's artistic production, see Natalie Naomi May, '"I Read the Inscriptions from before the Flood …" Neo-Sumerian Influences in Ashurbanipal's Royal Self-Image', in *Time and History in the Ancient Near East: Proceedings of the 56th Rencontre Assyriologique Internationale at Barcelona, 26–30 July 2010*, ed. L. Feliu et al. (Winona Lake, IN: 2013), 199–210; Alasdair Livingstone, 'Ashurbanipal: Literate or Not?', *Zeitschrift für Assyriologie und Vorderasiatische Archäologie* 97, no. 1 (2007), 98–118; Silvie Zamazalová, 'The Education of Neo-Assyrian Princes', in *The Oxford Handbook of Cuneiform Culture*, ed. Eleanor Robson and Karen Radner (Oxford: 2011), 313–30.

TABLE 14.1 *Selected sources for Ashurbanipal's account of Teumman and allies' defeat*

Medium	Type	Relevant sources
Textual	'Annals'	Prism B recensions, Prism A recensions
	Epigraph Tablets	Epigraph Text A, a few other tablets
Visual and Textual	Epigraphs on reliefs	Southwest Palace, Room XXXIII Epigraphs
Visual	Reliefs	Southwest Palace, Room XXXIII; North Palace, Room I.

epigraphs, short passages of cuneiform text serving essentially as captions to explain, comment on, or contextualise the visuals they accompany.[4] Related to these epigraphs on the stone wall reliefs are clay epigraph tablets, also excavated in Nineveh.[5] These tablets include some of the same epigraphs that appear on the wall reliefs, as well as many more epigraphs which together form a relatively coherent 'narrative' made up of a string of short statements. The purpose of these tablets is not known, and it may be that different epigraph tablets served different purposes.[6] Although they overlap with the content of the wall reliefs, I would argue that the tablets were likely also intended to function as coherent objects in themselves, rather than as 'drafts' for the script that would be carved in stone. Finally there are royal 'annals', long texts narrating the king's military achievements written on large clay prisms or cylinders and subsequently buried in the foundations of royal buildings and temples.[7] The term 'annals', borrowed from ancient Rome, is slightly misleading since the Assyrian annals were structured by campaign, rather than by years. These campaigns are, by Ashurbanipal's reign, a convention of the structure rather than a reflection of actual military tactics: events which appear as two separate

4 See Pamela Gerardi, 'Epigraphs and Assyrian Palace Reliefs: The Development of the Epigraphic Text', *Journal of Cuneiform Studies* 40, no. 1 (1988), 1–35.

5 John Malcolm Russell, *The Writing on the Wall: Studies in the Architectural Context of Late Assyrian Palace Inscriptions* (Winona Lake, IN: 1999), 154–209.

6 Russell, *Writing on the Wall*, 198–9.

7 Royal inscriptions dealing with some of the same content were also inscribed on publicly displayed steles, wall reliefs, or rockfaces, both at the centre of the Assyrian empire and the periphery, but they are not the texts we look at here. See Ann Shafer, 'Assyrian Royal Monuments on the Periphery: Ritual and the Making of Imperial Space', in *Ancient Near Eastern Art in Context: Studies in Honor of Irene J. Winter by Her Students*, ed. Jack Cheng and Marian H. Feldman (Leiden: 2007), 133–59.

campaigns in one prism will appear as one campaign in another prism later in his reign. For instance, the events discussed here are Campaign Seven and Eight in the Prism B account, but a unified Campaign Five in the later Prism A account. Although different versions of annals were composed during a king's reign, with regular updates about new military events, it would be misleading to think of successive versions as replacing previous ones, since the old prisms remained buried in the foundations of royal buildings, still testifying before the Assyrian gods. When I discuss the presentation of the campaigns against Teumman and his allies, I will note the origin of a quote or image, but I will treat these sources as aspects of an overall elite narrative in which separate sources exist in a single intellectual world and were seen by their creators as representing complementary and cohering versions of reality.

The question of audience for these various sources is a major debate within Assyriology. Early interpretations often focused on royal art and texts, and particularly on their portrayals of violence, as deterrent propaganda—'calculated frightfulness', in a famous phrase of A. T. E. Olmstead.[8] Today, most scholars would agree that these sources were written for an internal, elite audience, although the precise nature of this audience and its intended interactions with them is still a matter of debate.[9] I would emphasise a reading of these sources as written particularly for that most internal and elite audience, the Assyrian gods, for whom they were a testament to the king's correct prosecution of the duties they assigned him. As Ashurbanipal himself described the purpose of the images of conquered enemies he had carved in the Ishtar temple, 'By the craft of the god Ninzadim, I had drawn on it the villages of enemies that I had conquered with my own hands, the appropriate behaviour [*simtu*] of enemies which I repeatedly achieved at the command of her exalted divinity, and those

8 A. T. E. Olmstead, 'The Calculated Frightfulness of Ashur Nasir Apal', *Journal of the American Oriental Society* 38 (1918), 209–63.

9 Paul Collins, 'Gods, Heroes, Rituals, and Violence: Warfare in Neo-Assyrian Art', in *Critical Approaches to Ancient Near Eastern Art*, ed. Brian A. Brown and Marian H. Feldman (Berlin: 2013), 621–2; Ariel Bagg, 'Where Is the Public? A New Look at the Brutality Scenes in Neo-Assyrian Royal Inscriptions and Art', in *Making Pictures of War: Realia et Imaginaria in the Iconology of the Ancient Near East*, ed. Laura Battini-Villard (Oxford: 2016), 57–82; Steven W. Holloway, *Aššur Is King! Aššur Is King!: Religion in the Exercise of Power in the Neo-Assyrian Empire* (Leiden: 2002), 74–76; Mehmet-Ali Ataç, *The Mythology of Kingship in Neo-Assyrian Art* (Cambridge: 2010), 87–89; Hayim Tadmor, 'Propaganda, Literature, Historiography: Cracking the Code of the Assyrian Royal Inscriptions', in *Assyria 1995: Proceedings of the 10th Anniversary Symposium of the Neo-Assyrian Text Corpus Project, Helsinki, September 7–11, 1995*, ed. Simo Parpola and Robert M. Whiting (Helsinki: 1997), 325–38.

kings who were insubmissive to me'.[10] Ashurbanipal shows that he has performed the command of the exalted divinity Ishtar through his images of the 'appropriate behaviour' of enemies (i.e. submission, defeat, and death). In a secondary sense (and in both ideological and practical terms) the images' audience was also the Assyrian elites of the court, the current king, and his imagined successors, sometimes mentioned in codas to royal inscriptions.

Foreign visitors would have seen reliefs on the occasion of bringing letters or tribute, and it is possible that the palace, or at least its environs, was sometimes open to a wider public (the 'Banquet Stele' of Ashurnasirpal II claims that 69,574 people feasted at his palace in Nimrud, almost certainly an exaggeration but perhaps of real practices).[11] Impressive evidence for a range of situations in which a variety of visitors had access to the palace has been assembled by Russell and should not be overlooked.[12] Nonetheless, these visitors were incidental viewers, not the audiences *for whom* palace art was created.

Where written sources are concerned, there is no direct evidence for a much-speculated-upon practice of public readings of any texts in Assyria, and even the most convincing arguments for the practice suggest that only a few unusual royal texts may have had this treatment, not the prisms.[13] Primarily these texts would have been read by the scribes who composed and copied them, the king and other members of his court, and the gods who could read them even buried under royal foundations. If foreigners or ordinary Assyrians were sometimes given access to texts or reliefs, they were not part of the imagined, ideal audience. Despite their strong focus on the defeat and torture of Assyrian enemies and the might of the king, these texts did not serve a propagandistic

---

10 *da-ad-me na-ki-ri ša* ⸢*ik*⸣*-šu*$_2$*-da* ŠU.II-*a-a si-ma-a-ti na-*⸢*ki*⸣*-ri ša*$_2$ *ina qi*$_2$*-bit* ⸢DINGIR⸣-*ú-ti-ša*$_2$ *ṣir-ti aš*$_2$*-tak-ka-nu u*$_3$ LUGAL.MEŠ *la kan-šu*$_2$-[*ti*]-⸢*ia*⸣ *ina ši-pir* ^{d}*nin-za*$_2$*-dim*$_2$ UGU-*ša*$_2$ *u*$_2$-⸢*ṣir*⸣; Royal Inscriptions of the Neo-Assyrian Period (hereafter RINAP) 5, 'The Royal Inscriptions of Ashurbanipal and His Successors', ed. and trans. Jamie Novotny, online at <http://oracc.museum.upenn.edu/rinap/rinap5/pager>, accessed 8 August 2016, 21.33–35. This and subsequent translations follow Novotny.

11 A. Kirk Grayson, *Assyrian Rulers of the Early First Millennium BC. I, (1114–859 BC)* (Toronto: 1991), 288–93.

12 John Malcolm Russell, *Sennacherib's Palace without Rival at Nineveh* (Chicago: 1991), 223–40; see also Irene J. Winter, 'Royal Rhetoric and the Development of Historical Narrative in Neo-Assyrian Reliefs', *Studies in Visual Communication* 7 (1981), 32.

13 A. Leo Oppenheim, 'The City of Assur in 714 B.C.', *Journal of Near Eastern Studies* 19 (1960), 133–47; Kathryn F. Kravitz, 'A Last-Minute Revision to Sargon's Letter to the God', *Journal of Near Eastern Studies* 62, no. 2 (2003), 81–95; Tadmor, 'Propaganda, Literature, Historiography', 331–2.

or deterrent purpose.[14] When reading them, we must consider their meaning as a message by and for Assyria.

Severed Heads in the Narratives of Teumman and Allies

The Teumman narrative is, in full, an account of the defeat of Elamite king Teumman and his army at the Battle of Til-Tuba, at the River Ulai, followed by the defeat of further southeast Babylonian allies, including other Elamite leaders and the particularly significant Gambulu tribe, and culminating in victory celebrations in Assyria at which the living and dead enemies of these engagements are displayed. I will present a summary of the aggregate narrative here, focusing on incidents involving severing or severed heads. It should be noted that the captives of these campaigns suffer other types of mutilation and punishment, including ones that target the skin, the limbs, the bones, the tongue, and the flesh. The head is not then the only body part that could be targeted; and therefore when it is targeted, a deliberate choice has been made to harm the head in preference to other available body parts.

The set-up for the campaign against Teumman goes far back in time, through a long history of conflict involving Assyria, Elam, and the tribes between them, notably Gambulu, which served as a 'door' between the two.[15] Teumman had usurped the Elamite throne from his brother, with whom Ashurbanipal had also been at odds. Like his predecessors, Teumman was seen by Assyria as an enemy by virtue of his very existence, a contender for power and influence in the regions of Babylonia that Assyria wished to maintain as its own. Ashurbanipal's account in Prism B claims that Teumman was the aggressor in this particular war, marching to make battle against Assyria after Ashurbanipal had refused Teumman's repeated messages asking for the deportation of certain Elamite nobles, sons of the previous Elamite king, who were being given refuge in Assyria.

14 This is not to say that they do not sometimes describe enemy punishments which were intended to be deterrent spectacles for the defeated rather than celebratory affirmations for the victors. This is most clearly the case with depictions of impaling, as discussed by Karen Radner, 'High Visibility Punishment and Deterrent: Impalement in Assyrian Warfare and Legal Practice', *Zeitschrift für Altorientalische und Biblische Rechtsgeschichte* 21 (2015), 103–28.

15 Mark D. Waters, *A Survey of Neo-Elamite History* (Helsinki: 2000), 20; Grant Frame, *Babylonia 689–627 B.C: A Political History* (Istanbul: 1992), 118.

According to Prism Edition B, the earliest and longest account of the events, in the lead-up to the confrontation at Til-Tuba Teumman suffers some sort of physical event, perhaps a stroke, which causes physical omens, sent by the moon god Sin, to manifest in his body:[16] 'On that day, a misfortune came upon him; his lips became paralysed, his eye rolled back, and a contraction was set in its centre'.[17] Yet Teumman is unashamed of this affliction, which, to Assyrian eyes, is an obvious sign of his doom; he continues in his aggression. The Assyrian army begins to march to Elam. As they proceed, fear (according to epigraph tablets) overwhelms the officials of Hidalu, an area which appears to have been perhaps a semi-autonomous region of Elam. They cut off the head of Ishtar-nandi, king of Hidalu, bring it before Ashurbanipal's magnates, and swear fealty to him.

Battle is met at the Ulai River, outside the Elamite capital of Susa. Ashurbanipal is not personally present, a fact that is acknowledged, although he uses the first person to describe actions of his army and soldiers. The story of this battle and the beheading of Teumman in its midst is told in greatest detail in the Southwest Palace Reliefs and their accompanying epigraphs. The beheading is presented in a visually complex, non-linear narrative, moving across time and space on one visual field. The beheading takes place in the midst of a battle, depicted across three slabs of wall reliefs. The slabs were originally divided into two registers, with scenes of post-battle celebrations in the upper registers. Most of the upper register scenes have now been lost. The battle sequence is rendered without the strictly designed registers that are characteristic of other Ashurbanipal reliefs on a similar scale, although three pseudo-groundlines organise the space. In the thick of the battle scene, the organisation created by these lines largely breaks down. In contrast to the surviving post-battle sequences depicted elsewhere in the room, which are characterised by assemblies of ordered rows of soldiers or prisoners with clear focal points where events occur (for instance where prisoners are received, torture occurs, or booty is counted), the Til-Tuba battle is deliberately made to look visually chaotic.

Within this plane, the figure of Teumman appears seven times, either whole or as a head. These appearances are accompanied by carved epigraphs, narrating the events of the sequence. As a whole, events progress in a rough boomerang shape with a turning point at the moment that Teumman's head

16 Paul Collins, 'The Development of the Individual Enemy in Assyrian Art', *Source: Notes in the History of Art* 25, no. 3 (2006), 4.

17 *ina* u_4*-me-*$šu_2$*-ma mi-iḫ-ru im-ḫur-šu-ma* NUNDUM-*su uk-tam-bil-ma* IGI.II-$šu_2$ *is-ḫur-ma ga-ba-ṣu iš-*$ša_2$*-kin ina* lib_3*-bi-šu*; RINAP 5 3.v.11–13.

is severed from his body. In his first appearance, Teumman attempts to flee with his son Tammaritu, but his chariot overturns. Tammaritu tries to lead the wounded Teumman, who has been hit in the back by an arrow, away into the woods. Teumman crouches, ordering his son to raise his bow against the Assyrian soldiers who pursue them. However, they are set upon by 'a common soldier' (*a-ḫu-ru-u* ERIM.ḪI.A-*ia*) of Ashurbanipal's army, who kills Teumman and begins to sever his head and Tammaritu's, 'in front of one another' (*mi-iḫ-ret a-ḫa-meš*). The narrative now reverses 'direction' as the soldier, facing away from the beheading in his past, raises Teumman's head in the midst of battle; he is next seen in the Assyrian camp showing the head to be identified, seemingly by Elamites held in camp (perhaps captives or Assyrian allies, part of the Elamite faction which had been living at the Assyrian court).[18] Finally, the same soldier bears the head aloft in a chariot, on his way back to Ashurbanipal in Assyria. Describing the progression of events in this way reflects the chronological order in which events are meant to happen, but erases the effect of their presentation in art. By the nature of the genre, all these events occur simultaneously on the palace walls, and occur at the same time as other events depicted, although they are meant to evoke different locations in both space and time.

Also in the midst of the battle scene, two episodes occur, each accompanied by an epigraph describing the event depicted, each involving a deputy of Teumman, each represented as taking place roughly at the same time and in the same field as Teumman's own death. In one of these episodes, another Elamite, Ituni, voluntarily surrenders by breaking his bow (he is seemingly soon to be killed, a mace held over his head by an Assyrian soldier).[19] In the second episode, and the one more relevant to the question of severed heads, Teumman's relative Urtak, wounded with an arrow, calls out to an Assyrian soldier: 'Come, cut off my head, bring it before your lord, get a good name [for yourself]'.[20] In the relief, Urtak gestures with his hand to his throat. This incident is of particular importance, constituting as it does a shadow beheading incident within the grander narrative of Teumman's own beheading.

According to annals and epigraph texts, after the defeat of Teumman's forces at Til-Tuba Ashurbanipal immediately sets out (or more accurately, sends his

18 Chikako E. Watanabe, 'The "Continuous Style" in the Narrative Scheme of Assurbanipal's Reliefs', *Iraq* 66 (2004), 111.

19 This incident also survives in a fragment from the North Palace, suggesting that the entire sequence was likely repeated in that palace; R. D. Barnett, *Sculptures from the North Palace of Ashurbanipal at Nineveh (668–627 B.C.)* (London: 1976), pl. XXIV.

20 SAG.DU KUD-*is* IGI LUGAL EN-*ka i-ši-⸢ma le⸣-e-qi*$_2$ MU SIG$_5$-*tim*; RINAP 5 26.4–5.

army out) against Gambulu, an Aramean tribe located seemingly somewhere in the marshes of southeast Babylonia. (Visual depictions of this stage of the campaign(s) either do not survive or never existed, though the aftermath is depicted in Room XXXIII of the Southwest Palace and seemingly in North Palace Room I.) They conquer Sha-pi-Bel, the Gambulian 'stronghold' (URU *dan-nu-ti-šu*$_2$) whose 'site is placed in the midst of rivers' (*ša qe*$_2$*-reb* ID$_2$.MEŠ *na-da-at šu-bat-su*) in the marshy land of Babylonia. The Gambulian king, Dunanu, and his brothers are taken alive as captives, along with valuable booty (human, animal, and inanimate) and the entire surviving human populace. Also captured when the city is taken is the Elamite commander Massira, who had been left there by Teumman with an archery garrison to protect the city. According to Prism B, Massira is taken alive. Ashurbanipal then proclaims: 'I cut off his head and with it I beat the face of Dunanu: the ally who could not save him'.[21]

After the return to Nineveh, Dunanu is further ritually humiliated and punished—once again, via the use of severed heads. According to Prism B, Teumman's severed head is hung around Dunanu's neck. In epigraphs and in the wall reliefs the same event is recorded, with Dunanu's brother Samgunu also present and forced to wear the severed head of Ishtar-nandi, king of Hidalu, which had been given to Ashurbanipal's magnates. With music and rejoicing, Ashurbanipal enters Nineveh together with war booty and the macabrely adorned Dunanu. Ultimately, as reported in both Prism B and on epigraph tablets (though not depicted visually), Dunanu is slaughtered on a 'slaughterbench', like a sheep, and dismembered.

The use of Teumman's head as an instrument of punishment is not confined to its being worn as necklace: when it is brought into Nineveh, it is seen by (or shown to) Umbadara and Nabu-damiq, two Elamite nobles who were sent to the Assyrian court bearing messages from Teumman just before the outbreak of hostilities and have been detained there since.[22] At the sight of the severed head of their sender and king, 'a changing mind seized them' (*ša*$_2$*-ne*$_2$*-e ṭe*$_3$*-e-me iṣ-bat-su-nu-ti*). Umbadara tears at his beard while Nabu-damiq stabs himself in the stomach with his dagger, evidently attempting to commit suicide. This incident is recorded in Prism B and in epigraphs. A further epigraph and visual depiction shows the two messengers once again, being forced to read out the 'insulting messages' (*šipir mēreḫti*) they had brought from their now-dead king, in the presence of two visiting Urartian ambassadors. Although

21 SAG.DU-*su ak-kis*$_2$ *it-ti pa-ni* ^{m}*du-na-nu kit-ri la mu-še-zib-i-šu*$_2$ *ar-pi-is*; RINAP 5 3.vi.34–35, translation following RINAP 5.

22 See RINAP 5 3.iv.87–89 and RINAP 5 3.vi.51–52.

their ultimate fate is not mentioned, it seems unlikely that we should imagine it was a happy one.

At some point during these victory processions (the order of these events is not entirely clear) a highly fragmentary epigraph on a tablet suggests Teumman's head is mutilated by Ashurbanipal (the tendons of his face cut) and that Ashurbanipal then spits on it.[23]

Having taken Teumman's head from Elam through the capitals of Assyria and having used it as a weapon of punishment, Ashurbanipal dedicates it to the gods: 'In front of the city gate of the city of Nineveh, the severed head of Teumman—I offered it as an offering, in order to show the might of Assur and Ishtar, my lords, to the people: the severed head of Teumman, king of the land of Elam'.[24] This incident is apparently depicted in a now heavily damaged relief in the Louvre (AO 19914) from North Palace Room I, whose content is better preserved in drawings.[25] The head appears one more time in surviving reliefs from the North Palace, hanging upside down in a tree in the garden of Ashurbanipal while the king and his queen drink and attendants play music and bear food.

Other punishments of other enemies are also included in this sequence, but do not directly involve severed heads or beheading. One of these punishments should be noted, however, because it targets features of the head: two Gambulian officials, Mannu-ki-ahhe, the deputy of Dunanu, and Nabu-usalli, the city overseer of Gambulu, 'who uttered grievous blasphemies against my gods', have their tongues ripped out and are flayed in Arbela (the representation of this incident in the reliefs suggests that this is part of the same procession where Dunanu and Samgunu are forced to wear the severed heads). There is no explanation of what this blasphemy is; possibly their rebellion against Assyria is automatically interpreted as blasphemous, but in this case there would be nothing to distinguish them from the other enemies punished here. Given the ripping out of their tongues, it is likely that some disrespectful speech act of theirs was reported to Ashurbanipal. Although their heads are

23 Rykle Borger, *Beiträge zum Inschriftenwerk Assurbanipals. Die Prismenklassen A, B, C = K, D, E, F, G, H, J und T sowie andere Inschriften* (Wiesbaden: 1996), 301 (line 11); Ernst F. Weidner, 'Assyrische Beschreibungen der Kriegs-Reliefs Assurbânaplis', *Archiv für Orientforschung* 8 (1932–1933), 180; Russell, *Writing on the Wall*, 160.

24 *ni-kis* SAG.DU ^{m}*te-um-man ina* GABA KA$_2$.GAL MURUB$_4$ URU *ša* NINA.KI *u*$_2$-⌜*maḫ*⌝-*ḫi-ra maḫ-ḫu-riš aš*$_2$-*šu*$_2$ *da-na-an* AN.ŠAR$_2$ *u* ⌜d⌝15 EN.MEŠ-*ia* UN.MEŠ *kul-lu-me ni-kis* SAG.DU ^{m}*te-um-man* LUGAL KUR.ELAM.MA.KI; RINAP 5 3.vi.57–60.

25 Barnett, *Sculptures from the North Palace*, 42–43, pl. XXV–XXVI; Pauline Albenda, 'An Unpublished Drawing of Louvre AO 19914 in the British Museum', *Journal of the Ancient Near Eastern Society of Columbia University* 12 (1980), 1–8.

not severed, the targeting of facial features probably exists within the same conceptual sphere, as suggested by the frequent association between beheading and facial mutilation of statues.[26]

In summary then, we have: the cutting off of Ishtar-nandi's head and its presentation, in supplication, to Ashurbanipal's magnate; a severed head of the Elamite king Teumman depicted repeatedly in various situations as an object of public display, a weapon inspiring fear, harm, or humiliation, and an offering to the gods; a report of the severing of the head of Tammaritu, Teumman's son, before his own eyes; a discussion of the severing of the head of Urtak and its future presentation to the king; a severing of Massira's head and its reappropriation as a weapon against Dunanu; the use of Teumman's and Ishtar-nandi's heads as decorative objects hung around the necks of Dunanu and Samgunu; and the destruction of the faces of Mannu-ki-ahhe and Nabu-usalli.

The Severed Head and the Individual Enemy

The sheer diversity of the situations in which severed heads appear and the ways in which they are used should suggest that these objects can be made to do complex work and carry a wide range of meanings. Yet it is first important to note a common feature of all of these images of severed heads: the heads retain the identity of the specific individuals to whom they once belonged. When a head was severed from its body, the head, not the body (whose fate is not remarked upon in any of the cases discussed above) retained meaning, and meaning through its identity. This may seem obvious, but in fact it cannot be assumed that heads were necessarily the seat of identity, especially severed heads that were no longer part of a full body.

In Mesopotamia, heads did not have particular significance as the seat of thought or feeling. Across the ancient Near East, thought tended to be situated in the torso or heart (in Akkadian, one word, *libbu*, designates both).[27] Feelings could reside in several parts of the body, but primarily in the heart

26 Natalie Naomi May, '"In Order to Make Him Completely Dead": Annihilation of the Power of Images in Mesopotamia', in *La famille dans le Proche-Orient ancien: Réalités, symbolismes, et images: Proceedings of the 55th Rencontre Assyriologique Internationale at Paris, 6–9 July 2009*, ed. Lionel Marti (Winona Lake, IN: 2014), 701–26.

27 Moudhy N. Al-Rashid, 'Mental Symptoms in the Akkadian Diagnostic Handbook: A Study of Patterns in the Description of Depression, Anxiety, and Madness' (PhD diss., University of Oxford, 2014), 184–94.

and intestines (*kabattu*).[28] The head was not then the primary location of the thinking or feeling self, although recent research has suggested that a connection between the head and the mind is implicitly acknowledged in medical texts, which associate physical problems felt in the head with problems of thought and feeling.[29]

But even if the head was not normally understood as the seat of the inner self, it was understood as the seat of the *outer* self. Heads did identify a person as an individual through the Mesopotamian concept of *bunnannû*, a word alternately translated as 'face', 'features', or 'appearance'. The term appears to refer to the physical configuration of face or body that made someone (or something) what they were and nothing else. Although the term usually seems to refer specifically to the face, the *bunnannû* was also found in other aspects of the self. Like most questions of physical description and physical appearance, our understanding of how the Assyrians experienced these concepts is still uncertain. For instance, the king's 'features' are embodied in visual representations which look exactly like every other king, and also like the gods and spirits that surround him. The king's *bunnannû* then were clearly not what we would consider his *actual* facial features, but some other aspect of his appearance.

Indeed, the question of heads, features, and personhood are complicated by the fact that we are not here dealing with heads themselves, but with representations or discussions of them: not with the severed head of the Elamite king Teumman (long lost to us), but rather with an artistic representation and textual discussion of that head, repeated again and again. We must ask then not only where the identity of an individual resided in their body (in their head or clothing), but also how the identity of an individual was conveyed or created in Assyrian art and what depicting heads and faces meant. The concept of *bunnannû* when used in Akkadian sources is very frequently linked to the question of making images, which have their own *bunnannû* (including non-humanoid, fashioned objects, like chariots).[30] The *bunnannû* of fashioned objects is often singled out for praise. I would even go so far as to suggest that one of the best

28 See also Mark S. Smith, 'The Heart and Innards in Israelite Emotional Expressions: Notes from Anthropology and Psychobiology', *Journal of Biblical Literature* 117, no. 3 (1998), 427–36.

29 Al-Rashid, 'Akkadian Diagnostic Handbook', 257–8; Hanspeter Schaudig, '"Wahnsinn" im Alten Orient: Zum babylonischen Konzept eines stark von der gesellschaftlichen Norm abweichenden und selbstzerstörerischen Verhaltens', *Studia Mesopotamica: Jahrbuch für altorientalische Geschichte und Kultur* 1 (2014), 396–8; Joan N. Westenholz and Michel Sigrist, 'The Brain, the Marrow and the Seat of Cognition in Mesopotamian Tradition', *Le Journal des Médecines Cunéiformes* 7 (2006), 1–10.

30 CAD B: *bunnannû*.

ways of understanding *bunnannû* is as precisely what is represented in a fashioned object that gives that object its identity.

The question of images and their relation to reality is a topic of an ongoing discussion within Assyriology. Recent research has centred on delineating the precise relationship between representation and the real. It is generally agreed that images in Assyria had a power beyond mimesis in the strictly imitative sense. Rather, images truly embodied what they represented. This understanding of Assyrian images has been taken furthest by Zainab Bahrani, who sees all images in Assyria as inherently animated: 'there was a collapse of any clear distinction between the real and representation or, at least, the boundary between the two became blurred'. She maintains that images should be seen 'not as imitating the natural world but as participating in it and affecting it in supernatural, even magical ways'.[31] This last statement is of particular relevance with regard to her convincing analysis of the repeated depiction of Teumman's head as having performative power to recreate his defeat.[32] Others, including Fales and Collins, have argued that Bahrani somewhat overstates the point, stressing that not all images were inherently animated, as Bahrani assumes, a fact that is made clear by the existence of rituals specifically to animate some, but not all, images.[33]

In other words, in Mesopotamia, all images are created real, but some are more real than others. The 'realest', or better 'most animated', of these were undoubtedly cultic statues, which were animated through a ritual 'mouth-washing' (*mīs pî*).[34] Prior to this ritual, it seems cultic statues were indeed understood as mere dead objects which needed specific priestly knowledge and action to become the deities they were destined to be. We do not know of such rituals being performed in any other context, for instance with images of the Assyrian king.[35] From this, we might conclude that king images were not

---

31 Zainab Bahrani, *Rituals of War: The Body and Violence in Mesopotamia* (New York: 2008), 59, 57.

32 Ibid., 52–55.

33 Frederick Mario Fales, 'Art, Performativity, Mimesis, Narrative, Ideology, and Audience: Reflections on Assyrian Palace Reliefs in the Light of Recent Studies', *KASKAL* 6 (2009), 25–6; Paul Collins, 'Gods, Heroes, Rituals, and Violence', 636–7.

34 Michael B. Dick and C. B. F. Walker, 'The Induction of the Cult Image in Ancient Mesopotamia: The Mesopotamian *Mis Pî* Ritual', in *Born in Heaven, Made on Earth: The Making of the Cult Image in the Ancient Near East*, ed. Michael B. Dick (Winona Lake, IN: 1999), 55–121.

35 There are, however, clear similiarities between the mouth-washing ritual and rituals used in connection with non-human cultic objects such as drums, and possibly beds, although this is not clear. See Evelyne Koubková, 'Washing the Mouth of a Kettledrum',

animated at all. However, that appears not to have been true either, given both how such images are discussed in royal texts and the prevalence of iconoclastic destruction of non-cult images, designed not just to symbolically destroy, but to destroy specifically the life-giving regions of the image such as the nose, mouth, and throat.[36]

Instead, I would propose that there were degrees of animation to images. The doodles that scribes made on the back of tablets were likely not at all living, while the cult statues of gods were very real embodiments of a divine essence and presence.[37] King images probably sat closer to the cult image side, but were not exactly analogous, since they had not been ritually animated in the same way. Instead, royal images came to embody the essence of the king through their association with the court and the elite scholars who oversaw image-production, and the king's own approval of his image as officially him. In Assyrian royal inscriptions, kings celebrate the setting up of their own images, sometimes mentioning the meaning of the stylised poses used.[38] A revealing letter to either Ashurbanipal or Esarhaddon asks for the king to choose between two proposed designs for a future statue of himself (one drawn, the other a model in the round).[39] The king himself was involved in decisions

---

paper presented at the 62nd Rencontre Assyriologique Internationale, Philadelphia, 11 July 2016, <https://www.academia.edu/27202640/Washing_the_mouth_of_a_kettle drum_Rencontre_Assyriologique_Internationale_2016_presentation_>, accessed 3/7/2017; Barbara N. Porter, 'Feeding Dinner to a Bed: Reflections on the Nature of Gods in Ancient Mesopotamia', *State Archives of Assyria Bulletin* 15 (2006), 308–9.

36 May, 'In Order to Make Him Completely Dead', 719.

37 For scribal drawings on tablets, see Klaus Wagensonner, 'Non-Textuality in the Ancient Near East: Some Glimpses from the Mesopotamian Field', in *Non-Textual Marking Systems, Writing and Pseudo Script from Prehistory to Modern Times*, ed. Petra Andrássy, Julia Budka, and Frank Kammerzell (Göttingen: 2009) 33–67 at 42, 64; for examples also see CDLI P001686, P248578, searchable in the Cuneiform Digital Library Initiative database at <http://cdli.ucla.edu>, accessed 18/6/2017.

38 Examples from the texts of Neo-Assyrian kings describing the setting up of royal images include RINAP 1, *The Royal Inscriptions of Tiglath-pileser III (744–727 BC) and Shalmaneser V (726–722 BC), Kings of Assyria*, ed. and trans. Hayim Tadmor, Shigeo Yamada, and Jamie Novotny (Winona Lake, IN: 2011), 41.21'–25', 27'–29', 48.16'–18' for Tiglath-Pileser III; RINAP 3/2, *The Royal Inscriptions of Sennacherib, King of Assyria (704–681 BC)* ed. and trans. A. Kirk Grayson and Jamie Novotny (Winona Lake, IN: 2014), 153.r.1'–3' for Sennacherib; RINAP 4, *The Royal Inscriptions of Esarhaddon, King of Assyria (680–669 BC)*, ed. and trans. Erle Leichty (Winona Lake, IN: 2011), 60.r.26'-29' for Esarhaddon; RINAP 5 Tablet 02 L4=K 02694 + K 03050 for Ashurbanipal.

39 Steven W. Cole and Peter Machinist, *Letters from Priests to the Kings Esarhaddon and Assurbanipal* (Helsinki: 1998), n. 34; for discussion of another letter asking for a similar

about his image and gave his approval, making those images official. Nadali points out that there would have been situations in which the (living) king and his royal image were in proximity (most famously the throne room of Ashurnasirpal II in which the king in image appears twice above the throne itself). He suggests a nuanced and contextualised understanding of the relationship between the king and his images, that 'in that peculiar close acquaintance the king and the picture of his royal figure neutralize one another; in some way, we can say that the *alam šarrūtiya* ['statue of my kingship'] suspends its agency when the king in person is present and the king is in fact not affected by the picture of himself'.[40]

The general presumption of the animated power of royal statues seemed to have held throughout the region and between enemy cultures, explaining why various cultures, including Assyria's enemies, committed iconoclasm against *each other's* elite images. Assyrians 'believed in' the images of Elamite kings, as evidenced by the affective violence they did to them, for instance in Ashurbanipal's attack on a captive statue of the long-dead Hallusu, who had troubled his grandfather Sennacherib: 'his mouth which sneered, I cut off; his lips which spoke insolence, I sliced off; his hands, which grasped a bow to fight Assyria, I chopped off'.[41] However, in creating the image of Teumman they wished to do something novel: not to destroy an already-animated enemy king image, but to create and animate the image, not of their own king, who was there to impart his identity to the production, but of an enemy king (and one now dead). If the Assyrian king was created in image through his perfection and through official approval of the image capturing his *bunnannû*, how was the enemy king to be created in image?

It seems the solution reached with Teumman was likeness of distinct physical features, with their identifying divine judgment written into them. The relief-Teumman's distinctive ugliness and unusual features have been noted as

royal decision about statue design, see Irene J. Winter, 'Art in Empire: The Royal Image and the Visual Dimensions of Assyrian Ideology', in *Assyria 1995: Proceedings of the 10th Anniversary Symposium of the Neo-Assyrian Text Corpus Project, Helsinki, September 7–11, 1995*, ed. Simo Parpola and Robert M. Whiting (Helsinki: 1997), 359–81 at 367–8.

40 Davide Nadali, 'Interpretations and Translations, Performativity and Embodied Simulation: Reflections on Assyrian Images', in *Leggo!: Studies Presented to Frederick Mario Fales on the Occasion of his 65th Birthday*, ed. G. B. Lanfranchi et al. (Wiesbaden: 2012), 583–96 at 584–5.

41 KIR$_4$[-*šu*$_2$] *ša iš-ni-iṣ-ṣu ak-kis* NUNDUM.MEŠ-*šu*$_2$ *ša iq-ba-a me-ri-iḫ-tu*$_2$ *ap-ru-u* ŠU.II-*šu*$_2$ *u*$_2$*-kar-ri-it ša* ^{GIŠ}PAN *iṣ-ba-tu*$_2$ *a-na mit-ḫu-ṣi* KUR AN.ŠAR$_2$.KI; Borger, *Beiträge zum Inschriftenwerk Assurbanipals*, 54–55; trans. following May, 'In Order to Make him Completely Dead', 718–9.

a unique characteristic of this Assyrian antagonist;[42] they are certainly uniquely distinctive, although other enemies in Ashurbanipal's reliefs have features that mark them out from the norm (discussed below), if not as recognisable individuals. Collins has written of the development of Assyrian 'portraiture' in the depiction of Teumman, an attempt to individualise his image as a specific and real person. The purpose of this portraiture was to more fully ensure the destruction of the already-dismembered Elamite king by making an image that actually contained his essence, which would suffer eternally in stone representation. Collins sees this development as moving beyond the use of image as substitute in Mesopotamian art to something more: 'since the image was intended to represent the man himself, Teumman's *actual* defeat and death were constantly repeated by the narrative nature of the carvings'.[43] The features of Teumman were not mimetically represented; they were literally present in his image, through this innovative act of Assyrian portraiture rather than through animating ritual or royal approval.

The significance of Teumman's specific features must also be understood as related to the event reported to have befallen him just before the clash with Assyria's army, in which the god Sin deformed his eye and lips. These physical symptoms appear to be partially represented in Teumman's head after his death, with his eye squinted shut and curving downwards. As Collins points out, the deformity does not noticeably appear until after he has been beheaded, suggesting that the image-Teumman becomes even more the real, individual Teumman the more fully defeated he is.[44] The need to represent the head in its specific, divine-sent ugliness is also in part linked to the use of his particular body as a field of divine communication. His head needed to be recreated as a distinctive, 'real' object, and in such a way that the divine message inscribed upon it was clear.[45]

As mentioned above, the best testament to how Assyrians regarded images of individuals is the iconoclasm that was practiced against images when they

42 Julian Reade, 'Religious Ritual in Assyrian Sculpture', in *Ritual and Politics in Ancient Mesopotamia*, ed. Barbara N. Porter (New Haven: 2005), 7–61; Collins, 'Individual Enemy', 1–8.

43 Collins, 'Individual Enemy', 6; see also Bahrani, *Rituals*, 52–55.

44 Collins, 'Individual Enemy', 4–6.

45 I think it is likely that, at the time that these images were carved, Teumman's real head was still being kept by the Assyrian court. Although it would have been much changed in years of keeping, this might have given its visual representation an added reality: the real trophy was under Assyrian control just as the image trophy was, and could thus be linked to the image in the way that the real king was linked to his royal images in the throne room by bestowing his presence upon them.

were captured. May has surveyed iconoclasm against statues (in the round and in relief) of kings and gods and found that overwhelmingly the Mesopotamian images that we have today are found in states of intentional damage. Heads, and particularly mouths and noses, which connected individuals to the breath of life, were targeted for removal or damage. Hands that bore weapons or sustenance were also ritually damaged, because of their association with power, aggression, and strength.[46] In the representation of Teumman and his mutilation, a related set of assumptions is performed: instead of decapitating a representation, a decapitation is represented. The ultimate goal is the same: to repeat a death that has already occurred through the use of images (either images *of* death, or death *to* an image that had previously been animated).

Although Teumman is the most distinctive individualised enemy and the one most frequently depicted, the reliefs from the period of Ashurbanipal also feature other physically differentiated, and distinctively ill-formed, enemies and foreigners. In the post-battle segments of the SWP XXXIII reliefs, two Urartian nobles who have brought messages of supplication to Ashurbanipal are shown three separate times, cringing before scenes of torture and humiliation. The Urartians are much shorter than those around them, stooped with hands raised submissively, wearing fringed robes, floppy caps, and high sandals. One is clean-shaven while the other has a short beard. The bearded Urartian has a noticeably lined face, with lines around his cheeks, mouth, and forehead. The clean-shaven ambassador has no such lines. It is possible that this is a unique designation of adult age-differences in Neo-Assyrian art, with the lines indicating advanced age. Both have slightly misshapen eyes, which arc downwards rather than forming a perfect almond-shape, and sharply hooked noses. These are similar to the features that Teumman exhibits and may have been shorthand for age, infirmity, or merely for a physically unfitting look. These Urartian ambassadors are notably the most deficient figures, in size, and in their deviation from Assyrian-normal features, a fact that is perhaps surprising given that these ambassadors are voluntarily bringing news of preemptive supplication, and thus are not even enemies.

In the representation of the Gambulian leaders Dunanu and Samgunu's head-wearing punishment, Samgunu is also similarly physically distinctive

46 May, 'In Order to Make Him Completely Dead', 706–17. See also Carl Nylander, 'Earless in Nineveh: Who Mutilated "Sargon's" Head?' *American Journal of Archaeology* 84, no. 3 (1980), 329–33; Barbara N. Porter, 'Noseless in Nimrud: More Figurative Responses to Assyrian Domination', in *Of Gods, Trees, Kings and Scholars: Neo-Assyrian and Related Studies in Honour of Simo Parpola*, ed. Mikko Luukko, Saana Svärd, and Raija Mattila (Helsinki: 2009), 201–20.

(Dunanu's head falls in a damaged section of the relief, so we cannot say anything about his features). He is depicted with short stubbly beard, pouched chin, and lined and misshapen eyes. He wears the same floppy cap, fringed robes, and high sandals (underneath the fetters that bind his legs) of the Urartian ambassadors. The head of Teumman, visible hanging upside down above, is its usual distinctive, ugly self.

The individuality of these enemy leaders goes against the Assyrian ideal of standardised perfection. Assyrian kings look exactly like one another and their men look like slightly smaller versions of them (except for their eunuchs who are beardless with pouched chins, but who all look the same as each other). The ideal image achieved perfection, not individuation, and in achieving perfection achieved likeness to the king. Likeness did not derive from recreation of what we would consider the king's *actual* features but through perfecting his features into those of 'a king'. The appearance of 'a king' was a subject for which there was a long established and well-understood standard, in which his uniformity to other kings may have been related to a literal interference by the gods to shape his body such that 'the ruler's features convey qualities of ideal, divinely-sanctioned rulership, not just personhood'.[47] In contrast Teumman is not perfect and is in fact singled out (through Sin's omen deforming his face), marked out for death and humiliation by the specifics of his face.[48] The gods interfere in Teumman's body as they do in the Assyrian king's, but for a very different reason.

Bearing Heads, Bearing Messages

In each of the incidents relating to severed heads in this narrative, a concept of heads as messages is at work, although what the message is, who is sender, and who is receiver, change. I do not mean merely that these heads became signs, carrying meaning to those who saw the head, or saw its depiction in art—which would, by definition, be true. Rather, I mean specifically that concepts of how one sends messages and the status of messenger and sender are

47 Winter, 'Art in Empire', 373; and see 369–75 for an excellent discussion of the entire matter of kingly appearance, likeness, and perfection.

48 The ugliness of the other enemies is a culmination of a trend visible much earlier in Assyrian art in which enemies, although not 'individualised', are slightly and subtly different from Assyrians, usually conveyed through curved, not-quite-upright bodies. See Megan Cifarelli, 'Gesture and Alterity in the Art of Ashurnasirpal II of Assyria', *The Art Bulletin* 80, no. 2 (1 June 1998), 210–28 at 215.

governing paradigms for the severing and bearing of heads in these sources, with analogies to normal letter-sending deliberately invoked.

In the first place, the act of beheading is of course a message in itself, the ultimate message from Ashurbanipal of his displeasure, and simultaneously from the gods, also speaking of their displeasure, since their will ultimately underlies the strength of the Assyrian king. The common soldier who beheads Teumman is a messenger of Ashurbanipal, both in the sense that he delivers this displeasure and in the sense that, as messengers in the Near East often are, he is imperfectly distinguished from his sender. As with Yahweh and his angels, the distinction between Ashurbanipal and his messengers is fuzzy and sometimes inconsequential. Ashurbanipal in some places elides the detail of the common soldier who delivers his message (by taking credit for killing Teumman himself, with a first-person verb). And yet elsewhere and in equally valid royal narratives, he emphasises the very same detail (because of the indignity which death at the hands of a mere common soldier heaps upon Teumman). The two versions—that Ashurbanipal, in the first person, killed Teumman and that his soldier did it—are not incompatible descriptions of the event, because of the lack of distinction between messenger and sender. Which of the two equally valid tellings of the event is more suitable depends on whether the emphasis is Ashurbanipal's might or Teumman's weakness. The identification of the messenger/soldier with the king becomes especially strong during Ashurbanipal's reign, when the king is at his most distant, in art and text, from the physical locations of battle, but uses the first person to describe actions performed in reality by his army.[49]

In return, the common soldier who beheads Teumman bears back to the king a message made from Teumman's body but actually coming from the gods, who have written their will in Teumman's face. Although intended for Ashurbanipal, the head is a message to others as well, most notably Nabudamiq and Umbadara, messengers themselves of Teumman, for whom seeing the head delivers such an eloquent testament to their hopelessness that

49 It is possible to see in Assyrian reliefs a movement of the king away from battle over time: Ashurnasirpal II is shown participating in the battle, raising a bow against his enemies (WA 124545; WA 124555). Sennacherib places himself on a throne, receiving the spoils (human and material) of the conquest of Israelite Lachish in the enemy country (WA 124911). Ashurbanipal meanwhile has himself depicted receiving those spoils back in the heartland cities of Assyria (WA 135122). It is difficult to say how much of this is down to individual forces operating during a particular reign, but it seems that this is a general trend, and may reflect a real aversion towards direct participation in battle after the death of Sennacherib's father Sargon II in the field.

they self-harm at the sight. The head is both message and weapon. When Ashurbanipal ultimately receives Teumman's head, he reads in it a message from his army verifying the delivery of his message to Teumman, and at the same time a message from the god Sin about his judgment on Teumman, in which Teumman's head is merely a blank tablet that Sin has written on (i.e. via a transformation of his eye and lips).[50] In making the head an offering to the gods, Ashurbanipal sends back to them their message, another report confirming that he has carried out the judgment they had inscribed on that head. The message from the gods, conveyed through Teumman's ominous facial features, has been entered into the Assyrian royal record, into the sources that stand eternally before a divine audience, by being engraved on the palace walls in the form of an identifiable, and identifiably deformed, Teumman head.

The bearing of a head to Ashurbanipal is the central interest of the Teumman sequence, which uses the rendering of Teumman into a head as its climax and, in the visual sequence, its physical turning point. The head of Teumman's in-law Urtak is also understood to function literally as a message, but with a different emphasis. When Urtak is shown exhorting a soldier to kill and decapitate him, the epigraph focuses on the meaning of head-bearing to the one who will bear it: the messenger himself. In Urtak's case his head carries a different message than the one written on Teumman's by the gods. It will function (Urtak suggests), without divine writing but merely in its presence, to tell the story of an honourable action by a common Assyrian soldier in the field. Like cuneiform 'messenger texts' which entitle the bearer to certain rations at whatever official waystations they stop, Urtak suggests his head will function as such a message, bringing honour to its bearer. Urtak's head, then, is clearly not itself a trophy, but rather a message that will be exchanged for a real trophy, and 'a good name'. Perhaps we are to understand that Urtak (the character) also hopes that the head will be a message from him to the king: that he died honourably or that he died in supplication to Assyrian might. As Miller has noted, messengers were often expected to deliver information beyond the mere content of their text—something that was sometimes more desired by the sender, sometimes more by the recipient.[51] Urtak may be relying on the presumption that his voluntary surrender, in contrast to Teumman's ignominious flight, will be related to Ashurbanipal and perhaps to others (as presumably was the case, given that we have the story ourselves).

50 See Bahrani, *Rituals*, 80–96, on divination, semiotics, and the Mesopotamian body.

51 William Ian Miller, 'The Messenger', in *Frieden stiften: Vermittlung und Konfliktslösung vom Mittelalter bis Heute*, ed. Gerd Althoff (Darmstadt: 2011), 19–36 at 15–16.

The claim that the epigraph puts in Urtak's mouth—that bringing his head would make a name for the common soldier who does so—is an interesting one to appear in an Assyrian royal source, given the obvious namelessness of the common soldier who beheads Teumman (and the other common soldier who will soon behead Urtak). Assyrian royal inscriptions almost never give the names of any fellow Assyrians unless they are traitors and, therefore, enemies. The king is so fully identified with Assyria as an entity that further individuation is undesirable and indeed would be a violation of the perfection and unity of Assyrian identity (as with the enemy facial features that suggest imperfection and weakness, individuality was inherently weak). The glory of Teumman's death cannot be credited to a specific person, only to a proverbial 'common soldier', in which this commonness is used to denigrate Teumman, denying him a noble death. It is therefore hardly a flattering depiction of the soldier who did the deed, emphasising as it does the shame brought about by his low status.

The narrative itself does not, then, provide that 'good name' to its common soldiers. The words, put in the mouth of the Elamite Urtak, reference an entirely different discourse about war, one preserved in letters, administrative documents, and a few material objects but not in elite, royal narratives. As Radner has shown, there is ample evidence to testify to a system of prize-giving in which individual soldiers could earn both honour and material reward in battle.[52] Bringing severed heads of elites was one of the ways that prizes were won. Thus the claim by Urtak that his head will be a potent message for its bearer to deliver is probably historically accurate (even if that bearer's reward will not come in the form of named acknowledgment in elite, royal narratives).[53]

A different, very explicit message is delivered with the use of Massira's severed head as a weapon against Dunanu. His head has been transformed

52 Karen Radner, 'Fame and Prizes: Competition and War in the Neo-Assyrian Empire', in *Competition in the Ancient World*, ed. Nick Fisher and Hans van Wees (Swansea: 2011), 37–57, especially her discussion of earning 'names' (39–43) and of material rewards in exchange for high-status heads (47–49).

53 Although the execution of Teumman and Urtak on the field is celebrated in this narrative, it is worth noting that this is an exception to the preferred depiction of enemy defeat. The majority of Assyrian narratives emphasise the capture, display, torture, and execution of enemies after the battle, and often as part of a ritualised victory procession. This may reflect only a preferred narrative emphasis, but it may also mean that in Assyria killing an enemy in battle was in fact not the ideal outcome. The fact that bearing news of enemy death even to those who might be presumed to desire that death could be risky can be seen cross-culturally, and has been noted by Miller, *Messenger*, 31.

not only into a literal weapon with which to beat Dunanu but also, again in a literal sense, into a 'sign'—a message that repeatedly (presumably with each blow) communicates the phrase: 'the ally who could not save you'. That this is the meaning of the head is stated outright in the Prism B text.[54] As discussed above, the head retains the identity of Massira, the individual, even as it is transmuted in these ways: the message is communicated through a recognition of Massira's social identity and relationships. To Dunanu, the message is part of his punishment, humiliating him in suggesting the inadequacy of his allies, and by extension his own judgment on which great nation to rely. It seems certain that such a punishment would have been psychologically horrifying—being physically beaten in the face with the head of a former associate, ally, and perhaps friend—and that we are to understand this horror as part of the punishment.[55] The distress that accompanied the sight of severed human body parts might even have been greater in ancient Babylon or Assyria than it would be now. To a modern sensibility, the misuse of severed heads violates our sense of decorum and human dignity. In Assyria, the belief that this sort of mutilation would literally ensure misery in the afterlife might have made the act even more distressing.[56]

When Dunanu and Samgunu are forced to wear the heads of Teumman and Ishtar-nandi, a similar message is being communicated ('the ally who could not save him'), even if it is not so explicitly stated. Teumman was the great king

---

54 It should be noted that Assyrian cuneiform made extensive use of logograms, single signs which stood in for entire words or concepts. These same signs had syllabic value as well. Which meaning was intended in any given text must be determined from context. The cuneiform sign SAG, originally a clear picture of a human head, meant 'head' as a logogram (pronounced, when used as a logogram, by its readers not with its syllabic value 'sak/sag' but as the Akkadian word for head, either *rēšu* or *qaqqadu*). In conjunction with other logograms or in other contexts, it could generate a range of meanings, including political titles. Although I do not argue any direct connection between the cuneiform writing system and this incident, it is worth considering that the authors of this text existed in a world in which individual 'signs' (including a human head) had the ability to generate various and sometimes complex meanings.

55 For a text which does address the psychological implications of being forced to encounter severed heads, see Miller on the shepherd boy in *Njál's saga* who is handed the severed head of Sigmund by Skarphedin and told to take it as a message to Hallgerd. The shepherd boy throws the head away as soon as Skarphedin is out of sight. Miller has described this passage of narrative as one that 'gives an inner life to the shepherd-boy [...]. This terrified boy has his disgust briefly overwhelmed by his fear': William Ian Miller, *'Why Is Your Axe Bloody?': A Reading of Njáls Saga* (Oxford: 2014), 107.

56 A. R. George, *The Babylonian Gilgamesh Epic: Introduction, Critical Edition and Cuneiform Texts* (Oxford: 2003), Tablet XII, 102–53.

to whose empire Dunanu pledged himself in place of Assyria. He is forced to appear wearing a symbol of his allegiance. Again, we can also speculate with reasonable certainty that such a punishment would be psychologically devastating for the prisoner forced to wear the severed head of his former ally, evoking feelings of disgust, fear, and shame—and that the narratives take this aspect of the meaning of the display for granted. As they wear the heads, Dunanu and Samgunu are shown being slapped, grabbed, and spat upon. The display of prisoners with these severed heads facilitates and gives a justification for this casual violence and degradation.

I would suggest that the use of heads as 'necklaces' might even be intended to parody protective amulets of (frighteningly, powerfully ugly) heads like that of Huwawa/Humbaba, the monster destroyed by mythic heroes Gilgamesh and Enkidu, who was popular on plaques,[57] or the demon Pazuzu, whose snarling face was a popular subject during the first millennium for amulets worn round the neck.[58] Referencing charms of protection would add an ironic turn to the implicit message, 'the ally who could not save him': *these* protective charms have clearly failed to help their wearers.

A similar incident in the reign of Ashurbanipal's predecessor, Esarhaddon, in which two captives are also made to wear heads while being displayed in a victory procession is accompanied by what Tadmor has characterised as a unique example of a Neo-Assyrian 'victory chant' preserved in text:[59] 'In the month of Tashritu—the head of Abdimilkutti / In the month of Addaru—the head of Sanduaru'.[60] The circumstances under which it was performed are described thus: 'In order to show people the might of Assur, my lord, I hung them

---

57 It has been suggested that Teumman's death is intended to reference the Huwawa encounter in the Gilgamesh Epic, which it mirrors in location and subsequent treatment of the head as an offering and object for display; Dominik Bonatz, 'Ashurbanipal's Headhunt: An Anthropological Perspective', *Iraq* 66 (January 2004), 93–101 at 100. On Huwawa/Humbaba amulets, see Sarah B. Graff, 'The Head of Humbaba', *Archiv für Religionsgeschichte* 14, no. 1 (2013), 129–42; Eva A. Braun-Holzinger, 'Apotropaic Figures at Mesopotamian Temples in the Third and Second Millennia', in *Mesopotamian Magic: Textual, Historical, and Interpretative Perspectives*, ed. I. Tzvi Abusch and Karel Van Der Toorn (Leiden: 1999), 159–60.

58 Nils P. Heeßel, 'Evil against Evil: The Demon Pazuzu', *Studi e materiali di storia delle religioni* 77, 2 (2011), 357–68 at 361.

59 Hayim Tadmor, 'An Assyrian Victory Chant and Related Matters', in *From the Upper Sea to the Lower Sea: Studies on the History of Assyria and Babylonia in Honour of A.K. Grayson*, ed. Grant Frame and L. S. Wilding (Leiden: 2004), 269–76.

60 *ina* ITI.DU$_6$ SAG.DU ^{m}*ab-di-mil-ku-ut-ti ina* ITI.ŠE SAG.DU ^{m}*sa-an-du-ar-ri ina* 1-*et* MU.AN.NA *u*$_2$-*nak-ki-is-ma*; RINAP 4 1.iii.32–34.

[i.e. the heads] on the necks of their nobles, and with musicians and lyres I paraded past in the streets of Nineveh'.[61] The chant celebrates the heads specifically, allowing the severed head to stand in for a much larger narrative of enemy defeat. The heads encapsulate the story of defeat of enemies (and once again, the specific heads of specific, named enemies). The chant supplements the visual message of the heads' presence, although it proclaims little more than what is already obvious: that those heads are present in an Assyrian victory procession. From there it seems the heads speak for themselves.[62]

Heads are also significant means of bearing messages because of their connection to speech. This has been seen in Ashurbanipal's punishment of the Elamite king Hallusu's statue, discussed above, in which he targets sneering mouth and insolent lips, mentioned before even the arm which actually made battle. In the punishment of Nabu-usalli and Mannu-ki-ahhe, whose tongues are ripped out, a direct connection is made between their punishment and the (unspecified) blasphemous words that they spoke. The importance of words (spoken or written) in condemning enemies is further evidenced in the surrounding representation of punishment in the relief. The procession of punishment in which Nabu-usalli and Mannu-ki-ahhe are mutilated and flayed and Dunanu and Samgunu are forced to wear the heads of their allies, is completed by a third 'incident', in which offensive letters are read out by the detained Elamite messengers Nabu-damiq and Umbadara (the same ones who attempted to self-harm when they saw Teumman's head). This takes place before the eyes of the ugly Urartian ambassadors who have also been depicted witnessing the two other acts of punishment. Nabu-damiq and Umbadara being forced to recapitulate their king's insulting words is put on par with the other punishments—perhaps because it can be taken for granted that a similarly brutal punishment is automatically indicated by being identified with such words. It links together anti-Assyrian speech with punishment, and displays this before an audience of the two Urartians who, from their cringing forms and raised, supplicating hands, get the message.

---

61 *aš$_2$-šu$_2$ da-na-an ^{d}aš-šur* EN.*ia* UN.MEŠ *kul-lu-mi$_3$-im-ma ina ki-ša$_2$-di* LU$_2$.GAL.MEŠ-*šu-un a-lul-ma it-ti* LU$_2$.NAR *u$_3$* GIŠ.ZA$_3$.MI$_2$ *ina re-bet* NINA.KI *e-te-et-ti-iq*; RINAP 4 1.iii.36–38.

62 A third incident of head-wearing is also reported by Ashurbanipal, using the severed head of Nabu-bel-shumati, the grandson of Merodach-Baladan (Markduk-apla-iddina II) who had eluded Ashurbanipal through suicide and whom Ashurbanipal makes 'more dead than before' by beheading his corpse (RINAP 5 11.vii.38–50).

Conclusion

Severed heads preserve the identity of the defeated enemy at the same time that they dehumanise and transmute that enemy from human to object (whether letter, weapon, amulet, or offering). A dominant paradigm for the collection and use of severed heads is that of the messenger and message, in which the head can act as a message to and from multiple senders and receivers. The soldiers who actually bear these heads to the king are messengers, their own glory in playing this role a just-acknowledged discourse under the surface of the royal texts.

It is notable that a sequence centred around the one famous beheading of Teumman is in fact hedged about throughout the sources with (less visually prominent) depictions of severed heads and severing heads. The narratives treat these severed heads through an ideology of Assyrian might and divine support, but also with occasional psychological realism, in which the emotional power of severed heads and beheading is acknowledged along with the inner psyches of enemies who react to them, whether Urtak asking for his own beheading or Dunanu, Umbadara, and Nabu-damiq confronting their allies' heads in punishment. Although the Teumman beheading is usually examined for what is unique about it, its own sources present it in a way that instead emphasises its meaning as part of a tradition of taking, using, and recreating in narrative the heads of enemies.

Works Cited

Printed Sources

Albenda, Pauline. 'An Unpublished Drawing of Louvre AO 19914 in the British Museum'. *Journal of the Ancient Near Eastern Society of Columbia University* 12 (1980): 1–8.

Al-Rashid, Moudhy N. 'Mental Symptoms in the Akkadian Diagnostic Handbook: A Study of Patterns in the Description of Depression, Anxiety, and Madness'. PhD thesis, University of Oxford, 2014.

Ataç, Mehmet-Ali. *The Mythology of Kingship in Neo-Assyrian Art*. Cambridge: 2010.

Bagg, Ariel. 'Where Is the Public? A New Look at the Brutality Scenes in Neo-Assyrian Royal Inscriptions and Art'. In *Making Pictures of War: Realia et Imaginaria in the Iconology of the Ancient Near East*, edited by Laura Battini-Villard, 57–82. Oxford: 2016.

Bahrani, Zainab. *Rituals of War: The Body and Violence in Mesopotamia*. New York: 2008.

Barnett, R. D. *Sculptures from the North Palace of Ashurbanipal at Nineveh (668–627 B.C.)*. London: 1976.

Bonatz, Dominik. 'Ashurbanipal's Headhunt: An Anthropological Perspective'. *Iraq* 66 (January 2004): 93–101.

Borger, Rykle. *Beiträge zum Inschriftenwerk Assurbanipals. Die Prismenklassen A, B, C = K, D, E, F, G, H, J und T sowie andere Inschriften*. Wiesbaden: 1996.

Braun-Holzinger, Eva A. 'Apotropaic Figures at Mesopotamian Temples in the Third and Second Millennia'. In *Mesopotamian Magic: Textual, Historical, and Interpretative Perspectives*, edited by I. Tzvi Abusch and Karel Van Der Toorn, 149–72. Leiden and Boston: 1999.

Cifarelli, Megan. 'Gesture and Alterity in the Art of Ashurnasirpal II of Assyria'. *The Art Bulletin* 80, no. 2 (1 June 1998): 210–28.

Cole, Steven W., and Peter Machinist. *Letters from Priests to the Kings Esarhaddon and Assurbanipal*. Helsinki: 1998.

Collins, Paul. 'Gods, Heroes, Rituals, and Violence: Warfare in Neo-Assyrian Art'. In *Critical Approaches to Ancient Near Eastern Art*, edited by Brian A. Brown and Marian H. Feldman, 619–44. Berlin: 2013.

Collins, Paul. 'The Development of the Individual Enemy in Assyrian Art'. *Source: Notes in the History of Art* 25, no. 3 (2006): 1–8.

Dick, Michael B., and C. B. F. Walker. 'The Induction of the Cult Image in Ancient Mesopotamia: The Mesopotamian Mis Pî Ritual'. In *Born in Heaven, Made on Earth: The Making of the Cult Image in the Ancient Near East*, edited by Michael B. Dick, 55–121. Winona Lake, IN: 1999.

Fales, Federico Mario. 'Art, Performativity, Mimesis, Narrative, Ideology, and Audience: Reflections on Assyrian Palace Reliefs in the Light of Recent Studies'. *KASKAL* 6 (2009): 235–93.

Frame, Grant. *Babylonia 689–627 B.C: A Political History*. Istanbul: 1992.

George, A. R. *The Babylonian Gilgamesh Epic: Introduction, Critical Edition and Cuneiform Texts*. 2 vols. Oxford: 2003.

Gerardi, Pamela. 'Epigraphs and Assyrian Palace Reliefs: The Development of the Epigraphic Text'. *Journal of Cuneiform Studies* 40, no. 1 (1988): 1–35.

Graff, Sarah B. 'The Head of Humbaba'. *Archiv für Religionsgeschichte* 14, no. 1 (2013): 129–42.

Grayson, A. Kirk. *Assyrian Rulers of the Early First Millennium BC. I (1114–859 BC)*. Toronto: 1991.

Grayson, A. Kirk, and J. R. Novotny, ed. and trans. *The Royal Inscriptions of Sennacherib, King of Assyria (704–681 BC)*. RINAP 3/2. Winona Lake, IN: 2014.

Heeßel, Nils P. 'Evil against Evil. The Demon Pazuzu'. *Studi e materiali di storia delle religioni* 77, no. 2 (2011): 357–68.

Holloway, Steven W. *Aššur Is King! Aššur Is King!: Religion in the Exercise of Power in the Neo-Assyrian Empire*. Leiden and Boston: 2002.

Kravitz, Kathryn F. 'A Last-Minute Revision to Sargon's Letter to the God'. *Journal of Near Eastern Studies* 62, no. 2 (2003): 81–95.

Larsen, Mogens Trolle. *The Conquest of Assyria: Excavations in an Antique Land, 1840–1860*. London: 1996.

Leichty, Erle, ed. and trans. *The Royal Inscriptions of Esarhaddon, King of Assyria (680–669 BC)*. RINAP 4. Winona Lake, IN: 2011.

Livingstone, Alasdair. 'Ashurbanipal: Literate or Not?' *Zeitschrift für Assyriologie und Vorderasiatische Archäologie* 97, no. 1 (2007): 98–118.

May, Natalie Naomi. '"In Order to Make Him Completely Dead": Annihilation of the Power of Images in Mesopotamia'. In *La famille dans le Proche-Orient ancien: Réalités, symbolismes, et images: Proceedings of the 55th Rencontre Assyriologique Internationale at Paris, 6–9 July 2009*, edited by Lionel Marti, 701–26. Winona Lake, IN: 2014.

May, Natalie Naomi. '"I Read the Inscriptions from before the Flood ..." Neo-Sumerian Influences in Ashurbanipal's Royal Self-Image'. In *Time and History in the Ancient Near East: Proceedings of the 56th Rencontre Assyriologique Internationale at Barcelona, 26–30 July 2010*, edited by L. Feliu et al., 199–210. Winona Lake, IN: 2013.

Miller, William Ian. 'The Messenger'. In *Frieden Stiften: Vermittlung und Konfliktslösung vom Mittelalter bis Heute*, edited by Gerd Althoff, 19–36. Darmstadt: 2011.

Miller, William Ian. *'Why Is Your Axe Bloody?': A Reading of Njáls Saga*. Oxford: 2014.

Nadali, Davide. 'Interpretations and Translations, Performativity and Embodied Simulation: Reflections on Assyrian Images'. In *Leggo!: Studies Presented to Frederick Mario Fales on the Occasion of his 65th Birthday*, edited by G. B. Lanfranchi et al., 583–95. Wiesbaden: 2012.

Nylander, Carl. 'Earless in Nineveh: Who Mutilated "Sargon's" Head?' *American Journal of Archaeology* 84, no. 3 (1980): 329–33.

Olmstead, A. T. E. 'The Calculated Frightfulness of Ashur Nasir Apal'. *Journal of the American Oriental Society* 38 (1918): 209–63.

Oppenheim, A. Leo. 'The City of Assur in 714 B.C.' *Journal of Near Eastern Studies* 19 (1960): 133–47.

Porter, Barbara N. 'Feeding Dinner to a Bed: Reflections on the Nature of Gods in Ancient Mesopotamia'. *State Archives of Assyria Bulletin* 15 (2006): 307–31.

Porter, Barbara N. 'Noseless in Nimrud: More Figurative Responses to Assyrian Domination'. In *Of Gods, Trees, Kings and Scholars: Neo-Assyrian and Related Studies in Honour of Simo Parpola*, edited by Mikko Luukko, Saana Svärd, and Raija Mattila, 201–20. Helsinki: 2009.

Radner, Karen. 'Fame and Prizes: Competition and War in the Neo-Assyrian Empire'. In *Competition in the Ancient World*, edited by Nick Fisher and Hans van Wees, 37–57. Swansea: 2011.

Radner, Karen. 'High Visibility Punishment and Deterrent: Impalement in Assyrian Warfare and Legal Practice'. *Zeitschrift für Altorientalische und Biblische Rechtsgeschichte* 21 (2015): 103–28.

Reade, Julian. 'Religious Ritual in Assyrian Sculpture'. In *Ritual and Politics in Ancient Mesopotamia*, edited by Barbara N. Porter, 7–61. New Haven: 2005.

Russell, John Malcolm. *Sennacherib's Palace without Rival at Nineveh*. Chicago: 1991.

Russell, John Malcolm. *The Writing on the Wall: Studies in the Architectural Context of Late Assyrian Palace Inscriptions*. Winona Lake, IN: 1999.

Schaudig, Hanspeter. '"Wahnsinn" im Alten Orient: Zum babylonischen Konzept eines Stark von der gesellschaftlichen Norm abweichenden und selbstzerstörerischen Verhaltens'. *Studia Mesopotamica: Jahrbuch für altorientalische Geschichte und Kultur* 1 (2014): 391–423.

Shafer, Ann. 'Assyrian Royal Monuments on the Periphery: Ritual and the Making of Imperial Space'. In *Ancient Near Eastern Art in Context: Studies in Honor of Irene J. Winter by Her Students*, edited by Jack Cheng and Marian H. Feldman, 133–59. Leiden and Boston: 2007.

Smith, Mark S. 'The Heart and Innards in Israelite Emotional Expressions: Notes from Anthropology and Psychobiology'. *Journal of Biblical Literature* 117, no. 3 (1998): 427–36.

Tadmor, Hayim. 'An Assyrian Victory Chant and Related Matters'. In *From the Upper Sea to the Lower Sea: Studies on the History of Assyria and Babylonia in Honour of A. K. Grayson*, edited by Grant Frame and L. S. Wilding, 269–76. Leiden: 2004.

Tadmor, Hayim. 'Propaganda, Literature, Historiography: Cracking the Code of the Assyrian Royal Inscriptions'. In *Assyria 1995: Proceedings of the 10th Anniversary Symposium of the Neo-Assyrian Text Corpus Project, Helsinki, September 7–11, 1995*, edited by Simo Parpola and Robert M. Whiting, 325–38. Helsinki: 1997.

Tadmor, Hayim, Shigeo Yamada, and Jamie Novotny, ed. and trans. *The Royal Inscriptions of Tiglath-Pileser III (744–727 BC) and Shalmaneser V (726–722 BC), Kings of Assyria*. RINAP 1. Winona Lake, IN: 2011.

Wagensonner, Klaus. 'Non-Textuality in the Ancient Near East: Some Glimpses from the Mesopotamian Field'. In *Non-Textual Marking Systems, Writing and Pseudo Script from Prehistory to Modern Times*, edited by Petra Andrássy, Julia Budka, and Frank Kammerzell, 33–67. Göttingen: 2009.

Watanabe, Chikako E. 'The "Continuous Style" in the Narrative Scheme of Assurbanipal's Reliefs'. *Iraq* 66 (2004): 103–14.

Waters, Mark D. *A Survey of Neo-Elamite History*. Helsinki: 2000.

Weidner, Ernst F. 'Assyrische Beschreibungen der Kriegs-Reliefs Assurbânaplis'. *Archiv für Orientforschung* 8 (1933–1932): 175–203.

Westenholz, Joan N., and Michel Sigrist. 'The Brain, the Marrow and the Seat of Cognition in Mesopotamian Tradition'. *Le Journal des Médecines Cunéiformes* 7 (2006): 1–10.

Winter, Irene J. 'Art in Empire: The Royal Image and the Visual Dimensions of Assyrian Ideology'. In *Assyria 1995: Proceedings of the 10th Anniversary Symposium of the Neo-Assyrian Text Corpus Project, Helsinki, September 7–11, 1995*, edited by Simo Parpola and Robert M. Whiting, 359–81. Helsinki: 1997.

Winter, Irene J. 'Royal Rhetoric and the Development of Historical Narrative in Neo-Assyrian Reliefs'. *Studies in Visual Communication* 7 (1981): 2–38.

Zamazalová, Silvie. 'The Education of Neo-Assyrian Princes'. In *The Oxford Handbook of Cuneiform Culture*, edited by Eleanor Robson and Karen Radner, 313–30. Oxford: 2011.

Online Sources

Cuneiform Digital Library Iniative. <http://cdli.ucla.edu>, accessed 18/6/2017.

Koubková, Evelyne. 'Washing the Mouth of a Kettledrum'. Paper presented at the *62nd Rencontre Assyriologique Internationale* (11 July 2016), <https://www.academia.edu/27202640/Washing_the_mouth_of_a_kettledrum_Rencontre_Assyriologique_Internationale_2016_presentation_>, accessed 3/7/2017.

Novotny, Jamie R., ed. and trans. RINAP 5, <http://oracc.museum.upenn.edu/rinap/rinap5/pager>, accessed 8 August 2016.

Epilogue: Silence as a Weapon of Self-Defence in *Sense and Sensibility*

Nora Bartlett

> ... concealment, if concealment be possible, concealment is all that remains.
>
> Elinor took immediate possession of *the post of civility*.[1]

∵

A side of Bill Miller's interests that may not be widely known is his endless, absorbed, meticulous reading and rereading of the novels of Jane Austen. This has led to many exchanges, in person and by mail, between us over the years, including noisy disputes on street corners in St Andrews. In particular these have been about *Sense and Sensibility*, probably for both of us the favourite novel, and even more particularly about its heroine, Elinor, if not the favourite, the most significant character. In this brief discussion of *Sense and Sensibility* I'll be asking you to listen both to words and silence, wounding words that pass between sisters, and silences between them; and words that sharpen, and silences that sustain, the conflict between rivals.

For those who have not recently read the novel, it tells the story of two nicely brought-up sisters, Elinor and Marianne Dashwood, who have been made relatively poor by the death of their father, and are forced soon after the opening of the novel to move from their home in Sussex to a cottage in Devonshire, where they find themselves among a new, lively set of people who include the Middletons (stupid, kindly Sir John, his insipid wife, her well-meaning, vulgar mother Mrs Jennings, and a family friend, the melancholy Colonel Brandon) and John Willoughby, a devilishly attractive young man of the world. Marianne falls in love with Willoughby; Elinor has already fallen in love, back in Sussex, with Edward Ferrars, whose rich and grand family do not want him to marry 'a portionless young woman' like herself. I want to look at two moments in the novel, one in Sussex, between Elinor and Marianne, and one in Devonshire

1 *Sense and Sensibility* 160, 173 (italics added). Page references are to the R. W. Chapman edition, 3rd ed. (Oxford: 1933; repr. 1978) and hereafter will be placed in the text.

© KONINKLIJKE BRILL NV, LEIDEN, 2018 | DOI 10.1163/9789004366374_019

between Elinor and Lucy Steele, a cunning little vixen who is her rival for the affections of Edward.

The Dashwood home at the novel's opening is Norland, a substantial country house—but a house of mourning, for the Dashwoods' beloved father dies in Chapter One, and his death has followed that of the uncle from whom he inherited the house. Something not always remembered about the two heroines is that they and their mother must have been in mourning for a good long time when the novel opens. Mourning is what I want to start by looking at, but in Jane Austen, for whom the Chapter One death scene of Mr Dashwood is the only death scene in all of her major novels, it looks on the surface as if grief is sidelined by disappointment. As well as learning, in Chapter One, about a pile-up of Dashwood family deaths, we also learn that Norland is 'entailed': bequeathed only for life to Mr Dashwood, to be passed on at his death to his son John, Elinor and Marianne's brother. Mrs Dashwood and her daughters will have only a small income, and no home.

This is crucial to the plot, but let us ignore wills, money, and property for the moment and look at death, and grief, and the women who are living through it:

> Elinor … possessed a strength of understanding, and coolness of judgment … at nineteen … [she was] the counsellor of her mother.… She had an excellent heart;—her disposition was affectionate, and her feelings were strong; but she knew how to govern them: it was a knowledge which her mother had yet to learn …
>
> Marianne … was sensible and clever.… She was generous, amiable, interesting: she was everything but prudent. The resemblance between her and her mother was strikingly great (6).

This 'strikingly great' resemblance is shown most of all in their style of mourning:

> They encouraged each other now in the violence of their affliction. The agony of grief which overpowered them at first, was voluntarily renewed, was sought for, was created again and again. They gave themselves up wholly to their sorrow.… Elinor, too, was deeply afflicted; but still *she could struggle* (7; italics added).

I want us to keep in mind the language of 'giving up' to emotion versus the language of 'struggle', such a strong, evident contrast, but also to look at the language of creativity about emotion which characterizes Marianne and her mother: 'grief … was voluntarily renewed … created again and again'.

I should say right here that I am not going to be talking about 'performativity'; these woman have broken hearts, all of them. But for Marianne and her mother there is an excitement in the rituals of grief that is denied to Elinor: their suffering can find an outlet in the cultivation of what the eighteenth century—and Jane Austen, though she lived into the nineteenth—called 'sensibility'. Sensibility measured the strength of feelings by the flamboyance of their display. That is denied to Elinor: her experience of her father's death is of loss, the loss of a beloved person, of human company. There are no compensations. There is only 'struggle'. It is all work, and no play.

These crushed females—and there is another, a younger sister, who needs to be cared for—are invaded by the inheritors of the estate, the mercenary brother and his yet more mercenary wife, who bring with them the wife's brother Edward, the gentle, rather hapless fellow with whom Elinor will fall rapidly and deeply in love. (A standard way of reading the novel used to be that Elinor = sense, and Marianne = sensibility, but really both girls are hot-blooded and quixotic types.) A sign that Mrs Dashwood is coming out of the first phase of theatrical misery is that she notices a growing *tendresse* between Edward and Elinor and communicates it to Marianne, who is a little disappointed by Elinor's choice. Quiet Edward seems dull to a seventeen-year-old, but then, with a seventeen-year-old's arrogance, she comments that 'Elinor has not my feelings' (18) and proceeds to investigate what feelings Elinor has—and to trample on them.

The exchange takes place in chapter 4 of volume I: Marianne has mildly insulted the absent Edward—he reads aloud badly, he has no taste in art—in order to work Elinor up into defending him, which she does: '"his mind,"' she protests, '"is well-informed, his enjoyment of books exceedingly great, his imagination lively ... and his taste delicate and pure.... At present, I know him so well, that I think him really handsome; or at least almost so. What say you, Marianne?"' (20)

This tentative and private admission gets steamrollered by Marianne's dash to the finish line: '"I shall very soon think him handsome ... [w]hen you tell me to love him as a brother"' (20). Elinor reels back from this: she knows that 'what Marianne and her mother conjectured one moment, they believed the next' (21); and she has seen, over the six months since her father's death, the ways in which they turn real emotion into high drama. She cannot let them touch this: her feelings for Edward are too strong and too deep, and she instantly regrets 'the warmth she [has] been betrayed into, in speaking of' him (21). It is a mistake she will scarcely ever make again. In the long period—almost the whole novel—before Edward's 'sentiments are fully known' (21), Elinor speaks of him only when absolutely forced to.

So let us look at a point in the novel when she *is* forced to. Many chapters later, in Devonshire, Elinor learns the sickening fact that Edward has been secretly engaged for four years—since long before she met him—to an 'illiterate, artful, and selfish' (140) young woman called Lucy Steele. When she meets Elinor, Lucy takes pains, and obvious delight in giving Elinor pain, to inform her of this state of affairs. Elinor, once convinced that Lucy is not lying, might be expected to wish to avoid all contact with this cruel minx. But—and it might in passing be noted that the constraints of eighteenth-century socializing, as we see it in the country houses of Jane Austen's novels, would have made this difficult in any case, governed as they are by 'that kind of intimacy ... which consists of sitting an hour or two together in the same room almost every day' (124)—Elinor *does not try* to avoid Lucy, at least not at first, and this is interesting. In fact, once Lucy has broken the news of the secret engagement, Elinor positively seeks her out for further discussions, however painful she will find them, however fraught they may be. The narrative, which is intertwined for most of the novel with Elinor's thoughts, tells us that 'She wanted to hear many particulars of their engagement repeated again, she wanted more clearly to understand what Lucy really felt for Edward ... and she particularly wanted to convince Lucy, by her readiness to enter on the matter again, and her calmness in conversing on it, that she was *no otherwise interested in it than as a friend*' (141–42; italics added).

So, Elinor watches for an opportunity to achieve this bit of flummery. She must know—the reader knows—that Lucy, though low-class, is too smart, and too desperately determined to hold onto her man, to be fooled by this act for one minute. But the charade matters: it is *herself* Elinor needs to convince; she needs to show herself with what self-possession she can behave, whatever she feels. This is one of the things that, like dignified grief, counts as courage for women, and the novel gives many examples of it. In the face of pain and humiliation, believing she has lost Edward (and remember that in this time when marriage was not only the only life choice but the only job choice for women of this class), Elinor's situation combines a broken heart and a career flop, but she struggles on.

Let us look at the duel scene between the girls. It is in volume 2, chapter 2. As always, the more intense conflict is backgrounded in Austen's social comedy, which combines the mildly daffy stuff we enjoy with a Swiftean eye for everyday horrors. Lucy, another portionless young woman who, with her cruder, older, really desperate spinster sister 'Miss Steele', keeps herself in the social swim by staying at rich people's houses, and earns her keep there by flattering them and their children, has promised to make a 'filigree basket' for one of the spoilt Middleton children. Elinor sees that this crafty project of Lucy's offers the two of them some time alone together. '"Perhaps,"' says Elinor,

> 'I may be able to be of some use to Miss Lucy Steele, in rolling her papers for her.... I should like the work exceedingly'..... 'Indeed, I shall be very much obliged to you for your help', cried Lucy ... and the two fair rivals were thus seated side by side at the same table ... engaged in forwarding the same work ... without any risk of being heard at the card table. (145)

We will hear them, though, but I wanted first to make a small point about filigree work: it consists of little curls or scrunches of gold or silver paper, fitted together to emulate the real gold or silver filigree done by skilled craftsmen. It was a very popular female hobby in the late eighteenth and early nineteenth centuries. As this basket is for a small child, they are probably using glue: Elinor is folding, curling, scrunching, Lucy is gluing the curls, folds and scrunches onto a surface. But if they were doing this project for themselves they would both be using very sharp pins, and they must both—as the contemporary reader would—know that. The reader in 1811 could imagine quite a different scene, as could Jane Austen's first readers, her family, who knew her penchant for slapstick violence, and must have thought of the possibility of tough little Lucy (and, who knows, maybe even well-bred Elinor?) taking the opportunity for exchanging a few swift jabs, in an environment in which only children were allowed to scream out loud when they were attacked.

Here, though, Lucy has only her sharp tongue to aid her, and a very rich scene between the two 'fair rivals' takes place, backed by a 'very magnificent concerto' (149) from Marianne and the card-playing of the other women (it is an all-girl evening). Lucy pretends to express admiration and awe of Elinor. Something Lucy manages very adroitly is that, while Elinor is only nineteen and *she* is already at the more dangerous age of twenty-three, the older girl treats the younger girl as if, at nineteen, she were an elderly spinster whose function was to give advice to the young and marriageable. When Elinor resists this dubious opportunity, Lucy raps out her reason for wanting Elinor's advice: '"Tis because you are an indifferent person ... that your judgment might justly have such weight with me"'—she says this 'with some pique' and 'laying a particular stress on those words' (150). The reader knows what Lucy is up to: she is out to crush Elinor's confidence. Earlier she has said slyly that Edward regards Elinor and the other Dashwood girls 'quite as his own sisters' (130). Lucy is using her considerable energies to make a younger, prettier, higher-status woman feel old and ugly and sexless. Her motives are easy to read, for us as for Elinor.

What is going on, though, with Elinor? 'Elinor blushed for the insincerity of Edward's future wife' (150), the narrative comments; significantly, it is not Lucy who blushes, but Elinor, who is Edward's future wife. Surely here, if there were a meter to measure insincerity, Elinor, trying to convince Lucy she is indifferent to a man she deeply loves, would score pretty high? After this rencontre is completed, Elinor does try to snub Lucy's attempts to talk about Edward: 'she felt such conversations to be ... dangerous to herself' (151).

Which brings me to that deeper, longer, wider topic, of why it is so necessary for the heroines of Jane Austen's novels to keep their feelings hidden from everyone—everyone, that is, but the reader, who knows all, though may not—may not ever—quite understand it all. Why is Elinor so silent, for so much of the novel, about her feelings? It is not merely temperamental: there are moments when she shows a freer, more expressive side of her nature, the side of her that at one point leads Willoughby, Marianne's faithless lover, to comment 'you can even be saucy' (50). His practiced eye must have given Elinor the once-over along with Marianne, and seen that Elinor is not prim, is not 'reserved'—one of the words which ripples provocatively through the novel. She occasionally even tries to joke with Marianne, who usually misses the joke, as she misses the opportunities that make social life endurable to Elinor, as it must have made it for Jane Austen, opportunities for what Austen calls in *Pride and Prejudice* 'laughing at one's neighbours'.[2]

Hence derives Elinor's greater capacity to bear with the monstrous—to be polite to her selfish brother and his vicious wife—and with the foolish—to listen to Mrs Jennings's tasteless jokes and Mrs Palmer's laugh—which intense, somewhat humourless Marianne cannot manage at all. All this social competence of Elinor's surely originates in that tongue-in-cheek humour which Willoughby notes as her 'sauciness'. When characters in the novel are pompous, or self-contradictory, or absurd, we are not laughing at them by ourselves as readers; we are sharing the joke with Elinor.

But as the novel goes on, and the scene changes to claustrophobic London, and Willoughby deserts Marianne, and the secret of Edward and Lucy's engagement becomes public, Elinor finds her stance of grace under pressure rather harder to pull off; 'saucy Elinor' becomes 'silent Elinor'. In London Marianne is, the novel tells us, 'known to be unhappy' and treated accordingly by those among the other characters who are not fools or villains (producing some surprising reversals, which are beyond the scope of this paper). Elinor is treated, by the other characters, by the narrative, by herself in particular, rather as if

2 Jane Austen, *Pride and Prejudice*, 3rd ed., ed. R. W. Chapman (Oxford: 1932; repr. 1976), p. 364: '"For what do we live, but to make sport for our neighbours, and laugh at them in our turn?"'.

she were a soldier under battle conditions: England expects that she will do her duty.

So let us just end by comparing her courage with that of the novel's actual soldier, who has also learned to use silence as a weapon of self-defence. Colonel Brandon was as a boy tricked out of marriage to his first love, whose life was wrecked in consequence. When in volume 1, chapter 11 Elinor expresses to him an exasperated wish that Marianne's manners would display 'a better acquaintance with the world', Colonel Brandon, this apparently colourless older man willing to talk endlessly of the weather with strangers, radically disagrees: 'no, no, do not desire it' (56). The re-reader knows he is thinking of the story of his own beloved Eliza, the young woman destroyed by 'a greater acquaintance with the world': tremblingly he begins, '"I once knew a lady who in temper and mind greatly resembled your sister, who thought and judged like her, but who from an inforced change—from a series of unfortunate circumstances—" Here he stopt suddenly' (56–57). His silence continues. A hundred and fifty pages later he will tell the whole story, stating sadly that he is a 'very awkward narrator' (204). But in volume 1 he chooses silence, which one suspects has become his own weapon of choice over the years of loneliness and unhappiness which took him from Elinor's age, through years of active service in India, almost to her mother's. Unshown in the novel, but described, is *his* duel, with pistols, with the seducer Willoughby. Elinor shakes her head over the duel, reflecting, though, that he is 'a man and a soldier' (211). When the novel pairs her choice of silence with his, it is also comparing their courage.[3]

Works Cited

Austen, Jane. *Pride and Prejudice*. 3rd ed. Edited by R. W. Chapman. Oxford: 1932; repr. 1976.

Austen, Jane. *Sense and Sensibility*. 3rd ed. Edited by R. W. Chapman. Oxford: 1933; repr. 1978.

3 Nora Bartlett delivered this paper in Bill Miller's presence just before she was diagnosed with cancer, and one of her final requests to John Hudson before she died was that he take the paper through to publication. This is his lightly edited version of Nora's original text.

Bibliography of Books and Scholarly Articles by William I. Miller

Compiled by Lauren DesRosiers and Amanda Strick

1978

"The Middle English Ballad 'Robyn and Gandeleyn' (line 57)." *Notes & Queries* 223: 300–301.

1982

"Dorothy Thompson and the Court Packing Plan: Of Muse and Men." *Houston Law Review* 19: 695–711.

1983

"Choosing the Avenger: Some Aspects of the Bloodfeud in Medieval Iceland and England." *Law and History Review* 1, no. 2: 159–204.

"Justifying Skarpheðinn: Of Pretext and Politics in the Icelandic Bloodfeud." *Scandinavian Studies* 55, no. 4, 316–44. Reprinted with revisions as "The Central Feud in *Njáls saga*," in *Sagas of the Icelanders: A Book of Essays*, edited by J. Tucker (New York: Garland, 1989), 292–322.

1984

"Avoiding Legal Judgment: The Submission of Disputes to Arbitration in Medieval Iceland." *American Journal of Legal History* 28, no. 2: 95–134.

Review of J. L. Byock, *Feud in the Icelandic Saga*. *Speculum* 59, no. 2: 376–9.

"A Relic of Divine Dispensation." *The Explicator* 42, no. 4: 2–4.

1985

"Diebstahl, England." In *Lexikon des Mittelalters* (Munich: Brepols), 992–3.

Review of C. L. Gottzmann, *Njáls saga: Rechtsproblematik im Dienste soziokultureller Deutung*. *Scandinavian Studies* 57, no. 1: 84–85.

1986

"Dreams, Prophecy and Sorcery: Blaming the Secret Offender in Medieval Iceland." *Scandinavian Studies* 58, no. 2: 101–23.

"Gift, Sale, Payment, Raid: Case Studies in the Negotiation and Classification of Exchange in Medieval Iceland." *Speculum* 61, no. 1: 18–50.

Review of K. Hastrup, *Culture and History in Medieval Iceland: An Anthropological Analysis of Structure and Change*. *Scandinavian Studies* 58, no. 2: 183–6.

Review of J. Bossy (ed.), *Disputes and Settlements: Law and Human Relations in the West*. *The American Journal of Legal History* 30, no. 3: 266–8.

1988

"Beating Up on Women and Old Men and Other Enormities: A Social Historical Inquiry into Literary Sources." *Mercer Law Review* 39, no. 3: 753–66.

"Ordeal in Iceland." *Scandinavian Studies* 60, no. 2: 189–218.

"Some Aspects of Householding in the Medieval Icelandic Commonwealth." *Continuity and Change* 3, issue 3: 321–55.

1989

With Ted Andersson, co-translator and editor of *Law and Literature in Medieval Iceland: Ljósvetninga saga and Valla-Ljóts saga*. Stanford, CA: Stanford University Press.

"The Historical Setting." In *Law and Literature in Medieval Iceland: Ljósvetninga saga and Valla-Ljóts saga*, edited and translated by Ted Andersson and William Ian Miller (Stanford, CA: Stanford University Press), 3–62.

1990

Bloodtaking and Peacemaking. Chicago: University of Chicago Press.

1991

"Of Outlaws, Christians, Horsemeat, and Writing: Uniform Laws and Saga Iceland." *Michigan Law Review* 89, no. 8: 2081–95.

1992

"Sagas and Emotions." In *From Sagas to Society*, edited by G. Pálsson. Middlesex, UK: Hisarlik.

1993

"Hœnsa-Þóris saga." In *Medieval Scandinavia: An Encyclopedia*, edited by P. Pulsiano and K. Wolf (New York: Garland), 309–10.

Humiliation: And Other Essays on Honor, Social Discomfort and Violence. Ithaca, NY: Cornell University Press. "Giving the Gift of Humiliation," a short excerpt from Chapter 1, in *Harper's Magazine* 288 (Feb. 1994): 26–27.

1994

"'I Can Take a Hint': Social Ineptitude, Embarrassment, and the King of Comedy." *Michigan Quarterly Review* 33, no. 2: 322–44.

1995

"Deep Inner Lives, Individualism and People of Honour." *History of Political Thought* 16, no. 2 (February, 1995): 190–207.

1996

"Upward Contempt." *Political Theory* 23, no. 3, 476–99.

"Sanctuary, Redlight Districts, and Washington, D.C.: Some Observations on Neuman's Anomalous Zones (Symposium: Surveying Law and Borders)." *Stanford Law Review* 48, no. 5: 1235–46.

Review of B. Lincoln, *Authority: Construction and Corrosion*. *History of Political Thought* 17, no. 3: 453–4.

1997

"Gluttony." *Representations* 60, 92–112. Reprinted with substantial additions in *Wicked Pleasures: Meditations on the Seven "Deadly" Sins*, edited by R. C. Solomon. (Lanham, MD: Rowman & Littlefield: 1999), 19–49.

The Anatomy of Disgust. Cambridge, MA.: Harvard University Press. Spanish and Italian translations, 1999. Slovenian translation, 2006.

Co-translator, *The Complete Sagas of Icelanders, Including 49 Tales*, edited by V. Hreinsson, et al. Reykjavík: Leifur Eiríksson Publishing.

1998

"JOURNAL: Ann Arbor, December 1997." *The American Scholar* 67, no. 2: 143–6.

"Clint Eastwood and Equity: Popular Culture's Theory of Revenge." In *Law in the Domains of Culture*, edited by A. Sarat and T. R. Kearns. Amherst Series in Law, Jurisprudence, and Social Thought (Ann Arbor: University of Michigan Press), 161–202.

"Sheep, Joking, Cloning and the Uncanny." In *Clones and Clones: Facts and Fantasies about Human Cloning*, edited by M. C. Nussbaum and C. R. Sunstein (New York: W. W. Norton), 78–87.

"Focus on Faculty—William I. Miller," *Law Quadrangle Notes* 41, no. 3: 12–13.

1999

"Near Misses." *Michigan Quarterly Review* 38, no. 1: 1–15. Excerpted in *Harper's Magazine* 298 as "The Chagrin of the Near Miss": 26–27.

"Fear, Weak Legs, and Running Away: A Soldier's Story." In *The Passions of Law*, edited by S. A. Bandes. Critical America (New York: NYU Press), 241–64. A somewhat different version appears (as "Weak Legs: Misbehavior before the Enemy") in *Representations* 70 (2000): 27–48; and in *Demokratie, Recht und soziale Kontrolle im klassischen Athen*, edited by D. Cohen and E. Müller-Luckner. Schriften des Historischen Kollegs 49 (Munich: Oldenbourg, 2002), 15–35.

"In Defense of Revenge." In *Medieval Crime and Social Control*, edited by B. A. Hanawalt and D. Wallace. Medieval Cultures 16 (Minneapolis: Univ. of Minnesota Press), 70–89.

2000

The Mystery of Courage, Cambridge, MA: Harvard University Press. Spanish translation, 2005.

"Shapes of Courage." *Harper's Magazine* 301: 21–24. Excerpted with changes from *The Mystery of Courage*.

Review of J. Elster, *Alchemies of the Mind: Rationality and the Emotions*. *London Review of Books* 22, no. 15: 36–37.

2002

"Of Optimal Views and Other Anxieties of Attending to the Beautiful and Sublime." *Journal of Visual Culture* 1, no. 1: 71–85.

2003

Faking It. New York: Cambridge University Press.

Review of J. A. Burrow, *Gestures and Looks in Medieval Narrative*. *The Medieval Review* <https://scholarworks.iu.edu/journals/index.php/tmr/article/view/15405/2152>, accesssed 5/7/2017.

"Pretension and Pomposity in Academe." *The Chronicle of Higher Education*, no. 50, B7–B9.

2004

"Yale Kamisar: Up Close and Personal." *Ohio State Journal of Criminal Law* 2, no. 1: 65–67.

"Home and Homelessness in the Middle of Nowhere." In *Home and Homelessness in the Medieval and Renaissance World*, edited by N. Howe (Notre Dame, IN: University of Notre Dame Press), 125–42.

2005

"Oko za oko: obračunavanje s talionom." Translated into Slovenian by L. Učakar. *Pamfil*: 6–13.

2006

Eye for an Eye. New York: Cambridge University Press. Arabic, Chinese, and Italian translations, 2008.

2007

"Is a Gift Forever?" *Representations* 100, no. 1: 13–22.
"I'm sorry, so sorry, so very, very sorry." *The Globe and Mail*, December 22: D15.

2008

Audun and the Polar Bear: Luck, Law, and Largesse in a Medieval Tale of Risky Business. Leiden and Boston: Brill.
Review of A. Cuffel, *Gendering Disgust in Medieval Religious Polemic*. *Medievalia et Humanistica* n.s. no. 34: 161–5.

2009

"Death, Danger, and ... Dieting?: What is Courage? Who has it? Have We Debased its Meaning Since Plato Sought to Define It?" *Character* 4, no. 3: 4–11.
"Deceit in War and Trade." In *The Philosophy of Deception*, edited by C. Martin (New York: Oxford University Press), 49–66.
"Hatred." In *The Oxford Companion to Emotion and the Affective Sciences*, edited by D. Sander and K. R. Scherer (New York: Oxford University Press), 203–04.

2010

"Threat." In *Feud, Violence and Practice: Essays in Medieval Studies in Honor of Stephen D. White*, edited by B. S. Tuten and T. L. Billado (Farnham, England: Ashgate), 9–27.

2011

"The Messenger." In *Frieden stiften: Vermittlung und Konfliktlösung vom Mittelalter bis heute*, edited by G. Althoff (Darmstadt: WBG), 19–36.

Losing It: In Which an Aging Professor Laments His Shrinking Brain, Which He Flatters Himself Formerly Did Him Noble Service. New Haven: Yale University Press. "Losing It," excerpted from the opening chapters, *Michigan Quarterly Review* 50 (2011): 153–67. Korean translation 2014.

"Losing It: The Lament of an Aging Professor." *The Chronicle of Higher Education, The Chronicle Review*, October 30.

2012

"The Question of Courage." *SGI Quarterly* 69: 14–17.

"Conscience, Interest, Side-Switching, and Laxdæla saga, Chapters 59 and 61." In *The Creation of Medieval Northern Europe: Christianisation, Social Transformations, and Historiography: Essays in Honour of Sverre Bagge*, edited by L. Melve and S. Sønnesyn (Oslo: Dreyer Forlag), 373–88.

2014

"Feeling Another's Pain: Sympathy and Psychology Saga Style." *European Review* 22, no. 1: 55–63.

"What Book Changed Your Mind?" *Chronicle of Higher Education, The Chronicle Review*, November 7.

'Why is your axe bloody?': A Reading of Njáls saga. Oxford: Oxford University Press.

2015

With Helle Vogt, co-author of "Finding, Sharing and Risk of Loss: Of Whales, Bees and Other Valuable Finds in Iceland, Denmark and Norway." *Comparative Legal History* 3, no. 1: 38–59.

"May You Have My Luck." *The Chronicle of Higher Education*, no. 61, February 6.

2016

"Do I disgust you? (or, rather, you me?)—Mes frères, mes sœurs, mes semblables?" In *Le dégoût: Histoire, langage, esthétique et politique d'une émotion plurielle*, edited by M. Delville, A. Norris, and V. von Hoffmann. Collection Cultures Sensibles (Liège: Presses universitaires de Liège), 149–61.

"Where's Iceland?" In *The Making of Europe: Essays in Honour of Robert Bartlett*, edited by J. Hudson and S. Crumplin (Leiden and Boston, MA: Brill), 76–95.

2017

Hrafnkel or the Ambiguities: Hard Cases, Hard Choices. Oxford: Oxford University Press.

Index

www.ingramcontent.com/pod-product-compliance
Lightning Source LLC
LaVergne TN
LVHW010639300926
849161LV00005B/990